THE FAMINE IN WATERFORD 1845-1850

TEACHT NA bPRÁTAÍ DUBHA

Des Cowman, Editor
Donald Brady, Associate Editor

Geography Publications in association with Waterford County Council

Published in Ireland by
Geography Publications,
Templeogue, Dublin 6W
in association with Waterford County Council

ISBN 0 906602 60 2

Des Cowman is an historian and teacher.
Donald Brady is county librarian in Waterford.

Cover illustration:
Dawn Near Lismore
A work based on contemporary descriptions of life in this area in 1847, mostly taken from the reports of *The Cork Examiner* at that time. The idea behind it being the contrast with the hopelessness of the people's predicament at that time, and in an Ireland (and a world!) always capable, at least theoretically, of producing a glorious and optimistic 'new dawn', where famine and warfare will be things of the past. A clear target with little evidence of progress so far!

A.K. Maderson
27 April, 1995

Cover design by Christy Nolan
Typesetting by Phototype-Set Ltd., Dublin
Printed by Colour Books

Contents

Acknowledgements

This volume was planned as a contribution to the National Commemorations of the 150th Anniversary of The Great Irish Famine. Its production would not have been possible without the dedicated, continuous, and voluntary commitment of the contributors and the assistance of many organisations and individuals.

We are particularly indebted to

Anne Walsh, Eddie Byrne and other staff of Waterford County Library.

Richard Fennessy, Waterford City Librarian.

Donnchadh Ó Ceallacháin, who volunteered to share the editorial burden.

Arthur Maderson, for his magnificent painting used on the dust jacket.

John Young, local historian, Dungarvan.

James and Emily Villiers Stuart, for permission to use their portrait of Henry Villiers Stuart.

Ken Hanigan, National Archives.

Cork City and County Library Services.

The Irish Architectural Archive.

Anthony and Robyn Summers.

Sean Byrne, Photographer.

Tony Gyves, South Eastern Health Board.

The staff of the United States Embassy.

Sponsors, and in particular, Motor Distributors Ltd. and East Cork Oil.

In conclusion, this work would not have been produced without the support of the Members of Waterford County Council and the wholehearted commitment of the County Manager, Donal Connolly.

Foreword

It is an honour to introduce this powerful collection of articles. The essays included in this volume movingly tell the story of the Famine in County Waterford through the documents of everyday life. They reveal the reality of how this event touched all aspects of society. These articles are testimony to the universal suffering experienced between 1845 and 1849. The stories they tell are tales of utter hopelessness. But it is equally important, as these desperate years are commemorated, to remember the hope, courage and human dignity of Ireland's people.

According to Eugene Broderick's essay, early in the growing season of 1845 local authorities predicted a record potato crop. Hopes were high that "there never perhaps was a finer crop than the present". It was not until late fall of that year that the inroads of the blight were realised and the headlines read "Great Famine threatens the land".

The hopes of the spring of 1846 turned quickly to despair. The historical documents studied by the authors of this collection present vivid evidence of the hunger and sickness faced by the people of Waterford and of all Ireland in the following years. Rita Byrne describes workhouses filled beyond capacity. Joan Johnson writes of the Quaker Relief effort as it fought a losing battle against starvation and death until, as Jack Burtchaell states, "the Quakers, exasperated by government inaction, gave up relief work and stated the scale of the problem was beyond their means".

But in each article there is another story of people who struggled against the tragedy. People who helped the hungry and eased the suffering. Thomas Gregory Fewer describes the benevolence of William Cavendish and the often generous action of his agent Francis Currey. Tom Nolan concludes his description of the Lismore Poor Law Union by quoting the Cork Examiner: "To the Lismore Committee every credit is due for their exertions in relieving the destitution of the people. Liberality in their contributions, perseverance and industry in fulfilling duties of their position, have distinguished the Lismore Committee".

Joan Johnson tells the story of Rev. James Alcock who "worked ardently to save the fishing community at the time of the famine". He and Joshua Strangman formulated the vision that "relief was not just about feeding the starving but of enabling them to support themselves".

It seems that in the history of every nation there are tragic or violent events to which historians point as defining moments. Many historical events influence politics, economics and culture, but only the most traumatic define the national character. A nation's collective identity is formed by its experience of suffering. One such event in America was our civil war. Brothers fought against brothers as families were ripped apart. The long term effects of this bloody war can still be seen today in American society.

Many historians say that the course of Irish history was changed immeasurably by the potato blight. J.C. Beckett in *The Making of Modern Ireland* stated "One effect of the famine was to concentrate in a few brief years changes that would otherwise have been spread over generations...the very rapidity of these changes affected their character; and the immense burden of human suffering by which they were accompanied left an indelible mark on the popular memory". The Famine and its consequences are, as Mr. Burtchaell says in his article, "seared into the Irish conscience".

In 1960 my brother President Kennedy said: "The Chinese word 'crisis' is composed of two characters, one signifying danger and the other signifying opportunity". Great tragedy moves and shapes humanity because it is a combination of danger and opportunity, of despair and hope. While on one side of the famine there was only death and hopelessness, on the other side was the hope and courage of the Irish who found a way out of their plight by emigrating to America.

Those Irish who came to the United States during the famine years – my great, great grandfather was one of them – came without money, education or experience. What they did have was hope and a vision of a better life.

President Kennedy once said of the United States: "Ours is a nation of immigrants. The men and women who have come here from abroad built America into the greatest country in the world". Today 40 million Americans proudly claim Irish heritage. They are in all walks of life – artists, educators, entrepreneurs, labourers, professionals and politicians. According to the *Harvard Encyclopedia of American Ethnic Groups*, "The Irish experience in the United States was central to the country's social and economic development....Out of their interaction with the host society came a more diverse and tolerant American".

The Famine is part of Ireland's culture and national consciousness. On this 150th anniversary, the Nation is looking back to review the events and be reminded as Mary Robinson said "of the Irish strength to celebrate the people in our past, not for power, not for victory, but for the profound dignity of human survival".

It is especially appropriate to consider the interrelationship between hope and despair this year. Ireland entered 1994, as it had for 25 years, as an island plagued with violence. Now, thanks to the relentless efforts of people from all communities and backgrounds to end the killing, Ireland faces a peaceful and prosperous future. The peace process, while sometimes slow and cumbersome, will succeed. And Irish children face a future full of hope.

The work that Waterford's County Council have put into the production of this volume is commendable. The efforts of the writers are equally remarkable. This book will stand as a memorial to the lives lost during the famine. It will also serve to remind us of the goodness and generosity of those who sought to alleviate the suffering. Finally, this work will provide evidence of the dignity with which a nation faced its darkest moment.

Jean Kennedy Smith
[U.S. Ambassador to Ireland]

Contributors

Donald Brady
Donald obtained his B.A. in History and English at Maynooth. He has been County Librarian in County Waterford since 1982 and is particularly interested in the preservation and collation of the historical resources of the county. He was director of the West Waterford Heritage Week 1991 and 1992, and is co-ordinator of Waterford County Council's Famine Commemoration Programme.

Eugene Broderick
Eugene teaches in the Mercy Secondary School, Waterford. He obtained an M.A. from U.C.C. in 1991 on 19th Century Ecclesiastical History and is currently working on Protestantism in Waterford. His published work includes "The Blueshirts in Waterford" (*Decies*) and "Corporate Labour Policy of Fine Gael" (*Irish Historical Studies*).

Jack Burtchaell
A native of Ferrybank, Jack took his degree in History and Geography from U.C.D. and then spent a period as Junior Research Fellow in Queens University, Belfast. Among his published research in historical geography are items in *Waterford: History and Society* and in *Kilkenny: History and Society* as well as in *Decies*.

Rita Byrne
Teaches in Fenor. Rita's main historical interest is in folklore and tradition. She is author of *Fenor 1894-1994* and has also contributed to *Decies*.

Des Cowman
Edited *Decies* I to XXV; Associate Editor of *Waterford: History and Society* (1993). Amongst his published works are *The Abandoned Mines of West Carbery* (1987) and *Perceptions and Promotions: Waterford Chamber of Commerce 1792-1992* (1993)

Greg Fewer
Thomas Gregory Fewer graduated from U.C.C. with a B.A. (Hons.) in Archaeology and History in 1989 and an M.A. in History in 1993. He is currently a freelance writer with research interests in the history of Counties Waterford and Kilkenny.

William Fraher
A native of Dungarvan, Willie is particularly interested in, and has

published extensively on, the town. His "Dungarvan: An Architectural Inventory" and "A Calendar of the Minutes of Dungarvan Town Commissioners" are essential reference works on the area. He is a founder member and current President of Dungarvan Museum Society.

John M. Hearne

John teaches in St. Paul's Community School, Waterford. He has had works published on twentieth century local economic history; M.A. "The Waterford Economy 1945-62: The interaction of government policy and local initiative". He is currently working towards a Ph.D. on Waterford Society, Economics and Politics in the nineteenth century.

Joan Johnson

Joan Johnson is a Chartered Physiotherapist. She has previously worked in the Richmond Hospital, Dublin and in Waterford Regional Hospital. For the past 27 years she has been the physiotherapist in Airmount, Waterford Maternity Hospital. She is married to Roger Johnson, Vice Principal of Newtown School and has five children. She is currently working on further research on the Quakers in Waterford.

Tom Nolan

Tom's main area of interest is in medieval history and archaeology. He has been involved in "digs" in Dundrum Castle and Clonmacnoise. He has published works in *Decies* on aspects of the early history of Waterford City.

Donnchadh Ó Ceallacháin

Born in Cork, Donnchadh has been living in Waterford since 1980. He has a degree in History and Folklore from U.C.C. He is interested in ideological movements since the eighteenth century, particularly French influences on Irish nationalism.

Ted O'Regan

A drama teacher, Ted has written and directed *"The Stick Doll"*, a play on the famine in Waterford, produced in Garter Lane by Waterford Youth Drama. Apart from a number of articles in *Decies*, he has published *"Awareness through Drama"* (1982)

Dermot Power

Dermot Power has worked as a master-cutter in Waterford Crystal and as a professional musician. His published works include *"Ballads and Songs of Waterford"* (1992); *"The Street where you live"* (1993); *"Historical Photographs and Anniversaries of Waterford City"* (1994). He is also a regular contributor on local history topics to the *Munster Express*.

Preface

This is not a comprehensive history of the Famine in Waterford. Such can never be written. The best that we can strive towards is to record and interpret the faint and random echoes of a dark half-decade. But do we really want to know what it was like for a family to starve to death, and for that to be replicated over stretches of country? Do we want to know what the survivors felt when they first looked into the glazed eyes of the doomed, and how their hearts must have hardened as year followed year of apparently inevitable starvation?

Fortunately, perhaps, such voyeurism is not possible, and the contributors here are limited by the evidence at their disposal. Donnchadh Ó Ceallacháin captures the mixed and often ambivalent feelings of those who expressed opinions about agriculture in Waterford on the eve of the great crop failure. Generally, they thought things were improving. Ted O'Regan considers the reports to Dublin Castle over the first eight months of what we now call "the famine". About half of the potato crop had perished. Orderly measures were taken to deal with the resultant hunger and there was no panic.

There was panic, however, in the months following the total failure of the crop in August 1846. What happened in Dungarvan in conveyed by William Fraher in his description of the food riot on 28th September, while my own article looks at the desperate efforts made by those driven frantic in September and October 1846, by the need for sustenance. This was particularly so for the western portion of the county where the economy was most fragile. By November 1846 all was quiet again. Why? Eugene Broderick provides some suggestions on the evidence from the local newspapers. The rioters were now starving and freezing in the bitter winter of 1846-'47. His quotations provide some of the few local insights into this starkness. He also reveals the attitudes of newspaper correspondents and editors to what was happening around them over the worst years of the famine – attitudes which are at variance with what some famine historians have suggested. A more detached overview of the famine years is conveyed in the first of Jack Burtchaell's articles, which calendars the various stages of distress as reported from Waterford.

There are significant areas for which information is not available, particularly in the area of famine relief. The few surviving details of local relief committees raise many questions including, crucially, how many survived the famine due to their efforts. The same must be asked of the government-sponsored public works programmes. It would also help our appreciation to know what roads or other facilities we currently use were built under these famine programmes. The same questions must be asked of the workhouses. Rita Byrne and Tom Nolan interpret what survives of the records of that in the City and the Lismore Workhouse, respectively. That they catered for huge numbers by acquiring ancillary buildings is clear. Only when things go wrong, as Rita Byrne points out, do we get any glimpse of life within. The workhouse in Lismore was well run and if we were to judge from its records the famine there was a matter of clinical administrations. Greg Fewer's analysis of the management of the Duke of Devonshire's Lismore Estate shows a similar pattern with not a glimpse of the human tragedy around. The estate agent there helped the deserving; the fate of those deemed otherwise goes unreported.

One relief effort does stand out, however: that of the Quakers as recorded by Joan Johnson. Worthy as their short-term efforts were in providing practical help, particularly in "Black 47", their most egregious contribution was the saving of the Ring Fishing Community through helping to put long-term structures in place which enabled them not alone to survive but to flourish. It was a particularly good example of resource management where local vested interests could have little sway. Rights of ownership, leasehold arrangements and other landed interests were the inevitable structural barriers which prevented rational but radical changes to the agricultural resource on which most people depended. Such change was not part of the Official Response to the Famine, as recorded by John M. Hearne. Formulae were devised to cope with each stage of distress but the fabric of society in Waterford as elsewhere, must be kept intact. An alternative view of social organisation may be behind the anomalous, and indeed largely anonymous series of disturbances in Waterford in 1848-'49 as recorded by Dermot Power. It would seem to have been fuelled by the desire of surviving farmers, rather than cottiers, to consolidate what they had in the event of continued potato failure. It is strange, however, that this active response was confined to the hinterland of the Suir Valley rather than being a national movement.

Other anomalies abound. How could a Ladies Tenant Right Movement with a radical feminist agenda, for instance, have come into being around Kilmacthomas in 1848? This is amongst the questions posed by Eugene Broderick's analysis of the newspapers. What was the ratio of those who died to those who emigrated is another that must go unsolved for lack of evidence, as must the number of migrants drawn to the city but who died in the country en route. Jack Burtchaell's demographic study does at least provide some answers as to the estates which had the greatest number of casualties. What they had in common pre-1845 was bad management of land and people. The Famine solved the latter problem.

****

This book then has been a collaborative effort with much sharing of information. The inspiration for it came from Donald Brady, Waterford County Librarian, who lured me into editing it with the inviting offer, "What do you want? I'll get it". Thus, it was arranged that Donnchadh Ó Ceallacháin would spend a week in the National Archives researching what was available on Waterford 1845-'50 and ordering photocopies of all famine-related material. These arrived before, and after Christmas 1994, and were distributed to William Fraher, Dermot Power, and Ted O'Regan to be the basis of their articles. The County Library's own substantial resources included workhouse records put into the temporary possession of Rita Byrne and Tom Nolan, and records of the Devonshire Estate which were copied and given to Greg Fewer, while the Parliamentary Papers for the period were made available to Martin Hearne. Meanwhile the City Librarian, Richard Fennessy, had generously offered to do everything he could to forward the research and, amongst other areas of help, procured from Colindale the copies of the local papers which Eugene Broderick was thus able to use. Joan Johnson conducted her own research using largely Quaker sources, as did Jack Burtchaell and Donnchadh Ó Ceallacháin utilising secondary sources and Parliamentary Papers.

Before we started, none of us knew what was going to emerge from our sources. There were no precedents as nothing like this had been done before, to the best of our knowledge. Some sources proved much richer than others as is indicated by the lengths of the various articles. Questions were raised for which answers might eventually have been provided, given unlimited time. Time that we didn't have, and reluctantly some areas of research had to be left to future publications. Hence, for instance, there is nothing on the rich folk tradition of the famine in Waterford in song and story, and there is little on emigration.

As stated at the outset, this, therefore, is not a comprehensive history of the famine in Waterford, but a series of research essays put together under pressure of time. While it is incomplete and has some areas of overlap, we believe it to be important not only locally, but nationally. While studies have been carried out on some of the most publicised and badly affected areas such as the Skibbereen Union, nothing has been done on a relatively prosperous area such as Waterford. There was the danger, therefore, that in national histories, concentration on the famine in the West of Ireland might have exaggerated its impact over the entire country. However, it transpires that Waterford is itself a micro-version of the island as whole, with, coincidentally, the worst areas being in the west of the county (see Jack Burtchaell's maps) and the eastern barony of Gaultire being relatively unaffected.

****

This book commemorates the onset of a social disaster in the county 150 years ago. However, the fiftieth anniversary of it was not commemorated, nor is there a single article on the famine in the Journal of the Waterford and South East of Ireland Archaeological Society, which runs to over eighty issues beginning in 1894. Neither does it feature in Egan's history of the county in 1893 nor Downey's of 1914. However, these were written by the sons (almost exclusively) of the survivors of the famine generations. Their parents had seen sights that were best left unexpressed – to do otherwise would release an emotional cocktail of trauma, guilt and shame. This tacit conspiracy of amnesia would seem to have needed several generations to work out. The centenary of the famine was not commemorated although perhaps there were extenuating circumstances in 1945. From the 1970s on, sporadic items began to appear relating to the famine in Waterford but this is the first time that a systematic attempt has been made to research and present that period for the county. Almost all the information here and many of the illustrations, have been brought to light for the first time. The Famine was the single biggest event of the nineteenth century in Ireland and its consequences last to our own time, it's legacy being the tranquil countryside, the quiet roads and the wilderness areas now just used for leisure pursuits, which 150 years ago bustled with family life.

One of the awful features of the Famine in Waterford as elsewhere is the anonymity of those who died. No doubt there were great numbers of Pat Powers, Mary McGraths, Declan Dunphys and Margaret Morrisseys, living in reasonable harmony, despite hardships, until the food-source suddenly rotted in mid-August 1846. The records then show them as a hungry mob, desperate for food. Once hunger weakened them and they were no longer a threat, they became *"poor creatures", "objects of relief", "the destitute", "paupers", "inmates".* This veil of depersonalisation, as well as their distance in terms of time and culture is difficult to penetrate.

This is an apology to the hidden people whose lives, sufferings and deaths we have such little access, and to whom this book is dedicated. We only know what the official reports say about you collectively. It may be some small consolation to you that 150 years after the start of your tribulations we live in a society where, in theory at least, you would have been valued and that rigid class barriers which limited your options have now almost disappeared. However, the attitudes, actions, and, of course the names of your "betters", have survived. Yours have not. With the limited knowledge at our disposal, we present what we know from their records. You had no opportunity to record for us your experience, tar éis teacht na bprátaí dubha.

Des Cowman

Chapter 1

Waterford on the eve of the famine

DONNCHADH Ó CEALLACHÁIN

In the years leading up to the famine, Waterford was a county of contrasts. On one hand, its proximity to markets had led to a thriving export business in agricultural produce through the port of Waterford. Although the boom years of the Napoleonic wars were over when tillage farmers could expect very high prices, this trade in agricultural exports continued to prosper. The output of County Waterford farms rose as new farming methods were introduced by a class of improving landlords and agents. Many estates were well run and rents were relatively low. There was a darker side however. With an increasing population some landlords began to look for ways to clear surplus people from their estates. The majority of those living in the county were either landless labourers or cottiers, living in extreme poverty for much of the year, existing on potatoes and little else. As tillage began to decline after 1815, so also did the demand for the services of this labouring class. In spite of the problems of the county however, violence and crime rates remained low, particularly in comparison to neighbouring counties. This article will look at County Waterford society in the years before the famine and will examine some of the factors which led to the disaster of 1845.

Agricultural Practice
According to the majority of the witnesses appearing before the Devon Commission in County Waterford, agriculture was improving to some degree in 1844, only four out of twenty two witnesses believed it to be otherwise.[1] According to Sir Richard Musgrave agriculture had greatly progressed in the county, with better cattle, sheep and pigs, improved crop rotation, and the introduction of crops such as mangles and clover. He cited the number of new slate roofed houses as proof of the improved situation.[2] George Lane Fox and his agent were praised for introducing turnips as winter feed, a practice that would spare a large quantity of potatoes.[3] *Lewis's Topographical Dictionary* of Ireland described agriculture in Waterford as generally improving in 1837. Tillage occupied two thirds of the county, with a third comprising meadow, pasture and unimproved bogland. Wheat, barley, oats and potatoes were grown. Clover was becoming more widespread,

although turnips were seldom sown. Lime was the main type of fertiliser used, with seaweed and sand near the coast. Better implements and farm machinery were now in use.[4] Flax was grown in parts of the county for the domestic production of linen.[5] Seven years, later in 1844 turnips had not yet made a breakthrough as an animal feed, despite the best efforts of people like Lane Fox, only being *"grown in small quantities by gentlemen."* Potatoes remained the main winter food for animals.[6]

According to Michael Nolan, a farmer with 150 acres near Kilmeaden, agriculture was improving when the landlord encouraged farmers.[7] Father Patrick Treacy of Butlerstown thought that farmers were generally more industrious and were using better methods of agriculture, but the lack of capital was an obstacle to greater progress.[8] One land agent, James Galwey, believed that the River Suir was the boundary between good and bad agricultural practice, and complained about the neglect of landlords in Tipperary compared to Waterford.[9] Witnesses testifying before previous Parliamentary Committees also believed the state of agriculture was improving. John Musgrave told the Poor Enquiry of 1830 that he had seen great developments in the previous number of years. However he did not think that this improving state of things was going to result in any increase in employment. In fact he thought that better agriculture would lead to a decrease in the numbers of labourers, as superior implements were introduced.[10]

On the surface agriculture did seem to be improving in the region generally, with a large increase in the export of agricultural produce from the port of Waterford in the 1830's and 1840's.[11] This increase in production did not result in increased profits as the prices for agricultural products was either dropping or remained static during this time.[12] According to Francis Currey, Land Agent to the Duke of Devonshire, land rented at between £1 and £1.10s an acre was capable of producing ten to twelve barrels of oats and six to seven barrels of wheat.[13] An acre of the same land could produce 1,470 to 1,680 stones of potatoes.[14] In 1844 cows sold for between £8 and £10 and sheep between s £1 and £1.10s, potatoes fetched 3d. to 4d. per stone.[15]

The Devon Commission however can be a very unreliable source in investigating rural conditions in 19th century Ireland. Landlords were particularly cited as the source of problems in the country, and naturally wished to convey the impression that agriculture was improving. Not everybody who gave evidence before the Devon Commission was overly confident about the state of agriculture in Waterford in 1844. Piers Quarry Barron described the county as a *"great bulk, a barren waste of wretched pasture."* Farmers received no encouragement from landlords and Barron goes on to describe the system of farming as one *"calculated to reduce land to a maximum of sterility,"* with pigs and people sharing the same food – the lumper potato. With proper management, Barron suggested the county could have supported five times its population.[16] Writing in 1841, John O'Donnovan gave a vivid picture of the land and people around Sliabh gCua: *"The land is craggy, poor, unproductive, and the people are overworked. They are actually stunted or twisted (casta) in the earth with hard labour......they are not rich nor happy, but very quiet."*[17]

There were only two agricultural societies in the county, one at Lismore, and the other at Portlaw. The absence of agricultural societies in other parts of the county was seen as a great obstacle to progress by many of the Devon Commission witnesses. Landlords were criticised for not organising new societies or supporting those already established.[18] The need for agricultural education seems to have been recognised in many quarters. In 1841 *The Waterford Mirror* carried a letter from the Poor Law Commissioners in Dublin, stressing the importance of establishing Agricultural Societies in the country and pointing out the improved methods of agriculture that would result.[19] *The Waterford Newsletter*, published three times a week, gave detailed accounts of agricultural prices and markets. *The Waterford Chronicle, The Waterford Mirror, and The Waterford Mail* regularly published articles, mainly reprinted from such journals as *The Agricultural Gazette*, and *The Journal of Agriculture*, giving instruction on a variety of farming issues. An article on the 24th April 1844 had a strangely prophetic ring considering the events which were to unfold twelve months later. It dealt with diseases of the potato which can *"still injure or destroy our harvest."*[20] However before the famine 70.55% of the County Waterford population could not read or write (the third highest illiteracy rate in Ireland after Mayo and Galway).[21] This lack of education was recognised as an obstacle by many to increased improvements to agriculture. Nelson Trafalgar

Indicative of the strength of trade before the famine was the Waterford News Letter, a two page newspaper giving only commercial news.

Foley told the Devon Commission that the National Schools were not a success as the teachers were incompetent and very badly paid. He believed that agricultural schools should be established for the education of farmers.[22] Fr. Patrick Treacy thought that education alone without improving the conditions of the people was of no real use.[23]

On the eve of the famine there were 11,588 landholdings in County Waterford, and of these 35% did not exceed five acres.[24] Only 20% of farms in the county were over thirty acres.[25] County Waterford had the second lowest percentage of workers engaged in industry of any county in Ireland in 1841, at 14.4% after County Kilkenny with just over 9%[26] According to the 1841 Census the percentage of families engaged in agriculture rose from 62% in 1831 to 72% in 1841. In the Census of 1841, 7,423 people were returned as "*farmers*", (including 352 women). This was out of a total of 52,471 people generally engaged in agriculture of some kind. 42,061 were described as labourers and servants, with others engaged in other various agricultural pursuits, ranging from gardeners to land stewards. It is interesting to note that 3 women were returned as "*fishermen*".[27]

Tenants and Leases

During the first half of the 19th century the practice of land being held by middlemen began to disappear,[28] although a German visitor to Waterford in 1844 states that much of the area was still under their control.[29] This sysem was almost universally disliked by both landlords and tenants. According to Thomas Wyse in 1830, tenants holding land directly from their landlord often lived in "*comfortable cottages with good out-offices, their farms in a comparative state of agricultural improvement*", while those renting from middlemen lived in "*miserable hovels crumbling into ruins, the wretched inmates sometimes amounting to two or more families.*"[30] One large farmer, Thomas Fitzgerald from near Dungarvan tried to establish himself as a middleman in the 1840's. He sublet 12 acres of land at £12 per acre without the permission of his landlord Sir John Nugent Humble or his agent John Carew. The agent's reaction in this case was to make the sub tenants pay the rent directly to the landlord, and not to the middleman.[31]

For farmers renting land in the 1840's the main concern was security of tenure. The uncertainty of tenure was described as the "*bane of the country*" by Captain Edward Croker, a land agent living near Tallow.[32] In 1843 *The Waterford Chronicle* carried an editorial on the subject of tenure; arguing that this should be regulated, "*a man who dwells on land should have all advantages from its increasing value.*"[33] Tenants were generally anxious to have a lease, 21 years and a life concurrent being the normal formula, although Sir Richard Musgrave granted leases of 31 years, with the option to renew several years before it expired.[34] On the Duke of Devonshire's estate, leases were granted when asked for, and were for 21 years and a life, with covenants against sub-dividing and building without permission.[35] The practice of tenants paying a fee to an agent on being granted a lease seems to have been declining, although from evidence in the Devon Commission the practice continued on some estates, with £1 per acre paid to one agent, and in another case between £5 and £30 paid to agents to secure a lease.[36]

Many landlords were notorious for not granting leases, letting their land from year to year. On the Kiely Ussher estate in West County Waterford, no new leases were granted, the only tenants with leases being those holding one from previous owners.[37] George Lane Fox in the east of the county was equally reluctant to grant leases. He also seemed to have treated his tenants in rather a strange fashion, giving them presents of mirrors and beads when he visited them.[38]

There was a big variation in rent paid for land across the county. On the Devonshire Estate rents had been reduced by 25% in 1822. Between 10/5 and 11/9 per acre was being paid for average to good land, with permission to cut turf at 1d. per household.[39] One English visitor to Waterford before the famine quotes rents up to £7 per acre, although for smallholdings near the city this was exceptional.[40] Rent was fixed either by valuation or by proposal, and sometimes by auction. The average rent around Lismore was 15s per acre for good land. Many farmers paid from £1 to £2 an acre.[41]

Tenants were sometimes allowed to be in arrears with their rent, with a "*running gale*" on some estates. According to Inglis many tenants were in arrears that could never be paid off.[42] Patrick Hennebry told the Devon Commission of one 50 year lease in arrears for 30 years. He blamed sub division and joint tenancies for arrears building up.[43]

Evictions

Very few landlords were willing to admit that eviction was used for the non payment of rent. Most of the landlords speaking before the Devon Commission testified that eviction was rarely used; distraint being the preferred option, with perhaps a notice to quit served as a "*threat to induce payment.*"[44] In 1844 *The Waterford Chronicle* carried with almost obvious glee a notice which it described as "*of considerable importance.*" This was that the Devon Commission intended to find out and publish the number of evictions filed in Irish courts.[45] In 1843 there were 127 applications in Waterford to the courts to evict tenants, and of these 62 were granted.[46] Sir Richard Musgrave was of the opinion that "*under tenants were the main parties ejected.*"[47] James Galway, a land agent from near Carrick on Suir gave an example of five tenants evicted on Lord Cromorne's estate for non payment of rent, and because they were "*bad characters complained by other tenants.*" He gave them £8 each to help them emigrate. In his opinion very little assistance was given to those evicted. He gave an example of five or six evicted families living in one house. They were starving, and all they had to survive on was the proceeds of the women begging. He admitted that he evicted some tenants with very small holdings of half an acre.[48] Arthur Kiely Ussher had a policy of evicting tenants to add to his own demense.[49] Thomas Power, a farmer from Bungary told the Devon Commission that Kiely Ussher evicted 170 people from his estate at Ballysaggartmore to consolidate land holdings.[50] George Meara, agent to the Marquis of Waterford was very insistent that there had been no evictions on the estate after the 1826 election. However since some leases had "*fallen from time to time*" and since there had been some sub-letting, he had "*got out the under-tenants, mainly cottiers and paupers*", in the "*kindliest manner possible*", giving them all money, and keeping on those who were "*respectable*". When questioned about the fate of those evicted he was not able to tell if many of them emigrated. Some he believed were still in the neighbourhood, and some "*went to other places.*" There were no "*unkind feelings*" about the evictions, with many of those ejected "*pulling down their own houses.*"[51]

The Pill, an artificial river dug by the tenants of Geoge Lane Fox to link Waterford and Tramore.

On the Lane Fox estate near Waterford City, the tenants were said to have been in constant fear of eviction. Few had leases and many were in arrears. Some were able to pay off their arrears by working on a scheme to drain the marshes on the Tramore Waterford road in an attempt to construct a canal. The manager in charge of these works, Mr. Stuart was very harsh according to Fr. Martin Flynn, with workers being thrown into the river Pill for not working hard enough.[52] All of these charges were rejected by Joshua Keel, George Lane Fox's agent. He told the Devon Commission of the attempts made to improve the estate, stating that over £12,000 had been spent on the property since 1835.[53]

In 1843 it was estimated that there were 105,000 acres of unimproved pasture and bogland in the county, of which 50,000 were improvable.[54] Given the rising population and the general shortage of land, many landlords encouraged drainage on their estates. One landlord stated that between 20s and 50s were allowed in lieu of rent to farmers for drainage. Currey, agent to the Duke of Devonshire saw drainage as *"a most important branch of agricultural improvement."*[55] Some landlords, notably George Lane Fox got tenants to pay off arrears by carrying out drainage of marshy land – although in Lane Fox's case the result was not spectacular.[56]

Many of the improving landlords were anxious to help their tenants as much as possible; either by reducing rents in times of difficulty or by paying for improvements in times of relative prosperity. Some allowed their tenants timber and slates. Sir Richard Musgrave paid the wages of slaters, masons and carpenters for building on his estate, as well as donating timber and slates.[57]

Subdivision of Land

With increasing population during the 18th century and during the first half of the 19th century, the natural reaction among farmers was to subdivide their farms among their children, especially among their sons; there being no other employment available for the vast majority of the Irish people.[58]

John Musgrave pointed out the dangers of subdivision to the 1830 Poor Enquiry. In his opinion the constant splitting of land was leading to the small farmers becoming more and more impoverished, and unable to cultivate the land properly. He was reluctant to condone clearances of estates and consolidation of farms to solve the problems of tiny farms resulting from subdivision, pointing out that only the landlords and larger farmers would benefit. In his opinion the landlords of Ireland should be taxed on the rents they received to help pay for the distress caused by the policy of evicting cottiers to consolidate farms.[59]

William Sharman Crawford writing in 1839 took a different view. Although he recognises the problems with subdivision, he believes it would be wrong to prevent it. Describing the Irish people *"reduced to the lowest state of existence"* he stated that they had no other option, *"their condition is so bad it cannot be made worse. A small patch of ground insures food for at least a portion of the year, and thus subdivision goes on."*[60]

Landlords in general were keen to prevent subdivision and subletting, with most leases containing clauses preventing the custom.[61] However this continued on many estates without the permission of the landlords, and with many turning a blind eye to the practice.[62] Edmund Anthony Power who farmed sixty acres in the parish of Killronan for instance told the Devon Commission that his father originally had 700 acres but it was divided among the children.[63] In some old leases it seems that there were no clauses against subdivision.[64] On many estates joint tenancies existed. Between the Dungarvan and Lismore Poor Law Unions in 1843 there were 212 joint tenancies enumerated by the Poor Law Commissioners.[65]

Investment in Land

The general lack of investment in agriculture was of great concern during the 19th century. Thomas Wyse told the Poor Enquiry in 1830 that unemployment of labourers would be solved if more capital was invested in the land. He was especially referring to the middlemen who never re-invested rents in their estates.[66] By the middle of the century 35% of landlords in Waterford were absentees, and saw their Irish estates as a source of revenue only – with little interest in re-investing the rent in their land.[67] Certainly if one examines the estate of George Lane Fox, an estate according to one visitor to the county that was in a fairly deplorable condition, the

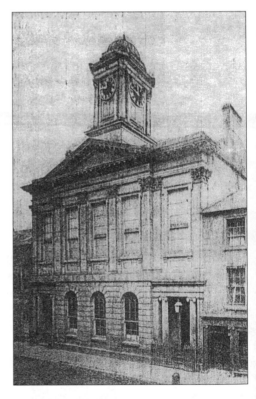

Waterford Savings Bank.

8

A Waterford beggar woman from Thackeray's *The Irish Sketch Book*.

general picture of the absentee landlord seems to be true.[68] One of the main conclusions of the Devon Commission in 1844 was that the landlords in Ireland had failed to live up to their responsibilities.[69] Many of the County Waterford witnesses to give evidence to the Devon Commission gave examples of what they described as "*objectionable management*" on estates. One land agent and magistrate, James Galwey admitted that in general little trouble was taken by Irish landlords with their land.[70]

In spite of the overwhelming evidence against landlords in general, and against absentee landlords in particular, one must remember that the Duke of Devonshire, one of the largest absentee landlords in the county had one of the best run estates managed by his agent Francis Currey. On the other hand *The Waterford Chronicle* in an editorial in 1844 complained about the Marquis of Waterford leaving the country to squander "*Ireland's riches for the benefit of the stranger.*" The editor had seen him on the boat to England "*in the very lowest society, flinging his sovereigns for the benefit of night walkers and others.*" He goes on to demand that this "*titled scamp*" should be taxed.[71] In June of the same year the paper renews it attacks on the Marquis, remarking that although he was not as wild as he used to be, "*he pays more attention to horses and hounds than to the interests of his people.*"[72] Some Devon Commission witnesses however were full of praise for Lord Waterford. While many tenants in the county were afraid to improve their farms, on the estate of the Marquis of Waterford, the agent was happy to see improvements carried out, and no tenant feared eviction as long as he paid his rent. As well as that, compensation was paid to tenants for improvements carried out, and the usual help was given for building.[73]

Many agents and landlords also felt that the larger farmers in particular were equally reluctant to re-invest their profits in their farms. This could be partly explained by the general insecurity of tenure of many farmers. Those farmers with leases feared large rent increases when the period of the lease was up, and were thus unwilling to invest money in land that they could never own.[74] One agent, Captain Croker from Tallow thought that landlords should only rent land to tenants with capital.[75] In 1830 Thomas Wyse stated that between £50,000 and £60,000 were invested in Waterford savings banks, much of it by farmers, and he believed that this prosperity would continue into the future.[76]

A number of witnesses before the Devon Commission were of the opinion that many large farmers were saving their money in savings banks. Captain Simon Newport, Lord Carew's agent spoke of large deposits by farmers in the banks, and he believed farmers would be encouraged to invest this money in their land if they had security of tenure and if landlords were willing to compensate farmers for improvements.[77] By the 1830's there were eleven banks serving the general south east region. Between 1828 and 1840, the amount of money on deposit in the Waterford Savings Bank was £100,000. However, the savings banks were investing in secure government stocks, and thus effectively, money which could have been used for agricultural development was being siphoned off to London.[78]

Furthermore it is difficult to imagine that large amounts of capital were available for investment by any except the largest farmers. It was stated in the *Parliamentary Gazetteer* in 1844 that there was very little difference between the lifestyles of farmers and cottiers; "*their enjoyments, their conveniences and manner of living very nearly resembling each other.*"[79] According to Fr. Patrick Treacy, tenants generally had no capital because the rents were too high, and that the "*respectable class of farmers are worse off than our servants, with meat no more than once per week...not many have deposits in savings banks.*"[80] According to Fr. Thomas Flynn, the farmers in his parish were very poor, with not more than seven able to give £100 as a dowry to one of their marriageable daughters. He did not think that there were twenty farmers in the district with £100 to spare. He was of the opinion that if there was security of tenure, farmers with money would invest it in their land and not leave it in savings banks or "*stick it in the thatch.*"[81]

Class Divisions

The "*small farmers of Ireland*" generally held between five and thirty acres of land. In the period before the famine, it was probably this class in conjunction with the landless labourers that was most involved in agrarian agitation at the end of the 18th century and the beginning of the 19th century.[82] The vast majority of farms in County Waterford were under thirty acres.[83] Thomas Wyse in 1830 outlined an ideal situation for the organisation of agriculture in the country. He believed that three classes of farmers would evolve with time, and through consolidation of farms; large farmers, average farmers and small farmers, (holding between one and two acres of land). This class of small farmers in his opinion would provide a constant supply of "*healthy labourers*" for the other two classes.[84] William Sharman Crawford identified this class of farmers as the one most at risk. At best they could maintain their position if they were lucky; at worst they would sink into the class of landless labourers through either subdivision of land or eviction. He identified six factors which could spell disaster for them: excessive rents, rents calculated unfairly, (usually by auction between small farmers), lack of security of tenure, no compensation on eviction, lack of industry, and lack of education.[85]

One of the main consequences of rising population and land shortage was the enclosure of marginal land, especially in the Comeragh mountains. This trend had begun in the 18th century, but had increased rapidly during the early 19th century.[86] Many landlords encouraged settlement of marginal land. Arthur Kiely Ussher tried to entice tenants to move to the mountains by giving them land free of rent for the first seven years.[87] On some mountain land tenants paid 1s. per acre for the first seven years, and after that, 2/6 per acre. In spite of these low rents their condition was described as *"wretched."*[88] George Lane Fox seemed to have been inspired by the notion of providing land for small farmers and landless labourers in his drainage schemes at Kilbarry.[89]

The building of the monastery at Mount Melleray, and the reclamation of waste land by the Cistersian Monks provided many with a concrete example of what could be done with unproductive land. *The Waterford Chronicle* in an editorial in April 1844 uses this as a practical example of what could be done if *"we had the benefit of a fostering or protective legislature."* It goes on to point out that the improvements brought about by the monks provided employment for twenty men at 9d. per day. According to *The Waterford Chronicle* it cost £60 to send an emigrant abroad, and it speculates on the improvements that could be achieved if that money could be spent on him in Ireland.[90] In all 120 acres of mountain land were enclosed at Mount Melleray, with eight acres for a kitchen garden. A school had been established for the poor, with plans to start an agricultural school.[91]

Compared to the poverty of farmers of all classes, that of the landless labourer was oppressive in the extreme. Hansard described the farm labourers in Ireland as the most miserable in the world, and goes on to state that nothing was more disgusting than the interior of an Irish cabin.[92] The condition of the cottier class in County Waterford was summed up in the following way in 1844; *"In their habitation, furniture, diet, clothing, in the education and provision for their children, they are not superior to the Russian boor...the lowest class in Ireland is the most miserable in the world."*[93] According to the Census of 1841 37.9% of houses in Waterford were mud cabins.[94] This compares to a national average of 50%.[95] Inglis in 1843 thought that *"farm house cabins were worse than in Wexford one without chimney, window only 2 broken stools.*"[96] In certain areas, families shared houses leading to gross overcrowding. Fr. James Power, the Catholic curate in Kill commenting on overcrowding because of high rents told the Devon Commission that in some cases two or three families had to share one house, *"and the consequence is that it is productive of the worst evils as regards morality."*[97] Many of the poor depended on private charity for much of the time. In 1844 *The Waterford Chronicle* described the work of the order of The Sisters of Charity in Waterford: *"both in Winter and Summer, coal, straw, blankets and clothes of every description are distributed, and on days when meat and soup are not given, potatoes and meal are supplied."*[98]

In most cases labourers were completely dependant on potatoes, both as a source of food and as a cash crop. Skimmed milk was the only other food to supplement potatoes. Meat was never eaten. Salt fish was sometimes available for those living near the sea.[99] Where skimmed milk was not available, salt was the only other accompaniment to potatoes.[100] Failure could mean disaster, and periodic failures of the potato crop were a regular occurrence before the famine of 1845. In October 1841 *The Cork Examiner* carried a warning about the state of the potato crop in County Waterford, stating that although the harvest had not as yet fully started, those potatoes already dug were found to be very wet. It was also feared that many of the seeds had failed, and farmers were advised to leave the remaining potatoes in the ground for as long as possible.[101] *The Waterford Mirror* in January 1842, carried a warning that a shortage of potatoes was to be expected later that year before the new crop could be harvested, as the 1841 crop was not as good or as plentiful as had been hoped. Foreign corn, oatmeal and surplus barley would make up the shortfall the article announced. The article made no reference to the human suffering that might accompany such a shortage, ending with the hope that *"money saved by temperance will be forthcoming for more solid fare."*[102] Fr. Fogarty told the Devon Commission that he had to buy potatoes for the poor around Dungarvan to prevent starvation.[103]

The potato was of course a perfect source of food; nutritious and easy to grow with little labour involved. A small amount of land only was needed to feed a family, providing the crop did not fail.

By the 1840's the potato seems to have superseded many other vegetables. The expansion of the potato as the staple food of the Irish people began in the middle of the 18th century in Munster taking the place of other foods such as grain and dairy produce.[104] Amhlaoibh Ó Súilleabháin writing in 1828 talks of peas and beans grown by farmers at the turn of the century, but *"do chuireadar na potátaí as data iad."*[105]

12

Piers Quarry Barron blamed the potato for the many improvident marriages in the country, as no other food was needed.[106] By 1845 potato cultivation had reached an all time high. In that year over 2.5 million acres, or a third of the arable land, were planted with potatoes.[107]

There was a realisation that the dependence on the potato crop alone was dangerous. Thomas Wyse told the Committee on the State of the Poor in Ireland in 1830 that one of the factors leading to the increase in pauperism in 1822, 1826 and 1827 were due to the partial failure of the potato crop. The only solution he saw to the problem of potato failure was increased production and better storage. In his opinion the Irish people were not beginning to use other food besides the potato, but he remarked that *"the dislike of oatmeal in institutions was passing"*.[108] According to the annual report of the Arthurstown Dispensary and Fever Hospital for 1840, there was a real connection between the diet of the labourers and typhus fever. Since 1826, according to the report, over dependence on the potato crop had led to the increase in fever cases in the area.[109]

In the annual report for the year 1841 lack of proper food and the recent scarcity of potatoes was seen as the reason for the rise in the number of typhus cases.[110] Nevertheless to note that between 1831 and 1841 only 3 deaths were recorded as a result of *"starvation"*. However,

Scene in Waterford Courthouse from Thackeray's *The Irish Sketch Book.*

as was the case during the famine itself, there was a great reluctance to certify that anyone died of starvation, with many such deaths classified as being as a result of various illnesses that would accompany hunger. Thus in the first six months of 1841, two thousand and thirty dive deaths were described as a result of contagious diseases, mainly from cholera and what was described as *"fever"*.[111]

Among the very poor hardship would have been equally shared between men and women, with women carrying out much of the work involved in the cultivation of the potato crop. According to a French visitor to Waterford before the Famine, *"women aged rapidly, subjected as they were to the sufferings and deprivations of poverty."*[112] In 1844 the following description was given of women in County Waterford: *"their strength and constitution yield at an early age to the destructive and unsuitable employments imposed upon them."*[113]

It was generally accepted that the condition of labourers was miserable, their lack of employment being the main problem. For the vast majority of labourers, employment was available for only a very short period of the year. The most difficult time for them was in early Summer before the early potato crop could be harvested. July was seen as a particularly difficult month, referred to as "*July an chabáiste*" in Irish – a month when the very poor depended on cabbage before their first crop of potatoes could be harvested. In 1836 in Ireland it was estimated that 585,000 labourers were unemployed for 30 weeks of the year, giving an estimated total of 2,285,000 living in extreme distress when dependants were added.[114] Also the overall numbers employed as farm labourers was declining since 1815. This was partly due to the depressed state of agriculture after the end of the war with France, and also because of a general improvement in tillage methods, and increased grazing.[115]

The average wage for a labourer was between 6d. per day with food, and 10d. per day without food, with the labourer paying between £2 and £3 for a cabin and small garden.[116] Those lucky to secure employment from benevolent landlords could expect to be paid up to 1s. a day, with a cabin rent free in many cases. On the Devonshire estate labourers were paid from 10d. to 1/2 per day. Farmers were also given assistance to provide better houses for their workers. Extra employment on the estate was given to labourers to carry out drainage work.[117] Landlords like Moore of Moorehill did as much as possible to give direct employment to landless labourers, spending according to one source £4,000 to £5,000 a year on labour.[118]

In the case of many labourers the possession of con-acre ground to grow potatoes for food or for sale was of vital importance. There was very strong competition among landless people for con-acre. Many farmers were reluctant to rent part of their own small farms. Others demanded payment in advance to guarantee against crop failure as potatoes could not be distrained in the event of inability to pay rent. The result was that many had to go into debt in advance of harvesting the crop.[119]

The rent paid for con-acre was enormous when compared to the rent paid for the land by the farmer to the landlord. The rent varied from £4 to £10 per acre, the land prepared and manured with lime by the farmer. There were cases of £20 paid for land manured with dung.[120]

Some were prepared to pay £12 per acre for land fertilised with lime only.[121] In some cases a labourer could pay off his con-acre rent in labour at between 6d. and 8d. per day. In one instance land could be rented for £6 per acre in labour or £7 in cash.[122] If we compare these prices to the £2 to £3 paid in rent to the landlord by the farmer, we can see that profits from this type of agriculture could be enormous for the farmer. While the farmer might expect some leniency from his landlord in times of difficulty, the same latitude was not granted to the labourer by the farmer. The rent was not reduced on the failure of the potato crop – in that case the advance payment was lost or the labourer was evicted.[123] As Michael Nolan, a large farmer from near Dungarvan told the Devon Commission, *"no people are so oppressive as the peasantry to each other."*[124]

The entire system was however a gamble. The farmer depended on the labourer's crop to get his rent – unless he could get payment in advance – while the labourer depended on the success of the crop for his life. If all went well, if the crop did not fail, he would be able to pay his rent to the farmer, or repay the money he borrowed from a moneylender, have food to last most of the year and sell part of the crop to finance the following year's gamble again. There was of course always the possibility of raising pigs on the surplus potatoes which could then be sold for extra cash. Captain Croker from Tallow cites an example of a labourer who made £11 profit from pigs in 1844.[125]

Dealing with the Poor

For many labourers without access even to con-acre ground, unemployment was the reality for much of the year. According to the Poor Enquiry of 1835, 75% of labourers in Ireland had no regular employment.[126] Captain Simon Newport told the Devon Commission that many farmers did not employ labourers except for digging potatoes.[127] The result of this was the large numbers of beggars to be seen on the streets of the cities and small towns. At a meeting of the Waterford Board of Poor Law Guardians on the 25th April 1844, a complaint was made about the numbers of destitute moving to the city to be looked after at the rate-payers' expense.[128] At a further meeting of the Guardians on the 15th of June they petitioned Parliament to amend the Poor Law Act, to increase the period of residency in a Poor Law Union from twelve months to seven years to qualify for admission to a workhouse, and for the inclusion of a clause providing for the transfer of paupers to be looked after by their own Unions.[129] According to the annual report of the Arthurstown Dispensary and Fever Hospital for 1840 each Spring *"the plentifullness of this region brought hundreds of poor"* who introduced fever.[130] Thackeray in his visit to Waterford before the Famine described Dungarvan as a town with *"beggars and idlers still more numerous than at Waterford."*[131] Amedee Pichot, a French visitor in Ireland in 1843 describes Dungarvan as the first Irish town where he met with large numbers of beggars. On reaching the town the coach in which he was travelling was surrounded by about thirty of them; describing them as a "*horrible spectacle*" with a "*dreadful stench.*"[132]

The official attitude of the government at the time was that the destitute should be supported from local taxation. Poor Law rates were collected in each of the Poor Law Unions for the upkeep of workhouses. We have seen how the Waterford City Guardians resented the fact that they had to support paupers from surrounding rural districts. Many farmers and landlords also objected to paying the rates in the first place. Tenants of Lord Carew in the townlands of Knockavelish, Harristown, Ballyglen, and Upper and Lower Woodstown presented the Devon Commission with a petition asking them to be exempted from the Poor Law rates. As there were no paupers in these districts, and as they guaranteed to provide "*employment for and maintain the destitute poor*" of their own area, they thought it unfair to have to pay for the upkeep of the poor from other less well managed estates.[133]

One of the solutions to the poverty of the unemployed labourer was public works. John Musgrave advocated this in 1830. Public works that were being undertaken at the time paid 8d. per day. However in Musgrave's opinion employment was not always offered at times of the year when it was most needed by the labourers. He was in favour of an extensive works programme, funded from a local tax on those who gained most from the land – the landlords. He believed that problems of labourers had been directly caused by landlords and large farmers through the consolidation of farms and extensive clearances on their estates. These clearances resulted in great benefits to the landlords and larger farmers. Therefore, it was this class that should pay for the relief of unemployed labourers.

A legal right to relief through the workhouse system would not solve the problems of labourers according to Musgrave. Such a legal right would only lead to increased poverty, as more landlords would make use of such a system to clear even more people from their estates. Also he believed that there were not enough capable people in many areas to administer the scheme. Instead he thought that a national system of public works should be established through the better use of funds already available, which would create a demand for labour. These public works would be administered nationally through a Board of Commissioners, aided by local Boards. He did not have a very high opinion of the ability of the Grand Juries, (the predecessors of County Council), to administer such a scheme of works. In times of emergency Local Boards could apply to the Commissioners for extra money to fund schemes. He believed that these works should include the

Waterford scene from Thackeray's *The Irish Sketch Book*.

building of roads, canals, piers, railways and the carrying out of drainage. A number of new roads had been built in the county, and had led to increased employment through the development of agriculture. All of these roads had been paid for out of local funds, with the cost borne as much as possible by the estates with the greatest number of unemployed labourers.[134] However Grand Juries did advertise the public works they carried out for tender.[135]

Except for those evicted from land, emigration did not seem to be a solution for many people before the famine. In Ireland as a whole, about 68,000 emigrated in 1844.[136] According to Fr. Treacy of Butlerstown, in 1844 very few emigrated from his area. Some went to Canada and the United States, and 2 families went to Australia. In his opinion landless labourers were looking forward to the coming of the railways and the employment that would be provided.[137] However in 1830 John Musgrave told the Poor Inquiry that many people wished to emigrate, especially to the United States.[138] Before the famine however, there were a number of free passages to Australia from Cork under the Colonial Government Bounty Scheme. These were opened to skilled tradesmen such as carpenters, smiths, wheelwrights and masons; as well as farm labourers, female domestics and farm servants. The passage included food and accommodation on board ship, free lodging in Cork until the ship was ready to sail, and free food and accommodation on board ship on reaching Australia. Matrons would travel on board to supervise "*single females.*"[139] There was opposition to emigration however before the famine. William Sharman Crawford estimated that there were 500,000 uncultivated acres in Ireland, and thought it would be cheaper and more humane to settle landless labourers and their families on this land instead of exporting them to Australia.[140] In June 1844 *The Waterford Chronicle* carried a politically motivated editorial urging people not to emigrate but to stay at home "*in anticipation of Repeal, which will supply money and employ labour in the development of Ireland's rich resources.*"[141]

Law and Order

In spite of the obvious poverty among large sections of the population in the years leading up to the Famine of 1845, it is surprising that there was so little agrarian violence in County Waterford.

Lewis remarked in 1837 on the relative peacefulness of the county.[142] Between 1831 and 1841, seventy three homicides took place in County Waterford.[143] In 1842, 302 people were committed for trial in the county, with 130 convicted and 172 acquitted. This number rose in 1843 to 500, with 207 convicted and 293 acquitted.[144] These charges included 136 offences against the person, thirty seven offences against property with violence, one malicious offence against property, and two offences against currency. The sentences of those convicted are interesting: seven people were sentenced to transportation; 131 were committed to prison; forty five were fined and five were sentenced to whipping.[145] In 1844 only seventeen agrarian outrages were reported to the Constabulary Office.[146] *The Waterford Mirror* in its report of the Dungarvan Quarter Sessions in January 1830 remarks on the fewness of assault cases, and cited this as proof of the improved state of the peasantry in the area. Only one assault case was tried, that of two brothers convicted of attacking a neighbour with a hatchet and slane. They were sentenced to two months in Waterford Gaol and fined £2 each. It is interesting to note that on the same day, and before the same Justice, a labourer named Cunningham was convicted of stealing three half bags of wheat from his employer, a large farmer. He was sentenced to seven years transportation, the Judge informing him that he intended to make an example of him to others to deter this kind of evil.[147] By 1843 similar notions of justice were still to be seen, with Catherine Hearn sentenced to 7 years transportation at the Waterford County Quarter Sessions for stealing £1.[148]

In fact between 1843 and 1844, the number of police stationed in County Waterford actually fell; from 161 in 1843 to 143 in 1844, although the numbers were to rise to 165 again in 1845.[149] This rise in the numbers of police in the county can probably be attributed to the transfer of police from the city of Waterford to the county because of the changes between the city boundaries in 1844.[150] In neighbouring counties agrarian violence was to remain a major problem. In Tipperary, for example, the Rockit movement reported to be still alive in 1830, and the Government *"determined to use severe measures with a view to restoring peace and quiet in the neighbourhood of Thurles."*[151] In 1832 *"Rockites"* destroyed weirs on the Suir, leaving threatening notices against anyone who repaired them.[152]

Secret societies such as the Whiteboys, Caravats and Shanavests that developed in much of East Munster during the 18th century, had by the beginning of the 19th century largely died out in the Waterford region.[153] By then, under the increasing influence of O'Connell and the

18

Catholic Church the agrarian violence of the previous century began to give way to tithe agitation, and the campaigns for Catholic Emancipation and Repeal. Random violence continued however for a number of years as the Poleens and the Gows fought each other at fairs and other gatherings. In fact one family, the Connerys of Sliabh gCua, achieved almost legendary notoriety in their long confrontation with the authorities between 1831 and 1838.[154]

There were, however, a number of isolated agrarian outrages in the county in the years leading up to the Famine. According to Piers Quarry Barron a public subscription was raised to shoot one unpopular landlord, John Keefe. He raised rents on his estate after tenants had made improvements.[155] Another landlord, Charles Welsh was murdered after he evicted tenants for non-payment of rent and "*bad cultivation.*"[156] Other minor outrages also took place such as the destruction of ploughs, burning of a farm cart, and breaking a horse's leg. These were generally because of disputes between farmers – usually over land.[157] Francis Currey mentioned two examples of house burning – one however was a family dispute, and the other was to intimidate a witness in a court case in Tipperary involving horse stealing.[158] Compared to the extensive violence in Tipperary, reports of "*outrages*" in Waterford seemed mild in the extreme. In 1843, what were described as two "*ruffians*" entered the house of John Power in Clonea-Power, ordered dinner, and after eating broke everything in the house. On the same day the coastguard reported that they had put an end to illegal fishing on the Suir.[159] In 1842 *The Waterford Mirror* carried a report of a meeting of "*the gentry of the county expressing regret and indignation at the poisoning of the Marquis of Waterford's hounds.*"

There were many, however, who saw the seeds of revolution all about them, remembering perhaps the excesses of 1798. In 1840 The *Waterford Mail* believed that there was "*a deep well, a widely extended system of Ribbonism, a system directed against life and property,*" with the state of the country "*alarming...increased as it is by the shapeless apathy of a faithless government who would give up the Protestants of Ireland bound hand and foot to gratify the demon demagogue.*"[160] The "*demon demagogue*" was Daniel O'Connell. He died in Genoa in March 1847. The revolution anticipated by so many, was preceded by signal fires on the hills in West Waterford, led by proto-republicans inspired by barricades in Paris and petered out in a squalid exchange of gunfire in Cappoquin. (see Dermot Power's article).

For most people in County Waterford, as in the country as a whole, other events were of more significance. The potato crop partly failed in 1845, and failed totally in 1846.

REFERENCES

1. Devon Commission Report: Evidence taken before Her Majesty's Commissioners of enquiry into the state of the law and practice in respect to the occupation of land in Ireland (hereafter Devon Commission) (U.K., 1845), Vol. III, p.24.
2. ibid, Musgrave, Witness 813.
3. *The Cork Examiner*, 1 Oct. 1841.
4. Lewis, Samuel, *A Topographical Dictionary of Ireland* (London, 1837) Vol. II, p.678.
5. Butler, Matthew, *A History of the Barony of Gaultier* (Waterford, 1913) p.122.
6. Parliamentary Gazetteer of Ireland 1843-1844 (Ireland, 1844) p.478.
7. Devon Commission, Nolan, Witness 907.
8. ibid, Treacy, Witness 914.
9. ibid, Galway, Witness 903.
10. Poor Inquiry (1830), p.81.
11. Solar, Peter, "Agriculture and Trade, 1809-1909", in Nolan, W. & Power, Thomas P. (eds.) *Waterford History and Society* (Dublin, 1992) p.500.
12. Cowman, Des, "Trade and Society in Waterford City, 1800-1840", in Nolan, W. & Power, T. (eds.) *Waterford History and Society* (Dublin, 1992) p.433.
13. Devon Commission, Currey, Witness 812.
14. ibid, Foley, Witness 816.
15. *The Waterford Chronicle*, 8 May 1844.
16. Devon Commission, Barron, Witness 912.
17. O'Donnovan, John, *Letters containing information relative to the antiquities of the county of Waterford collected during the progress of the Ordnance Survey in 1841* (Ireland, 1841) p.45.
18. Devon Commission, Musgrave, Witness 813.
19. *The Waterford Mirror*, 8 Dec. 1841.
20. *The Waterford Chronicle*, 24 April 1844. The article also gives a list of potatoes suitable for cultivation in Ireland and lists varieties such as: Shaw's Early, Bread Fruit, London Purple, Pink Eye, Magpie, China Orange, Red Kidney, Lankeshire Kidney and No Blow. Irish White Apple was recommended as a pig feed.
21. Ireland: Census of Population 1841 p.xiv.
22. Devon Commission, Foley, Witness 816; Vol. 3 p.195.
23. ibid, Treacy, Witness 914.
24. ibid, Appendix 90, Table of Landholding Sizes, 1841 Census, Vol. p.274.
25. Woodham-Smith, Cecil, *The Great Hunger: Ireland 1845-9* (London, 1962) p.29.
26. O Grada, Cormac, *Ireland before and after the Famine: Explorations in Economic History, 1800-1925* (Manchester, 1993) p.44.
27. Ireland: Census of Population 1841, p.90
28. Burtchaell, Jack, "19th Century Society in County Waterford", *Decies* XXX, (Autumn 1985), p.40
29. "As others saw us, Waterford in Kohl's Travels in Ireland, 1844", *Decies 47*, (Spring 1993), p.23.
30. Poor Inquiry 1830, p.631.
31. Devon Commission, Fitzgerald, Witness 825, Vol.3, p.209; Witness 826, Vol. 3, p.210.
32. ibid, Witness 803.
33. *The Waterford Chronicle,* 24 Jan. 1843
34. Devon Commission Musgrave, Witness 813.
35. ibid, Currey, Witness 812.
36. ibid, Vol.3, p.184.

37. Feeney, Patrick, "Ballysaggart Estate: Eviction, Famine and Conspiracy", *Decies* XXVII, (Autumn 1984) p.6.
38. "As others saw us, Waterford in Inglis's Journey through Ireland in 1834", *Decies* 45, (Spring 1992) p.2.
39. Devon Commission, Currey, Witness 812
40. "As others saw us, Waterford in Inglis's Journey through Ireland in 1834", *Decies* 45, (Spring 1992) p.4.
41. Devon Commission, Vol 3, p.341-342.
42. "As others saw us, Waterford in Inglis's Journey through Ireland in 1834", *Decies* 45, (Spring 1992) p.2.
43. Devon Commission, Hennebry, Witness 916.
44. ibid, Witness 1038, p.294.
45. *The Waterford Chronicle,* 6 May 1844.
46. Devon Commission, Appendix 100, 101, 104, Summary of evictions brought to courts: Queens Bench, Court of Common Pleas, Court of Exchequer, and Civil Bill Ejectment.
47. ibid, Musgrave, Witness 813.
48. ibid, Galway, Witness 903.
49. Feeney, Patrick, op. cit. p.6
50. Devon Commission, Power, Witness 832.
51. ibid, Witness 1041.
52. ibid, Flynn, Witness 906.
53. ibid, Kill, Witness 1038, Vol.3; p.764.
54. ibid, Appendix 96, p.290.
55. ibid, Currey, Witness 812.
56. Carroll, J.S., "The Estate of George Lane-Fox", *Decies* XXVI (Summer 1984) p.52.
57. Devon Commission, Summary, p.38.
58. Woodham-Smith, Cecil op. cit. p.27.
59. Poor Inquiry (1830) p.71.
60. *The Cork Examiner,* 30 Sept. 1839.
61. Devon Commission, Summary, p.373.
62. ibid, Witness 814.
63. ibid, Power, Witness 828, Vol.3, p.216.
64. ibid, Nolan, Witness 907.
65. ibid, Appendix 94, p.285.
66. Poor Inquiry (1830) p.645.
67. Proudfoot, Lindsay, "The Estate System in Mid-Nineteenth Century Waterford", in Nolan W. & Power, Thomas P. (eds.) *Waterford History and Society* (Dublin, 1992) p.519
68. "As others saw us, Waterford in Inglis's Journey through Ireland in 1843", *Decies* 45, (Spring 1992), p.2.
69. Woodham-Smith, Cecil, op. cit. p.42.
70. Devon Commission, Galway, Witness 903.
71. *The Waterford Chronicle,* 20 May 1844.
72. *ibid,* 5 Jun. 1844.
73. Devon Commission, Flynn, Witness 909, Vol.3, p.441.
74. ibid, Flynn, Witness 906.
75. ibid, Croker, Witness 803.
76. Poor Inquiry (1830) p.642.
77. Devon Commission, Newport, Witness 905.
78. Cowman, Des op. cit. p.439.

79. Parliamentary Gazetteer of Ireland 1843-1844 op. cit. p.482.
80. Devon Commission, Treacy, Witness
81. ibid, Flynn, Witness 909; Vol. 3, p.442.
82. Clark, S. & Donnelly, J. *Irish peasants, violence and political unrest 1780-1914*, (Manchester, 1983) Introduction pp.17-18.
83. Devon Commission, Appendix 90, p.274.
84. Poor Inquiry 1830 p.632.
85. *The Cork Examiner,* 27 Sept. 1839
86. Ketch, Katherine, "Settlement and Colonisation in Marginal Areas of County Waterford, Part III, Early Evidence", *Decies* XXXIV, p.71.
87. Feeney, Patrick, op. cit. p.6.
88. Devon Commission, Foley, Nelson Trafalgar; Witness 816, Vol. 3, p.194.
89. Carroll, J.S., op. cit. p.52.
90. *The Waterford Chronicle,* 15 April 1844.
91. Lewis, Samuel, op. cit. p.677.
92. Hansard, Joseph, *The history, topography and antiquities (Natural and Ecclesiastical), with biographical sketches of the nobility, gentry and ancient families, and notices of eminent men, &c., of the County and City of Waterford: including the towns, parishes, villages, manors and seats.* (Ireland, 1870)
93. Parliamentary Gazetteer of Ireland 1843-1844 op. cit. p.482.
94. Devon Commission, Appendix 89, p.273.
95. Woodham-Smith, Cecil, op. cit. p.14.
96. "As others saw us, Waterford in Inglis's Journey through Ireland", *Decies* 45, (Spring 1992) p.2.
97. Devon Commission, Power, Witness 911.
98. *The Waterford Chronicle,* 27 April 1844.
99. Hansard, Joseph, op. cit. pp.444-445.
100. Parliamentary Gazetteer of Ireland 1843-44, op. cit. p.482.
101. The *Cork Examiner,* 1 Oct. 1841.
102. *The Waterford Mirror,* 31 Jan. 1842.
103. Devon Commission, Fogerty, Witness 810.
104. Whelan, Kevin "Post and Pre-famine Landscape Change" Póirtéir, Cathal, (ed.): *The Great Irish Famine,* (Dublin, 1995) pp.19, 20
105. O'Sullivan, Humphrey, *Cinn Lae Amhlaoibh* (Dublin 1973) p.37.
106. Devon Commission, Barron, Witness 912.
107. Kinealy, Christine, *This Great Calamity: The Irish Famine 1845-1852* (Dublin, 1994) p.6.
108. Minutes of Evidence before Select Committee on the State of the Poor in Ireland p.638.
109. *The Waterford Mirror,* 25 Jan 1841.
110. ibid, 24 Jan. 1842.
111. Ireland: Census of Population (U.K., 1841) p.96.
112. Holt, Eileen "A 19th Century French Traveller's visit to Waterford", Part I; *Decies* XVIII, (Sept. 1981), p.16.
113. Parliamentary Gazetteer of Ireland 1843-44, op. cit. p.483.
114. Poor Inquiry (1836)
115. Devon Commission, Barron, Witness 904.
116. ibid, Croker, Witness 803.
117. ibid, Currey, Witness 812.
118. ibid, Croker, Witness 805.
119. ibid, Galway, Witness 903.

120. ibid, Nolan, Witness 911.
121. ibid, Power, Witness 911.
122. ibid, White, Witness 820.
123. ibid, Treacy, Witness 914.
124. ibid, Nolan, Witness 824, Vol. 3, p.208.
125. ibid, Croker, Witness 803.
126. Woodham-Smith, Cecil op. cit. p.27.
127. Devon Commission, Newport, Witness 905.
128. *Waterford Chronicle,* 27 April 1844.
129. ibid, 15 June 1844.
130. *The Waterford Mirror,* 25 Jan. 1841.
131. Thackeray, William Makepeace, *The Works of William Makepeace Thackeray,* Vol. VIII, p.302.
132. Holt, Eileen, op. cit. p.61.
133. Devon Commission, Newport, Witness 905.
134. Poor Inquiry (1830) pp.84-85.
135. *The Waterford Mirror,* 15 April 1841.
136. Woodham-Smith, Cecil, op. cit. p.204.
137. Devon Commission, Treacy, Witness.
138. Poor Inquiry: (1830) p.76.
139. *The Waterford Mirror,* 13 Jan. 1841.
140. *The Cork Examiner,* 30 Sept. 1839.
141. *The Waterford Chronicle:* 1-6-1844.
142. Lewis, Samuel, op. cit. p.677.
143. Ireland: Census of Population (1841) p.97.
144. *The Waterford Chronicle,* 1 May 1844.
145. The Parliamentary Gazetteer of Ireland 1843-44, op. cit. p.484.
146. Devon Commission, Appendix 36, pp.118-119.
147. *The Waterford Mirror,* 13 Jan. 1883.
148. *The Waterford Chronicle,* 3 Jan. 1883.
149. Devon Commission, Appendix 83, p.266.
150. *The Waterford Chronicle,* 6 April 1844; following a reduction in the area of Waterford city, Stuart de Decies as Lord Lieutenant of the county asked magistrates to request the overall numbers of police in the city to be reduced and the numbers in the county to be increased.
151. *The Waterford Mirror,* 4 Jan. 1830.
152. O'Connor, Emmet *A Labour History of Waterford* (Waterford, 1989) p.50.
153. Roberts, Paul E.W., "Caravats and Shanavests: Whiteboyism and Faction Fighting in East Munster, 1802-11" in, Clark, S. & Donnelly, J. (eds.) *Irish Peasants, Violence and Political Unrest 1780-1914* (Manchester, 1983), p.97.
154. For a detailed account of faction fighting between Poleens and Gows, and of the Conneries, see, Kiley, M.B. *The Connerys* (Dublin, 1994).
155. Devon Commission Barron, Witness 912.
156. ibid, Witness 814.
157. ibid, Summary, p.303.
158. ibid, Currey, Witness 812.
159. *The Waterford Chronicle,* 10 Jan. 1843.
160. *The Waterford Mail,* 23 March 1840.

Chapter 2

An overview of the famine in Waterford

JACK BURTCHAELL

The potato blight spread stealthily across the potato fields of Europe in the summer of 1845. By September it had made its appearance in County Waterford. The degree of destruction was highly variable in the 1845 crop, but Waterford seems to have been badly hit losing over 40% of its potato crop by the Spring of 1846.[1] By the beginning of December 1845, occupancy in Dungarvan workhouse had increased by 63% over the same week the previous year, Lismore saw a 26% increase in inmates, and the city area seems least affected with an occupancy rise in the Waterford Union workhouse of only 2%.[2]

By the Spring of 1846 efforts were being made to provide relief by employing people on public works, but no public works had actually commenced by the end of March 1846. Local relief committees also made collections which were augmented by donations from the British Government via the Lord Lieutenant. My mid July 5,237 men were employed on public works in the county, having risen dramatically from 2,951 on July 4th, and rising to 5,403 by July 25th 1846. Employment began to decline by August 1st as men were laid off in expectation of the harvest. On August 1st 1846, 3,623 men were still engaged throughout the county on public works as follows. Coshmore and Coshbride had 1,233 employed, Decies within Drum 644, Decies without Drum 1,104 and Upperthird 742.[3] Along with the rise in occupancy in workhouses, these figures point to the impact of the crop failure in Waterford of 1845 as falling most heavily on the western half of the county. It had been a terrible year, but Ireland had weathered similar years before. It is doubtful if anyone died of actual hunger during the first year of the famine in Waterford. Mortality rates did rise as seen on table 3 (chapter 12), but deaths were probably due to other ailments prematurely carrying off the most vulnerable age groups.

The vital potato harvest of Autumn 1846 was almost a complete failure, and the months that followed saw the country slide from crisis into catastrophe. Terror spread among the hungry, faced with the prospect of absolute famine, and among the elite confronted by social conflict, public disorder and violence. In October, 1846, the government made further grants to relief committees to support those out of work; for each head of household out of work, £4.00 was

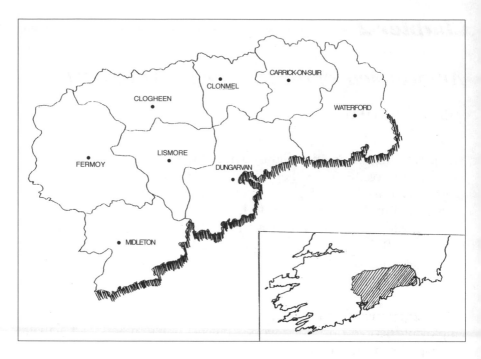

Poor Law Unions.

granted. The estimated numbers of destitute households in County Waterford was as follows: Glenahiry 962 households; Gaultier 1,831 households; Middlethird 2,529; Decies within Drum 3,996 households; Upperthird 4,603 households; Coshmore and Coshbride 4,743 households and Decies without Drum 6,378 households.[4] By this reckoning 25,042 households in the county were at risk; if average family size was four persons it put 100,168 people, or if average family size was five persons it put 125,210 people at immediate risk in the county, or between 45% and 50% of the total population of the county.

Public works, particularly road building and improvement, continued throughout the autumn and winter of 1846, but the scale of demand for work and the demands for supervision and administration swamped the system. The change from day wage rates to task work put further strains on an overworked administrative staff and impeded action, under an avalanche of paperwork and red tape. For the workers it led to lay offs and delays in payment. Government policy severely limited the availability of rations and food prices soared. Even those in employment could not afford sufficient food. Small farmers were forced to eat their corn seed, and labourers begged, borrowed, stole or starved.

The Inspecting Officer Captain Hay wrote in January 1847 of the eastern part of the county, "*the relief committees are besieged by applications for employment on the public works*".[5] Accusations of jobbery and favouritism were rife, and there is evidence that larger farmers used the public works as a means of ridding themselves of labourers and cottiers traditionally dependant upon them for work and conacre. The employment offered on public works was a lifeline to those facing starvation, but as food prices continued to soar the lifeline metamorphosed into a garotte. Captain Hay said of those on the works "*their food is most scanty owing to the high price of meal*"; he went on "*labourers are unable to accomplish a day's work from want of sustenance*".[6]

Farmers themselves were in very straitened circumstances due to increased rates and seed shortages; and with no potatoes, they could not in many instances afford to employ labourers in early 1847. Lieut. Downman was now told "The *farmers have dismssed all their servants*". A little later he noted, "*A plough is now occasionally seen on the farms, but instead of labourers being employed, the farmer's sons guide the plough*".[7] For the smaller farmers even this substitution option was not available. Reporting from Waterford in February 1847 Captain Mayne stated, "*the farmers of from 5-15 acres, who hold so much of it, have not the money to expand on their farms, or seed to sow, and must probably all become labourers, as many are now, their land being given up*".[8]

Early in 1847, the long standing government policy of not providing outdoor relief was reversed and soup kitchens opened. Tied to this was another policy shift, the phasing out of public works as a relief measure, and the provision that almost all relief measures were in future to be financed by the union concerned. This marks the start of the government's disengagement from the crisis. By the autumn of 1847 the process was accelerating apace and by early 1848 was in full swing.

The Temporary Relief Act of 1847, which provided for soup kitchens, administered to huge sections of the Irish population. However the needs of the population varied immensely from place to place. It varied from Unions in Ulster where less than 1% of the population required outdoor relief, to large parts of the west where over 60% of the population were on the Relief Lists. In Ballinrobe the figure reached over 93% of the total population at one point.[9] The experience in Waterford lay between these two extremes. The Waterford Union had 44% of its population eligible to receive soup, Dungarvan had 47.8% at the height of the crisis, Carrick-on-Suir Union which included part of County Waterford had 28% and Clonmel 35.8%. Lismore Union stood out with 66.7% of its population on temporary relief lists. This figure is

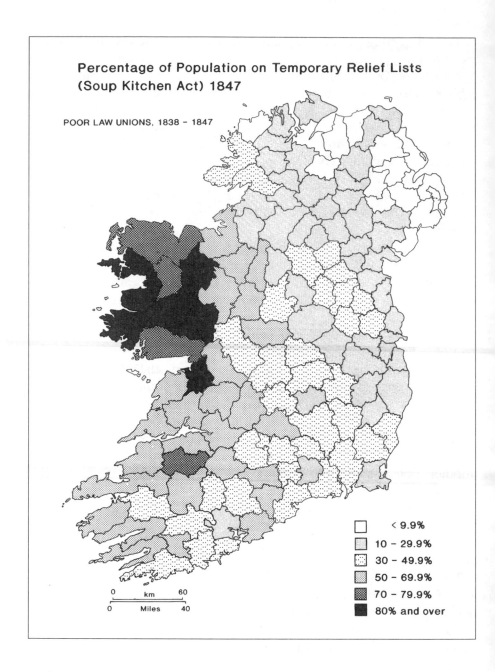

Percentage of Population on Temporary Relief Lists (Soup Kitchen Act) 1847

POOR LAW UNIONS, 1838 – 1847

☐	< 9.9%
☐	10 – 29.9%
☐	30 – 49.9%
☐	50 – 69.9%
☐	70 – 79.9%
■	80% and over

0　　km　　60
0　　Miles　　40

higher than for any union in the provinces of Leinster or Ulster and is on the scale of west Cork and Kerry, west Limerick, Clare and Connacht. Lismore was the only union east of a line from Cork City to Sligo which exceeded the 60% figure.

The change of government policy with regard to relief works swung rapidly into action. On March 20th 1847 20% of those on the works

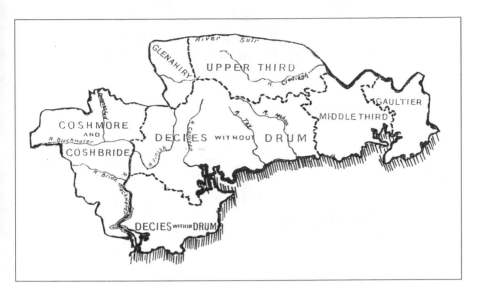

Waterford Baronies.

were discharged, while a further 10% were discharged on April 24th and the remainder a week later. The complete abandonment of public works relief on May 1st several months before the potato harvest in the autumn is either an admission that public works were totally inadequate, or signal the intention of government disengagement.

While the Temporary Relief Act undoubtedly saved thousands from starvation, it came too late for many. Weakened by hunger, poorly housed and only partly clothed, many died. Estimates of mortality vary, S.H. Cousens[10] estimated 3.3% of the 1841 population of Waterford died 6,474 deaths in total.

Throughout the summer of 1847, food flowed into Ireland and prices dropped as a result. The potato harvest of 1847 was largely free from blight, but the acreage planted had been severely restricted for the reasons outlined above. Estimates put the 1847 acreage at about one third of the usual potato acreage.

The good harvest provided a brief respite, but now another by-product of the distress and economic dislocation was to come centre stage in the experience of the poor in County Waterford. Since 1843 landlords had been eligible for the payment of rates due on properties whose land was valued at less than £4.00. Faced with inflated rates bills and high rent arrears many landlords proceeded to evict. The Gregory clause of the Temporary Relief Act forbade relief at the expense of the union to anyone holding over a quarter of an acre. These two legal provisions caught the labourers and cottiers in a pincer movement.

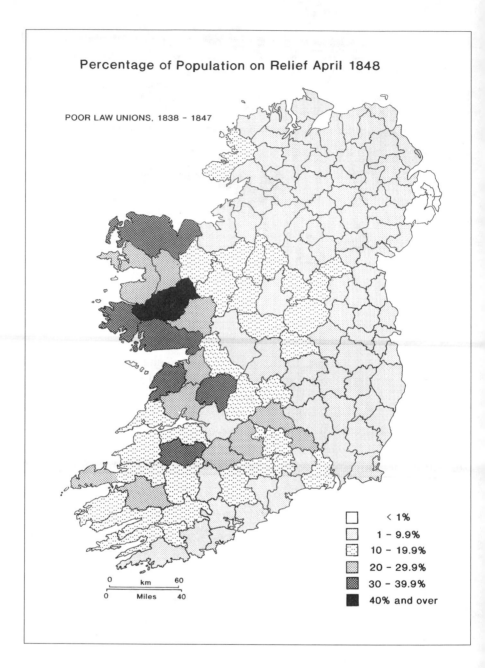

Percentage of Population on Relief April 1848

POOR LAW UNIONS, 1838 – 1847

0 km 60
0 Miles 40

☐	< 1%
☐	1 – 9.9%
▦	10 – 19.9%
▨	20 – 29.9%
▩	30 – 39.9%
■	40% and over

While the 1843 act may have inadvertently led to unforeseen consequences, the Gregory clause could only have had malice aforethought.
Landlords evicted or "*encouraged*" tenants to surrender their holdings,
so that they could avoid having to pay rates on them. People holding
small acreage's could only obtain relief when they had surrendered
their land. The result was an exodus of the rural poor which changed

forever the face of the Irish landscape. Such a huge transformation was only possible, without massive agrarian disorder, amid the despondency and helplessness of famine conditions.

From now on all Irish poverty was to be relieved by local rates. As Cecil Woodham Smith states *"from this point onwards good intentions on the part of the British Government became increasingly difficult to discern".*[11] Joel Mokyr is more blunt, *"when the chips were down in the frightful summer of 1847, the British Government simply abandoned the Irish and let them perish".*[12]

As Government support declined and local responsibility increased during late 1847 and into 1848, the percentage of those receiving relief dropped dramatically. The need for relief had declined somewhat due to death and emigration. The partial harvest of 1847 had helped for some months. By the spring of 1848 hunger and destitution were increasing again but access to relief had tightened dramatically due to the Gregory Clause, and its financing fell on local resources. In April 1848 we can measure this using the parliamentary papers.[13] Again marked regional contrasts are apparent. Three Ulster unions Gortin, Newtownard and Downpatrick had less than 1% of their respective populations in receipt of relief. Across Ulster the average was 3.88%. In Connacht the provisional average was 19.8%, with Ballinrobe the national blackspot with 41.75% of its population in receipt of relief. Waterford was a little better than the Munster average of 14%, Dungarvan stood at 8%, Lismore at 7.8% and Waterford city at 10.9%, neighbouring Clonmel was at 11.95% and Carrick-on-Suir at 3.7%.

Death rates from starvation rose again in the Spring of 1848,[14] accelerated by very cold weather, but by now it was a famine that dares not speak its name, at least in official circles. Charitable donations began to dry up after the extraordinary charity of 1846-7. Following the non-blighted but small potato crop of 1847, most people believed the pestilence had passed, and massive effort was expended on putting in the 1848 potato crop. But from mid June, wet weather made extensive blight inevitable and the resultant crop failure was as devastating as in 1846.[15] The abortive Young Ireland Insurrection was used in Britain to popularise a policy decision which pre-dated the insurrection. Ireland was to be left to her own devices. What followed during the Winter of 1848 and Spring 1849 was as bad or worse than two years earlier. In the face of huge rate increases, even previously solvent tenant farmers fled the prospect, and emigrated. Landlords faced with empty farms, no rent and huge rates went bankrupt.

Thomas Carlyle visited Waterford in 1849 and commented on the ruined commerce and empty shops and warehouses. Another blow fell with the arrival of cholera in the Spring of 1849. By June even the

Quakers, exasperated by government inaction, gave up relief work and stated the scale of the problem to be beyond their means. Mortality in Waterford City and County peaked in 1849 (see table 4 in my article on demography). Some 31% of total famine deaths in Waterford occurred that year. Throughout the country, workhouse occupancy peaked in June of 1849 with some 227,329 inmates. In July 1849 out-door relief peaked for the year at 784,370 recipients, far less than had availed of soup kitchens two years earlier, but death, emigration and local financing of relief had seen to that.

The 1849 potato harvest was quite good except in parts of the west, and outdoor relief was wound down in most areas. By the Spring of 1850, rate collection nationally was exceeding expenditure.[16] The 1850 harvest was again mostly healthy, with the exception of parts of the west of Ireland. The famine was over locally: it's grim legacy had begun.

REFERENCES

1. Kinealy, Christine, *This Great Calamity: The Irish Famine 1845-52* (Dublin 1994), p.42.
2. British Parliamentary Papers, *Copies or extracts of correspondence relating to the state of the union workhouses in Ireland: First Second and Third series.* (Shannon, 1968) p.415.
3. British Parliamentary Papers, *Correspondence relating to the measures adopted by Her Majesty's government for the relief of distress arising from the failure of the potato crop in Ireland with similar correspondence.* Commissariat series (First Part) and an Index 1846-47 (Shannon, 1970).
4. British Parliamentary Papers, *Correspondence relating to measures adopted for the relief of distress in Ireland: Board of Works series (First Part) with an Index 1847* (hereafter Famine Ireland 6) (Shannon, 1970).
5. ibid, Jnl. of Capt. Hay Inspecting Officer Co. Waterford Jan. 1847.
6. ibid, Jnl. of Capt. Hay Inspecting Officer Co. Waterford Jan. 1847.
7. ibid, Jnl. of Lieut. Downman Inspecting Officer Co. Waterford Jan. 1847.
8. ibid, Report of Capt. Mayne Co. Waterford Feb. 1847.
9. British Parliamentary Papers, *Papers relating to proceedings for the relief of distress and the state of the unions and workhouses in Ireland:* Seventh and Eight series 1847-48 (hereafter Famine Ireland 4) (Shannon, 1970).
10. Cousens, S.H. "The Regional Variation in Mortality during the Great Irish Famine" in *P.R.I.A.* lxiii section c No. 3 1963.
11. Woodham Smith, Cecil, *The Great Hunger* (London 1966) p.319.
12. Mokyr, Joel *Why Ireland starved: A quantitative and analytic history of the Irish economy 1800-1850* (London, 1983) p.291.
13. Famine Ireland 4.
14. Kinealy, Christine, op.cit p.229.
15. Woodham Smith, Cecil, op.cit p.363.
16. Kinealy, Christine, op.cit p.270.

Chapter 3

First responses to blight

TED O'REGAN

With hindsight, the partial failure of the potato crop in 1845 was an augury of distress. But did the people of the time, particularly those in official positions, have a premonition of the cataclysmic events to come? In preparing this essay I examined a small block of Relief Commission Papers from the National Archive, which comprised letters and reports to Dublin Castle between the Autumn of 1845 and Spring 1846. These were mainly from Boards of Guardians in the County of Waterford, but there were also letters from Electoral District Committees, Resident Magistrates, Relief Committees, Town Clerks and private individuals.

Reports on the failure of the potato crop

The first recorded reference to the blight was on 19th October, 1845, when G. Fitzgerald R.M. (Dungarvan) wrote to the Under Secretary that the *'potatoe* (sic) *crop appears to be universally blighted'*. He immediately qualified this however *"on the general digging of potatoes – crop found much better than expected"* and *"early potatoes considered safe"*. And again: *"People believe that the diseased potatoes have become sound again and they are in better spirits about their crop"*. Then the report see-sawed between gloom and optimism: *"Potatoes in some areas destroyed to a frightful extent"* but *"Apprehension about potatoe crop subsiding"*.[1]

The next day, 20th October, 1845, by unanimous resolution, the Board of Guardians of the Waterford Poor Law Union, reported that *"Potatoes, failure of, to a great extent"*.[2] while on that same day, Lord Stuart de Decies, Chairman of the Poor Law Guardians, Dungarvan Union, reported: *"Failure of potato crop very general. Disease spreading while crop remains in the ground. If not checked the worst consequences as regards provision to the people to be apprehended."*

Thanks to experiments at the workhouse, Lord Stuart de Decies, had a practical suggestion:-

"No. 1. Diseased potatoes housed ten days, when boiled, unfit for use.

  No. 2. Diseased potatoes pitted in earth ten days, very little better than No. 1.

  No. 3. Pitted in lime and earth, better than Nos. 1. and 2.

  No. 4. Pitted in lime decidedly best."

Armed with this knowledge he made some further suggestions:

> *That potatoes should be pitted in lime to arrest the progress of disease. The immediate digging and careful separation of the sound from unsound potatoes and storing them in small narrow heaps. That dry pulverised earth or sand would be a good substitute for lime. The conversion of diseased potatoes into starch and the preservation of the sound ones for seed.*[3]

Soon, reports of potato failure began to arrive thick and fast from many parts of the county. By the 19th January, 1846, returns from Waterford Poor Law Union showed that David Walsh, a Guardian from Kilkeasy had lost three quarters of his crop as also had David Holden of Killahy and Patrick Madigan of Clonassay. Thomas Griffin and Michael Dooley (both of Newcastle) and Thomas Dillon, a Guardian from Rathmoylan, had lost two thirds of their crop.[4] These could be regarded as pretty extreme losses when compared with Ardmore – one quarter diseased, Abbeyside – one third, Ring – one half to two thirds, Aglish – a third and at Kilgobinet – half the average crop.[5]

The assimilation of such facts took time. Lord Stuart de Decies' suggestion on 15th November, 1845 *"that the different Boards of Guardians.....in the County be made the medium for collecting information as to the state of the potato crop"*.[6] Two weeks later he reported that *"The three Poor Law Unions have agreed to appoint local committees consisting of the Electoral Guardians to report every week or every fortnight."*[7] March and April saw a series of reports reflecting crop loss, labourers idle and vacancies in the Workhouse.[8]

Requests for the provision of Public Works

Pressure for "Public Works" for the unemployed started early. Lismore Union urged, on 3rd November, 1845, *"that Government should adopt means for an increase of employment for the population, and adopt any other measures which may seem best to avert the threatened evil of a year of scarcity."*[9] James Galwey, J.P. wanted Public Works *"and at sufficient wages, not less than 9 shillings a week."*[10]

Requests and suggestions poured in. The Electoral Division Committee of Crooke (Waterford Union) urged that

> *Government employ the labouring poor (who are likely to suffer most) in cleansing the docks and town of Passage and building a small pier to prevent future accumulation of sand and gravel and restore Passage as a harbour of shelter, which would give employment. Also the repair of roads by the Board of Works*

Henry Villiers Stuart, Lord Stuart De Decies (1803-1874)
Champion of catholic emancipation and M.P. for Waterford.

*particularly those passing through Kilmacomb Hospital Estate
leading to Ballymacaw.... That great relief would be afforded to the
labouring class by another important public work, the taking in of
the Back Strand of Tramore and formation of road thereto, this
project has been favourably reported on.*[11]

December, 19th 1845, saw a suggestion by "the Landlords etc."
forwarded by James Galwey, J.P. as: "*a new line of road through the
mountains of Knockambraindane, Lyre, Knockanafrinn, Carrigthalure
and thence through the Gap of Barra Vila Valla (from the ford of
Kinackhan in the Barony of Decies Without to the new line of road
from Carrick-on-Suir to Dungarvan) which would open the Barony of
Glenahiery and part of Decies Without etc. and thus afford employment
to a great number of labourers who will shortly be in great distress from
failure of potato crop.*"[12]

There were other suggestions for a canal to Tallow,[13] the repair of
footpaths of the mail coach road,[14] for improvements to harbours and
navigable rivers, draining, new roads, provision of materials for future
repairs of roads, improvements in fisheries. There were great hopes for
the planned Waterford to Limerick Railway.[15] Patrick Hayden of Carrick-
on-Suir, suggested on 10th February, 1846, "*that the distressed areas of
the south are proposed to be intersected by railway (Bill before
Parliament), their immediate operation would be the means of saving
the people*".[16] Edward Elliot of 7, South Parade implored His Excellency
to issue orders to the Board of Works and 'the Post Office' "*to set
forward works to give immediate employment*" through building the
railway to Limerick, but was told it could not commence until March
1846.[17]

Richard Osborne, Resident Engineer for the Waterford and Limerick
Railways thought that work on the Railway project would give
employment to more than 3,200 men – labourers, masons, carpenters,
smiths, overseers, clerks and timekeepers in the first six months of
1846.[18]

Alternatives

Some sought alternative uses for the potato: Dungarvan Guardians
suggested making Farina from unsound potatoes.[19] They also "*stated
that pigs and cattle thrive on diseased potatoes*".[20] The making of potato
starch was recommended. C. Darby Griffiths Esq., of Morrisson's Hotel,
wrote on 4th November, 1845, that he, in conjunction with Mr.
Cornelius Power of Cappoquin made experiments in the manufacturing
of potato starch.

The results are as follows:-

> *1d. per stone cost of damaged potatoes might be had for less. Total cost of rasping, straining and washing so as to produce perfect starch in an undried state 1d. per stone. This work was done by three women by task work earning each 9d. per day. The price obtained for the starch 15/- per cwt., would not be sufficiently remunerative to repay the actual expense exclusive of drying – so as to induce it being carried on in a continuous manner.....*

Griffith suggested: *"that Government purchase up the produce at a certain price, or undertake the drying gratuitously and also supply mills for rasping on loan under such circumstances the manufacture could be carried on to an extent to form a suitable relief to districts of poorest classes."*[21]

George Hill of Cappoquin writing on 3rd November 1845 stated that he had tried some potato starch mixed with flour in equal parts which made bread differing in quality very little from the best wheaten bread and that *"prime wheat flour entirely out of reach of the poor."*[22]

In October, 1845, the corn crop was reported as *"fair average"* or *"above average".*[23] Hill proposed that *"as many farmers as possibly can may sow Siberian oats early in Spring, which possess many good qualities and come in earlier than any other grain".* Also that *"those that cannot obtain Siberian Oats to sow Bere Barley as it is the grain best adapted for poor man's bread and comes in before the general harvest."*[24]

Edward Galwey, J.P. suggested on 26th December, 1845 that *Government establish granaries in principal towns in Ireland and stock them with oats and barley, to arrest anticipated calamity of famine.* There was, he stated, "a considerable quantity of oats and barley in farmer's haggards beyond what required for their own consumption."[25]

On March 3rd, 1846, William White & Co., of Waterford offered the firms services to Government in the Importation and Sale of Indian corn in which they have been engaged for several years and stated – *"that about 10,000 quarters of Indian corn are in Waterford of which writers hold 4,600 quarters."*[26] On 21st March, 1846, P. Phipps., of Clonmel Poor Law Union, Co. Waterford asked that the guardians be instructed to use Indian corn.[27]

Local Subscriptions and Government Grants
There were many local efforts to raise funds. "A public meeting is about to be held for the purpose of raising subscriptions" wrote Robert Maxwell, of Moorehill, Tallow on March 24th. 1846. He asked if the

Government *would "grant an equal or a proportionate sum in addition to the amount subsidised in any locality."* The non-committed response, in a margin note, was that *"the rate of Government donation will depend upon the circumstances of the district with* (illegible) *disposition to be liberal".*[28] On March 30th, 1846, the Castle authorities authorised Sir Randolph Routh to advance to the Lismore Relief Subscription the sum of £75.[29]

G.E.H. Evans., writing from Kilmacthomas, suggested that each parish raise funds and that the Government should match the amount raised.[30] Patrick Hayden, of Carrickbeg wrote on 20th March, 1846 *"the Carrickbeg subscription now exceeds £160 and a liberal donation from Government is expected."*[31]

Conclusion

At the end of the Spring of 1846, the plight of the people varied in the different communities across the county. The population of Carrickbeg 3,017 souls," *chiefly labourers and tradesmen are in abject distress, for want of employment, three have died of starvation".*[32] Yet in Waterford City there was *"nothing approaching famine in district. The workhouse not so full as usual. Fever Hospital does not contain within 40 patients as many as in December. General sickness less prevalent than usual."*[33]

Yet, despite the earnest concern and initiatives of many, the vast chasm between the big farmers and gentry on the one side, and the conacre tenants and labouring cottiers on the other, itself brought disaster ever nearer.

In the world of commerce, business remained business. On 26th February, 1846, James Leahy of Tallow offered on sale to the Government *"2,000 barrels of seed potatoes warranted sound on delivery at 15/- per barrel. (current price being 17/6d. per barrel)."* He asked for *"an answer soon (if at all) as the fearfully increasing want of food would render dangerous his keeping them beyond a month or 5 weeks from the probability of personal attacks etc."*[34]

Meanwhile, the Famine was tightening it's grip on those most in need.

REFERENCES
1.   Relief Commission Papers, Ref. as date (only some have Reference Nos.).
2.   ibid.
3.   ibid.
4.   ibid.
5.   ibid, Z. 1664.
6.   ibid, Ref. as date.
7.   ibid, do.

8. ibid, D 589, Z 4174, Z 5216, 928,872, 1049, 1413, 1524, 1581, 1631, 1763, 1708.
9. ibid, Ref. as date.
10. ibid, 19/12/45.
11. ibid, 1/12/45.
12. ibid, Ref. as date.
13. ibid, 13/10/45.
14. ibid, D. 371.
15. ibid, 12/1/45.
16. ibid, Z 2766.
17. ibid, 12/1/46.
18. ibid, 514.
19. ibid, 25/10/45.
20. ibid, 1/1/46.
21. ibid, Ref. as date.
22. ibid, (Illegible).
23. ibid, 25/10/45.
24. ibid, 30/10/45.
25. ibid, Ref. as date.
26. ibid, do.
27. ibid, 872.
28. ibid, 970.
29. ibid, 1084.
30. ibid, 1049.
31. ibid, 1631.
32. ibid, 1413.
33. ibid, 0866.
34. ibid, 3794.

Chapter 4

The official view of the famine: Waterford, a regional dimension

JOHN M. HEARNE

Official Thinking

The first confirmation in September 1845 of scattered outbreaks of the potato-killing fungus *'Phythophthera Infestans'* in Dublin and Waterford, initially caused little or no public concern. It was, many felt, too late in the growing season for the disease, already detected in Belgium and England, to make serious inroads into a flourishing crop.[1] Indeed, the outbreak of potato blight in the Autumn of 1845, while unexpected, was not exceptional. Minor regional famines had been experienced in 1816-17, 1822, 1831, 1835, 1837, 1839, and 1842. These famines had been mainly confined to the western seaboard and significant loss of life had not resulted. Government response to these endemic food crises was reasonably effective and not ungenerous.[2]

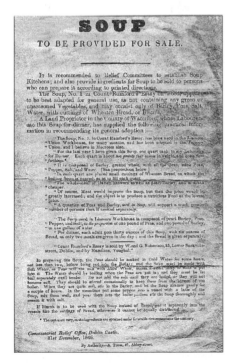

Official soup recipe.

Persistent food shortages between 1816 and 1821 led the young Chief Secretary, Sir Robert Peel, to initiate the establishment of a commission to administer famine relief. Relief works were inaugurated enabling the needy to earn money to purchase food. But a precondition for assistance for these relief schemes was an insistence on local contributions towards them, and upon local committees to organise the actual relief.

After 1822, a long-term government programme of public works was enacted designed to relieve distress by creating employment to bring long-term improvements to remote areas. Between 1822 and 1845 a major government programme of road works, land drainage and harbour and pier

41

improvements was embarked upon aimed at relieving poverty and initiating new economic activity. In 1832 when control of these government projects was handed over to the Irish Board of Works (set up in 1831), an estimated one million pounds had been spent on public works.[3] Thus, by the eve of the Great Famine, in response to Ireland's vulnerable economy, where food shortages were endemic and where the dietary dependence of at least one-third of the population was dominated by the potato, an effective administrative organisation had been established. But Government response to any crisis or crises which necessitated interference in the economy was conditioned by the prevailing constraints of classical or orthodox economic thought.

Classical economists like Smith, Say, Malthus and Ricardo were adherents and indeed proponents of government non-intervention in economic affairs. This 'laissez-faire' policy which was underpinned by Say's Law of Markets was consolidated by the Labour Theory of Value and Malthus's Iron Law of Wages. By the 1840's, however, the new practitioners of this school of economic thought, led by Nassau Senior, Lewis, Torrens and Archbishop Richard Whately, were anxious to translate this economic theory into policy. Within this movement there was a consensus that Ireland could not follow the English path to development without assistance. Government action was thus thought legitimate to build a public infrastructure and provide education. In this respect both the Irish Board of Works and the National Education System had the support of orthodox economists. However, for orthodox economic thinkers the relief of destitution, whether endemic or caused by exceptional circumstances, was a much greater philosophical question.[4]

As early as 1795, when the British Prime Minister, William Pitt, was coming under increasing pressure for government intervention following the harvest failure of that year, Edmund Burke produced an economic pamphlet, "Thoughts and Details on Scarcity". Contained in this pamphlet was a thundering denunciation of governmental interference in the food trade, stating that

> Such acts were worse than impolitic, they were immoral: It is not in breaking the laws of commerce, which are the laws of nature and consequently the laws of God, that we place our hope of softening the Divine displeasure to remove any calamity under which we suffer or which hangs over us.[5]

This moralistic interpretation of economic theory which evolved alongside and within the traditional political economy had by the 1840's developed into a coherent ideology – Providentialism. When this ideology interacted with the more radical economic theories of the day which were imbued with the ethos of evangelical protestantism of the clerical economists, Sumner, Whately and Chalmers, it had profound influence on British political and economic attitudes.

Hence, blame for the condition of Irish society was put clearly on the moral failings of Irishmen of all classes, with the landlords, receiving special attention. Thus, direct acts of providence, such as the potato blight could be interpreted in this tradition as special *'mercies'* sent to oblige men to remove artificial obstacles to the Divine Order. According to Gray, Peel's linking of the potato blight of 1845 to the policy of removing the corn laws can be read in this light.[6] Consequently, the famine was welcomed as a God-given opportunity to enforce a policy that would transform Irish behaviour. The obsession with free trade in food from 1846 reflected the power of this ideological connection.[7] That Peel's government fell as a result was not only an indication of political tensions; it also reflected unease within the body politic that such an ideology could be used to justify interference with such a fundamental law of commerce.

It was in this climate of ideological flux and political instability that official government policy to address the Irish famine was framed and implemented.

Response to Partial Famine of 1845

When the potato crop failed in the Autumn of 1845, Sir Robert Peel acted promptly. Although the prevailing evidence did not point to an unprecedented disaster, Peel had already made his mind up that Ireland did in fact face a major crisis. Traditional relief measures were invoked similar to those which he had introduced in 1817 and which had been implemented with some success during the endemic food shortages of the pre-famine years. Firstly, a Relief Commission was set up with commissioners instructed to form local committees in order to raise subscriptions to buy food which would be resold to the distressed. Secondly, the Board of Works was to create employment by engaging in making new roads or improving old ones. Thirdly, experience had taught Peel that disease followed in the wake of hunger. Thus, fever hospitals were to be secured, outside of the workhouse itself. Finally, Peel was aware of the need to keep food prices down. In this respect, the Government procured Indian corn and as prices increased, quantities of this corn would be sold on the market in an effort to stabilise prices.[8]

In order to obtain an accurate assessment of the scale of the crop failure Peel commissioned local constabulary reports. In the meantime, however, he, along with his Chancellor of the Exchequer, Goulburn, ordered the Merchant bankers, Baring Brothers, to purchase over £100,000 worth of meal and maize from America. Eventually, over £185,000 was spent on this food scheme. Much of this was spent secretly, against Treasury advice or prior to receiving Treasury sanction.[9] In the event, this expenditure was criticised as being extravagant especially when it was revealed that the potato failure was but partial, with almost two-thirds of the crop unaffected.[10] While the 1845 potato failure was ultimately used by Peel to justify repeal of the Corn Laws, the reports commissioned by him did highlight the regional dimension of the crisis. This is clearly illustrated in Table 1 below.

Statement of the Average Produce per Acre of late Years, and also of the present Year, of Wheat, Barley, Oats and Potatoes, in each of the Counties of Ireland, with the Average for the whole of Ireland: as shown by the Returns received from the Constabulary Office in Dublin.

COUNTY	Average Produce per Acre of late Years of each of the following Crops, viz.-								Average Result of the present Year per Acre							
	Wheat		Barley		Oats		Potatoes		Wheat		Barley		Oats		Potatoes	
	Cwt.	lbs.	Cwt.	lbs.	Cwt.	lbs.	Cwt.	lbs.	Cwt.	lbs.	Cwt.	lbs.	Cwt.	lbs.	Cwt.	lbs.
Antrim	18	58	19	58	18	37	153	0	16	67	18	28	16	45	2	45
Armagh	16	28	16	89	15	89	172	89	17	35	14	100	13	44	3	37
Carlow	18	28	20	0	17	58	153	28	18	0	16	84	14	28	17	84
Cavan	22	28	18	74	15	49	176	0	21	93	15	89	13	27	5	37
Clare	18	25	20	12	19	37	190	37	17	51	19	0	14	87	4	0
Cork	11	13	13	21	13	48	118	48	12	28	13	4	11	0	11	64
Donegal	31	18	21	48	16	48	147	32	20	58	20	18	16	32	5	32
Down	19	18	19	37	19	0	135	0	17	93	19	37	17	0	--	
Dublin	23	67	23	89	22	100	198	0	21	95	22	22	19	5	6	35
Fermanagh	23	0	25	0	19	93	181	18	22	74	23	58	18	74	4	0
Galway	16	80	19	80	17	44	176	18	16	21	18	100	15	28	13	99
Kerry	15	84	16	58	17	89	136	0	13	70	13	84	13	67	15	84
Kilkenny	18	42	19	105	18	70	174	42	16	40	17	70	14	32	3	105
King's	15	0	17	89	17	67	145	0	15	100	15	20	14	7	15	58
Leitrim	20	0	20	0	16	0	157	42	19	42	20	0	12	108	2	28
Limerick	20	40	23	20	38	47	177	81	22	20	21	40	19	50	8	0
Londonderry	18	84	16	28	17	70	132	58	18	28	15	58	16	0	1	37
Longford	24	42	28	0	21	28	201	42	23	42	24	93	17	0	0	74
Louth	23	58	22	58	20	18	145	0	24	45	20	22	18	22	7	22
Mayo	34	74	34	14	32	0	231	37	33	74	46	42	20	37	2	98
Meath	19	7	19	84	21	31	164	42	19	84	19	48	17	84	17	104
Monaghan	18	37	17	0	15	28	161	84	18	74	13	74	11	0	2	74
Queen's	15	52	21	60	18	80	155	0	15	42	18	28	15	51	9	0
Roscommon	20	58	17	58	18	67	154	0	20	84	17	84	17	0	2	0
Sligo	28	44	22	78	19	102	164	18	23	74	23	74	15	14	8	44
Tipperary	14	42	17	8	16	62	147	25	15	8	15	84	12	100	18	93
Tyrone	18	88	17	67	16	22	138	0	17	88	16	40	15	14	5	67
Waterford	13	58	15	98	12	84	134	84	13	11	13	44	10	11	8	14
Westmeath	21	64	23	82	21	86	150	88	22	4	18	51	18	70	2	18
Wexford	16	32	20	3	18	20	167	44	15	32	16	72	8	44	14	52
Wicklow	21	0	21	41	17	89	198	89	19	67	16	58	13	11	6	100
	614	8	606	13	589	91	4958	28	598	70	596	60	447	102	227	37
Average for the whole of Ireland, exclusive of Kilkenny	19	58	20	58	19	2	159	98	19	34	19	27	15	46	7	37

October 24, 1846.

This statement includes the returns from all the counties in ireland except Kildare, which has been omitted in consequence of the returns from that county being evidently incorrect.

Table 1.

Many counties lost between 30% and 40% of their average crop in 1845. Some counties, like Wexford, were virtually unaffected,[11] while its south eastern neighbour, Waterford, sustained the largest loss. Yet distress in Waterford City and County was minimal, initially, with the workhouse being less than half-full up to the middle of 1846.[12] Indeed during his fact-finding tour of Ireland during the Autumn of 1846, Lieutenant-Colonel Tullock observed that...

The failure of the crop appears to have been greatest in those parts where the culture is of the most primitive description, and the same ground has been under a succession of potato crops. Wherever superior agriculture and a variety of crops prevail, as around Carlow, Kilkenny, Fermoy, Clonmel and Waterford, the potatoes are more plentiful and the quality superior; indeed it forms one of the most serious features of the present famine, that wherever the population has hitherto depended entirely upon potatoes for subsistence, there the failures have been greatest.[13]

This statement in many ways highlights the peculiarities which characterised the regional impact of the famine on Waterford. The city, more used to consumption of bread than potatoes, escaped comparatively lightly; while within the county, were densely populated areas which experienced extreme hardship.

It was not until six months after the potato blight was first reported that the first food depot was opened. The government had delayed opening depots until as late as possible in anticipation of a favourable early potato crop in 1846. Growth of the winter planting of potatoes would have been sufficiently advanced by March to indicate how good the crop would be. However,

In Waterford the March pits have been generally, not universally, opened, and I can bear witness to the fact that in the immediate vicinity of this place, a proportion of one-third to one-half, and in some cases the whole, has been found totally injured, fetid, and only fit for the dunghill (there might be strong reasons for not using it even as manure).[14]

This was only echoing the information Trevelyan was getting from the rest of the country. The writer, Deputy Commissary General Dobree went on to state that while the Wexford crop had been saved, Carrick-on-Suir was already in a state of distress, and that "*Some of the crops of potatoes planted in January have been examined, and the seed has been found to have generally rotted.*" Further investigations of forty one electoral divisions in Waterford revealed twenty seven had lost 70% to 80% of the early crop and the other fourteen had lost half.[15]

Thus, by the end of March, such countrywide observations suggesting a second successive crop failure, the food depots were opened. An important assertion in Dobree's letter was his belief that the landlord class was clearly to blame for this looming disaster.

> *It appears evident that those persons on whom the moral responsibility is constitutionally vested are doing nothing more than thinking upon what Government is going to do, intending thereby to oblige Government to take the initiative, and to throw the onus upon their shoulders.*[16]

This was in line with official government policy. Thus, this crisis was providential in that it would allow policies be implemented to transform Irish landlord behaviour.

It was decided in February 1846 to locate a food depot at Waterford with D.C.G. Dobree appointed to supervise its operation.[17] However, the actual stocking of the Waterford depot was more by accident than necessity. Dobree arrived in Ireland on 5th March 1846 intending to go to Dundalk.[18] However he was ordered to *Waterford* the following day to supervise the repairing of the *Harriet-Rockwell* which had overshot Cork due to a shifting cargo. Dobree was under clear instructions that the ship, carrying a cargo of Indian Meal, should not be unloaded at Waterford. However, because it had also sprung a leak it was decided to unload part of the cargo and use it to stock the local food depot; the remainder was to be returned to Cork for grinding.[19] The Waterford depot was not officially opened until the 20th May: a branch depot was opened at Dungarvan two months later.[20]

Within a few weeks of his arrival in the city, Dobree had acquired an accurate overview of the plight of its citizens. In mid-March he communicated to Trevelyan that "*the price of potatoes is so high and they are of so hard a quality that they are no longer used in the poor-house here, bread being substituted...at 6d per stone of 14 lb...is quite beyond the reach of the poor.*"[21] He also castigated the local merchants who had raised their prices by 6/- per ton and thus created a false impression of scarcity, when in fact, the real problem was that the two steam mills in the city had such a large stock of corn that they were having difficulty grinding sufficient quantities to meet demand.[22] In April he reported that the price of potatoes had risen to 8d, but that he had "*succeeded in introducing here a quality of bread which the bakers are retailing at 1d a loaf with sufficient profit to themselves, and the greatest benefit to the poor, who buy it up faster than it can be made.*"[23]

While Dobree agreed with and indeed complimented the Government's intervention, he nonetheless (initially at any rate) believed that there was plenty of food, with the exception of potatoes, in both Waterford and the county as a whole. This was borne out by the fact that by early July, of the 200 tons of Indian Meal originally deposited in the Waterford depot, only 23 tons had been disposed of. Furthermore, prices in the City were considerably lower than in the adjacent counties,[24] suggesting that supply was adequate to meet prevailing demand. Also, in June, oatmeal requested by Dobree for the Waterford depot was redirected to Galway by Routh *"as demand is not so general or urgent as at Galway"*.[25] However, Dobree was at one with the government in accepting that such intervention should only be used to stabilise prices, and in extreme circumstances, could be used as a threat to unscrupulous corn merchants to control their prices. As he said –

> *If Government would now and then at large towns or elsewhere place at the disposal of the authorities or committees a supply of meal, to be sold with discretion at cost price...the dealers express the greatest disquietude as to the effect which the Government relief may have on their importations, and a broad hint of this kind now and then would keep the market at its fair level.*[26]

But Dobree, who initially, was perhaps one of the more *'conservative'* commissioners, and an adherent of the more orthodox economic philosophies of the day, seemed to undergo an ideological change of heart while in Waterford, as can be gleaned from his letter to Trevelyan thus...

> *If there were a doubt in any reflecting man's mind on the correctness of Burke's "Thoughts and Details on Scarcity", he need only come to Ireland to have it removed, and to be satisfied that the greatest evils may arise from Government being depended upon for the subsistence of the people, or meddling with it if it can be avoided.*[27]

While this part of Dobree's statement seems to, and has in fact been used by some commentators to illustrate the Government's adherence to economic orthodoxy, a continuation of his statement shows clear signs of a deviation from the principles of Government non-intervention in the economy. Dobree continued –

> *but since Government has, at this present juncture initiated such interference to meet the impending distress throughout this*

country, I deemed that they might do much moral good by making occasionally a legitimate use of their 'reserve' to keep down the prices of the markets, without at all interrupting the importations of private account, or allowing themselves to be brought into the field before the season of extreme distress for which their provision was made.[28]

This liberal or flexible interpretation of Classical Economic Thought was, one commentator suggests, more attuned to what Burke himself would have advocated if confronted with the Irish crisis.[29]

The ideological amelioration of Dobree at Waterford quickly wrought official disdain. In June of 1846 Peel's Conservative Government fell and was replaced by a *'minority whig'* government led by Lord John Russell. Russell's government was more intransigent towards direct government importation of food. In a letter to Routh in early July, Dobree informed him that the stock of ground corn at the Waterford depot was quickly diminishing, yet the supply of unground corn in the city exceeded demand. Dobree further stated that if another grinding machine could be procured that merchants would be willing to sell the excess supply for £9.6s.8d a ton; much cheaper than the £10 a ton he was forced to pay for ground corn from Cork to meet local demand. Routh curtly replied –

It will occur to you that it is not our object to interfere with trade, but only to step in where the trade price is too high for the people, or to act under circumstances where the trade have no supply or land.[30]

But Routh, acutely aware of the mounting anger of the small traders against Government intervention in the food trade was not yet prepared to countenance closing the depots. Confiding in Dobree he did, however, concede that, *"We may safely begin to prepare for the period when our services at the harvest ought to be discontinued."*[31] However, there was to be no potato harvest that year. Nevertheless, with Treasury approval the instruction for closure was transmitted.[32] Thus, the Waterford depot was closed on the 15th August 1846; Carrick-on-Suir followed on the 22nd, Clonmel on the 29th and Dungarvan on the 31st, just at the time that the full consequences of the potato failure became apparent. In total, these depots had issued 1,247,186 lbs of Indian Meal, 415,946 lbs of oatmeal and 2,884 lbs of biscuit[33] and were responsible for the alleviation of extreme destitution in the city (in particular) and county in the three critical months they remained open.

Crises after August 1846: (i) Provision of Corn

The disastrous decision to close the Waterford depot was criticised by Dobree. On 19th August, aware that the potato crop was in danger of failing completely, he pleaded that the food depots be kept open. He told Trevelyan "*In a circuit of 200 miles, I have not seen a field free from it (blight). My belief is that scarcely any of the late potatoes will be fit for human food.*"[34] He also refuted Routh's assertion that the relief measures were interfering with trade, stating that he had never heard such complaints in Waterford.[35] This is a clear indication that Dobree's adherence to orthodox economic theory had undergone a fundamental ideological transition while in Waterford; and given that his letter is addressed to Trevelyan not Routh illustrates his depth of feeling on this issue.

When it became evident that the potato crop had in fact failed for the second successive year, the full implications of the depot closures became apparent. In a memorial from the Waterford Board of Guardians in October, the Mayor, Sir Benjamin Wall, outlined the distress envisaged in the City because of the depot closures. He also issued a veiled warning of impending civil unrest should adequate quantities of Indian Meal not be made readily available.[36] Indeed Dobree had already reported (April 1846) that grain coming from Clonmel to Waterford needed an escort of fifty cavalry, eighty infantry and two artillery pieces![37] Nevertheless, Stanley maintained orthodoxy: "*It is not in contemplation to establish in any part of Ireland depots of food to be sold under current trade prices.*"[38] Stanley went on to inform Wall that a food depot would not be established in the City or indeed in any part of the eastern division of Ireland.[39]

This policy stand regarding cheap food was re-asserted in December 1846 when an application from the Waterford Relief Committee inquired whether £50 from the Relief Fund could be used to provide cheap food. A terse reply from the Relief Office commented that "*It is presumed (that) the intention of the committee is to provide food for sale under cost; and as this involves partial gratuitous relief, it cannot be sanctioned.*"[40] An application by Ardmore Relief Committee to have a depot established there was also rebuffed even though it was acknowledged by Routh that this part of the county was in a lamentable state.[41]

A Memorial from the Waterford Poor Law Union in October 1846 suggested that, "*Exports should be stopped for six months, distillation suspended, and Irish produce purchased by the government, to supply extensive public granaries.*"[42]

Although a general European scarcity existed by the end of the year, leading to higher prices being commanded by Irish grain exports, by the summer of 1847 Irish markets were flooded with foreign corn and maize.[43] Thus, the suggestion from the Waterford Poor Law Union was impracticable given the simple economics of the situation – suppliers will supply more at higher prices. Given that any continuing relief scheme depended on the co-operation of landlords and commercial interests, the Waterford suggestion was ignored. As the table below illustrates, net exports of grain from Ireland declined in any case during 1846-'47 while imports rose, thus in a way justifying the government's economic policy, whatever about its social policy.

Table 2[44]

Grain Exports and Imports 1844-48 (Thousands of tons)

	Exports	Imports	Net Change
1844	424	30	+ 394
1845	513	28	+ 485
1846	284	197	+ 87
1847	146	889	− 743
1848	314	439	− 125

Russell's government did in fact face many practical difficulties in continuing Peel's food policy. The Autumn and Winter of 1846-47 was a time of considerable scarcity in Britain, and Europe. Higher continental prices witnessed grain shipments being landed in Belgium and France rather than Britain.[45] And with higher prices obtaining in England, Irish exports were attracted to that market, thus giving rise to accusations that food left for Britain while Ireland starved. But whatever the problems, either real or illusory, associated with food distribution and storage, the main burden of famine relief rested with the tried and trusted remedy of public works, which had been used regularly since 1817.

Crises from August 1846: (ii) Public Works
Early in 1846 Peel, having completed arrangements for controlling food prices, attempted to solve the Irish unemployment situation. Four Bills were introduced to increase employment, and on March 5th they received the Royal Assent. The first and most important dealt with public works which the government decided should be jointly financed; half from the Treasury by way of a Grant and the balance coming from local taxation. A second Act addressed road repairs, drainage and sewage. The remaining two Acts dealt with pier and harbour construction.[46] Local grand juries would forward applications

for government finance and having examined the proposed schemes, the Board of Works (on whom the administrative burden for supervising public works primarily fell) either approved or rejected these loan applications. Employment was given to those in possession of relief tickets from their local relief committees.[47] By April of 1846 many of these relief schemes had commenced throughout Ireland.

Despite the decision by the British Government to place the burden of relief works on local taxation, the failure of the potato crop in 1846 led to an increased demand for employment on relief works. But in an attempt to halt the exodus from the land the Treasury instructed local Board of Works inspectors that no person should be employed on any relief works who could obtain employment on other public works or in farming. Furthermore, wages for those employed on relief works *"should, in every case, be at least 2d a day less than the average rate of wages in the district"*, with pay being in proportion to work actually done.[48] And with regard to task-work, the officers of the Board of Works were instructed that "the sum to be paid for each portion of work should be sufficient to enable an ordinary labourer to earn 10d to 1/5 per day and a good labourer who exerted himself from 1/4 to 1/6."[49]

These instructions adhered not only to the parameters within which relief was administered but also to the Iron Law of Wages. While these wage levels may have been adequate in pre-famine years, by the Autumn of 1846 the escalating price of food made them look insignificant and led Fr. Matthew to conclude that *"A shilling a day or even 1/6 is nothing to a poor man with a large family if he has to pay 2d a lb for Indian Meal."*[50] Captain Pole in Banagher concurred, stating that the wages proposed by the Board of Works would not prove enough to buy food.[51] Moreover, payment by results of task work only widened the gap between the healthy labourer with some capital and those most in need; and by placing the burden of relief works on local responsibility, only mitigated against those areas least equipped to fend for themselves.[52]

Most of the Relief Committees in Waterford had been set up between late Spring and early Summer of 1846. In August, a circular was issued to all Relief Committees

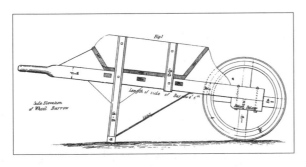

The officially approved design for a wheelbarrow to be used in public works.

requesting a detailed analysis of local conditions and especially on how public monies were being expended.[53] Eighteen committees from Waterford replied. From these replies a reasonably accurate picture of conditions in County Waterford during the Autumn of 1846 can be gleaned. It would seem that the areas which suffered greatest hardship were the baronies of Coshmore and Coshbride, Deices without Drum and the mountainous regions of Glenahiry; Carrick-beg in particular was suffering great hardship at this time. Local subscriptions raised by these committees came to almost £3,729 and were matched by Government donations of £2,475 with a further £141 coming from other sources such as the Calcutta Relief Fund. By in large this money, £6,345 in total, was used to buy Indian Meal, which was then either sold at, or below, cost to the local inhabitants; more often than not meal was distributed gratuitously while a small portion of the money was expended on public works. It was no surprise, therefore, that all but one of these committees lost money on the purchase and sale of meal.

Arising from these transactions, the Relief Committees were £2,638 in debt by August, ranging from a high of £379.13.11 by the Whitechurch, Affane, Modeligo Committee to a low of £28.1.2. in Ballyduff. Not all committees undertook public works. In Ardmore, which was in a destitute state,[54] all monies were expended on meal for 350 families. In Ringagonach where another 350 families were in receipt of weekly relief, no one was required to work. Instead, one member in each family was given a ticket for work and meal was given 'gratis'. Of the 2,300 in receipt of weekly relief at Clashmore, only 17 were required to work as a condition of relief. Although the rate of payment per day was 10d, the Clashmore Committee compensated the labourers at the rate of two stone of meal for three days work. Indeed, of the eighteen replies to the Relief Commission Circular, only ten had introduced task work, with the average rate of payment being 10 1/2d per day; much lower than the country average of 1/- per day.[55] The Stradbally-Clonea Committee, where the daily payment was also 10d, paid 3d in cash and 7d worth of meal. In Kilmacthomas-Bonmahon where 3,520 were in receipt of relief, all payment was in meal. What these replies illustrate is that the implementation of relief and public works programmes in County Waterford in general were undertaken with leniency and compassion and administered with a good deal of common -sense. Treasury instructions, while not totally ignored, certainly were subject to much improvisation and in some cases, abuse.

Prime Minister Russell had intended discontinuing the Public Works Schemes by early August, but was forced by pressure from the Relief Commission to keep them open. He allowed landlords sponsor works that would improve their properties provided they accepted all financial responsibility,56 though this had little impact. In Waterford, numbers on public works more than doubled between August and December. By the end of January 1847 numbers in receipt of Public Works relief still remained high, though it was to be discontinued and replaced by outdoor relief. Government expenditure on public works nationally during the Autumn and Winter of 1846-'47 had cost £4,848,235.[57]

Table 3[58]

Numbers of Able-bodied Employed on Public Works in Waterford and Selected Counties from 1st August 1846 to 30th January 1847.

	Waterford County	Waterford City	Limerick County	Limerick City	Cork County	Cork City	Galway
Aug. 1st	3,623	—					
Aug. 8th	4,495	—					
Aug. 29th	520	—					
Oct. 17th	1,894	—					
Nov. 8th	3,110	—	18,282	—	10,566	199	14,714
Nov. 8th	6,108	254	24,354	643	19,974	209	24,222
Dec. 12th	7,890	170	27,488	591	34,410	247	29,588
Dec. 19th	7,362	245	29,426	578	30,944	366	28,101
Dec. 26th	8,555	255	31,200	690	31,840	437	42,245
Jan. 30th	6,338	568	30,328	837	57,045	805	36,911

Table 3 illustrates clearly the increasing dependence on public works during the Autumn and Winter of 1846-'47. Between August and December 1846 the numbers dependent on such work in Waterford almost trebled – especially if one takes into account that a considerable amount of women and boys, and the infirm, also were employed. These latter categories increased dramatically during the Winter of 1846-'47. Indeed, total employment on public works in Waterford during the week-ending the 30th January, 1847, as illustrated in Table 4 gives a reasonably accurate account of the distribution of the various categories on public works in Waterford.

By late January 1847, 10,125 were dependent on public works employment in the city and county. This represented approximately three per cent of County Waterford's total population of 196,187.[60] This was a relatively low figure, especially if compared to either Cork, Limerick, or Galway. It does, however, fail to highlight the extreme hardships experienced in many peripheral areas of the county. Nor are these figures a true representation of public works being distributed in accordance with a particular district's needs. In reality the eastern part of the county did not experience the same degree of hardship as the

Table 4[59]

Daily Average Numbers of Persons Employed on the Roads for Week-Ending 30th January, 1847, in Waterford.

	Labourers Able-bodied	Infirm	Women	Boys	Population in 1841	% Employment
Coshmore and Coshbride	1,729	22	243	311	32,986	6.98
Decies-within-Drum	130	—	50	30	26,566	.79
Decies-without-Drum	107	7	42	8	54,412	3.02
Gaultiere	589	2	68	149	13,615	5.93
Glenahiry	375	7	51	16	6,271	.71
Middlethird	1,422	8	239	280	17,151	2.60
Upperthird	1,986	108	1,068	462	21,970	16.49
Total County Waterford	6.338	154	1,761	1,256	172,971	5.49
Waterford City	568	3	27	18	23,216	

western or mountainous parts of the county. Yet as Table 4 indicates, the relatively prosperous Middlethird in the east had over twice the proportion (11%) employed on public works than had Glenahiry (5%) which Lieut-Colonel Douglas described in January 1847 as "*being deserted, with the destitute living on turnips*".[61] Relief in many cases depended on the existence of a relief committee in the area, with committee members sympathetic to the plight of people, or by having an influential or progressive landlord.

Daly has observed that although Waterford suffered the largest crop failure following the initial outbreak of blight in 1845, the county failed to attract much government financial aid during the following year.[62] While the replies to the Relief Commission's circular (Appendix I) showed that Waterford had received just over £6,000 in relief assistance (most of which was spent on food) up until August 1846, between September of that year and the end of January 1847, another £53,25963 was allocated to various Waterford relief committees.[63] Most of this money was spent on public works, as illustrated in Table 5. However, this only represented one per cent of the enormous sum of £4,848,235 spent on public works during the Autumn and Winter of 1846-'47. As table 5 shows, 60% of all relief funds allocated to Waterford during this period was spent in three Baronies, Coshmore and Coshbride, Decies without Drum and the Barony of Upperthird. The single most badly hit area Decies within Drum, west of Dungarvan received only a fraction

(.79%) of the allocation that its more prosperous neighbour to the north, Coshmore and Coshbride, received (7%).

Table 5[64]

Government Financial Aid for Public Works in Waterford
September 1846 to January 1847 (inclusive)

District	Amount Sanctioned	% of Total
Decies without Drum	£9.031	17%
Coshmore and Coshbride	£13,417	25.20%
Middlethird	£7,010	13.15%
Upperthird	£9,669	18.15%
Decies within Drum	£4,450	8.35%
Gaultiere	£3,384	6.35%
Glenahiry	£3,531	7%
Kilculliheen	£255	.05%
Waterford City	£2,512	4.75%
TOTAL	£53,259	100%
Figures rounded.		

Appendix I sets out in greater detail the money raised locally and the extent to which this was matched by government grant. Most committees received only about two thirds of what they'd raised and this they spent mainly on the purchase of meal.

These monies do not include government assistance for drainage schemes which amounted, in Waterford, to £22,529 during the same period. If one compares the public works allocation of £53,259 with the county's population of 196,187 it shows that Waterford received £0.27 per capita; if the sum allocated for drainage schemes in the county is added to this, then Waterford obtained £0.39 per capita; and if the initial £6,345 is also included it shows that Waterford's total per capita financial allocation for relief measures amounted to £0.42 up until the end of January 1847. For a family of six, this relief (based on public works relief) amounts to £1.63, or £2.17 for a family of eight. When compared to the national average of £5.23 for every family in Ireland[65] Waterford's allocation of relief by way of public works was miserly. Overall Per Capita relief in Waterford was also well below the national average of £0.59.

The above sums exclude financial assistance by the Government (under the amended Drainage Act) to assist Irish Railways through relief works. The alteration, in providing loans for private drainage schemes also covered railways. However, only one company, the

Waterford and Limerick Railway Company, in which the Malcolmsons had a major shareholding, took advantage of this provision.[66] Indeed the Railway only reached Waterford City ten years later. During the Famine years almost all government expenditure on this railway line was expended in Counties Limerick and Tipperary and Kilkenny.[67] To judge from a detailed memorandum, the Chamber of Commerce in the city was certainly aware of the commercial potential of the railway in advancing the prosperity of Waterford and its hinterland.[68]

The Application of the Public Works Programme

The introduction of task work on public works was resisted violently in many parts of the country. However, in Waterford, while tensions were never far from the surface, few outrages occurred. This was due, primarily, to the liberal interpretation of the rules by the relevant inspecting officers. Reporting from Waterford Capt. Hay stated -

> *works progressing satisfactorily. Labourers are industrious and quiet. The applications for employment, except in the City of Waterford, are numerous and pressing in consequence of the high price of food and the necessity of employing as many as are capable of work to enable them subsist.*[69]

This was the common theme running through the reports of the Inspecting Officers of the Board of Works in the Waterford district. Lieutenant Primrose reported from Glenahiry and Upperthird, that the works progressed favourably once the workers were paid regularly.[70] This referred to the shortage of coinage created by such a large number of workers being in receipt of payments of small denominations. It was also the cause of unrest. To address this problem, a ship, *The Comet*, was dispatched from Portsmouth in early September with coinage of various denominations to selected ports in Ireland. Waterford received £900 in crowns, £2,000 in half-crowns, £3,000 in shillings, £2,000 in sixpences, and £2,100 in fourpences.[71]

But shortage of coin was not the only cause of trouble. Lieutenant Downman, one of the Inspecting Officers in Waterford, stated that *"Much trouble arises from the incompetency of overseers and stewards"*. He also commented that the task-work had not yet been implemented in the Barony of Decies without Drum.[72] But as the severe Winter progressed, resistance to task-work increased as did the inability of labourers to work efficiently. In early January 1847 Capt. Hill reported that a few robberies of a trifling nature had taken place in the Barony of Coshmore and Coshbride and that there appeared no great objection on the part of labourers to work by task, *"if the task were set"*,[73] suggesting a lack of organisation . However, when task-work was actually implemented some labourers refused to work, threatening to attack a local goods depot and take sheep, but they were prevented by other labourers.[74] In general however, "*destitution is so great that the workers are quiet and show no disposition to insubordination*".[75] This was due, no doubt, to the physical incapacity of many labourers who, because of the spiralling price of food and the inadequacy of the wage rate, were too weak to work let alone rebel. This was corroborated by Capt. May in late January who stated that there were in Upperthird and Middlethird "*Many instances of labourers unable to accomplish a day's work for want of sustenance; they are quiet and well disposed and the works are fairly executed.*"[76]

Downman stated that while the people were quite reconciled to task-work, in many instances it was very unfairly set. Furthermore, all inspectors in the Waterford area reported that while labourers were increasingly incapable of performing work efficiently, they were also neglecting farming operations. By late February, the Finance Inspector, William Hyde, reported on the apathy to all farming operations around the Kilmacthomas area where, the surface of the land "*presents the same blackened appearance as it did in September last*". Kilmacthomas, he believed, was one of the most distressed parts of this country and he added "*has always been notorious for its wretchedness*".[77]

Violent resistance to task-work was not a common feature in Waterford during the Autumn and Winter of 1846-'47. Threats of violence were more common and often achieved their objective. But abuse of the public works schemes was endemic. On inspecting quarries in the vicinity of Waterford City in November 1846, Downman found the wage rate too high and immediately reduced it from 1/6 to 1/3. There were also thirteen too many employed. But instead of dismissing them he put them on labourers wages.[78] In Kilrossenty, Ross found several men employed on the roads who were receiving 10d for themselves, and 2/6 for a horse and dray. He ordered that when a horse from a house at 2/6 is employed, no other work should be given to that house. In some cases he also found two and three from a house employed at 10d each. Again he ordered that not more than one man at 10d, and one boy at 6d should be employed from the same house.[79] However, by January, Downman, because of the increasing price of provisions, was admitting two and even three from a family to relief works.[80] This again, similar to the common sense approach of the relief committees in early Autumn of 1846, indicates that the Board of Works Inspectors, in general, adopted a sympathetic approach when administering relief. Rules were implemented to suit local conditions. But this flexible approach was adopted as much to prevent social unrest as to alleviate destitution. In Waterford while this approach was successful in preventing social disorder, its success otherwise cannot be measured.

Food and Health

While County Waterford, in general, was perceived in official circles to have escaped the extreme rigours of the Famine, the City of Waterford in particular was seen as an oasis of normality in a sea of destitution. Capt. Mayne on inspecting the City in February 1847 commented that -

> a *fortnight ago in the town of Waterford when the inspecting officer and I agreed that about 25 only of upwards of 100 recommended by the Relief Committee need have work supplied by us, the Bishop of Cashel announced to the remainder that, while without work they should have each daily a loaf of bread and a quart of good soup, never more than 30 came for it.*[81]

He thus dismissed reports of destitution in the City as exaggerated. Mr. Forster was of like mind. In a letter to Trevelyan he observed that having visited New Ross, Knocktopher and Waterford, that "*Waterford is of course much better off, having more resources to fall back on: the other places depend principally on the Government Works.*" He related how he had seen very few without clothes and observed that their shoes and stockings were in tolerable order. "*They look well*" he stated, "*and their health is as high or higher than is general at this season. I saw before leaving London worse cases than I have seen round here.*"[82] Forster also informed Trevelyan that the farms between Knocktopher and Waterford were better stocked with grain than he had seen elsewhere. The Society of Friends had been very active in the City having already begun a soup kitchen. (See Joan Johnson's article.)

A much more distressed situation pertained at Carrick-beg where by late January two soup kitchens were in operation. Lieut. Colonel Douglas reported that, "*there exists a most painful amount of misery and destitution in Carrick-beg...the workhouse is full (220 refused admittance on Saturday 19th) and there is a great run on the soup kitchens.*"[83]

Soup was being dispensed gratuitously while those with means could purchase a quart of soup and 1/2 lb loaf of bread with a 1d ticket. In September 1846 it was reported that the inhabitants of Clashmore were living on blackberries.[84] The violence which accompanied such distress in the months of September and October is recorded elsewhere (see William Fraher and Des Cowman).

Unlike the English Poor Law, the Irish Poor Law of 1838 did not provide for outdoor relief. Thus, the decision in early 1847 to feed that part of the Irish population most in need breached one of the major tenets of the 1838 Act. The Temporary Relief Act, passed in March 1847, changed the thrust of British social policy towards Ireland. But the introduction of official soup kitchens, which did not occur until the Summer of 1847, only formalised what had already been the norm in Waterford City and its hinterland since the early days of the Famine. Cooked food also had the ideological advantage of being immune from pilferage, or financial speculation.[85] It also meant that following the passing of the Irish Poor Law Extension Act in June, Government aid for relief in Ireland was to cease. Local rate-payers were now made entirely responsible for relieving destitution in their areas. This was to cause much hardship throughout the country. But in Waterford 75% of the rate due had been collected by March 1848.[86] Although most of the well-known business people in the City and surrounding area were in varying degrees of debt, the high collection rate would seem to corroborate the earlier impressions of Forster, Mayne and Routh. Disease, however, respects neither class nor creed. And as the rural destitute sought refuge in urban centres from late 1846 onwards, they brought with them a multitude of diseases which found their new urban environment conducive to rapid advancement.

Public Health Provisions

As early as February 1846, George Walker reported that there had been a great increase of fever in Bonmahon.[87] From Tramore, M. Quinlan, M.D., observed that there had been an increase of bowel complaint. Similar complaints came from Lismore and gastric fever was prevalent in the prosperous village of Portlaw. From Dungarvan and Carrick came reports of dysentery and diarrhoea. It was not until March 1847 that Dr. Mackesy in the City reported that "*fever has been steadily on the increase since November last, but it is not of a malignant character*". By September, however, Dr. Courtenay reported the prevalence of

Table 6[89]

Town	Population	No. of cases	No. of deaths	%	First case	Last case
Waterford	29,288	522	294	56.3	15 April 1849	07 Sept. 1849
Dungarvan	12,382	723	344	47.6	29 April 1849	11 Sept. 1849
Portlaw	3.647	72	13	18	13 May 1849	21 Aug. 1849
Lismore	3,007	91	53	58.2	02 May 1849	31 July 1849
Tallow	2,696	35	19	54.3	29 April 1849	27 Aug. 1849
Cappoquin	2,341	17	8	47	25 April 1849	12 Sept. 1849

typhoid in the Waterford Union and that "*dysentery at present prevails to a great extent*".[88]

At the end of 1848 the cholera epidemic sweeping through Europe reached Ireland. In April 1849 the first case was reported in Waterford. In all, 731 people died from the disease in the county. Table 6 shows the impact of the disease in various centres in the county.

What is noticeable from the table above is that the prosperous town of Portlaw was hardly affected by the disease, while Waterford City, Lismore and Tallow had a mortality rate exceeding 50%. This was much higher than most urban centres nationally.[90] Thus, the cholera epidemic only exacerbated an already difficult situation in the county. Indeed mortality in Waterford peaked in 1849 as did workhouse occupation.

Conclusion

While the Government's response to the Irish Famine was neither complacent nor reckless, British Civil Servants, and Trevelyan in particular, viewed Ireland in British terms. As such the administrative set-up in Ireland, of which the Poor Law was an important element, was geared to deal with endemic food shortages of a short duration and not with successive harvest failures. Government response to the Famine was also inhibited by a strict adherence to economic orthodoxy which had by the 1840's become pervaded with providentialism. While Waterford was but a regional dimension of this great calamity, it did witness many of the ideological tenets being questioned and eventually being abandoned.

Furthermore, many of the inspectors assigned to the Waterford district showed remarkable compassion and flexibility in dispensing government relief. Many of the rules and regulations which governed the administration of relief measures were more often than not modified to suit local conditions or dispensed with completely. Although this policy may have been pursued as much to prevent social unrest as it was to alleviate hardship, these actions by the inspectors did nonetheless contribute to the changing of British social policy towards Ireland.

From an official perspective Waterford was perceived to have escaped lightly from the harsher realities of the Great Famine. While this may have been true for the eastern part of the county, the west of the county did contain many areas which were subject to extreme distress. Thus, in the regional dimension of the Famine in Waterford, and in the official response to the inherent contradiction therein, the county can, in many respects be advanced as a microcosm of the Famine in general and of the Government's response to that crisis in particular.

REFERENCES

1. Bourke, P.M. Austin, "Apologia for a Dead Civil Servant", in *The Visitation of God: The potato. and the Great Irish Famine.* (Dublin, 1993) p.171.

2. Daly, Mary E., "The operations of Famine Relief, 1845-47", in Poirteir, Cathal (ed.). *The Great Irish Famine.* (Dublin 1995) p.124.

3. ibid; p.125.

4. Gray, Peter, "Ideology and the Famine", in Poirteir, Cathal (ed.) *The Great Irish Famine.* (Dublin, 1995) pp.188-189.

5. Bourke, P.M. Austin, op.cit. p.72.

6. Gray, Peter, op.cit. p.92.

7. ibid.

8. Woodham-Smith, Cecil, *The Great Hunger.* (New York, 1989) p.61.

9. Daly, Mary E., *The Famine in Ireland.* (Dundalk, 1986) p.70.

10. British Parliamentary Papers, *Correspondence relating to the measures adopted by Her Majesty's government for the relief of distress arising from the failure of the potato crop in Ireland with similar correspondence: Commissariat series (First Part) and an Index 1846-47* (hereafter Famine Ireland 5) (Shannon, 1970) p.479 This table is derived from Constabulary. Reports on the state of agriculture in Ireland in 1845 and 1846. What is interesting is that with the exception of Cork and Londonderry, Waterford's potato yield per acre in 1845 was one of the lowest in the country at 134 cwt. 84 lb. In 1846 the yield was one of the highest in the country albeit at a very low level.

11. Ó Gráda, Cormac *The Great Irish Famine* (Ireland, 1989) pp 58-59. O'Grada states that while Munster and Connacht were badly hit by the Famine, Wexford escaped lightly.

12. Kinealy, Christine, " The Workhouse System in County Waterford 1838-1923", in Nolan, W. & Power, T.P. (eds.) *Waterford history and Society,* (Dublin 1992) pp.583-584 Kinealy observes that the Waterford Workhouse, established in 1844, was in good condition, but the guardians were criticised for employing too many staff and paying them high wages.

13. British Parliamentary Papers, *Correspondence relating to measures adopted for the relief of distress in Ireland: Board of Works (First Part) with an index 1847* (hereafter Famine Ireland 6) p.244 Letter from Mr. Tullock to Trevelyan, November 1846; Tullock goes on to say that. Waterford City was supplied by Wexford potatoes – and as the crop in Wexford was only slightly affected by blight, the city did not suffer serious want.

14. Famine Ireland 5, p.73 Letter from D.C.G. Dobree to Trevelyan, March 21, 1846. It was quite evident that Dobree was already becoming alarmed that a second successive crop failure was a possibility.

15. ibid, Dobree's thinking was conditioned to apportion blame for the crisis on inefficient and lazy landlords, given the official policy on this matter.

16. ibid.

17. ibid, pp.64-65 Letter from Sir R. Routh to Trevelyan, 21 Feb. 1846 – It is quite clear from this correspondence that Routh was not unduly worried about conditions in Waterford City even though he was aware that the county had been severely hit by the initial crop failure in 1845. This is a common theme in much of the official correspondence regarding Waterford and one would be justified in observing that the favourable situation in the city coloured the official mind regarding the situation in the county.

18. ibid, pp.79-80 Letter from Sir R. Routh to Trevelyan, 7 Mar. 1846.

19. ibid, It was made clear to Dobree that Cork was the centre for grinding the

Indian corn. Routh was also afraid that unloading corn in Waterford would increase the supply in the city and thus depress the price. If this was allowed happen he could be accused of interfering with Trade.

20. Ibid, p.422.
21. ibid, pp.88-89 Letter from Dobree to Trevelyan, 19 Mar. 1846 – Dobree was aware that.
no scarcity existed in the city and yet prices were increasing.
22. ibid, p.210 Letter from Dobree to Routh, 2 July, 1846.
23. ibid, Letter from Dobree to Trevelyan, 4 April, 1846.
24. ibid, pp.219-220 Dobree to Trevelyan, 8 July, 1846; – Even though prices in the city were escalating, they were still much lower than in Cork and Limerick.
25. ibid, p.167 Routh to Trevelyan, 1 June, 1846.
26. ibid, Dobree to Trevelyan, 4 April, 1846; p.109 – This letter witnesses Dobree questioning the 'laissez faire' policy. He was aware that in a situation where supply was greater than demand prices should not increase.
27. ibid, Dobree to Trevelyan, 24 April, 1846 – Bourke in his "Apologia for a Dead Civil Servant" uses Dobree's statement thus: "Dobree in Waterford also drew the Treasury's attention to the correctness of Burke's views". (p.173) This gives the impression that Dobree was in total agreement with government non intervention in the economy. However, Dobree, as his statement continues, questions seriously the morality of this stance and states that intervention (albeit limited) should be allowed to alleviate the distress the 'Laissez Faire' policy was causing.
28. ibid, Above all, Dobree's argument was based on morality; and given the prevalence of providentialism it was an interesting counter argument against this ideological theory.
29. Bourke, P.M. Austin, op. cit. p.172; Burke had earlier implied that Edmund Burke had indicated that in exceptional circumstances Government intervention in the economy was permissible.
30. Famine Ireland 5: Routh to Dobree, 4 July, 1846 – Routh was ever sensitive to accusations of Government interference in the market.
31. ibid, p.216 7 July, 1846.
32. ibid, p.216 Treasury Minute: Re above 7 July, 1846.
33. Famine Ireland 5 p.424.
34. ibid, Dobree to Trevelyan 19 Aug. 1846 – In this letter Dobree's adherence to Classical Economic Orthodoxy has clearly ended. Fearful of a major disaster, and aware that a second crop failure had occurred, he pleaded with Trevelyan to keep the food depots open.
35. ibid.
36. ibid, Memorial from Waterford Poor Law Union to Sir R. Routh, 22 Oct. 1846; p.647 – What is interesting about this correspondence from Waterford is not the fact that the mayor was in favour of abandoning the Laissez Faire policy, but the observations of Routh in a letter to Trevelyan 3 Nov. 1846, where he stated that Waterford could be left to its own resources, and while "we must look after the poorhouses, but without encouraging them to reply.".
37. ibid, Dobree to Trevelyan 29 April 1846.
38. ibid, Stanley to Wall, 16 Oct. 1846.
39. ibid.
40. ibid, p. 867 – In a letter to Routh, Stanley reasserts the Governments policy regarding interfering in the market.
41. ibid, p. 649 26-31 Oct. 1846 – Even though Routh acknowledged the distress at

Ardmore, it seems that adherence to an Orthodox Economic Ideology was more important than the lives of the inhabitants at Ardmore.

42. ibid, p.703 9-11 November 1846; p.703.
43. Ó Gráda, Cormac, op.cit. p.61.
44. ibid, p.62, Table II. This table refutes the criticism that food left the country while people starved.
45. Daly, Mary E., *The Famine in Ireland*. (Dundalk, 1986) p.72.
46. Woodham-Smith, Cecil, op.cit., p.78.
47. Daly, Mary E., *The Famine in Ireland*. (Dundalk, 1986) p.74 – Many of the Board of Works Inspectors who visited the Waterford district found that on many of the public works schemes in the county, tickets were not issued – thus making it easier to employ more workers than was necessary.
48. Famine Ireland 6, Treasury Minute re. wages on public works schemes, 31 Aug. 1846; The officials were worried that if too many labourers were enticed to public works that they would neglect their farming work.
49. ibid, p.171, Letter from Relief Commission to Trevelyan – Instructions to Board of Works officers re. wages to be paid for task-work.
50. ibid, p.75, Letter from Fr. Matthew to Trevelyan concerning the inadequacy of the wage rate in the face of escalating prices, 30 Sept. 1846; p.75.
51. ibid, Captain Pole to Trevelyan re. above, 8 Sept. 1846.
52. Ó Gráda, Cormac, op.cit., pp.54-55.
53. Relief Commission Papers 1845-7, 2/442/13: Circular issued by Relief Commission Office, Dublin on 12 Aug. 1846 – See Appendix 1. The replies would seem to indicate that many of the rules governing the operation of relief were being openly breached.
54. ibid, According to the 1841 Census, Ardmore had a population of 706, which meant that if 350 families were in receipt of relief that the population had increased dramatically or that it serviced a large hinterland.
55. Ó Gráda, Cormac, op.cit., p.54.
56. ibid.
57. Daly, Mary E., *The Famine in Ireland* (Dundalk, 1986) p.82.
58. Famine Ireland 6 Table III is derived from employment figures in this volume. It only gives able-bodied male employment. However, as will be shown elsewhere, many women and boys were also employed.
59. ibid, Table IV shows all those employed on Public Works in the various baronies in Waterford for one particular week ending on 30th January 1847.
60. Census of Ireland 1841.
61. British Parliamentary Papers, *Correspondence relating to the measures adopted for the relief of distress in Ireland: Board of Works series (Second Part) with Index and Commissariat series (Second Part) with Index 1847* (hereafter Famine Ireland 7) (Shannon, 1970). Letter from Lieutenant Colonel Douglas to Lord Stradbroke, 27 Jan. 1847 p.405. This is a letter which clearly shows the compassion of the Board of Works Inspector for a community which he believes has been abandoned by their landlord, Lord Stradbroke. Douglas, in advocating the establishing of a soup kitchen went on to "press upon all classes above indigency their duties in aiding this work." In a letter to Trevelyan on this matter, 30 Jan. 1847, Douglas goes on to state "I cannot see how property can be relieved from the moral obligations which devolve upon all above indigency in such a crisis as this." Trevelyan's reply is a classic example of the Providentialist Theory – "As justly observed by you, we must do all we can, and leave the rest to God". (1 Feb. 1847); p.407.

62. Daly, Mary E., *The Famine in Ireland* (Dundalk, 1986) p.75.

63. See Appendix 1.

64. Famine Ireland 6, Table 5 derived from information regarding monies sanctioned regarding public works relief.

65. Daly, Mary E., *The Famine in Ireland.* (Dundalk, 1986) p.82 Daly's figure of £5.23 was based on families dependent on labour for their living. No comparative figure could, during the the course of research for this article, be found; therefore, the figures derived for Waterford may in fact be too low.

66. This Railway Line had been mooted as early as 1825.

67. British Parliamentary Papers, *Reports from the Relief Commissioners and other papers on Famine Relief in Ireland with Appendices 1846-53* (hereafter Famine Ireland 8) (Shannon, 1970) p.386: By September 1847 Presentments for earthworks on this line to the value of £65,694 had been received by the Commissioners of Public Works, of which £22,000 was sanctioned. All of this was to be expended in the Baronies of IFFA and OFFA West, IFFA and OFFA East and Clanwilliam in Tipperary and Iverk in Kilkenny.

68. Famine Ireland 5, p.311.

69. Famine Ireland 6, p.482 Cpt. Hay – "Extracts from Inspectors' Reports", 12 Dec. 1846.

70. ibid, 12 Dec. 1846; Lieut. Primrose.

71. ibid, p.98.

72. ibid, Lieut. Downman "Extracts", 12 Dec. 1846 – Downman comes across as a very compassionate inspector and one who was also very fair.

73. ibid, Taskwork was uncommon in Ireland and overseers, fearing violence if introduced, often did not introduce it in order to ensure productivity on the works.

74. ibid, Cpt. Ross, "Extracts", p.86.

75. ibid, Cpt. Hay, "Extracts", p.86, 9 Jan. 1847.

76. ibid, Cpt. Hay, "Extracts", p.86, 27 Jan. 1847.

77. ibid, Report from William Hyde, Inspector of Finance, 22 Feb. 1847, writing from Kilmacthomas Writing from Kilmacthomas a week earlier Douglas stated that the Mining Company of Ireland at Knocmahon were employing 400 men for four days a week @ 2/6 a day. The Company was however making a loss of £50 a week by selling provisions below cost to miners for six months – even though there was no demand for copper.

78. ibid, p.288 – Extracts from Journals of Inspecting Officers week ending 14 Nov. 1846. Downman also found that a man reported by the Parish Priest Fr. Casey, to have died from starvation had in fact died from fever, and cautioned the priest for sending such letters.

79. ibid.

80. Famine Ireland 7: 16 Jan, 1847 – Downman was by January employing two and three of a family on the 'works' because of increasing provisions prices and because "the small farmers are as badly off, in many instances, as the labourer, their own corn being consumed.".

81. ibid, Feb. 1847.

82. ibid, p.479 – Mr. Forster to Trevelyan, 13 Feb 1847 – Forster, a Quaker, like Tuke undertook a tour of Ireland to ascertain the condition of the country. While his observations were favourable regarding Waterford City, the Quakers in general were against providing food free of charge. They were also unwilling to interfere with the economic and social order; they were also unwilling to criticise the government.

83. ibid, Douglas to Routh 28 Jan. 1847.
84. Woodham-Smith, Cecil, op.cit. p.125.
85. Daly, Mary E., The Famine in Ireland (Dundalk, 1986) p.87.
86. Famine Ireland 8, p.685.
87. ibid, p.393 Medical Officers Reports for the four provinces.
88. British Parliamentary Papers Papers relating to proceedings for the relief of distress and the state of the unions and workhouses in Ireland: Sixth series 1847-48 (hereafter Famine Ireland 3) (Shannon, 1968) p.684 – Extracts from Minutes of proceedings of Board of Guardians 16 March 1848. The Poor Law Inspector also stated that the Waterford City Workhouse was dirty and noted a defalcation of £500 which was 12 months overdue.
89. Famine Ireland 8, pp. 440-441.
90. In Cork City the figure was 41.8%, Limerick City 49.7%; Carlow Town 50.1%; New Ross 53.3%, and Carrick-on-Suir 47.3%.

Appendix 1
Relief Commission Circular

Relief District	Barony	Amount of local subscription	Total amount from Govt.	Total amount from other sources	How was money expended	How much meal purchased	Price sold a. price £	To have many individuals was money paid/otherwise and when die relief commence (weekly)
Dunhill/Fenor	Middlethird	£76	£55	£ s d / 22 5 0	Purchasing meal and/or public works	20 21/2 / 9.68 / 2d-6d per stone	1 cwt. gratis	— / 9 June 1846
Clonlea	Middlethird	£ s d / 118 7 2	£ s d / 85 - -	—	Meal and labour	T. cwt. £ / 14 10 / 10.60	None sold	— / 6th May 1846
Ardmore	Decies within Drum	141 3 6	91 2 -	22 5 0	Meal £10.10.0	58 tons @ 1/3 per stone	1/- to	350 families / 19th May 1845
Clashmore	Decies within Drum	224 13 11	149 15 0	9 15 0	Meal and payment to Secretary	69 1/2 tons @ £10.15.0	—	2,300 / 13th May 1846
Ringagonah	Decies within Drum	136 5 0	91 0 0	35 0 0	Meal and on poor	42 tons @ £10.10.0	1/- per stone	350 families / 13th May 1846
Villierstown	Decies within Drum	160 14 0	96 11 4	5 0 0	Meal and sick	T. cwt. 72 10 @ £10.10.0	8d/9d per stone	1,824
Lismore	Coshmore/Coshbride	237 11 0	138 - -	25 - -	Meal and labour	86 tons @ £10 and £15 for oatmeal		',025 / 20th July 1846
Ballyduff	Coshmore/Coshbride	114 - -	25 - -	- - -	Meal and labour	20 tons @ £10 and £15 for oatmeal	1/3 per stone or 2/- for oatmeal	— / 10th July 1846

Place	Barony	£ s d					Purpose	Quantity / Price	Price per stone	Population / Date
Dungarvan	Decies without Drum	523 12 6	365	-	-	-	Meal and labour	211 tons @ £10.2.9	—	1,200 individuals or 980 families 5th March 1846
Kilrossanty	Decies without Drum	136 2 6	100	-	-	-	Meal	18 tons @ £10.10.0	6d per stone	180 individuals 5th May 1846
Stradbally Clonea	Decies without Drum	149 15 0	100	-	-	None	Meal and selling below cost	59 tons @ £10	1/2 per stone 4d stone rice	2,000 6th May 1846
Whitechurch Affane Modeligo	Decies without Drum	271 17 0	180	-	-	-	Meal and selling below cost	T. cwt. 74 12 @ £10.10.0	6d/8d per stone and 1d to destitute	2,531 1st May 1846
Colligan Kilgobnett	Decies without Drum	190 - -	120	-	-	-	Meal and selling below cost	T. cwt. 54 18 @ £10.10.0	8d-10d per stone and 1d to destitute	2,000 15th May 1846
Rathgomack	Upperthird	138 17 3	85	-	-	-	Meal and labour	T. cwt. 16 10 @ £10.6.0	None sold	780 11th May 1846
Bonmahon and Kilmacthomas	Upperthird	493 2 6	325	-	100	-	Meal and labour	T. cwt. 131 15 @ £9.17.6	1/2 to 1/10 per stone and 6d to 8d	3,520 (791 families) 2nd June 1846
Portlaw	Upperthird	244 14 0	160	-	-	-	Meal and labour	25 1/2 tons @ £9.18.0	6d to 1/- per stone	170 but 1,020 on relief 14th May 1846
Carrick-beg	—	248 9 9	178	-	50	-	Labour	None purchased, funds too limited	1d per stone small quantities	— 7th June 1846
Glenahiry	Glenahiry	114 - -	75	-	-	-	Meal	22 tons @ £10	19 tons 1/2 price 1 ton cost 2 tons 'gratis'	1,030 2nd June 1846

Chapter 5

Poverty and patronage: responses to the famine on the Duke of Devonshire's Lismore Estate

THOMAS GREGORY FEWER

Introduction

William Cavendish, sixth duke of Devonshire, is noted by some historians to have been a leading example of the benevolent landlord in Ireland (and an absentee one at that), especially during the Famine.[1] However, individual dealings between Devonshire's agent, Francis Currey, and the tenants on his Lismore estate during the Famine have not received any detailed treatment. This article will attempt for the first time to provide a detailed assessment of Currey's relationship to the tenants on the estate against the background of general landlord/tenant relations during the Famine.

The source used in this assessment are two of the Lismore Application Books deposited in Waterford County Library at Lismore.[2] These ledger-sized books were used by Francis Currey to record both the applications made by tenants and others for some kind of assistance and his own responses to them. Written in Currey's own hand (for the most part),[3] these books give the names and townland addresses of each applicant. This information would be of major value to genealogists researching a family whose members had emigrated or died during the Famine (especially when alternative sources such as the 1841 and 1851 census returns are not available for the Lismore area). Also, references to a family dispute, a family suffering from fever, or a parent's need for a child's coffin lend pathos to what might otherwise be a dry account of someone's family tree.

Particular themes have been selected for analysis including applications regarding crop seeds, farm and building improvements, charity, work, emigration, voluntary surrenders of holdings, evictions and new lettings. Graphs have been constructed of the applications falling under most of these headings on a monthly or bi-monthly basis (between March and December 1847). Since applications for August and December are very few, they have been statistically amalgamated with those of July and November, respectively. Since there were no applications recorded for September, this month is represented by a gap in each graph. The graphs are intended to show both the chronological variation in the number of applications and the proportional importance of each type of application against the monthly or bi-monthly total.[4]

Applications for seed

As can be seen from the graph, applications for seed predominated in March and April as would be expected for the sowing season. This indicates a level of confidence amongst some of the stronger farmers at least that they could pay their rent (and often their arrears) after harvesting the crop.

Indeed, Francis Currey was usually amenable to applications for seed but expected payment for it. For example, when Patrick Cotter of Ballybreedy [unidentified] applied for some seed on March 29th 1847, he was told that only turnip seed was available and that he would have to pay for it similarly[5] William Donoghue of Ballymartin was told on applying for seed oats on the same day that there was none available and that *'he ought to give up his land if he cannot buy seed'*.[6] Currey was more flexible with some tenants, allowing them to obtain grain on his own guarantee that payment would be made at a later date. Such flexibility was shown to James and John Flynn of Carrignagower who on 12th April applied for seed to sow 2 acres of oats and 1.5 acres of turnips. Currey told them that he would *'give them as much Turnip seed as will sow their lands and will guarantee P. Heffernan for 3_ [Barrels] [of] Oats at 22s/- per Barrel to be paid [by] 29 Sept. If they do not Heffernan is to take their 2 acres for it'.*[7] On 26th April, three tenants –

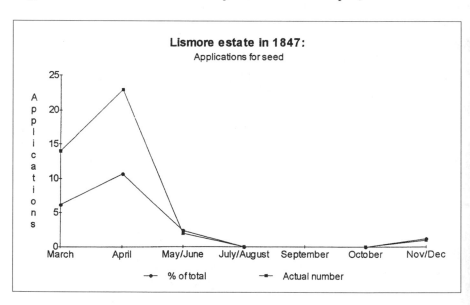

Edward Hurley of Knocknamuck, Michael Nugent of Ballyin and James Duggan of Tournikipogue [Toornagoppoge] – were each told to make out an I.O.U. to Heffernan for oat seed, promising to pay the supplier by 29th September or simply after the harvest.[8] On one occasion (12th April), Currey actually advanced £5 to Darby Byrne of Lyre a Callee [Lyrenacallee][9] to purchase 6 acres' worth of seed oats due to *'the peculiar circumstances of his case'* (whatever they were!) for which he was to repay the loan by 6th June *'when he [Byrne] will be selling some cows'.* On the other hand, five tenants (John Hale [12th April; address unknown], Michael Corcoran of Lackbrack [?-unidentified] – *'he has not been at all a satisfactory tenant since he went to Lackbrack'* – John O'Donnell of Ballynoe [either Co. Cork or Co. Waterford], John Morrissy of Ballyin and John Fitzgerald of Ballylug [all 26th April])[10] were denied seed or assistance to obtain it because they had not yet paid their rents or were deeply in arrears. Others were encouraged to give up their holding instead such as William Doolan of Ballyknock[11] and John Ronayne of Killasseragh (Co. Cork)[12] (both 29th March).

Though most (9) of the applications for seed in March were unspecific, three were for oats while another two were for turnips. In April, however, seventeen applications were for oats, two for oats and turnips, one for clover and one for turnips alone, while the single application for seed in November/December was for barley. The high number of applications for oat seed reflects the predominance of oats in grain exports from Waterford in 1847 (109, 866 barrels compared to 40,557 barrels of wheat and 5, 763 barrels of barley).[13] Indeed, there had been a *'major shift from wheat to oats and barley'* during the 1830s in the south-east of Ireland.[14] Previously, the oat was the most important food cereal in the eighteenth century, especially in the form of oaten bread.[15] A number of late eighteenth/early nineteenth century agricultural surveys enumerated the oat's predominance in this period.[16] Cormac Ó Gráda, using sources such as the 1841 census, the Poor Inquiry and guesses at pre-Famine crop acreages estimated that, among crops, the output of oats in Ireland as a whole during 1840-45 amounted to £8.1 million, second only to the production of potatoes (£8.8 million).[17] Nonetheless, applications for oat seed were not always successful for reasons already discussed as well as for their lack of availability (for which Currey might offer turnip seed instead). In one case, however, three tenants (James[?] Farrell of Ballyrafter Mountain and Denis McCarthy and W. D. Duggan of Monaman) stated that P. Heffernan's oats were *'not good'* and they were to enquire where they might get better seed. Currey told them that *'when they can ascertain where they can get the oats on credit till the Harvest[,] if given to them on their I.O.U.s I will be security for their paying at that time'.*[18] Overall,

71

Lismore Castle from *Dublin Penny Journal* 1833, Francis Currey had his office here.

Francis Currey was happy to assist those of his tenants whom he felt could continue farming, but he was eager to encourage less successful tenants to leave their holdings.

Farm/building improvements

Historians generally recognise the poor interest that landlords showed in improving the quality of their tenants' holdings or in land reclamation, which was usually left up to the middlemen and the larger farmers to carry out.[19] Where landlords did contribute directly to improvements, it tended to be *'devoted to drainage schemes for which they could borrow on favourable terms from the Board of Works'.*[20] The Duke of Devonshire was no exception as a landlord, at least before 1849 when he began to visit his Lismore estate on an annual basis until his death in 1858.[21] Until this time, the duke's improvements were concentrated on embellishing Lismore Castle (especially in 1811-22).[22] However, in 1814, he also built a canal on the River Blackwater that extended for one mile to Lismore.[23] During the 1850s, on his visits to Lismore, the duke *'dispensed a great deal of money to schools, churches, chapels and charities, Catholic as well as Protestant [and] he would suffer no religious prejudice, if anything favouring the Catholics because they were oppressed'.*[24] During the Famine however, Devonshire spent £11,700 on drainage and a further £4,500 in compensation for improvements made by tenants.[25]

Francis Currey, on the other hand, was concerned with at least some improvements prior to the Famine. His testimony to the Devon Commission on the management of the Lismore estate reveals both a concern for ending agricultural practices which exhausted the soil and a desire to consolidate holdings. This he did by expelling the weakest tenants on the expiration of old leases and amalgamating their holdings with those of the stronger farmers.[26] He had little success, however, in enforcing covenants inserted into leases which required tenants to adopt agricultural practices that prevented soil exhaustion. Occasionally, there are references to Currey's concern in conserving the land in one place or another. When, on October 4th, Thomas Darcy of Kilnacarrigy [Kilnacarriga] complained that he could not get sand at Youghal *'as usual'*, Currey explained that he *'was obliged to stop sand being taken in consequence of the injury it would do to the works going on there, but [would] inquire if there is any other place from which it could be taken'.*[27] The following month, Mary Bryan of Tallow asked for charity and *'to be allowed to remove the Clay from the Garden'*, but was told that *'she must not on any account move any of the Clay from the Garden'.*[28] On 3rd April, Michael Morrissy of Crooked Bridge wanted to

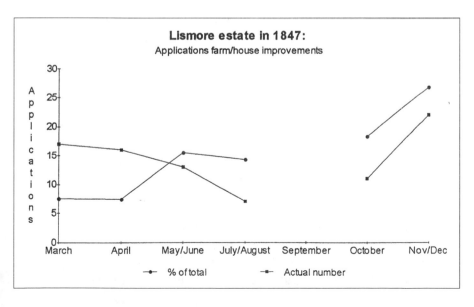

sell his manure to John Cunningham of Round Hill. Currey told him that he could sell only his turf and limestone but not the manure,[29] while on July 26th, Currey refused permission for Thomas[?] McGrath of Ballyknock to cut turf on his land.[30] Landlord Arthur Kiely-Ussher's steward similarly forbade tenants on the neighbouring Ballysaggart-more estate to sell turf from March 25th 1847 (gale day) to make it difficult for the tenants to raise the cash needed to pay their rent.[31] It's unlikely that Currey was using Kiely-Ussher's strategy with regard to McGrath because of the date – two months before the September 29th gale day and in advance of the harvest season when McGrath might be able to earn money in wage labour. Currey's usual tactic, however, was to delay carrying out or finishing improvement works such as drainage in order to encourage the tenant to pay the rent or do some other duty. For example, on October 4th, the Widow Donovan of Shrugh [Sruh] wanted her drains filled in, complaining that her horse had fallen into them and drowned. She also wished to be paid for *drawing the stones* (from the newly-drained field?). She was told, however, that the drains would only be finished once she had drawn the stones – for which she would not be paid.[32] Biddy Farrell of Bishopstown also asked for drains to be filled on 8th November, but was reminded that she was not paying her rent.[33]

The graph shows a steady decline in the number of applications for farm and building improvements from March to July/August, though they peak later in November/December. The applications are dominated by requests for windows (22) and doors (22) for the tenants' dwelling houses followed by drainage (14). While many of the applications for doors and windows probably resulted from a simple need to replace damaged or rotting fittings, some may have been due to a concern for security. Such a concern is reflected in two applications. Denis Dawley of Monalour applied for a door and frame on 8th March *'to secure his home'* while Michael Cahill of Toornagoppoge wanted shutters and a door on 4th October *'having been robbed lately'*.[34]

Joel Mokyr has related how contemporary writers found farm buildings to be backward in Ireland:

> *Barns, stables, and pigsties were described repeatedly as miserable hovels. Tools, implements, and carts were often left on the fields, carts left in gaps in ditches.*[35]

Mokyr considered that such *'backwardness'* was due partly to *'the general low capital intensity from which Ireland was suffering'*. Nonetheless, there were a number of applications on the Lismore estate for various improvements, the more common of which were:- for one or more pairs of gates (7); for ploughs, harrows or rollers (or the timber for making them) (6); for fencing (5), for the ribs and couples needed in roofing the dwelling house (5), for the ribs and couples of outbuildings (4); and three each for shutters, barn doors and timber for dwelling houses.

Many nineteenth century travellers and commentators strongly recommended the use of plants such as clover, vetches and turnips in a system of crop rotation with cereals in order to improve grain yields, and they often berated the Irish farmer for not doing so. Leguminous plants such as clover and vetches restore nitrogen to the soil while turnips clean the soil by breaking the life-cycles of cereal pests and diseases. Since potatoes share this property with the turnip, many farmers in Ireland saw no need to abandon them until the ravages of potato blight in the mid-1840s.[36] Though thought of by contemporary writers as typical features of backwardness, the lazy-bed method and the spade used in cultivating potatoes were far cheaper than using draught animals and heavy ploughs.[37] Furthermore, though one third of the total potato crop before the Famine was used as animal fodder,[38] the potato was the main subsistence crop for many cultivators.

Turnip cultivation was long resisted for a variety of other reasons. Drainage was often required in parts of the country in order to allow turnips to be grown, making the plant's cultivation more expensive than potatoes.[39] Turnips were cited as the reason for requesting drainage in three applications on the Lismore estate – John Crotty of Sruh (on April 12th), John Mullowny of Glountain (Glentane, Co. Cork) (April 20th) and Michael Hurley of Knocknamuck (May 10th). Currey's response to these requests varied – he told Crotty that he didn't think he could do it *'this year'*, that he would *'get the drains cut'* for Mullowny so long as the latter drew the stones *'without payment but not otherwise'*, and that he would *'speak to Mr. Hutchinson* [the middleman?]' about Hurley's application.[40]

Tenants also greatly disliked landlord/agent interference in the day-to-day running of their farms particularly for *'their patronising manner and their tendency to regard all tenants as deficient in intelligence and education'*.[41] Mokyr states *'that turnips tended to be stolen from the fields'* as a direct consequence of landlord interference and was an effort to reduce interest in adopting the new farming practices.[42] This may have been the case prior to the Famine, but in the late 1840s, such theft must have been carried out in desperation by hunger-stricken peasants. Whatever the reason for the theft, strong farmers continued to prosecute the starving for such theft during the Famine years.[43] Some farmers even acquired guns to protect their crops and shot people caught stealing any turnips![44] On the Lismore estate, Denis Dawley of Monalour requested *'Sticks for [a] Cabin to watch his Turnips'* on October 25th, while William (or Widow) Prendergast of Cooladallane wanted *'timber to repair a turnip house'* on November 8th.

Family matters

A few of the applications at Lismore between March and December refer to various family problems. A number of the more serious of these involved cases of family violence and financial disputes.

The Widow Neville of Mutton Lodge complained to Currey on March 8th that her father had *'swindled her out of £40 that was in Mr Gumbleton's hands'*. The following month, the Widow Neville (now of Ballyrafter Mountain) stated that her father had not yet *'given her the Notes promised for the money of hers taken by him from Mr Gumbleton'*.[45] On the first occasion, she was simply told to come in to see Currey again the following Monday. On the second occasion, she was told to come in yet again – this time with her father. A note inserted after this and dated April 28th records that *'Mangan agrees to give a Note at 9 Months for £5 and at 12 Months for £10'*. (Nothing was said about the remaining £21...).[46]

Three women had difficult relationships with their sons. Mary Collins of Tallow (stated to be the wife of Patrick Collins) complained *'of ill treatment by her 2 younger sons who have beaten her and taken her money out of her box'*; Widow Leahy of Tallow reported that *'her son Patrick forces himself upon her against her will, he having a House of his own'*; and Widow O'Donnell of Killahally who complained *'of treatment of* [i.e. by] *her Son'*. The first and last of these three applications are marked *'No app.'*(?) but Currey's response to Pat Leahy's behaviour was to tell him: *'that I consider he is acting improperly in forcing himself into the House as she does not wish it to be so'*. One wonders whether this statement of the obvious had any effect in dissuading the son from continuing to harass his mother(!).[47]

Brothers could also cause trouble. The brother of Mary Sullivan of Mass Lane was *'keeping all the money sent from America and not giving her any of it'*, while Mary Cotter of Ballybrady complained *'of the conduct of her brother and will not let her reside in the house'*.[48] Complainants regarding troublesome brothers were not all women as (?) Curran of Ballygalane Mountain found fault with 'his *brother Andrew [who had] turned him out of his house'*.[49] Although Curran's application is marked *'No app.'*(?), Currey responded to Sullivan's plea by sending for her brother who then paid her *'the £1'* on his arrival. Currey's reply to Cotter was less helpful, saying he could not *'interfere between them – the brother is tenant to the place'*.

If fathers and brothers were not bad enough, in-laws could add further problems. Notable among the Lismore applicants was John Flynn of Glenshask who, on four occasions between March and May 1847, complained about his brother-in-law Pat Sweeny of Ballyrafter Mountain or asked for assistance regarding his sister (Sweeny's wife).[50] More specifically, the second application on March 15th reveals that Flynn had *'lost £24.14.0 by [the] marriage of his Sister to Patrick Sweeny who has sent her away and now Widow [?] Sweeny wants to bring in another son in law'*. Indeed, a Mary Sweeny of Ballyrafter Mountain wished *'to be allowed to bring in a Son-in law O'Donnell of [Glendeish?]'* on March 8th.[51] On April 26th, it was stated in Flynn's third application that his sister *'was married to Sweeny who has gone to America and left his wife behind'*. Flynn's last application about this matter (on May 10th) was simply a request to Currey for any assistance he could give to *'his sister who was married to Sweeny'*. This was obviously not a happy marriage! Currey's response to the first application on March 8th seemed promising – *'I have a fund[?] to allow them to bring in any son-in-law [but] I cannot do more at present'*. *'No app.'* was placed next to the second application (and that of Mary Sweeny) while Flynn was told to return on the Wednesday following his third application. Unfortunately, an entry inserted directly after this response and dated April 28th is too faint to understand. The last application merely provoked a straight forward *'cannot interfere'*.

Another John Flynn, this time of Carrignagower, wanted *'to bring in a Son in law'* in March as well as obtain two barrels of oat seed to sow his land. Currey had no seed and told Flynn that he could not *'permit him to bring in any Son in law, but if he gives up the place [he] would give him ['£' sign crossed out] some assistance to emigrate'*.[52]

Still on the matter of the family and property, Michael Cotter of Glenreigh told Currey in July that his son William was *'about to sell his farm to his Uncle James Cotter for £10 and leave the country without paying him £40 as agreed'*.[53] Currey stated that *'as he* [? Michael or William?] *chose to give the place up without first coming to the Castle I cannot interfere between them – this only relates to the farm [while] James Cotter holds the rest under a division made between themselves and not sanctioned by me'*.

When Pat Kennelly of Monalour, accompanied by his brother Malachie, informed Currey in April that both of their parents had died of fever, he indicated his desire to keep the land. Kennelly was only fifteen years old, and Currey noted down –

> *I shall take up the land – he is not of age nor has he the means to hold land at all – if they give it up and the three children go into*

the Poor House for a time [!] I will pay £5 for each (£15) into the Savings Bank for them when they are of an age to emigrate or to do any thing for themselves.[54]

Mary Daly has noted the 'disproportionate number [of workhouse inmates that] were women and children'.[55] Some children were orphans while others were simply abandoned at the workhouse by their parents. Either way, many children *'remained a long-term burden on the poor law. Already by February 1847 children under fifteen years, though some would have had parents in the workhouse, constituted a majority of all workhouse inmates; they also constituted a majority of inmates in 1851'.*[56]

Getting property back from the pawn-broker could be difficult as two applicants found – whether they had placed items in pawn themselves or not. On May 10th, John Flannigan of Chapel Lane reported that William Conway had *'his wife's cloak in pawn and will not give it up'* to which Currey remarked – *'Conway is desired to give Flannigan the duplicate for the cloak and is told I am very much displeased with him for taking lodgers and unless he gets rid of them I shall give him a notice to quit'.*[57] Currey, however, was not able to help Mary Kiely of Monaman who wanted *'money to get her things out of pawn'* on April 26th.[58] One other rather curious application was made by Michael Gorman of Monatarriv who enquired *'about [the] execution put in by Pat Mangan'.* Currey told Gorman that *'Anderson will attend the court tomorrow if necessary'.*[59] However, nothing more is mentioned about the matter in the applications.

Applications for charity
Although some applications, such as for work, might have been what Mary Cullen calls *'a disguised form of begging'*,[60] forty-four of them between March and December 1847 were specifically for charity. Seven other applications were for more specific kinds of charity – Mary Kiely of Monaman wanted, on April 26th, *'money to get her things out of pawn'* (Currey replied: *'I cannot do it'*),[61] three people wished to be sent to Cork Infirmary (Thomas Hallahan of Tallow on March 13th,[62] the *'nearly blind'* Bridget Coleman of Ballysaggartmore on April 27th[63] and John Keeffe of Garraneribbeen [Co. Cork] on July 9th),[64] and two individuals (Thomas [or Nicholas?] Coleman on April 3rd[65] and Garrett Norris on March 13th[66] – both were of Lismore) desired a coffin, for a child in Norris's case.

Of the forty-four requests specifying only *'charity'*, thirty-two (73%) of them received favourable responses from Francis Currey, while eight were negative and four mysteriously marked *'No app.'*. The high success rate contrasts favourably with the proprietors of Skibbereen, Co. Cork, who were berated in January 1847 by Sir Randolph Routh (Commissary General and chair of the Relief Commission) for not using their substantial wealth to alleviate suffering on their property.[67] The Duke of Devonshire himself donated £1,000 to *'The British Association for the relief of the extreme distress in the remote parishes of Ireland and Scotland'* founded on 1 January 1847.[68] The amounts that Currey donated to the applicants varied from 6 pence to 10 shillings. The amount most frequently given was 1 shilling (nine times), followed by 2/6 (seven times), 2/- (six times), 10/- (five times), 5/- (four times) and 6d. (twice).

Some of the applications for charity give more information on the condition of the applicants or of their families. This helps us to understand the wide variation in money given by Currey. The 10/- amount was given to the Widow Flahavan of Newport who sought both *'charity and employment for her boy'* on March 29th;[69] to two men (Garrett Roche and James Ryan on May 10th) whose houses were burned down in Glengarra (they were presumably neighbours) – one of them losing £15 in paper money to the flames[70] to Kitty Keeffe of Newport who, on October 25th, asked for *'assistance for her sister Mary Dudley'*;[71] and also to Margaret Ryan of Ballyin, eight members of her family suffering from fever on July 26th.[72] The 5/- amount was given to the wife of Pat Dynas of Monalour who was ill on April 3rd[73] and to the Widow Flahavan of Newport who (again) wanted charity and *'a son employed'* on July 26th.[74]

Curiously, lesser amounts were handed out to people who seem to have been in no less distress than some of those receiving larger sums. John Dawley of Ballyrafter Mountain received only 2/6 on April 3rd despite having three children sick with fever at a time when (he claimed) the fever house was full, while Catherine Mack of Chapel Lane (Lismore) whose *'family [was] in fever'* got just 2/-.[75] When Mary Toomey of Ballyrafter applied for *'relief'* on April 12th, she told Currey that *'her husband has been in bed for a fort'night'*,[76] while the Widow Carroll of Newport applied on October 25th for charity *'her husband having died lately'*. Both women received only 2/- each. Nonetheless, when James Toomey of Mountain Farm asked for charity on April 26th, his *'wife sick in fever'*, he was given just 1/-.[77]

Currey was generally not happy with people who returned for more aid when they had already received some. On November 22nd, Mary Bryan applied for charity, and although she was given 1/-, Currey remarked that her aunt had been promised *'a trifle [sum] if she gave up the house and went into the poor house which she would not do and I cannot support her out of it'*.[78] To Timothy Nugent of Monaman on

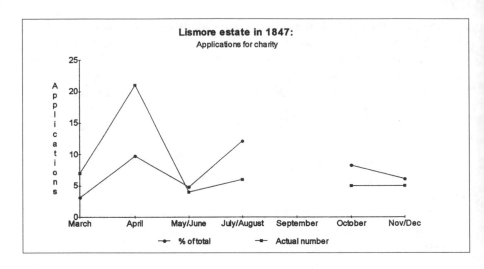

Lismore estate in 1847:
Applications for charity

Applications

—•— % of total   —■— Actual number

March   April   May/June   July/August   September   October   Nov/Dec

April 12th, Currey gave 1/- and commented that *'they were told to apply at the Poorhouse and as they will not do so I cannot relieve them any longer'.*[79] At least these two applicants got a shilling – others who had previously received aid were not so lucky.

Widow Sophie Walsh of Chapel Lane, Lismore, was told by Currey on April 26th that he *'gave money to send her sons to America and cannot do more for her – she must apply to the Committee for Relief'.*[80] Mary Mansfield of Ballyin Mountain was informed on November 8th that her family had *'received £20 on giving up the place and [that Currey could not] do more for them'*, while the Widow Cunningham was told the same day that as she *'Has one son employed [she was] told [that he] cannot do more'.*[81] Mary Griffith of Tallow Bridge was simply told *'to apply to the relief committee'* on July 26th,[82] while others were told either to give up their holdings for a sum of money – compensation for the unexpended duration of the lease – (Michael Power of Glengarra on April 12th and John Fitzgerald of Ballylug [?] on May 24th)[83] or simply that Currey could not help them (Mary Molowne of Sruh on April 26th and Kitty Power of Glengarra on May 24th).[84]

The two applicants who each received the smallest sum (6d.) were Nancy Morris of Tallow on March 13th and Thomas Murray of Church Lane on April 12th, neither of whom had a *'claim'* and so could not be further assisted.[85] Such individuals without a claim might have been subtenants living on the estate without Currey's approval as the estate agent. Alternatively, they could have been migrant beggars from some place outside the Lismore estate who thought that they might strike it lucky if they begged at Lismore Castle. There were many reports during the Famine period of migrant beggars who would flock towards the towns and villages where either work or relief might be available for them.[86] Many of those forced to beg were not only poor but had depended almost entirely on the potato for sustenance. The potato failure of 1846 forced many starving peasants into the towns. By December, many of the starving were dying within the limits of cities such as Cork where it was reported that 100 deaths occurred each week that month. By April 1847, the number of weekly deaths in Cork had risen to 500.[87]

In the mid-1830s, according to evidence collected for the Poor Inquiry of 1835-6, *women greatly outnumbered men among the destitute [...] especially among the aged'.*[88] Women also dominated the numbers of those adopting vagrancy as a form of relief, and many of these had husbands classified amongst the able-bodied unemployed. At the point of destitution, whole families left the home with *'the wife supporting herself and the children, [while] the husband saved to re-establish the family back at home'.* Normally, summer was the season in which this migration was most likely to occur, a period when the potato reserves from the last harvest had been used up and little employment was available.[89] One historian states that witnesses who gave evidence to the Poor Inquiry

> *agreed that the vast majority of the seasonal yearly invasion of strolling beggars in their locality was comprised of able-bodied women accompanied by young children. Some of these women were identified as widows but the majority were the "wives of labourers". Estimates of the proportion of all strolling beggars these women represented ranged from two-thirds to nine-tenths.*[90]

Of the Lismore applications for charity from March to December 1847, 30 (or 68%) of them were by women, 12 (27%) by men and 2 (5%) by persons of unknown sex. Of the 42 applicants who can be sexed, 71% were female and 29% male. Taking into account that three women returned for charity on one other occasion between March and December (giving a total of 41 people making applications for charity in this period), the proportions become 66% female, 29% male and 5% unknown (or 69% female and 31% male amongst the sexed population only). These figures agree with the estimates of the Poor Inquiry of a decade earlier. The major distinction between 1835-6 and 1847 was the time of the year when begging for charity occurred – peaking in springtime (especially April) on the Lismore estate rather than in the summer months. This peak is no doubt linked with the problems many of the poor faced in paying their rents on March 25th.

One might have expected a greater number of males applying for charity at Lismore since bands of starving men were reported in

November 1846 to be roaming about the country begging for food, *"more like famishing wolves than men"*.[91] It was usually explained by the Poor Inquiry witnesses that the low number of male beggars in the mid-1830s happened because men were more ashamed to beg than women![92] It would appear, from the Lismore evidence at least, that despite the more extreme conditions of the Famine, this attitude continued to prevail into the late 1840s.

It is not possible to say from the evidence of the Lismore applications whether children accompanied their mothers to Lismore Castle or not.[93] Certainly, nothing as horrific as the report of a woman carrying a dead child in her arms at Skibbereen, Co. Cork, in December 1846[94] was noted amongst the Lismore applications! It is possible to say, though, that eleven of the women applying for charity at Lismore Castle were designated as widows. Though Poor Inquiry witnesses identified some women beggars in the mid-1830s as widows, this high proportion (41%) of the 27 women applicants at Lismore is an indication of the hardship suffered during the Famine.

Geographically, the applicants' addresses were dominated by urban areas (Lismore, including Chapel Lane [5], Tallow [6], Church Lane [?Youghal or Lismore] [2], Ferry lane [?Youghal] [1], and Tallow Bridge [1]) and upland[95] townlands with agriculturally marginal land, including Glengarra (4), Monalour (3) Monaman (2), and 1 each for Ballygalane, Ballyin, Ballyin Mountain, Ballylug, Ballyrafter, Ballyrafter Mountain, Cooldrishoge, Glengarra, Glenshask, Glountain (Glentane, Co. Cork), Monalour, Monaman, Mountain Farm and Sruh. Another four applicants were from Newport. Though this townland is on lower ground and beside the Blackwater estuary, some or all of the applicants from Newport may have lived among the poor *"squatters"*, who had put up a hut of sods in a bog, or on the seashore, for the sake of seaweed for potato manure'.[96]

Relief work
Much has been written elsewhere about the Whig government's decision in February 1847 to end the public works relief system and replace it with soup kitchens. The main reasons for this change of policy were that the availability of the schemes and the funds to support them varied considerably from one area to another, that many of the people in most need of relief work were turned away in favour of those more well off (such as farmers' sons), that the waged labour the works provided drew workers away from farm employment (conacre and the rent would be paid for by labour rather than with cash), that the wages were either insufficient to cover the cost of the grossly-inflated food prices of late 1846/early 1847 or were irregularly

paid, and that consequently, many of those employed on the public works became too weak to work or even died from lack of food. The public works were therefore to be phased out from March 1847 and replaced with a system of direct relief – providing soup to the poor.[97] Currey was both estate agent and a member of the relief committee: there seems to be a certain overlapping of roles in dealing with the tenants between March and July 1847.

On the Lismore estate, the number of applications for work dropped from 21 in March though 9 in April and 7 in May/June to just one in July/August. Currey's response to a number of the applications on March 8th was to tell the applicant to apply to the Relief Committee directly or that he would bring up their name at its meeting on the Wednesday following. However, owing arrears could make getting relief work rather difficult. When Mary Cullinane applied for work *'on the publick roads'* on behalf of her husband Pat, she was told that he *'would* 'get no work there unless he gives up his land[.] He owes a large arrear of rent'.[98] Having a member of the family already employed on the works also seems to have been a basis for exclusion as John Boyle of Sruh (a sub-tenant) found out that day.[99]

By March 13th, the bad news of the government's decision to bring an end to the public works system was being disseminated among that day's applicants. Daniel Ryan of Ballyin was *'told the Board of Works will not give any more employment'* while John Keeffe of Middle Quarter was informed that there were *'no more taken on public works'.*[100] Pat Brennach of Ballyin Mountain, applying for work on the roads was told by Currey *'I cannot do it. I have no power',* though it was suggested to John Mangan of Bridane to *'apply to the Committee'.*[101]

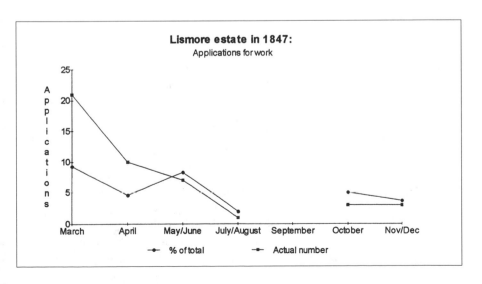

83

Ellen Flaherty of Ballyin's applications for work, first for her husband ('*on the work*') on March 13th and then for her children (on the roads) on March 29th met with a similar though contradictory response. On the 13th, she was told that her husband had already been given money to help *him* go to Wales and so no more assistance could be given *him*. Since Currey had noted that her husband had not yet left for Wales by March 13th, Ellen may have thought that no further aid would be given while he was still around. On the 29th, Currey refused further assistance again, stating that '*the husband got money to take them to England and has now gone and left them*'.[102] It would appear that Currey was confused over the terms of the assistance previously given this family, or perhaps, for some unrecorded reason, he wished to wrangle himself out of paying more money than he felt he needed to.

Work does seem to have been made available (or was at least promised) on estate improvements instead during the month of March. Although '*No app.*' was placed beside the application of Michael Tobin of Moanfune for a job as '*Steward of drainage*',[103] a number of others simply seeking employment were told that they could get work when the drains were being made. Examples include the Widow Fleming of Monatarriv (for herself) and two women (Nelly Brien of Glenshask and Widow Morrissy of Ballylug) who applied for work on behalf of their two daughters.[104]

That women and children were among those applying for work at Lismore was a widespread feature of famine relief works in Ireland.[105] Less usual was a mason's widow from Tallow, Margaret McNamara (or Macnamarra), whose request for assistance to set up in business gained her a donation of 5 shillings on the second attempt.[106] The only other observed request for help in setting up a business was made by (?) Power of Newport in July who wanted to be set up in butchering. Currey was not able to help him.[107]

From March 29th, a number of applicants (including James Barry of Carrignagower, James Hynes of Newport, James Flaherty of Newport, John Dawly of Glengarra, William Ryan of Monatrim, Pat Morrissy of Ballyin, Pat Keeffe of Mass Lane and Widow Milligan of Monaman)[108] found that no work was available at all. More specific responses were not much better – Widow Flahavan of Newport was told to try the workhouse, Thomas Byrne of Lyrenacallee was told (regarding employment on the Glenribbeen road) '*to apply when the work is recommenced*', while David (or Daniel) Barry of Newport heard that enquiries would be made on his behalf.[109] Currey's optimism that work on the Glenribbeen road would be restarted is further reflected in his May 24th response to John Dynas of Monalour to whom he said that he would '*try and get his name on the [relief committee's] list*'.

Some of the more successful applicants were offered work for only two or three weeks, such as when James Morrissy of Ballyin applied for work on behalf of his son so that he could afford to buy seed, or when David Geary of Ballyrafter Mountain requested employment for *his* son.[110] Another applicant's son was given work on the drains while his own holding was taken up. The tenant (Michael Power of Glengarra) was allowed to remain in his house as (an unpaid) caretaker.[111]

Some applications for work were more specific and indicate the range of jobs that were potentially available on the Lismore estate. Patrick Ahern of New Street asked for work in the garden (at Lismore Castle), James Burtin[?] of Moanfune requested a job as a *'wood ranger'* on behalf of his brother, and William Ryan of Bridane applied for employment at Ballinvally Fort. The mysterious designation *'No app.'* unfortunately accompanies these applications.[112] For other applicants, we have more information. Michael Cahill of Toornagoppoge asked for work at *'the Bank'* for his daughter (to which Currey responded with *'Order given to Corbett'*); William Ryan of Monatrim (the William Ryan of Bridane who made a similar application some months earlier?) is recorded as *'wanting work at the Fort'* (Currey stated 'I *cannot give it him'*); and John Clancy of Garrycloyne.[113] Clancy had apparently taken the initiative to look after a wood in Garrycloyne though Currey remarked that he had never appointed him to do so. Nonetheless, Currey told Clancy that *'if he looks after the place properly and there is no trespass committed, I will pay him £2 a year from Lady day last during pleasure'*.

A few applications for work inadvertently reveal something of the conditions of the time. Currey told Laurence[?] Byrne, recorded as being one of the twelve children of Thomas Byrne of Lyrenacallee, that he would *'see if [he could] get him work on the drains [he says he cannot work on them'is crossed out] for himself and [his] brother John'*.[114] Could Byrne have felt that he was too weak to work on the drains only to hastily put such anxiety aside when he realised that the alternative would be unemployment? The only other application of a person who *may* have been too weak for work was made by Ellen Moynihan of Ballyin who wanted work on the roads but was told by Currey that he would not recommend her to the relief committee (no explanation recorded).[115] Given the frequent references in the contemporary press and other records to weak or starving labourers on the public works, it is surprising that virtually no reference to such hardship is made in the Lismore Application Books for the period analysed.

When Brian Fitzpatrick wished *'to be taken into the employ many again'*, Currey proclaimed that he would *'never take any person into the employment again who is detected in stealing'.*[116] In applying for work, John Dawly of Glengarra declared *'that the Soup [i.e., that provided by the soup kitchens] is no good to them'.*[117] The only other reference to food given out as relief occurred when Widow Power of Monalour complained *'about the quantity of meal she is getting'.* Currey suggested that she apply to the relief committee.[118]

Finally, regarding employment, when Pat Geary of Crooked Bridge wanted *'to get a character [reference] to take to America',* Currey pointed out that he *'never give[s] characters to any one'.* Yet, less than two months later, Currey gave *'a Note to the Recruiting Serjeant of the 34th Regiment'* for Daniel Farrell of Cooladallane who wanted to enlist and *'to get a letter of recommendation'.*[119] But then, Currey's ability to contradict himself has been noted before.

Emigration, 'giving up', farm consolidation and eviction

Emigration during the Famine has received much attention from historians with regard to the number of emigrants, their social origins, destinations and mortality level either at sea or following arrival in the new country. Prior to the Famine, emigrants seem to have been 'a *largely proletarian outflow'* since *'over two-thirds of those who went to New York and Boston in the 1820s and 1830s were labourers or displaced textile workers, and only one-sixth were artisans'.*[120] This proletarian dominance continued into and followed the Famine years, though many recorded as labourers in ships' manifests were the sons or daughters of farmers.[121] The fare to Canada, however, was lower and probably attracted many more of the poorer emigrants.

Emigrants to Canada suffered a higher mortality rate than those going elsewhere due to the poor shipboard conditions resulting from

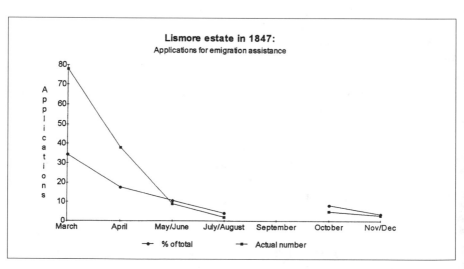

the cheap fares and unenforced shipping regulations.[122] Indeed, some of the most distressing descriptions of mass death and suffering during the Famine were of emigrants arriving at Grosse Isle in Québec.[123] All the same, many poor people could not afford to emigrate, particularly in Munster, and Waterford had one of the lowest emigration rates in Ireland between 1841 and 1851.[124]

The United States was the destination of first choice for most famine emigrants followed by Canada and Great Britain (in terms of those permanently settling in these countries).[125] The preference for the United States is born out by the Lismore evidence as America was specified as the destination in 61% of cases. British North America (namely Newfoundland and Québec) is represented in only 3% of cases while Britain was the destination (temporary or permanent) for 21% of applicants (many of these may have departed for America and elsewhere from British ports). No destination is given in 15% of emigrant applications.[126]

Many landlords, facing bankruptcy as a result of the heavy financial burden of paying rates for tenants with holdings valued under £4 (imposed by the Whig government in 1846) and from falling rental incomes, decided to either evict their tenants or to compensate those '*voluntarily*' giving up their holdings.[127] Although some of the larger farmers emigrated to avoid paying rates themselves,[128] smallholders and labourers were given what McCartney calls '*small bribes to clear out*'.[129] Speculator Francis Spaight '*emigrated*' 1,400 people from his Derry castle estate around Killaloe by 1849, compensating each tenant with £3.10s. In 1849-50, William Steuart Trench, the agent for the Marquis of Lansdowne's Kenmare estate in County Kerry, convinced his employer that many of the poorer tenants should be assisted to emigrate. As a result of Trench's policy, more than 4,600 tenants were given an average of £3.14s. to give up their holdings.130 The O'Callaghan proprietors of Clogheen in South Tipperary (Viscounts Lismore) gave the considerably smaller compensation of just £1 '*for persons throwing down their houses and giving up their holdings [while] a small minority of this group were to receive subsidies to emigrate*'.[131] Some landlords or their agents were even worse, deluding their tenants to demolish their own houses in return for '*a few shillings and an assurance of outdoor relief*' as was reported for Kilrush Union in County Clare.[132]

Arthur Kiely-Ussher of Ballysaggart is also reported to have deceived his tenants in the three decades or so prior to the Famine. In the process of expanding his demesne, he would take up holdings close to his residence on the expiration of their leases and let new plots of ground to the displaced tenants on poorer mountain soil. Promising, but failing, to give the tenant a lease for the new plot (usually for a 21-

year term), he would take up the mountain holding after just a few years once it had been made productive by the tenant's improvements, and placed him/her on still more unproductive bog and heath.[133]

In contrast to these examples, Currey offered an average of £9 to tenants giving up their holdings and emigrating between March and December 1847. Others simply asking for *assistance* to emigrate (but not necessarily to give up a holding in the process – either they had already given it up, they never had one on the estate or were subtenants and therefore not entitled to aid from the Duke of Devonshire's agent) were offered an average sum of £1.12s.

On the Lismore estate, applications about giving up holdings (without any reference to emigrating) met with various responses. Two (made by Peter Hennessy of Ballyrafter Mountain and John Hallahan of Barrits [sic] Land) were put on the long finger while two other applicants (John Noonan of Tallow and Thomas Lyons of Monatarriv) were told to return after they found *'respectable'* tenants to take their place.[134] Two further applications were essentially by tenants wishing not to give up their farms *per se* but to exchange them with another tenant (the widow of David Lawlor of Longaville and John Power [Corkeran] of Glengarra) while another (Denis Carthy of Monaman) wished to receive 3 acres back under a new tenancy after giving up his holding.[135]

Four applicants wanted to sell a house (having constructed it themselves on the holding) but each was received differently – Currey could not buy the house offered; he would not allow the sale of the house; the lease had already expired two years before; and Currey just *'gave 2/6d'* (presumably charity) to the fourth applicant instead.[136]

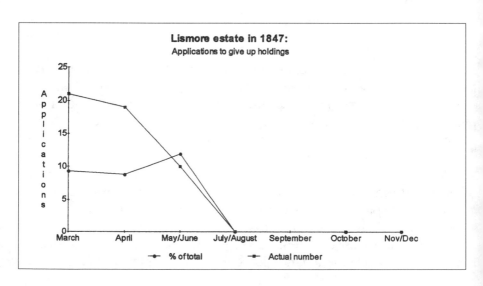

Lismore estate in 1847:
Applications to give up holdings

Although in two cases (Pat Mahony of Glentrasna, County Cork, with Denis Connell of Rathdrum, and James Cotter of Ballyrafter),[137] the compensation to applicants was not specified, there are twenty-three in which the sum is given. The amount of compensation offered varied from £1 to £22, with the most frequent offers being £20 (six times), £10 (four times) and £16 (3 times).[138] The average amount offered, at £13.12s., compares extremely favourably with the paltry sums given by those landlords discussed by Donnelly, Smyth and Feeney mentioned above.

In other cases, incoming tenants were to compensate the outgoing tenant. Usually, this meant that the new tenant would have to pay part or all of the arrears of the previous tenant as well as an additional amount as compensation for the loss of the holding. When Michael Ryan of Ballygalane wished to give up his 7 acres, 3 roods and 38 perches of land, the new tenant was to give him £34 (of which £7.15.0 were to cover the arrears).[139] Twenty pounds was the sum offered to Patrick Fitzpatrick of Glenribeen for his land and also to John Morrissy of Glenshask (by his brothers) for giving up his house in addition to paying off his arrears.[140] One woman (Mary Morrison of Killasseragh, County Cork) made an arrangement whereby an incoming tenant would give her £60, out of which she had to pay £20 to cover the arrears.[141] This large sum contrasts markedly with the meagre £1 received by Mr Higgins of Cooladallane for his land, especially when Currey reminded him that he had to pay arrears of £15.19.7.[142] In one case, Currey agreed to pay £5 to John Hickey of Bishopstown while a further £5 would be paid by the incoming tenant.[143]

While some tenants made arrangements to give up their holdings, others applied for additional land (largely made available by those who had just vacated it). Many applicants were turned away because the land had already been let or was not yet surveyed and re-arranged, while others were told to come back at a later date. One tenant (John Wynn of Coolygoodys(?)) was denied further land because Currey thought that he held 'quite as much land already (about 40 acres) as he has the means of managing' (!).[144] Some applicants may have been desperate for land such as Edmd. Bigby of Cooladallane who declared that he would 'pay as much as any one'.[145] Those that got new land were usually made 'yearly tenants' such as John Cody and Denis Dawley (both of Monalour) who separately made applications on April 12th, or Catherine Curreen of Dungarvan who applied on October 4th.[146]

Some applicants were warned not to bring in any 'lodgers' or 'strangers' into their house or else they would be given notice to quit.[147] One tenant, Julie Lane of Tallow, was even required 'to get the tenant *out of the adjoining house and add it to her own at once'* when she moved in!¹⁴⁸ If the incoming tenant did not need to move into the outgoing tenant's former house, the building would have to be turned over to some other use, whether as an 'outhouse', 'offices', or as a cattle shed.¹⁴⁹

As might be expected from reading Currey's testimony to the Devon Commission (mentioned earlier), applications regarding upcoming evictions of tenants are comparatively few. Of twenty-two such applications, only eleven holdings were affected, and not all of the tenants were evicted as a consequence. Even when evicted, tenants on the Lismore estate might still be offered some compensation which they would have been wise to accept promptly or else forsake it altogether. When Mrs Moynihan and Timothy Moynihan (her son?) of Ballyin enquired about giving up their lands on April 9th, they found that *'an Ejectment [had] been obtained and [that] the decree [would be] executed in a few days'*. Even though they were to be evicted, Currey said that he would give Mrs Moynihan £25 *'to assist her in taking her[self] to America'* while giving Timothy £5.¹⁵⁰ Three days later, Widow Moynihan asked for £30 rather than the £25 she was offered. Currey retorted *'I shall not do so and shall execute the ejectment next Wednesday and she will then get nothing'*.¹⁵¹ Currey had previously reported to the Devon Commission that failure to quietly surrender a holding resulted in the loss of any compensation which, at that time, usually consisted of a year's tenure of the house and land rent-free and the permission to take the timber and thatch of their houses on leaving.¹⁵²

There are two other cases where tenants were given the choice of either accepting a cash payment for giving up their holding or being

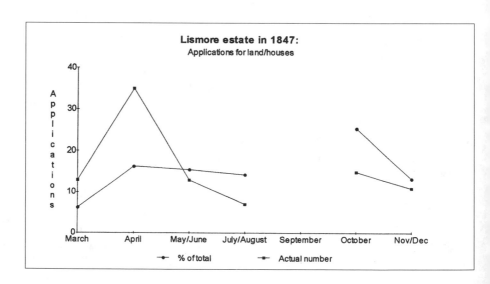

Lismore Castle, seat of the Duke of Devonshire with part of his estate stretching along the river Blackwater.

evicted. The Widow Geary of Tallow was told on October 25th by Currey that he had *'an Ejectment against the place but if she [gave] up at once [he would] give her 10/-'*. However, Currey reported that *'she is not satisfied with this and is told the Ejectment will be executed and she will get nothing'*. When Geary returned a month later asking for money for giving up her house, Currey told her that *'she was offered 10/- and as she will not take that I shall execute the decree'*.[153] The other case was the rather long drawn-out affair of the Foulke family of Bishopstown and Youghal.

Initially, Thomas Foulke of Bishopstown (accompanied by Richard Foulke of Bishopstown and William Foulke of Youghal) related *'that he has expended a large sum in manuring the farm and produces three Wheat Tickets which he states have been forged by his Nephew and by which he was robbed of over £5'*. Currey responded by saying *'I cannot interfere in their family quarrelling but that I find an arrears of £150 now due which as the farm was let for the value [sic] and all old arrears forgiven ought not to be the case – that I shall therefore have the crops sold under the distress'*. Thomas Foulke returned ten days later, this time accompanied by Thomas Walsh of Bishopstown who offered to give security for £65 to be paid in December (Archdeacon Power having declined to act as security). Currey was not particularly impressed with this proposal and did not think that Foulke could *'by any possibility'* pay off the debts and arrears. As a result, he offered him £50 and a further £25 to each of his two nephews if he gave up the farm and all the crops thereon. Otherwise, he would continue distraining the crops and also *'bring an ejectment against the place'*. Thomas Foulke (accompanied by Thomas junior, his nephew) came again on November 12th to discuss giving up the farm. Since the Foulkes could not agree among themselves to give up the farm, Currey told them that *'the Ejectment must be proceeded with'* but this time offered £35 to *'each of the young Foulkes'* as well as the £50 previously offered to Thomas senior. Currey declared that he would not offer anything higher and gave the Foulkes two days to consider his proposal. At last, the two Thomas Foulkes returned on November 26th and asked for more money(!) Currey replied that unless the amount he offered previously was accepted, he would proceed with the eviction. Amazingly, perhaps, the younger Foulke then proposed to give his uncle £50 and a further £10 *'for the Straw which with the turnips and all other things [are] to remain on the farm'*. Even more amazingly, Currey recorded that *'He [Thomas junior] is told I will in this event make him Tenant from Lady Day next if he can give me solemn security for payment of the arrears due at 25 March'*.[154]

In May and July, some tenants suggested paying part of their arrears, but these applications were not generally welcomed by Currey. He told James Duggan of Monatrim Farm on May 19th that paying the rent at the next harvest was no good (but he relented on May 22nd, accepting a cash payment of £40 with the promise of a further £60 at harvest-time).[155] On May 24th, John Barry of Glenreigh offered to pay half the year's rent but was told that he would be evicted unless all of the rent and the arrears were paid. His later offer (made on July 26th) of £100 to be paid before Christmas was similarly dismissed and he was informed that the eviction would take place on August 3rd. John Barry's third proposal (made on August 1st) that both Martin Noonan of Cullinagh and Mr Higgins of Glenreigh give security to harvest the crops and pay the arrears up to May was, however, welcomed by Currey though he did not think that Noonan was good security when he was himself in arrears. Still, he decided to let the holding to Noonan and Higgins for six months on their written agreement that all of the crops on the land would be sold by them and that the money from the sale would be deposited at Lismore Castle to cover Barry's arrears. If they failed to pay the full amount indicated in the written agreement, Currey would then *'certainly sue them for whatever may be deficient'*. Currey also warned Barry that if the crops did not pay for the rent and [harvesting?] costs, he would not let the farm to him again.[156]

Though Currey thought in July that the farm of Patrick Barry of Rathdrum was *'so deeply in arrears'* that he should evict him, he stated that he would consider the tenant's proposal to let the holding to his son-in law so long as the latter paid the arrears. On Barry's subsequent application in October, he said that he would pay a year's rent in a week. Since his arrears stood at £65.3.5, Currey thought that this would *'not do'* and decided to evict him.[157] Other tenants who suggested bringing in temporary tenants to act a security for the payment of part or all of the arrears (all of whom were successful in at least postponing the threat of eviction) include Mrs Collins of Curraheen, Edmd. Barry of Ballinvella, Richard and Thomas Driscoll of Killasseragh, County Cork, and Edmd Cotter of Ballyerin, County Cork.[158]

While Barry's earlier proposal obviously fell through, Currey was willing to consider a similar offer from Denis Higgins of Longaville who applied in November for his brother David's land. Currey stated that he *'must bring an Ejectment against'* the property unless Denis could pay his brother's arrears (even if he paid only £30 initially and *'gave security for the remainder [Currey] would give him a trial'*).[159]

Usually, evictions took place on the Lismore estate because the tenant had fallen too deeply into arrears to have much chance of paying them. In one case, Currey wished to evict a family in Cooldrishoge whose head "old Thos. Donovan' had died (though there was no mention of a decree being sought to bring about the eviction). Thomas Donovan's widow was living on the farm in July along with another Thomas Donovan, Biddy Donovan and two grandchildren. They were told that *'the House must come down, the land to go to Andrew Crotty and the crops to be taken in hand by Andrew Crotty who is to pay the debts'*. Biddy Donovan returned to Currey in November asking him if the house could be kept but was told *'this cannot be – the House must come down and the matter settled by Andrew Crotty as before arranged'*.[160]

Generally speaking then, Currey (acting on the duke of Devonshire's behalf) avoided carrying out evictions, preferring to make some kind of deal with the tenant instead. Only when the tenant refused to accept the terms offered or was thought to be unable to pay off their arrears was he/she evicted. This contrasts sharply with both the traditional image of Irish landlords (especially absentees and their agents) and the general rise in the number of evictions which occurred during the Famine period (mentioned earlier).[161]

Conclusion

Francis Currey, acting on behalf of the duke of Devonshire, distributed seed to tenants sometimes on the strength of an I.O.U.; he provided assistance to tenants seeking to improve their houses and outbuildings by the addition of new windows, doors or roofs and their land by drainage; he gave charity to virtually anyone who asked for it – though less was given to those with no 'claim' (i.e., non-tenants); in the wake of the demise of the public relief works in the spring of 1847, he made some work available to those looking for employment (largely on estate drainage schemes); he avoided directly evicting tenants who were in arrears, usually offering them compensation to give up their holdings on terms that far exceeded those of a number of other landlords and their agents during the Famine; and he assisted many people wishing to emigrate, some of whom were not his tenants. On the negative side, he disliked tenants taking in lodgers (probably people who had vacated their own holdings) and occasionally was unrelenting to tenants whom he felt were unable to farm their land, had rejected his offer for compensation to give up or had been caught stealing.

As a land agent, Currey had to balance the needs of the landowner with those of the people who actually lived on the land. Although Currey could be inflexible with some applicants, he generally comes across as a conscientious man who was generous in the handing out of charity whether to tenants or to people without a 'claim'. Considering the low-cost estate clearances by agents such as William Steuart Trench in Kenmare and the unpopularity of other agents including Mr Smith (steward of the Kiely-Ussher estate at Ballysaggart)[162] and Mr Hackett (described as "*this Man of Sin*" in an anonymous letter of 1838 on behalf of his "*much persecuted and oppressed tenants*" to their landlord Walter Mansfield),[163] Currey appears to have been a human and even sympathetic agent.

REFERENCES

1. Woodham-Smith, Cecil, *The Great Hunger* (London, 1962) p. 21; Donnelly, James S. Jnr. *The land and the people of nineteenth-century Cork: the rural economy and the land question* (London 1975) p. 109; and Lees-Milne, James *The bachelor duke: a life of William Spencer Cavendish 6th Duke of Devonshire 1790-1858* (London, 1991)

2. The Application Books were catalogued and enumerated by the Public Record Office of Northern Ireland which assigned the prefix "T" to the number given to each book (for example, T1, T2, T3 and so on). The two Application Books examined (for the period March-December 1847) are numbered T15 and T16. There is no Application Book for 1848, volume T17 commencing with entries dated January 29th 1849.

3. Two applications dated 5th June are signed "HWH" (T16, p. 26).
4. In the course of constructing the database on which the statistics are based, there were a few applications encountered which could not be read clearly while the nature of some applicants' requests to Currey were not specified. These were excluded from the statistical analysis.
5. T15, p. 38.
6. T16, p. 2.
7. T16, p. 7.
8. T16, p. 16.
9. T16, p. 8.
10. T16, pp. 9, 15, 16, 17 and 18, respectively.
11. T15, p. 37.
12. T16, p. 2.
13. Solar, Peter M., "The agricultural trade of the port of Waterford, 1809-1909", in Nolan, W., Power, T.P. and Cowman, D. (eds.) *Waterford: History and society* (Dublin: 1992) pp. 495-518 (Appendix Table 2, p. 511). However, exports from Waterford of flour that year amounted to 320,324 cwt compared to 3,453 cwt of oatmeal (ibid.). In the eighteenth century, Ireland was "a net importer of wheat". Cullen, L. M. *An economic history of Ireland since 1660* (London, 1987) p. 68. The flour exported from Waterford in the nineteenth century was probably largely imported from County Kilkenny's many corn mills (*ibid.*, p. 70).
14. Solar, Peter M., "Harvest fluctuations in pre-Famine Ireland: fluctuations from Belfast and Waterford newspapers", *Agricultural History Review* 37(ii), pp. 157-65 (p. 159) (1989)
15. Cullen, L.M., op. cit. pp. 68, 70.
16. Ó Gráda, Cormac, *Ireland before and after the Famine: explorations in economic history, 1800-1925* (Manchester, 1988), pp. 60-1.
17. ibid, p. 48 (Table 10); cf. Ó Gráda, Cormac, "Poverty, population, and agriculture, 1801-45", in W. E. Vaughan, (ed.) *A New History of Ireland. V: Ireland under the Union, 1801-70* (Oxford, 1989) pp. 108-36 (p. 123).
18. T16, p. 13.
19. Ó Gráda, Cormac, "Poverty, population, and agriculture, 1801-45" pp.108-36 (p. 128) (Oxford, 1989); Mokyr, Joel, *Why Ireland starved: a quantitative and analytic history of the Irish economy, 1800-1850* (London: 1983), pp. 83, 173.
20. Daly, Mary E., *Social and economic history of Ireland since 1800* (Dublin, 1981), p. 40. cf. Smyth, W.J., "Estate records and the making of the Irish landscape: an example from County Tipperary", *Irish Geography* 9, pp. 29-49 (pp. 37, 41), (1976) and Currie, E.A., "Land tenures, enclosures and field-patterns in Co. Derry in the eighteenth and nineteenth centuries", *Irish Geography* 9, pp. 50-63 (p. 53) (1976)
21. Lees-Milne, James, op. cit. p. 184.
22. ibid, pp. 22, 147; Proudfoot, Lindsay, "Landlords and politics: Youghal and Dungarvan in the 1830s", *Decies* 34, pp. 35-47 (p. 41) (1987)
23. Freeman, T. W., "Land and people, c. 1841", in W. E. Vaughan (ed.) *A New History of Ireland. V: Ireland under the Union, 1801-70* (Oxford, 1989), pp. 242-71 (p. 257).
24. Lees-Milne, James, op. cit. pp. 185-6. Improvements at Lismore Castle, however, continued during the same period (*ibid.*, pp. 190-2).
25. Donnelly, James S. Jnr., op. cit. p. 109.
26. ibid, pp. 38, 56. Many of those forced to give up their holdings were subtenants living on a former middleman's holding (*ibid.*, p. 57).

27. T16, p. 33.
28. T16, p. 42 (November 22nd).
29. T16, p. 2.
30. T16, p. 28.
31. Feeney, Patrick, "Ballysaggart estate: eviction, famine and conspiracy", *Decies* 27, pp. 4-12 (p. 8) (1984)
32. T16, p. 35.
33. T16, p. 39.
34. T15, p. 28; T16, p. 34.
35. Mokyr, Joel, op. cit. p. 168.
36. Mokyr, Joel, op. cit. pp.163-4; Ó Gráda, Cormac, "Poverty, population, and agriculture" pp. 124, 126. Nonetheless, following the potato failures of 1845-6, turnips were quickly substituted wherever possible. [Ó Gráda, Cormac *Ireland before and after the Famine*, (Manchester, 1988) p. 66].
37. Ó Gráda, Cormac, *Ireland before and after the Famine* (Manchester, 1988) p. 56.
38. Mokyr, Joel, op. cit. p. 165.
39. Mokyr, Joel, op. cit. pp. 165, 169.
40. T16, pp. 8, 17 and 22.
41. Daly, Mary E., op. cit. pp. 40-1.
42. Mokyr, Joel op. cit. p. 168.
43. Hoppen, K. Theodore, *Ireland since 1800: conflict and conformity* (London, 1989) p. 56. To the farmers' dismay, a magistrate at Kildorrery, Co. Cork, dismissed all cases of turnip theft on compassionate grounds in October 1846 (Donnelly, James S. Jnr. op. cit. p. 87).
44. Donnelly, James S., Jnr. op. cit. p.87
45. T16, pp. 37, 38. Prendergast's address is difficult to decipher.
46. T15, p. 28 (March 8th); T16, p. 16 (April 26th).
47. T15, p. 31 (March 9th); T16, pp. 33 (October 4th) and 19 (April 27th).
48. T16, pp. 35 (October 4th) and 36 (October 25th).
49. T16, p. 14 (April).
50. T15, pp. 27 (March 8th) and 36 (March 15th); T16, pp. 16 (April 26th) and 21 (May 10th).
51. T15, p. 30 (March 8th).
52. T15, p. 39 (March 29th).
53. T16, p. 28 (July 26th).
54. T16, p. 5 (April 9th).
55. Daly, Mary E., *The Famine in Ireland* (Dublin, 1986) p. 93.
56. ibid, p. 93.
57. T16, p. 20 (May 10th).
58. T16, p. 16 (April 26th).
59. T16, p. 42 (November 22nd).
60. Cullen, Mary, "Breadwinners and providers: women in the household economy of labouring families 1835-6", in M. Luddy and C. Murphy (eds) *Women surviving: studies in Irish women's history in the 19th and 20th centuries* (Dublin: Poolbeg, 1990), pp. 85-116 (p. 107).
61. T16, p. 16.
62. T15, p. 35.
63. T16, p. 19.
64. T16, p. 30.
65. T16, p. 3.
66. T15, p. 37.

67. Woodham-Smith, Cecil, op. cit. pp. 163-4.
68. ibid, pp. 169-70.
69. T16, p. 2. Currey "recommended her to go into the Poor house".
70. T16, p. 20.
71. T16, p. 37. Currey told Keeffe that "Mr Bennett gave her 10s/- a short time ago & also some clothes – I will give her 10s/- more now & told [her] it is the last time I can so".
72. T16, p. 29.
73. T16, p. 2. Currey told her "that if her husband is in so bad a state he had better come in as soon as he is well enough and arrange about giving it [the holding] up." It would seem that Currey was sceptical that this tenant's illness was genuine, perhaps perceiving it to be a ploy to delay paying overdue rent.
74. T16, p. 29. Currey said nothing about the son's employment.
75. T16, pp. 3, 29.
76. T16, pp. 8, 43. Currey also told Carroll that "she should apply at the poor house".
77. T16, p. 17.
78. T16, p. 42.
79. T16, p. 9.
80. T16, p. 17.
81. T16, pp. 38, 40.
82. T16, p. 29.
83. T16, pp. 9, 24.
84. T16, pp. 16, 25.
85. T15, p. 35; T16, p. 8.
86. Hoppen, K. Theodore, op. cit. p. 55 (quoting an un-named Derry proprietor); Litton, Helen, *The Irish Famine: an illustrated history* (Dublin, 1994) p. 59 (reproducing a letter of Constable John Norris of Aughrim, Co. Wicklow, 16 June 1847).
87. Woodham-Smith, Cecil, op. cit. p. 144; Donnelly, James S. Jnr., op. cit. p. 87.
8. Cullen, Mary, op. cit. p. 87.
89. ibid, pp. 107, 109.
90. ibid, pp. 109-10.
91. Woodham-Smith, Cecil, op. cit. p. 140.
92. Cullen, Mary, op. cit. p. 113.
93. Unless Widow Flahavan of Newport who twice applied for work for her son (on March 29th and July 26th) was accompanied by him on each occasion. Considering that Newport (located near the mouth of the river Blackwater) is some distance away from Lismore, this may have been the case.
94. Woodham-Smith, Cecil, op. cit. p. 163.
95. A substantial portion of the Lismore estate was located on the lower slopes of the Knockmealdown Mountains
96. Woodham-Smith, Cecil, op. cit. p. 144.
97. Ó Tuathaigh, Gearoid, *Ireland before the Famine 1798-1848* (Dublin: 1972) pp. 213-14; Daly, Mary E., *The Famine in Ireland*, (Dublin, 1986) pp. 78-84; McCartney, Donal, *The dawning of democracy: Ireland 1800-1870* (Dublin: Helicon, 1987), pp. 168-9; Ó Gráda, Cormac, *Ireland before and after the Famine*, (Dublin, 1988) pp. 114-16; Litton, Helen, op. cit. pp. 36, 39-40, 55-6; Donnelly, James S. Jnr., op. cit. pp. 84-5; Daly, Mary E., *Social and economic history of Ireland since 1800*, (Dublin, 1981) p. 22.
98. T15, p. 27.
99. T15, p. 29.

100. T15, pp. 34 and 33, respectively.
101. T15, pp. 36 and 35, respectively.
102. T15, p. 34; T16, p. 2.
103. T15, p. 30 (March 8th).
104. T15, p. 36 (March 8th) – for all three applicants. To Fleming, Currey gave 6d. in charity.
105. Daly, Mary E., *The Famine in Ireland*, (Dublin, 1986) p. 79; Litton, Helen op. cit. p. 40.
106. T15, pp. 30 and 34 (March 8th and 15th). The earlier application was marked 'No app.'.
107. T16, p. 28 (July 26th).
108. T16, pp. 8 (April 12th), 22 (May 10th), 24 (May 24th), 34 (October 4th), 39 (November 8th) and 42 (November 22nd). Barry, Flaherty and Dawly were given 1/- each in charity, while Pat Keeffe received 2/-.
109. T16, pp. 2 (March 29th), 24 (May 24th) and 34 (October 4th).
110. T15, pp. 39 (March 29th); T16, 7 (April 12th).
111. T16, p. 3 (April 3rd).
112. T16, pp. 14 ('April') and 19 (April 27th).
113. T16, pp. 25 (May 24th), 34 and 35 (both October 4th).
114. T16, p. 21 (May 10th).
115. T15, p. 29 (March 8th).
116. T16, p. 21 (May 10th).
117. T16, p. 24 (May 24th).
118. T16, p. 24 (May 24th).
119. T15, p. 39 (March 29th); T16, p. 24 (May 24th).
120. Ó Gráda, Cormac, "Poverty, population, and agriculture, 1801-1845" in W.E. Vaughan (ed.) *A New History of Ireland V.: Ireland under the Union, 1801-70* (Oxford, 1989) p. 121.
121. Donnelly, James S. Jnr., "Excess mortality and emigration", in W. E. Vaughan (ed.) *A New History of Ireland. V: Ireland under the Union, 1801-70* (Oxford, 1989) pp. 350-6 (p. 353).
122. ibid, pp. 353, 356; Woodcock, George, *A social history of Canada* (*London*: Penguin Books, 1988), p. 238.
123. Woodham-Smith, Cecil, op. cit. pp. 218-25.
124. Donnelly, James S. Jnr., "Excess mortality and emigration", in W.E. Vaughan (ed.) *A New History of Ireland. V: Ireland under the Union, 1801-70* (Oxford, 1989) pp. 354-5.
125. ibid, p. 353.
126. In analysing only those emigrant *applicants* with specified destinations, the profile becomes 72% (America), 4% (British North America) and 24% (Great Britain).
127. Ó Gráda, Cormac, *Ireland before and after the Famine*, (Manchester, 1988) pp. 113, 115; Ó Tuathaigh, Gearóid, *Ireland before the Famine*, 1798-1848 (Ireland, 1972) pp. 213, 216; Daly, Mary E., *Social and economic history of Ireland*, (Dublin, 1981) pp. 23-4; McCartney, Donal, op. cit. p. 169.
128. Daly, Mary E., *Social and economic history of Ireland*, (Dublin, 1981) p. 24.
129. McCartney, Donal, op. cit. p. 169.
130. Donnelly, James S. Jnr., "Landlords and tenants", in W. E.Vaughan (ed.) *A New History of Ireland. V: Ireland under the Union, 1801-70* (Oxford, 1989), pp. 332-49 (pp. 338-9).
131. Smyth, W.J., op. cit. p. 46.

132. Donnelly, James S. Jnr., "Landlords and tenants", in W.E.Vaughan (ed.) *A New History of Ireland V: Ireland under the Union, 1801-70* (Oxford, 1989) p. 340.
133. Feeney, Patrick op. cit. p. 6.
134. T16, p. 18 (April 26th and 27th); T15, p. 33 (March 13th); T16, p. 22 (May 10th).
135. T15, p. 31 (March 9th); T16, p. 12 (April 23rd); T15, p. 28 (March 8th).
136. Bridget Gorman of Chapel Place, T15, p. 31 (March 9th); William O'Neill of Ferry Lane and another, T15, p. 39 (March 29th); Michael Anderson of Mountain Lodge, T16, pp. 21 (May 10th); and Ellen Higgins of Tallow, T16, p. 22 (May 10th).
137. T15, p. 37 (March 26th), and T16, p. 8 (April 12th).
138. The least frequent offers were £1, £5, £7, and £22 (one offer each) and £8, £12, and £15 (two offers each).
139. T15, p. 31 (March 9th).
140. T15, pp. 32 (March 13th) and 39 (March 29th).
141. T16, p. 4 (April 9th).
142. T16, p. 19 (April 29th).
143. T16, p. 25 (May 24th).
144. T15, p. 38 (March 29th).
145. T16, p. 15 (April 1847).
146. T16, pp. 7 and 33.
147. In the cases of Richard Smith of Tallow (T16, p. 7, April 12th), Pat Cunningham of Kilmakoe[?] (T16, p. 15, April 26th), Pat Ryan and Widow Kerins of Monalour (T16, p. 28, July 26th) and David Comins of Tallow (T16, p. 44, November 26th).
148. T16, p. 25 (May 24th).
149. T16, p. 7, April 12th (William Coleman of Toornagoppoge); T16, p. 26, June 28th (Pat Linneen of Ballyrafter Mountain); and T16, p. 11, April 16th (John Cahill of Ballyrafter Mountain).
150. T16, p. 5.
151. T16, p. 5.
152. Donnelly, James S. Jnr., *The land and the people of nineteenth-century Cork: the rural economy and the land question* (London, 1975) p. 57. Indeed, both Daniel and Timothy Dinneen of Ballyknock were told on their separate April 9th applications (both T16, p. 4) to give up their land that they could take the timber and thatch of their houses in addition to the receipt of a cash sum (£16 and £20, respectively) so long as they gave up "at once".
153. T16, pp. 38 and 42 (October 25th and November 22nd).
154. T16, pp. 32 (October 4th), 36 (October 14th), 41 (November 12th), and 44 (November 26th).
155. T16, p. 23.
156. T16, pp. 25 (May 24th), 27 (July 26th) and 29 (August 1st).
157. T16, pp. 31 (July 9th) and 36 (October 18th).
158. T16, pp. 27 (July 26th), 31 (August 10th), 32 (August 29th), 45 (November 26th); T15, p. 38 (March 29th) and T16, p. 32 (August 17th).
159. T16, p. 43 (November 22nd).
160. T16, pp. 31 (July 9th) and 43 (November 22nd).
161. Ó Tuathaigh, Gearóid, op. cit. p. 217.
162. Feeney, Patrick, op. cit., pp. 6, 8.
163. Ainsworth, John F., and MacLysaght, Edward, "Survey of documents in private keeping, second series", (1958) *Analecta Hibernica* 20, p. 106. Mansfield owned estates in the barony of Upperthird, the liberties of Waterford, County Kilkenny and elsewhere.

Chapter 6

The Lismore Poor Law Union and the famine

TOM NOLAN

Introduction

The Lismore Poor Law Union was established in accordance with the terms of *"An Act for the more effectual relief of the destitute poor of Ireland"* which had passed into law on 9th April 1838. The Union was declared on 30th March 1839 and comprised an area of 95,397 acres, which contained in 1831 a population of 34,376. A Board of Guardians of 24 members and 8 ex-officer members was elected comprising 4 members for each of the divisions of Lismore, Cappoquin and Tallow and 2 for each of the other divisions. The Board included Sir Richard Musgrave, Sir Richard Keane, Francis Currey representative of the Duke of Devonshire, and Arthur Kiely-Ussher who was to gain notoriety and infamy due to the treatment of tenants on his own estate at Ballysaggartmore. In general terms the Board fulfilled its role diligently and effectively and minimised the distress and death rate during the famine.

The total Poor Law Valuation of the Union was £64,708.5.0 and the total number of persons rated was 3,943. A workhouse was contracted for erection on 11th November 1839 and was scheduled for completion by 18th May 1842 at a cost of £5,500 with £1,000 for fittings and contingencies. It occupied an area of 4 acres at Townparks East and had accommodation for 500 people. The first admissions of paupers occurred on 18th May 1842.

Minutes of meetings of the Board of Guardians were recorded by the Clerk. It is from these minute books, which are held by the County Library Service, that the following account of the famine has been compiled. The account is, therefore, one-sided and gives only occasional glimpses of what was happening outside the workhouse.

Arrival of the blight:

Blight was first noticed on the potato crop in September 1845, although its fuller implications were not obvious until the following month. The officers of Lismore Workhouse acted with commendable promptness as a minute of 11th October records: *"A letter was sent to each guardian to* attend a meeting on 20th October 1845 to consider the state of the potato crop and what steps were to be taken to prevent spread of the disease or how to convert the affected crop into starch". As a clear picture had not emerged by the time of that meeting, "various and contradictory" views were put forward and the meeting was adjourned for a fortnight "when the crops would be dug and the extent of the disease understood".

At the adjourned meeting of 11th November, Mr. Currey submitted a seven-point proposal which so impressed his fellow guardians that they decided to send a copy to the Prime Minister and to the Lord Lieutenant as well as having it published in the Waterford Mail and in the Cork Examiner

Amongst the proposals were:

1. To dig out as quickly as possible in dry weather only and to endeavour to have the potatoes as dry as possible before storing them either in houses or in any other way.

5. ——. It has been satisfactorily ascertained that until the decay has advanced very far they may be safely used for human food, and given to fowl, pigs and cattle, but when used for human food they will be greatly improved by cutting away the unsound portion before boiling.

6. If the rot should be found to proceed faster than the potatoes can be consumed in this way, cutting the unsound ones into two or three parts if large, and drying them by artificial means, either by lime-kilns or placing them on raised hurdles above a slow turf fire as recommended by the Government Commissioners, will probably preserve them for a considerably longer period.

7. If this should be impracticable, the only other means of preserving any portion of the diseased crop for food appears to be by reducing them to starch. This process is familiar to most people, but any unacquainted with it will be shown how to do it at the Union Workhouse every weekday at the hour of 12 o'clock. The starch obtained cannot be used alone for food but when mixed with an equal or greater weight of oat-meal and made into cakes it affords a wholesome and palatable food. The pulp, if squeezed into flat cakes and dried will keep for a considerable period and makes a very good food for pigs and cattle.

At the meeting the guardians, anticipating that "great want and scarcity will ensue", decided to write to the government urging it to "take steps to devise means for an increase in employment for the population and other means to avert the evil of scarcity.

Accommodating the destitute

From the records of the Lismore Union, the picture that emerges is of the workhouse as a large, bleak, walled in refuge in the midst of a countryside devastated by poverty, famine, disease and hopelessness. People arrived at the Porter's lodge singly and in family groups; ragged, starving, and frightened. On admission, they were immediately subjected to the house rules and became "paupers" with a number.

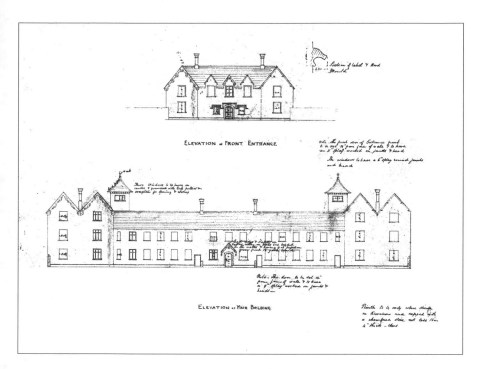

ELEVATION of FRONT ENTRANCE

ELEVATION of MAIN BUILDING

**Top: Elevation of Lismore
workhouse with smaller
entrance block and main
block.
Right: Plan of first floor of
workhouse showing
entrance block, main
block and buildings.**

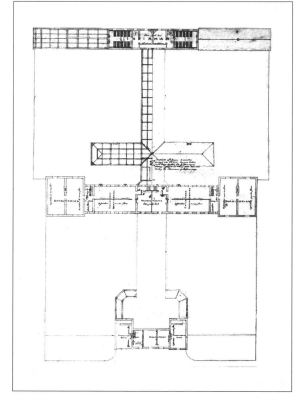

Every vestige of independence was taken from them. They worked, they ate, they slept, only when and where the rules permitted. Their own clothes were taken from them and each was given a pauper's uniform. Husbands, wives, children were separated to specific areas of the workhouse and mingling was almost non-existent. Breaches of the house rules were severely punished by deprivation of food, periods in the black hole or, as a last resort, by expulsion.

At their weekly meetings the master, clerk and guardians never alluded to the *"outside"* horrors. They carried out their duties to the house and to the paupers just as had been done since the setting up of the union. They discussed numbers, they decided on food, they issued tenders for materials and they judged cases of indiscipline; everything was cold, clinical and according to the rules of the Poor Law Commissioners. (An entry in the Minutes of 10th July, 1850 is as follows: *The porter of this workhouse died this morning. Resolved: That the clerk advertise for a porter, at £10 p.a.*).

Adding to the unpleasantness which was part of the workhouse regime were additional elements peculiar to the building in Lismore. Built only in 1842, the litany of flaws and shortcomings in its construction makes depressing reading. As early as 20th February, 1846 the Visiting Committee complained to the guardians of *"the shameful manner in which the house was built. The rain, this week, has penetrated the walls to such an extent as to render the dormitories scarcely fit for the paupers to inhabit, and unless some repairs are done the principal timbers must very shortly decay"* ... *the dormitories and other chambers are being flooded by the recent rain"*. (They blamed lack of rendering for this.) They also complained that *"the sewers appear to have been built without a proper fall, so they are full of stagnant water giving off an offensive smell."*

On 29th September, 1849 the Medical Officer complained that *"the smell from the privies attached to the Probationary Ward was so offensive that he regarded it as a danger to the health of the patients. The effluvium was so substantial that it extended over the high road"*. Again, on 12th December, 1849 he reported that *"the water pours in torrents down the staircases in the Infirmary whenever there is much rain and wind."* Also, *"the manure pit is much too near the Infirmary."* On 1st May, 1850 the Visiting Committee reported that *"the boys' and girls' privies give off an intolerable stench"*; and the following week the Medical Officer reported that *"the smell from the privies of the Probationary Ward is so great that he deems it positively dangerous to the general health. The atmosphere in the Tailors' and Shoemakers' shops is quite pestilential and the walls in the Infirmary are so damp, that the bedding becomes damp also."*

While Lismore workhouse had been designed to accommodate 500 inmates, it's population did not reach half that number until the end of November 1846. During 1844 the number of inmates fluctuated between 100 and 140. During 1845 it ranged between 130 and 170. By the end of 1846 389 paupers were being cared for by the Lismore Union.

By the beginning of 1847 the full horrors of famine had arrived, with any stock of food held by the small farmers and labourers now gone. In most cases they had sold anything that would realise money, and they now faced the stark choice of starvation, emigration or the workhouse. The number of inmates in January 1847 was 472, by March it had risen to 577, in July it was 600 and during December 1847, the workhouse that was designed for 500, was catering for 700.

The guardians and officials did their best to remedy the overcrowding. In January 1847, they requested plans from the Poor Law Commissioners to erect *"sleeping galleries"* in the house. At the same time plans were prepared to increase the size of the complex by building in the men's yard. As a temporary measure, they procured a store in the town from a Mr. Michael Riordan to house some of the paupers. It was proposed to use the store as a dormitory for some women who would be marched back to the workhouse each morning and returned to the store in the evening.

Feeding the starving

Even by 1st November, 1845 the workhouse was finding difficulty in procuring sufficient stocks of potatoes for the inmates and the Board of Guardians discussed *"what food could be used as a substitute for potatoes in the dietary."* By 6th December 1845 potatoes were almost completely unobtainable in the local markets and for the first time, the Master's Estimate of Provisions for the house made no mention of potatoes. Instead, 15 cwts. of oat-meal were ordered. The Poor Law Commissioners in Dublin were notified that *"potatoes are so scarce in the markets that the paupers had to be given bread."*

At their meeting of 13th February, 1846 the clerk was directed *"to obtain copies of the several dietaries in use in English workhouses, so the guardians may consider how far they may be introduced into this house, in case potatoes become completely unobtainable."* On receipt of the dietaries a number of experiments on soup were carried out using such ingredients as Indian flour, peas, barley-meal, wheaten bread etc. The Provisions Committee reported, on 25th March, 1846 that, *"they had carefully examined the work of Count Rumfort (of Munich) on nutrition in workhouses and they had followed his directions in making his "Soup No. 1."* The committee claimed that they found the soup *"extremely*

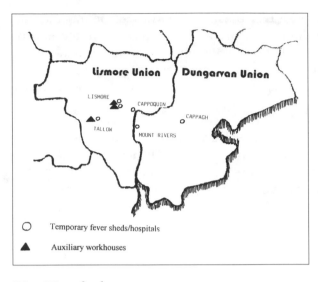

West Waterford.

○ Temporary fever sheds/hospitals

▲ Auxiliary workhouses

palatable and highly nutritious." The Medical Officer for the house stated that *"the health of the paupers would not be impaired by it."* To prepare this soup for 200 paupers, it was estimated that the following quantities of ingredients would be needed: 23½ lbs. of pearl barley, 22 lbs. of split peas, 11½ lbs. of wheaten bread, 3½ lbs. of salt, 84 quarts of water and some vinegar. From this quantity of soup each adult would receive 20 ounces (¼ pint). The total cost came to 12/9½ or 3½ pence per person. This soup was to be served for dinner on alternate days. Owing to complaints from the inmates the ration of soup was increased, first to 25 ounces and later to 30 ounces per adult.

In April 1846 Indian meal (supplied by Messrs. Grubb of Clonmel, at 11/- per cwt.) made an appearance on the dietary of Lismore Workhouse, when it was reported in the Minutes of the meeting of 10th April, 1846 *"Indian meal instead of oat-meal for breakfast on the days when bread and oat-meal gruel was served for dinner."* But two weeks later the guardians ordered *"8 ounces of Indian meal stirabout be now given to the paupers every day."* By July of that year, dinner every day consisted of soup.

As the potato crop again failed in 1847 the Poor Law Commissioners suggested that the workhouse land be planted with cabbage, rye and turnips. The Board ordered seed and followed these instructions. In September the turnips became available and a decision of the guardians during their meeting of 1st September, 1847 was reached that ... *"the turnips grown on the workhouse land be used in lieu of peas. They would be mixed in equal measure with Indian meal and served for dinner."* During the winter the workhouse found it very difficult to obtain sufficient milk, so the Medical Officer ordered that new milk be given only to the sick, the aged and the very young, and that the others be given skimmed milk. But he also suggested that every person over nine years be given one ounce of molasses per day as a supplement to the milk.

By early 1848 the house had developed a dietary that was used, with only minor changes, until the food crisis ended three years later. It is noticeable that potatoes were completely missing and that meat was not mentioned. Even before the Famine, meat was served on only two days in the year, at Easter and Christmas, although there are some entries in the Minutes that suggest that meat was served to patients in the hospital wing. At their meeting of 12th April, 1848 the Board of Guardians endorsed the following:

Proposed scale of dietary for all classes of paupers in Lismore Workhouse

CLASS	BREAKFAST	DINNER	SUPPER
Adults	8 ounces meal and 1 pint of skim milk or ½ pint sweet milk	6 ounces of bread and 4 ounces of meal and 2 lbs. of turnips as soup*	None
Children (10-15 yrs.)	5 ounces of meal (Milk as above)	4 ounces of bread 3 ounces of meal and 1½ lbs. of turnips as* soup	4 ounces of bread
Children (6-10 yrs.)	3½ ounces of meal (Milk as above)	4 ounces of bread Soup (as above)*	4 ounces of bread
Children (2-6 yrs.)	3 ounces of meal ½ pint sweet milk	4 ounces of bread 2 ounces of meal and 1 lb. of turnips as* soup	4 ounces of bread
Infants (Weaned)	½ lb. of bread and 1 pint of sweet milk, daily		
Infants (Suckling)	¼ lb. of bread and ½ pint of sweet milk, daily		

*When peas are used in soup for dinner instead of turnips, they may be used in equal portions with Indian meal for the 4 upper classes.

The diseased and the dead

The arrival of new inmates, already ill or in fever, added to the horror of the workhouse. The hospital rapidly became overcrowded and by the middle of February 1847 there were 100 patients being treated. But worse was to follow. On 17th March, the Medical Officer reported cases of Typhus Fever and the number of deaths increased. An entry

Top: The workhouse from the rear drawn by Robert Armstrong in 1842. The entrance block is on the exteme right.
Bottom: The front of the entrance block as it is in 1995.

for 19th March stated that the Lismore Fever Hospital, located at South Lane adjacent to the Workhouse, refused to accept any more patients from the workhouse. By April, the doctor was reporting the presence of diarrhoea and dysentery in the house. To try to segregate the fever patients from the other inmates, an application was made to the parish priest, Dr. Fogarty, for the use of his barn as a temporary fever hospital.

At the same time (25th March, 1847) a Mr. John Slattery was approached to rent his store to the union as an auxiliary workhouse. Nurses and infants were transferred there and any spare space there was to be allocated to female inmates and children.

The death rate continued to rise and during March and April it averaged 12 per week with 26 dying in the the week ending 17th April, 1847. These numbers, added to those in the town who were not included on the union list, caused serious problems for burial. As early as 25th February, 1847 the guardians received a letter from the Dr. Cotton (acting Dean of Lismore) complaining of the numbers being interred in the Cathedral grounds. He suggested that other burial grounds be obtained. The Guardians assured him that every effort was being made to do so. They proceeded to procure two fields adjoining the workhouse but before the legalities could be completed, the Duke of Devonshire presented two acres to the Roman Catholic clergy on condition that half an acre of this land be allotted as burial ground for paupers from the workhouse. At their meeting of 14th April, 1847 the Guardians decided to refuse admittance to any more patients (except in the most extreme cases) until the number already installed could be reduced below 600. They also decided, that for the sake of public health, no more burials from the workhouse would take place in the church yard and they appealed to Fr. Fogarty to have the recently acquired land consecrated and walled in at once to be ready for use.

To increase hospital space in the house, a decision was made at the meeting of 21st April, 1847 to build a second floor over the *"Idiot Ward"*. This, however, was not ready for occupation until the end of 1849 and even then the Medical Officer complained at the meeting of 30th January, 1850 that *"the rain penetrates the south wall and renders the ward, just opened, very liable to dampness"*.

Meanwhile, Mr. Currey had been in contact with the Duke and he was able to report on 12th May, 1847 that the Barracks at Tallow could be rented from the Devonshire Estate, to be used as a fever hospital. The Guardians accepted this offer but decided (27th November, 1847) to use it, not only as a hospital, but as an auxiliary workhouse. When fully commissioned, 1000 paupers could be accommodated there. It had its own Master, and staff but remained under the control of Lismore. To transport food and materials between Tallow and Lismore, the Guardians sanctioned – at the above meeting – the purchase of a mule. A year later – 8th November, 1848 – it was proposed and passed *"as the mule is not sufficiently strong to do the work of the Establishment, a larger mule should be procured!*

Towards the end of 1847 the minutes record one of the extremely rare accounts which give a view of what was taking place outside the workhouse. "The workhouse was besieged by a starving crowd demanding food or employment. A delegation was admitted to explain their demands. On being told that the only way they could be given relief was to be admitted as paupers to the workhouse, they dispersed." (3rd November 1847)

The "work-house"

The inmates were effectively imprisoned in what was intended as a work-house. One of the duties of the Master was "...to see that the able-bodied paupers are kept regularly employed and to provide employment for the aged and infirm, as far as their circumstances admit of it."

Work for the men and boys was varied. They tilled the farm of the workhouse to produce food for the whole establishment. Prior to the Famine, it appears that potatoes were the main crop grown, but, as recorded earlier, the Poor Law Commissioners encouraged the growth of various vegetables (29th August, 1846) and this appears to have been done quite successfully as can be judged from the dietary of the union. At the end of 1848 the farm was producing beans, turnips, peas and rye, and these were being used in the soup on which the inmates were surviving. An entry in the Minute Book for 30th October, 1850 gives a miserable picture of the children working in the union fields in winter. The Master suggested that "the school-boys should get shoes or they will not be able to work on the farm in cold weather." So we may assume that many of the children normally worked bare-footed. (When the Master passed on his suggestion to the Poor Law Commissioners he received a reply on 6th November, 1850 instructing him to examine the possibility of making the shoes in the workhouse but to discover if wooden soles could be used.)

Besides outdoor work, the inmates were occupied with the production of practically everything needed in the house. Many of the men and boys spent full working days in the tailors' and shoemakers' shops. Carpentry was carried out on the premises as was blacksmith work on the repair of farm tools. With the advent of Indian corn, special mills had to be procured (8th November, 1848) for the grinding of this excessively hard grain, and this work was also done on the premises.

In October 1848 an entry stated that "...the Master is to spend two days in the Waterford house to study their manufacturing methods (for cloth)" and at the same meeting it was decided to "...apply to the Royal Exchange Insurance to ascertain if the spinning of flax and the carding and spinning of cotton would be allowed in the house." The reply seems to have been favourable as at the next meeting (1st November, 1848) tenders were issued "...for flax wheels, woollen wheels, cotton and

Lismore Fever Hospital in 1842 by Robert Armstrong. This was built before the workhouse and functioned independently of it.

woollen cards and spindles." Also ordered were *"two looms and a supply of flax and cotton".*

Work for the women consisted of cooking, cleaning, laundry work, nursing, spinning, knitting and repair of clothing. With disease rampant in the hospital wards, the washing and replacing of bedding became so constant and time-consuming that the Board of Guardians – at their meeting of 21st April, 1847 – ordered that *"...extra rations of bread (6 oz.) and milk (1/2 pint) be given to the women working in the laundry because the work there is very heavy owing to the numbers in hospital."*

That the house was almost self-sufficient in clothing at least, may be seen from an entry in the Minute Book for 18th October, 1848 where it is recorded that *"...as the workhouse has now sufficient clothing of all kinds for any emergency, the Guardians instruct the clerk to ask the opinion of the Poor Law Commissioners as to what ready-sale articles could be produced so as to keep the female inmates employed and the children trained."*

The goods produced during the week ending 9th August, 1848 are listed as follows and give a good idea of the variety of tasks performed in the Lismore house:

69 girls' shifts	40 mens' shirts
49 womens' shifts	20 pairs mens' shoes
14 womens' wrappers	21½ pairs mens' stockings
16 pairs womens' stockings	16 pairs sheets
40 girls' bibs	40 lbs. yarn

A year and a half later (20th August, 1850) when the flax and woollen wheels had been installed, the week's production was:

2 Rugs	376 womens' caps
40 ticks	85 yards flannel
10 pairs mens' shoes	52 yards sheeting
15 pairs womens' shoes	82 yards frieze
10 womens' wrappers	52 yards linen
60 aprons	

Financing the relief effort

The finance for the maintenance of the building and the inmates had to be procured from the rate-payers of the Lismore Union. The union consisted of 9 Electoral Divisions and these were combined into four groups with a Collector assigned to each group. In January 1848 the groups and collectors were as follows:

Lismore, Ballysaggartmore, Mocollop ....Richard Farrell
Cappoquin, West Modeligo...Francis D. Hudson
Castlerichard, Tallow, Templemichael ....Thomas Hayden
Kilcockin ....John Flynn

The Poor Law Valuation of the union was between £64,692 (in 1841) and £59,691 (1851) and the rates averaged 3/8d in the £ (in 1848). The expenditure was heavy, as can be judged from the House Orders for the week (picked at random) ending 26th June, 1850:

4 stone malt	3 tons Indian meal	6 cwts. salt
3500 qrts. boiling milk	630 qrts. sweet milk	3 pounds tea
60 qrts. sour milk	24 pounds sugar	16 bags flour
12 pounds pepper	1 gallon whiskey	3 tons coal
2 tons barley meal	3 cwts. soap	40 pounds candles
	12 pounds mould candles	

The Lismore Union Officers appear to have managed to balance their books very efficiently during the period under discussion. This may have arisen from the fact that the union contained many very substantial land-owners and rates seldom failed to be collected. The Minute Books record, each week, the *"balance in favour of the house."* For the years 1848, 1849 and 1850 when inmate numbers were huge and when outdoor relief was being given, the balance in favour fluctuated between £4,019 and -£427 in 1848; £2,232 and £576 in 1849; and £3,252 and -£822 in 1850. When the workhouse was forced into the red loans were arranged from the banks, using as collateral the rates that were due.

Outdoor relief was a severe drain on union funds, but became a duty of the Board of Guardians of each workhouse after the passage of the "*Temporary Relief Act 1847*" (popularly known as the Soup-Kitchen Act). Each ration of food was to consist of one pound of biscuit, meal or flour, or one quart of soup thickened with meal and four ounces of bread or biscuit. When the ration was bread only, 1½ pounds were given. Each person was obliged to bring a bowl or a pot and stand in line until his turn came to have soup or stirabout ladled into it.

The Lismore Union was divided into 4 Relief Districts, each served by a Relieving Officer:

District 1.	Lismore, Castlerichard, Drumroe	Mr. Ross
District 2.	Cappoquin, Modeligo, Ballinamult, Ballyhane	Mr. Phelan
District 3.	Mocollop, Ballyduff, Gortnapeaky, Ballyin, Ballysaggartmore	Mr. O'Grady
District 4.	Tallow, Kilcockin, Kilwatermoy East and West	Mr. Hudson

After March 1848 outdoor relief was available by calling to the workhouse in Lismore, and by March 1850, when the Famine was coming to an end but homelessness seems to have become a problem, the union developed another method of relieving hardship. This consisted of giving over-night lodging to paupers; it must have been a completely new concept if we may judge from the fact that it was very thoroughly questioned by the Poor Law Commissioners. Any person availing of this facility was compelled to do three hours work in the house on the following morning, was then given breakfast and immediately discharged. It is difficult to see how these over-night callers were accommodated when the Records for March 1850 show that the numbers of inmates for that month varied between 1,816 and 2,000, the hospitals had between 220 and 240 patients and there was an average of 5 deaths per week in the workhouse.

The human dimension

A facet of the Famine that is seldom alluded to is the effect that workhouse conditions had on the unfortunate poor incarcerated there. In most cases they were country folk, used to open spaces, privacy and the frugal comforts of a family life. Suddenly, they were confined in overcrowded, squalid conditions where their every action was monitored. It was a monastic life without any of its advantages. Each one developed his or her own survival plan and being human, they displayed the good and bad sides of human nature. The Minute Books record very many sad, noble, strange and mean little episodes that were discussed, judged, and, in many cases, punished by the Board of Guardians. Among the inmates were people who tried "to beat the system" and survive in this alien environment. When we consider the surrounding horrors, both inside and outside the house, it is amazing to read of the Officers sitting down to their weekly meetings and ponderously dissecting the "crimes" brought to their attention.

8th December, 1847. *Mary Troy and her three children were ordered out of the workhouse because her husband was discovered to be earning 1/- a day.*

12th February, 1848. *The Medical Officer reported that Mary Russell, an inmate, was made pregnant by Michael Brohan, an inmate."*

Resolved: Mary Russell, Michael Brohan and his wife and children be expelled.

29th April, 1848. *The Matron complained Ellen Coughlan for disobedience, Biddy Foley for absconding, Mary McMahon for refractory conduct and Joanne Dwyer for stealing a sheet.*

Resolved: Ellen Coughlan to be confined to the Refactory Ward.

The others to be brought before the Magistrates at the next Petty Sessions.

7th June, 1848. *The Master discovered a man named Troy, an inmate, wearing two shirts. Troy admitted that the extra shirt was for his wife who was in the Fever Hospital.*

There is no record of punishment!

23rd August, 1848. *The Master complained that Michael Hogan got permission to leave the house to go bury his wife who had died in the fever hospital. He did not return." Information was sworn against him for deserting his six children.*

9th January, 1850. *An inmate, Mary Tobin, is reported to be pregnant. Her husband is dead since March 1849. On being questioned by the Board of Guardians, it was discovered that she was the mother of nine children and that she did not know the name of the father of the present child. She claimed that when she was on an errand for the Master she met the man on the road between Lismore and Tallow. The Officers expressed indignation at her conduct and ordered that her ration of milk be stopped every other day until*

	her lying-in, providing the Medical Officer approved.
8th May, 1850.	*An inmate, Mary Barry, was found to have £14.11.2d on her person. She claimed that she had received it from her brother in Malta." However, the "Malta" letter was proved to have been written by an inmate, John Harty.*
	Resolved: Harty to be confined to the Black Hole each day for a week (not during working hours!!) and be deprived of soup every other day for a week. Mary Barry to be punished in the same way, and after her week's punishment she was to be handed her money and dismissed from the house. (It emerged that Mary – who was helping in the hospital – got the money by taking more soup than was needed into the wards. This extra soup she bartered for bread. She then sold the bread for cash.)
17th July, 1850.	*Ellen Parker was found with £9.11.2d. She was dismissed.*

Even inter-religious stresses made their appearance among the inmates of the workhouse. On 4th March, 1848 it is reported that, as there were eleven Protestants in the house, a permanent Protestant Chaplain should be appointed. This was agreed, but to avoid having a similar appointment in the auxiliary house in Tallow, the Board of Guardians decided to move all Protestants to Lismore. The first report of inter-religious strain is mentioned at the meeting of 12th February, 1848. The R.C. Chaplain of the Union, Dr. Fogarty, complained that the Archdeacon of Lismore and Rev. Merric had contacted John Medcalf, an inmate of the house and a R.C. and "*had led him away from his faith and he became a Protestant.*" However, on being questioned, Medcalf claimed that he had changed religion voluntarily. The following week the Rev. Chaplain was again complaining that not only had Medcalf become a Protestant, but that "*he was distributing controversial Tracts among the inmates and even among the children.*" There is no record of any action being taken by the Board. One month later (10th March, 1848) an entry in the Minute Book states: "*Anne and William Donovan demand that their two children be enrolled and educated as members of the Church of England.*" Strangely, there is no mention of whether the parents changed religion also. On 28th November, 1849 the Minute Books report: "*Johanna Neal – an inmate – registered as a Roman Catholic, has expressed a desire to become a Protestant.*" This change of religion seems to have caused some bitterness among her house companions, because at the weekly meeting of 20th March, 1850 the Protestant Chaplain complained that "*Mary Nugent, a R.C. inmate, used offensive language to Johanna Neal and struck her.*" Nugent was severely reprimanded by the Chairman of the Board and was deprived of milk every other day for a fortnight.

Changing religion was not confined to the house in Lismore alone. The meeting of the Board on 23rd January, 1850 was informed that "*three inmates of the auxiliary workhouse in Tallow stated before the Master and the Wardmistress that they desired to leave the Roman Faith and to become Protestants.*" There is no recorded case in the Minute Books of any member of the Church of England converting to the Roman Catholic faith.

The Guardians chose the House Officers carefully and came down heavily on any who were less than thorough. In their advertisement for a new Master (12th April, 1848) they laid down their parameters very plainly:

> *Wanted by the Guardians of this Union, a Master for the workhouse. He must be a person of strict moral character and be of active habits. He must also have a competent knowledge of Accounts. The principle duties he shall have to perform are, to keep the accounts appertaining to his office in a neat and correct manner; to enforce Order and Regularity among the Workhouse inmates; to see that the able-bodied paupers are kept regularly employed; to provide employment for the Aged and Infirm as far as their circumstances admit of it and to superintend generally the management of the house. He will be required to reside in the Establishment. Salary £60 per annum, with rations of coals, candles and apartments.*

The smooth running of the house and the welfare of the unfortunate inmates was much higher in the Guardians priorities than the comfort and sensitivities of the Officers. When circumstances demanded it, they could be ruthless as may be seen:

8th November, 1848.   *A Guardian (Mr. Kiely) discovered that the Master of Tallow Auxiliary Workhouse, Mr. O'Brien, helped by his wife and son, removed iron and timber from the house and brought it home. Kiely had the house searched and the goods were discovered. O'Brien was dismissed forthwith and summoned to appear before the Quarter Sessions in Lismore.*

6th October, 1849.	*Michael Lennon, Relieving Officer for Cappoquin, was dismissed. He was accused of taking part in an attack on the Police Barrack in Cappoquin.*
20th February, 1850.	*The Medical Officer reported that meat got for the hospital was so bad as to be unfit for human food. The Board sampled it and found it most inferior and tainted. The Master was called before the Guardians and so severely censured that he offered his resignation. The Clerk was instructed to advertise for a new Master.*
9th January, 1850.	*The Master applied for three days leave of absence and a character testimonial. The Guardians granted the leave but until the stock be ascertained to be correct, they could not grant a testimonial.*

Care of the house and all its contents was very high on the Guardian's priorities. A very simple rule existed to safeguard the stock: e.g. if bedding (sheets, pillows, etc.) could not be produced when stock-taking was in progress, the Matron was held responsible, and she had to replace or pay for the missing articles. The same simple rule covered all goods in the house; in case of loss or damage some one was responsible and that person paid. Contractors supplying goods to the Union came under the same rule. For example, if milk supplied was found to be sub-standard, the Master simply procured suitable milk elsewhere, and presented the bill to the defaulting contractor.

In one of their more far-reaching schemes to improve the Union (as distinct from the house) the Guardians proposed (11th October, 1848) that *"local landowners make a collection of £50 and ask the Lord Lieutenant and the Royal Agricultural Society for an equal amount to have the services of an Instructor in Agriculture (who could speak Irish) to work the Union area for ten months."* A Mr. William Wall was appointed, with the title of Practical Instructor, and besides managing the workhouse land and training the boys in farm management, he also visited every holding in the Union area to instruct and encourage the local farmers to diversify their agricultural methods and to experiment with new crops. Wall's appointment was a huge success and when his term of office was completed, pressure was exerted and he was retained. So great was the demand for his services that (13th March, 1850) he had to *"recommend the appointment of a person to superintend the boys of the Workhouse while employed on the land and to carry out his instructions for cropping etc."* On 26th June, 1850 he reported the necessity to provide portable privies for the men and boys working on the land. The Master ordered two such privies.

Conclusion

By the end of 1850 the Famine (or its cause – potato blight) had run its course and the production of food was no longer a problem. Untold damage had been done to the country. Large areas had been cleared of their population, especially of the very small farmers and the labouring folk. The Lismore Union seems to have fared significantly better than unions west of the Shannon. It managed to remain solvent, and in spite of enormous pressure on its resources, the workhouse fulfilled its duties to the poor and starving quite efficiently. We have recorded cases of dreadful squalor and unspeakable filth in the house, but that was inevitable when its shoddy construction and appalling over-crowding are taken into consideration. With a few exceptions, its officers were men of character and principle and earned a well-merited encomium from a newspapers of the day:

> *To the Lismore Committee every credit is due for their exertions in relieving the destitution of the people. Liberality in their contributions, perseverance and industry in fulfilling the duties of their position, have distinguished the Lismore Committee...Amongst these are Sir Richard Musgrave, Mr. Currey (agent of the Duke of Devonshire), Mr. John Bowen Gumbleton, Mr. Burchell, Mr. Barry Drew and Lord Stuart De Decies." ("Cork Examiner." Monday, May 3rd., 1847.)*

Chapter 7

The workhouse in Waterford city, 1847-49

RITA BYRNE

Introduction

This is not a comprehensive account of the workhouse on John's Hill but is based on limited evidence. No workhouse books are available about for 1845, 1846 or 1850. This study is based mainly on the following:

1847:	Incoming letters and questionnaires from the Relief Commission in Dublin[1] (this is a one sided correspondence as the replies from Waterford are not extant).
March 1847-March 1848:	Burke's published reports of his inspections of the workhouse.[2] It includes summaries of missing minutes.
1848:	March-September – nil. Sept.-Dec. – Minutes of Board of Guardians.[3]
1849:	January-June, Minutes of Board of Guardians.[4] June-December – nil.

These are supplemented to a certain extent by parliamentary reports and by some of the minutes of the Board of Guardians published in a local newspaper. Other memoranda may be in private hands and it is hoped they will be forthcoming to flesh out this first tentative account of Waterford workhouse during the most crucial years of famine.

Workhouse extensions and out-buildings

The workhouse in Waterford city was built to serve a *"union"* area comprising most of east Waterford and south Kilkenny as indicated on the accompanying plans. Costing £7,850 (plus fitment costs £1,577) and designed to house 900 people, it was opened on 15th March 1841. It covered an area of just over six acres. While its plans are not extant, presumably it conformed to the standard design. Within six years its size had to be increased by one third: in January 1847 permission was given to extend the building including the creation of a hospital.

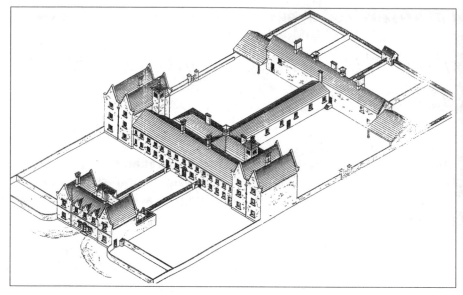

The layout approved for workhouses, 1838.

Medical concern was expressed that this was being built on the site of a cess-pool.[5] Permission was also given for the

> *hiring of buildings to be converted into workhouses – for meeting the immediate pressure of application for relief while the building is carried on.*[6]

Despite the extensions, the *"pressure of application for relief"* grew greatly over the next two years and hired buildings became an important part of the workhouse institution. Consideration was given to getting alternative ancillary accommodation in January 1847 and the following month *"somewhat angry discussions took place relative to the additional buildings"*.[7] Therefore it was not until later in the year that positive steps were taken. The Presentation Convent was the first Auxiliary Workhouse rented in October 1847 for £80 p.a.. Grady's tanyard in Michael Street, Clarke's two stores in Alexander Street and White's malthouse were taken for the same purpose that December.[8] Hayden's store along with White's malthouse and Store in John Street were likewise commissioned in 1848 as auxiliary workhouses as were unspecified buildings in Michael Street and Hennessy Road.[9] Despite this, by early February 1848 the workhouse was said to be *"crowded to suffication. Sixty four died during the last fortnight; they were dying like rotten sheep"*.[10]

Few details survive of these ancillary buildings. Grady's tanhouse was to take three weeks to refurbish for workhouse purposes but after three months still was not ready.[11] Between October and December 1848 new floors were being installed in the Hennessy's road establishment.[12] Most interesting, perhaps, is the Michael Street auxilliary workhouse which, with the approval of the Commissioners in Dublin was attached to the city's gas main providing seven lights which *"will enable females employed in this establishment to continue their several different works to a reasonable hour in the evening with less danger and at cheaper rate than if candles were used."*[13]

The dangers referred to were very real because on the 25th November 1848 a fire occurred in the drying room of the female laundry in the main workhouse. It burned for most of the night destroying roof and other timbers plus other combustibles valued at £300 by the Guardians. The insurers, Sun Fire and Life, paid £250 compensation.[14]

As workhouse numbers increased in the winter of 1846-7 it became necessary to provide separate accommodation for the sick and dying. Early in March 1847 the medical officer reported an increase in fever and dysentery, the following week there were twenty nine deaths. Hence plans were requested from the Poor Law Commissioners for an emergency fever hospital.[15] These duly arrived with a standard plan for a wooden building, a hundred feet long to accommodate fifty persons. It could be built for £300 for which a loan was provided. Fitting it out was at the expense of the local guardians but a design for an *"economic bedstead"* was provided.[16]

This temporary fever hospital or fever shed was in commission by the early summer of 1847 but quickly proved inadequate. In June the guardians applied for a loan for a second shed which they intended to use as a hospital. This was turned down as *"only buildings which are for fever patients only (sic) can be funded".*[17] Requirements may have quickly changed, however, as by 1848 the guardians had opened three other fever sheds. One was on the grounds of the Infirmary and there were two outlying ones in Kilmacthomas and Bunmahon.[18]

Despite the temporary nature of these sheds they seem to have had a better than ninety per cent success rate if official statistics are to be accepted. In 1847 2446 patients were treated with only 236 deaths and the following year 1854 were treated with 174 fatalities.[19] The fever in 1847 was described as *"mild typhoid"* lasting about fourteen days but tending to recur. There was also much dysentery.[20] In September 1848 the order was given from Dublin that the outlying fever sheds were to be closed so presumably the sick were transported back to the grounds of the main workhouse. Nevertheless treatment continued effectively

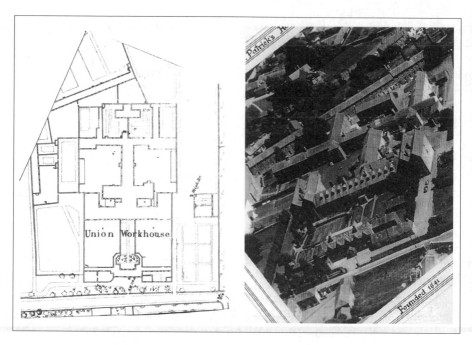

Waterford workhouse as it was about 1870 (from O.S. sheet FX99) and photograph taken approximately one hundred years later (courtesy Mr. T. Gyves, St. Patrick's Hospital) the main blocks were then unchanged.

with only 127 deaths out of 2077 treated in 1849 rising rapidly in 1850, however, to 482 deaths out of 2184 persons treated.

Numbers catered for by Waterford Workhouses[21]

Per week	In workhouse(s)	In hospital(s)	Deaths
Jan. 1845	816	54	3
Jan. 1846	854	59	7
Jan. 1847	1056	83	12
May 1847	1056	136	19
March 1848	2034	?	?
June 1849	2752	273	12

There were further medical structures within the county though it is not clear whether they were directly run from the workhouse. A listing for the union of the workhouse, however, gives an extraordinary total of twenty five temporary hospitals catering for 250 patients and serviced, somehow by sixteen nurses and eight wardsmaids.

There were also three dispensaries.[22] Certainly the workhouse took responsibility for the storage of medicines as is clear from one of their minutes of February 1849:

> *depots of medicine be placed in charge of medical officers in Dunmore, Tramore, Bonmahon, Kilmacthomas, Kilmeadon, Kilmacow and Glenmore with the understanding that they are not to be used unless upon urgent necessity caused by the appearance of extensive epidemic disease.*[23]

There is no surviving evidence of them ever having been used.

In 1849 additional provision had to be made against an anticipated outbreak of cholera. Negotiations were entered into with the trustees of the Infirmary to use a wing of that hospital. Permission was granted provided that the Guardians removed the abandoned and unsightly fever shed on their grounds.[24] On 15th April 1849 the first case of cholera struck and it raged over the following six months, the last case being on 11th September. The fatality rate was high – 249 died out of 522 cases.[25]

One other structural aspect of the workhouse was its cemetery. While there may have been provision in the workhouse grounds initially for burials to take place, by late 1846 other locations had to be utilised. Thus the graveyard attached to the medieval ruined church of Kill St. Laurence less than a mile away was recommissioned. In the first five weeks of 1847 ninety two people had been buried there so that by mid February 1847, it *"was so overcrowded that the coffins in many instances are only a few inches under the surface"*. Another medieval church at Kilbarry was also considered but it too was equally crowded.[26]

Thus it would appear that the Board of Guardians of the workhouse on John's Hill adapted themselves to the growing emergency through a programme of building and renting. By 1848-'49, as Appendix I shows, they were dealing with vast numbers and maintaining a relatively low mortality rate, except perhaps, for the Spring of 1849. Such figures say nothing about the quality of life amongst the inmates which were not intended to be pleasant but must have been rendered much worse by bad administration.

Administration

It was said that wandering paupers avoided the Waterford workhouse if at all possible and headed instead for New Ross or Dungarvan.[27] What their perspective on it was we do not know. Certainly the Poor Law Commissioners in Dublin had great trouble getting accurate information

The churchyard of the medieval ruin of Kill St Laurence was used for famine burials but had to be abandoned early in 1847 being overcrowded.

on the operation of the workhouse in Waterford during 1847.[28] In March 1847 they appointed an inspector named Lloyd to investigate the problems in Waterford.[29] He found that too many people were getting outdoor relief and that there was *"laxity of discipline".*[30]

Over the next twelve months the workhouse seemed at one level to be working smoothly. The new buildings mentioned above were commissioned, difficulties were overcome and a programme of outdoor relief successfully implemented. Attendance at these decision-making meetings was generally low, particularly from early November 1847. For the forty seven meetings held during the next twenty weeks, only four attracted attendance of twenty or more of the sixty three Guardians and about half had less than nine with the number frequently falling to three or four.[31] Matters came to a head however, when one of the local Guardians, Sir Henry Winston Barron who happened to be in Dublin, received letters from two of his fellow guardians critical of the way Waterford workhouse was being run. He chose to write a most intemperate letter to the Commissioners, apparently uninhibited by the fact that he had missed sixty of the seventy eight meetings, had not inspected the workhouse for a least twelve months[32] and that serious questions had been raised about his suitability to be a Workhouse Guardian as he had not paid in full his poor law rates.[33] In the letter he urged *"the absolute and pressing necessity of either dissolving the Board of Guardians or appointing an inspector"* and gave his reason,

> *the jobbing and neglect of the relieving officers and the total inefficiency of the master, together with the negligence and jobbing of a portion of the guardians, are altogether incredible if not witnessed; and ultimately these matters combined are fast bringing the law into disrepute and rendering it most unprofitable for all parties.*[34]

The Commissioners responded immediately by sending a Mr. Burke to investigate. Following an inspection, Burke listed nine irregularities that to him seemed gross. These included paupers having some of their own possessions in the workhouse, some wearing their own clothes, floors not fully cleaned and the ticks or mattresses in need of repair. The workhouse had a back gate which was somewhat irregular and gave rise to some dubious practices. Some windows were nailed up which interfered with ventilation.[35]

The most serious implications of Burke's investigation as far as the lives of the inmates were concerned was about food. At best, there was massive negligence; at worst, peculation. Whatever contracts were entered into with outside suppliers were not subject to any quality control. For instance, good quality beef was to be supplied, for the making of soup. Instead *"shins of beef which consisted of eight pounds bone and only five pounds of meat"* were provided. The resultant broth was *"to prove actually pernicious to many who partook of it, especially the children"*. Two doctors forbade its continued use. Likewise, there was no contract made for the supply of bread with a Mr. Thompson who had been supplying the workhouse since 1844. However, what he was providing up to March 1848, *"frequently disagrees with those who use it"*.[36]

The main problem was lack of commitment by the sixty or so members of the Board of Guardians. They failed to adjust themselves to the enormous social problems that arose in 1847/8. Their task was an onerous one. They frequently were called on to attend up to four meetings per week. Seventy eight meetings were held between March 1847 and March 1848: there were twenty five meetings in sixty days in January and February 1848 each starting at midday.[37] The guardians, as well as this, were expected to carry out regular inspections of the workhouse and draw up reports on it. And probably, most demanding of all, they were obliged to meet the applicants and to decide who was destitute and who was not. Most guardians responded to these demands by simply not turning up.[38] This put further pressure on those who did attend. At a meeting of the Board attended by only eleven of them in December 1847 it was resolved that –

> *As applications for relief are becoming more numerous and impossible to dispose of in one day, the board will, until pressure of business eases, meet on Mondays, Wednesdays, Thursdays and Fridays.*

In support of this motion it was said

> *there were five or six hundred paupers seeking for admission of*

relief —-. (Also) it was most important that they should give outdoor relief, it would be a means of keeping poor persons from becoming inmates of the house for life.[39]

Illustrating this difficulty is a description of what happened as the Guardians were meeting some weeks earlier when –

An unusual number of persons of all ages and sexes, (the majority women) to the number of upwards of five hundred, assembled around the gate of the workhouse, led there, we suppose in the hope of getting outdoor relief—-. Up to a late hour in the day the board was occupied in investigating the claims —-.

They got around to dealing with only two-thirds of them.[40] What became of the other one hundred and seventy or so is not reported. An exchange of notes is most revealing in this regard. Only one Guardian, Roger Hayes, turned up on Patrick's Day, 1848 to decide on admissions to the workhouse. There should have been a minimum of three. Since the inspector from Dublin, Joseph Burke, was in town Hayes sent a note to his hotel:

My Dear Burke,
I wish you could spare a few minutes to walk up here to witness with your own eyes the effects of no attendance and the house surrounded with poor objects shivering in the cold.

Burke sent the messenger back with this reply:

My Dear Hayes,
I am so occupied that I cannot find time to go out today, but although not strictly legal, you should, assisted by the relieving officer, decide on the applications of the poor who should not be allowed to go away unrelieved.

The next day Hayes sent the following stark note:

My Dear Burke,
What a job you assigned me yesterday – had to sit alone until eleven o'clock last night – 600 persons relieved.[41]

During the months of deepest distress from June to December 1847 only two of the sixty or so Guardians had bothered to carry out their duty of inspecting the workhouse – Roger Hayes and Simon Newport.

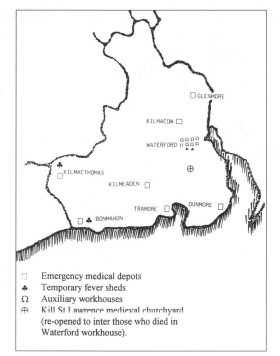

Emergency medical depots
♣ Temporary fever sheds
Ω Auxiliary workhouses
⊕ Kill St Lawrence medieval churchyard
(re-opened to inter those who died in
Waterford workhouse).

Waterford Union.

The latter, at a meeting attended by only nineteen of them, proposed a motion, politely stating that:

> *the general superintendance of this establishment —- requires a much more vigilant and constant daily inspection than the Board of Guardians can conveniently or satisfactorily give.*

He proposed that they request that the running of the workhouse be taken over by full-time officials and was backed by Hayes. They were opposed by a clique who wanted only one full time official and they lost the vote. The amended request was accepted by the Poor Law Commissioners in Dublin despite the advice of Burke. He had simply pointed to the failures of those who had accepted the role of Guardians of Waterford workhouse to live up to their responsibilities.[42]

Thus the inmates suffered for what was, at best administrative inefficiency and which had led to the resignation of a master of the workhouse in October 1848.[43] Most serious of all perhaps was his failure to ensure the full collection of rates to finance relief. Five rate collectors had been appointed for the entire union, each having entered into a surety against any default on their part. About April 1847 a collector named Phelan made off with £500 which he had collected in Poor Law rates, yet no attempt was made to collect on his surety. According to Burke the city area needed two collectors but only one was appointed. As a result he had failed to collect £2178 of the £7309 due, the second biggest defaulter being Waterford Corporation. £1150 from the rural areas had also gone uncollected.[44]

Nevertheless, the surviving minute books show that administrative detail was not overlooked despite some slips. Tenders were put out for cloth of different kinds in order that the two tailors employed by the workhouse (Messrs FitzGerald and Walsh at 8/- per week in 1848) could make clothes for the inmates and ticks for mattresses. The cloth bill in December 1848 from J. & E Maher was £300 per month. Cotton was bought from Malcomsons of Portlaw, presumably for bedding.[45] Something of the scale of the administrative operations can be seen from the following record of what clothes were to be reused and what discarded

28 Mar 1849

32 sheets	17 blankets 18 ticks	
49 waistcoats	125 trousers	225 shirt
119 pairs of shoes	3 pairs of stockings	105 caps
108 gowns	108 petticoats	128 shifts
200 aprons	150 handkerchiefs	88 pairs of shoes
200 womens caps	59 boys shirts	75 pairs of boys shoes
100 boys caps	30 girls frocks	10 girls petticoats
30 shifts	10 childs petticoats	10 frocks
10 girls caps		

The largest organisational effort, however, was to procure, cook and distribute three meals per day to up to four thousand people as well as providing food for outdoor relief for up to a further two thousand people per day (Appendix 1).

Life in Waterford Workhouse
The official plan for a temporary fever hospital. As these were wooden structures they have not survived.

Applicants to the workhouse were "*tested*" to ensure their complete destitution by a committee comprising a relieving officer and at least two guardians. If they passed they were given an admission ticket and presented it to the porter. They then were led behind the high walls of the workhouse, the men being directed one way, the women another and the children led off. All were stripped, told to wash and were given workhouse clothes. Their own clothes were taken and labelled. Those who were ill were taken to the infirmary: "*idiots, lunatics and epileptics*" were conducted to their own area. Only nursing mothers were allowed to keep their infants. However, from mid February 1847 each new entrant was to be fed after these rituals of arrival had been completed, "*as it is a fact that not a few of them are two days without food*".[46]

Work was demanded of the adults capable of it. Women were employed in the never-ending tasks of washing, cleaning, cooking, scrubbing floors with freestone or sand, repairing clothes and changing the straw in the ticks (mattresses) weekly. Some were employed in the

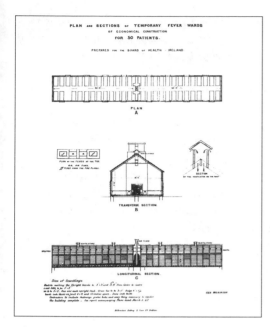

PLAN AND SECTIONS OF TEMPORARY FEVER WARDS
OF ECONOMICAL CONSTRUCTION
FOR 50 PATIENTS.

PREPARED FOR THE BOARD OF HEALTH - IRELAND

The official plan for a temporary fever hospital. As these were wooden structures they have not survived.

oakum room, unravelling old rope to be dipped in tar and used for caulking ships.[47] It seems to have been more difficult to have the men thus gainfully employed. Some, to the horror of Inspector Burke, were to be found wandering around the town. The majority however were in *"overcrowded"* dayrooms or –

In a shed in the men's yard there was scarcely more than standing room for the men and boys in it and it would be most desirable for their health's sake, if instead of being allowed to remain in such a fetid atmosphere, the people were employed in the open air on some work in the ground, however useless it might be.[48]

However, when it was suggested that men from the workhouse be put to productive work sweeping and cleaning the streets of the city, this would not be countenanced by the Commissioners in Dublin.[49] Nevertheless some work was found in the workhouse garden and out of it in September 1848 strangely, £27 worth of potatoes were sold to outsiders (potatoes do not feature in the workhouse diet) with a pig being sold in December. This operation must have been greatly expanded from May 1849 when farmland worth £450 was purchased nearby.[50]

For children, two schools were provided, one for boys (schoolmaster paid £40 p.a.) and one for girls (mistress paid £25 p.a.) with many changes of teachers. A report on these early in 1847 is a little ambivalent:

Since the date of the previous inspection the male school has much improved in the several branches of instruction and in the female department some progress has been made. The literary

129

*acquirements of both teachers are tolerable. The boy's school is well
conducted but in the female school there is not the same degree of
efficiency and no rolls have been kept by the schoolmistress.*[51]

At the same time, due to overcrowding it was reported that five or six
children were sleeping in one bed.

By the end of the following 1848 it was decided to give some
practical training to the boys, "*in the several operations of agriculture
and kitchen gardening*". Twenty small spades and ten small shovels
were purchased towards this end and Peter Cleary was employed at
ten shillings per week to provide instruction and to supervise the
workhouse land.[52] For a number of girls, motherhood in Australia was
the career path chosen for them (see below).

Nothing really survives, however, to give any real insight into the
experiences of an inmate of Waterford workhouse. One wonders about
the purchase of a cupping machine (used to draw blood) and of a
wooden leg (cost 11/-).[53] There also seems to have been some
disciplinary problems with some of the inmates to judge from the
decision to implement a "*refactory dietary*" for those who misbehaved.
It comprised of three meals of bread per day for three days, eaten in
isolation.[54] The Catholic chaplain asked that

> *a separate place might be provided for the females of loose
> character in the house as intercourse or contact with those of
> regular habits would be productive of evil consequences.*[55]

That some people did not see commitment into a workhouse as a last
resort is indicated by Mrs. Mary Nolan who in 1849 was appointed
ward mistress to Hayden's Store auxiliary workhouse. On enquiries
being made as to where her child was, it transpired that she had
deposited him in the workhouse which was deemed "*incompatible
with the employment of the mother as a paid officer*".[56] Odd anomalies
come to light. What is one to make of the following incoherent letter
from the Catholic Chaplain to one of the Guardians in April 1849 in the
expressed hope that the unidentified abuse will be rectified –

> *I beg to restore to you your boy as his having a bed in your
> quarters may be against the act of Parliament; or worse – against
> the conscience of zealous and pious men (I don't mean myself).
> And furthermore, it will if you permit it, venture an advice – 'tis
> this; that you and Mr. Craddick keep always well within the act,
> more especially whenever it will enable you to play the churl or
> mortify a popish priest. Crush, incommode us them, but feed upon*

them, that's the plan. Enforce the rule against one and I shall see whether by so doing you serve your friends.

Outdoor Relief and Emigration

From March 1847 each workhouse was allowed to feed the destitute of their own Union areas provided strict criteria were adhered to. The official instructions were that a ration of cooked food be given to each destitute person applying. This could be –

1½ lbs of bread	OR
1 lb of biscuit	OR
1 lb of meal or flour of any grain	OR
1 quart of soup thickened	
with meal and one quarter ration of bread.	

In May 1848 an instruction was issued from Dublin,

that one pound of meal is not sufficient for able bodied men who are required to work. The daily allowance to an able bodied man should be not less than one and three quarter pounds of raw meal or two and a quarter pounds of baked bread.

It is not clear when the Board of Guardians in Waterford commenced their programme of outdoor relief but its provision dominated their meetings in the early months of 1848. By March 1848 one relieving officer stated that he found it impossible to cope with the numbers applying. Many families had gone twenty four hours without food. He states *"The poor people have sold out clothes and furniture and the applicants are hourly, even daily increasing on my books."*[57] What is striking from such figures as are available is that so many could be fed so cheaply. The recipe for the meatless soup (really a form of watery porridge) is given in John M. Hearne's article.

Outdoor Relief 1848 [58]

March	6283	
April	7116	£181-9sh.
June	8965	
July	8995	£164-5sh.
December	1293	

Thus it would seem that once the crop of 1848 was harvested, the problems eased. By January 1849, however, the numbers increased. Some of these were victims of eviction: a *"great number of small landowners under ejectment and all classes feel the severe pressure of the times".* An example was given of the Osbourne evictions in Ballycashin, County Kilkenny.[59]

Emigration was one option for these displaced people. Many had gone from various parts of the country to the English ports which faced with a tide of Irish paupers decided to send some back. One shipload arrived in Waterford in July 1847 and made their way to the over-crowded workhouse. The guardians anxiously wrote to the Commissioners in Dublin asking whether they had the power *"to forward poor persons landed at Waterford from Liverpool and other ports to the locations to which they belonged."* They were told they did not have that right.[60]

One other group that did not have any rights were the orphan girls sent to Australia from Waterford in 1849. Twenty five of them were selected that Spring, examined and vaccinated by Dr. Burchett, provided with a hat, clothes, boots, comb (total cost £100-8-4) and a box *"strong and of good material so as to bear the strain of a long sea passage —- well and strongly corded and properly secured."* (cost 4/6d) to put their modest possessions in. The twenty five left Waterford by sea for Dublin which they reached at 4.00 p.m. on April 18th. Two hours later they were en route for Plymouth from where they were transhipped to South Australia. Details of the modest accomplishment of the twenty five are listed in the minutes (Appendix II). One wonders what the future held for the likes of 15 year old orphan Catherine Foran who had spent six years of her life in the Workhouse. Another forty five of her colleagues followed her five months later (17th August) with a further batch of twenty three being sent a month later (18th September).[61] The names of these sixty eight are not recorded and their fate remains unknown. However, one hopes they were better behaved on the boat than their colleagues from Clonmel who went out there at the same time. Not alone was their language *"vile in the extreme",* but their behaviour was

> *refractory, insubordinate and extremely troublesome during the passage, setting at defiance all authority, mixing with the sailors and threatening that if extreme measure were resorted to for the purpose of restraining them, they would get the sailors to help them.*

Perhaps the description which was given of some of the 2219 orphan girls in Australia did not apply to any of those from Waterford. Many were in a state of *"extreme filthiness and unimaginable indelicacy."*[62] However, from the evidence available on Waterford workhouse it is hard to see how some at least would have avoided being traumatised by the experience which had not only brought them there but rendered them orphans, or how they could have survived without being hardened by the utilitarian regime inside. However, at least they were alive which they might not otherwise have been.

REFERENCES
1. Relief Commission Papers 1845-7 (in County Library, Lismore).
2. British Parliamentary Papers, *Papers relating to proceedings for the relief of distress and the state of unions and workhouses in Ireland: Sixth series 1847-48* (hereafter Famine Ireland 3) (Shannon, 1968) pp.681-691.
3. Waterford Union: Minute Book, 9 Sept. 1848 – 15 June 1849.
4. ibid, These minutes and RC letters are in the County Library, Lismore. (ed. note: these three workhouse books have been fully indexed by Rita Byrne. This index plus a fuller version of this article is also in the County Library).
5. *Waterford Mail*, 10th April 1847 p.2. This and all other references from this paper are reports of meetings headed BOARD OF GUARDIANS.
6. Relief Commission Papers 1845-7, op. cit.
7. *Waterford Mail*, 16 Jan. 1847, p.2. and 13 Feb. p.2.
8. Famine Ireland 3, p.684 – Burke's report and The *Waterford Mail* Board of Guardians Report, 29 Dec. 1847.
9. Waterford Union: Minute Book, Dec 8th 1848, op. cit. Dec 15th 1848 (passim).
10. *Waterford Mail*, 5 Feb. 1848, Mr. Delahunty.
11. Famine Ireland 3, Burkes report March 16th 1848.
12. Waterford Union: Minute Book, 9 Sept. 1848 – 15 June 1849.
13. ibid.
14. ibid.
15. ibid, 3rd March 1847.
16. British Parliamentary Papers, *Reports from the Relief Commissioners and other papers on Famine Relief in Ireland with Appendices 1846-53* (hereafter Famine Ireland 8) (Shannon, 1970).
17. Waterford Union: Minute Book, 9 Sept. 1848 – 15 June 1849, op. cit. letter 3rd June 1847.
18. ibid, Sept. 27th 1848, Oct. 28th 1848.
19. Famine Ireland 8.
20. ibid, p.416, reports Drs. Mackesy and Courtney.
21. British Parliamentary Papers, *Copies or extracts of correspondence relating to the state of the union workhouses in Ireland: First Second and Third series* (hereafter Famine Ireland 1) (Shannon, 1968) pp.105 and 186; Famine Ireland 3 p.1008; British Parliamentary Papers, *Papers relating to proceedings for the relief of distress and the state of the unions and workhouses in Ireland: Seventh and Eight series 1847-48* (hereafter Famine Ireland 4) p.267 and 524; Waterford Union: Minute Book, 9 Sept. 1848 – 15 June 1849 op. cit. 1849 figure 9th June.
22. Famine Ireland 1 p.124 reports of the Relief Commissioners with a further report for 1848, p.177.
23. ibid, 21 Feb. 1849.
24. Infirmary Minutes (in WML) 13th April 1849. In granting this permission the trustees there strangely note, "the most stringent disciplinary arrangements be made and enforced to prevent the recurrence of such disorder as occurred on a former occasion when that part of the hospital was so used.".

25. Waterford Union: Minute Book, 9 Sept. 1848 – 15 June 1849, op. cit.
26. *Waterford Mail*, 20 Feb. 1847, p.2.
27. Per Tom Nolan, reference found by him in Lismore Workhouse Books.
28. Relief Commission Papers 1845-7, op. cit. contain a series of requests from the PLCs, daily asking for information.
29. ibid, 27 March, a reference without details.
30. *Waterford Mail*, 5 Feb. 1848. It is not clear whether this is the March 1847 report or a later one.
31. Famine Ireland 8, pp.687-8, abstracts from minutes.
32. ibid, p.686, meetings and attendance; p.689, inspections.
33. *Waterford Mail*, 17 April 1847, complaint by County Collector Phelan.
34. Famine Ireland 8, p.683, letter.
35. Waterford Union: Minute Book, 9 Sept. 1848 – 15 June 1849, op. cit. 2 Jan 1849.
36. ibid, 16 & 17 March, 1848.
37. Famine Ireland 8, pp.687-8, listing and abstract of meetings.
38. ibid, p.686, meetings and attendance; p.689, inspections.
39. *Waterford Mail*, 22 Dec., 1844.
40. ibid, 4 Dec., p.2.
41. Famine Ireland 8, p.688
42. ibid, pp.683 and 689 with details of debate from the minutes 18 March 1848, p.690: p.691, immediate reply of commissioners, 22 March 1848. Burkes advice, pp.681-2 is dated 17th March and must have been what he was writing in his hotel when he could not respond to Hayes' note.
43. Waterford Union: Minute Book, 9 Sept. 1848 – 15 June 1849, op. cit. mins 3rd Oct., 1848.
44. Famine Ireland 8, p.681 and 685-6, figures.
45. Waterford Union: Minute Book, 9 Sept. 1848 – 15 June 1849, op. cit. e.g. 9 Dec. 1848.
46. *Waterford Mail*, 13 Feb. 1847, p.2.
47. Waterford Union: Minute Book, 9 Sept. 1848 – 15 June 1849, op. cit. e.g. January 1849, £4-8/- for sale of oakum.
48. Famine Ireland 8, p.684, report Burke's inspection.
49. Waterford Union: Minute Book, 9 Sept. 1848 – 15 June 1849, op. cit. 9 Feb. 1849.
50. ibid, 23 Sept. and 30 Dec. 1848 and May 1849.
51. Relief Commission Papers 1845-7, op. cit. 8 Feb. 1847
52. ibid, 9 Dec., 1848
53. Waterford Union: Minute Book, 9 Sept. 1848 – 15 June 1849, op. cit. 13 Sept. and 18 Oct. 1848.
54. ibid, Feb. 1849.
55. *Waterford Mail*, 10 April 1847, p.2.
56. *ibid*, April 1849.
57. Famine Ireland 3, p.688 and O'Grady's report.
58. Famine Ireland 3, p.1008 and 1037 and Famine Ireland 4 pp.263, 267 and 524.
59. ibid, p.351, reports Fitzgerald and O'Connor.
60. Relief Commission Papers 1845-47, op. cit. July 1847.
61. Waterford Union: Minute Book, 9 Sept. 1848 – 15 June 1849, op. cit. as per dates in text.
62. Kinealy, Christine, *This Great Calamity: The Irish Famine, 1845-52* (Dublin 1994), pp.323-4.

Appendix 1
Numbers obtaining relief Sept 1848 – June 1849

Date	In Fever Hospital	Relieved out of workhouse	In workhouse
09 Sept	41	1220	2331
16 Sept	40	1094	2063
23 Sept	47	1033	1980
30 Sept	40	823	1577
07 Oct	32	377	666
14 Oct	37	463	819
21 Oct	34	501	837
28 Oct	31	535	881
04 Nov	32	562	927
11 Nov	47	543	883
18 Nov	50	546	890
25 Nov	47	578	944
02 Dec	44	615	1048
09 Dec	47	646	1122
16 Dec	27	701	1261
23 Dec	34	705	1290
30 Dec	36	762	1487
06 Jan	41	804	1556
13 Jan	54	904	1870
20 Jan	45	996	2047
27 Jan	46	1129	2388
03 Feb	48	1194	2507
10 Feb	61	1380	3085
17 Feb	75	1602	3432
24 Feb	60	1613	3689
03 Mar	65	1574	3588
10 Mar	63	1599	3797
17 Mar	67	1605	3687
24 Mar	69	1583	3617
31 Mar	53	1128	2404
07 Apr	59	1350	3042
14 Apr	53	1378	3005
21 Apr	84	1387	3177
28 Apr	76	1391	3223
05 May	81	1419	3352
12 May	84	1431	3458
19 May	92	1467	3574
26 May	111	1571	3651
02 Jun	94	1589	3810
09 Jun	110	1659	3673

Appendix 2

	Names	Age	Qualifications	Time spent in Union
1	Mary Ann Sullivan	15	Cannot read nor write – can sew	6 Mnths
2	Ellen Drea	15	Can read – can sew	2½ Yrs
3	Margaret Verekers	15	Can read – can sew	7 Mnths
4	Catherine Foran	15	Can read write – can sew	6 Yrs
5	Biddy Murphy	15	Can read – can sew	1 Yr
6	Biddy Ryan	15	Can read write – can sew	2 Yrs
7	Ellen Kennedy	16	Cannot read nor write – can sew	1½ Yrs
8	Biddy Brogan	17	Cannot read nor write – can sew	1½ yrs
9	Catherine Toole	19	Can read – can sew	2 Yrs
10	Mary Carr	17	Cannot read nor write – can sew	8 Mnths
11	Catherine Walsh	17	Cannot read nor write – can sew	1 Yr
12	Mary Ryan	18	Can read – can sew	1 Yr
13	Biddy Fitzgerald	17	Can read write – can sew	1 Yr
14	Mary Power	18	Cannot read nor write – can sew	9 Mnths
15	Catherine Sullivan	17	Cannot read nor write – can sew	1½ Yrs
16	Ellen Donovan	18	Cannot read nor write – can sew	2 Yrs
17	Mary Wallace	17	Cannot read nor write – can sew	1 Yr
18	Mary Tobin	18	Cannot read nor write – can sew	1 Yr
19	Catherine Duggan	18	Can read write – can sew	2 Yrs
20	Mary Thompson	18	Cannot read nor write – can sew	1½ Yrs
21	Ann Walsh	18	Cannot read nor write – can sew	1 Yr
22	Mary Sheehan	19	Can read write – can sew	1½ Yrs
23	Ann Keys	19	Cannot read nor write – can sew	2 Yrs
24	Mary Martin	19	Cannot read nor write – can sew	2 Yrs
25	Margaret Conroy	16	Cannot read nor write – can sew	1 Yr

Chapter 8

The Dungarvan disturbances of 1846 and sequels

WILLIAM FRAHER

Introduction

On the eve of the Famine there was no intimation that there would be any particular difficulties in the area of Dungarvan. By and large, as Donnchadh Ó Ceallacháin points out, the countryside had been tranquil and there was a mood of modest optimism. The workhouse had been opened in 1841 with accommodation for six hundred; over two thirds of its capacity lay unused in the Summer of 1845. While the partial crop failure in September 1845 posed no substantial threat for the east of the county, there were danger signals in the Dungarvan area by January 1846 to judge from the provisions being made by the Board of Guardians there to monitor its implications.[1]

Particular concern was expressed about the four hundred fishing families in the town. Superficially, they should have been the least vulnerable to potato failure. However, it is likely that what happened in Ring was also true in Abbeyside and Dungarvan. There, the fishermen, having pawned their boats and nets, would have starved were it not for the intervention of the Quakers (see Joan Johnson's article). There was, it seems, no such long term intervention for those in Dungarvan (graphic details of their fate is given by Eugene Broderick in his article). Short term relief measures proposed for them and for those in the coastal hinterland included the building of piers and harbours at Dungarvan, Ballinacourty, Ballinagoul, Stradbally, Ardmore and Whiting Bay. Schemes were also initiated for marsh drainage and the building of a canal to link Dungarvan to the Blackwater.[2]

A Famine Relief Committee was set up in Dungarvan in January 1846. Within two months nine other committees were set up in the local union area. The medical officer in Dungarvan meanwhile, had noted widespread cases of dysentery as a result of eating diseased potatoes.[3] By April 1846 there were strong intimations of the trouble to come. At a meeting of local landlords convened by the resident magistrate Patrick C. Howley, one of the local corn merchants complained that he was being intimidated to the extent that he was afraid to export corn. Not only could he not tell who was threatening him, but even the offer of army protection would not induce him to export.[4]

Summer was the traditional period of shortage and Howley was obviously concerned that there would be further intimidation. He considered the fifty five marines stationed in the castle inadequate security and wanted dragoons to be sent to Dungarvan as well as marines who would protect shipping leaving the harbour. He reconsidered this and was prepared to compromise in May 1846 accepting that reinforcements from the 170 strong garrison in Youghal could be rushed to Dungarvan if necessary.[5]

Tensions in September 1846

Thus matters stood over the Summer of 1846 which promised an excellent potato harvest. In August the blight struck again; a stunned population realised that their staple diet was destroyed. The food deposit in Dungarvan closed on 31st August and public works provided insufficient income to meet the soaring cost of cereals. By the middle of September hungry crowds began to gather in the countryside around Dungarvan. There seems to have been some organisation behind the unrest, to judge from Howley's report,

> About the hour of eight o'clock on last evening the country was lighted up as far as eye could see with signal fires...I went out to inquire into the object of them and heard horns blowing and numbers of persons traversing the county shouting and making the most hideous noises.[6]

This was on September 13th; the following day there was to be a meeting in Dungarvan to decide on the rates for public works. Howley explained that the labourers wanted one shilling a day wages, but were only offered eight pence.

A large crowd was expected to gather for the sessions and reinforcements had been sought from Youghal to augment the local constabulary. Howley reported that about 4,000 people crowded around the courthouse in Bridge Street: "*towards the evening they commenced using the most frightful threats against some of the gentry whom they said were opposed to the granting of the several works.*" The crowd blocked up the iron railings in front of the building to prevent people leaving until their demands for a pay increase on the public works schemes were met. When the military and constabulary arrived the crowd reacted by throwing stones. The ringleaders were arrested and with great difficulty were put into the Bridewell (adjacent to the courthouse). "*Several clergymen exhorted the unfortunate people to*

138

desist but all to no purpose, as they said 'Life was a burden to them and the sooner they lost it the better.'" Howley ordered all the public houses in the town to close. He then read the riot act and ordered the military to load arms. This had the desired effect and the crowd dispersed. One man was arrested for throwing a stone at the County Inspector of Police, John Clarke. Constable Wall was hit with a stone and a soldier of the 27th Regiment received a serious wound to his face.[7]

On the night of 16th September Howley reported that for the third successive night signal fires had been lit and horns blown. He had 60 constabulary and 66 men of the 67th Regiment and 30 of the 8th Dragoons on standby to prevent tar barrels being lit in the streets. The next day two or three thousand labourers wandered around the courthouse and streets but left the town without incident that night. Howley stated that some outrages had occurred and felt that the situation could not improve until the public works commenced and the cost of provisions was reduced.[8]

On Monday, 21st September another Presentment Session was held in Dungarvan. For some days before, fires were lit on the surrounding hills and trouble was expected. However, on the day of the sessions the P.P. of Lismore, Father Fogarty, delivered an address in Irish to over 1,000 people:

> *I am authorised...to address a few words to you in the language which you will better understand... The disorder which you have created in this court by your turbulent and riotous conduct...is highly disreputable... The magistrates and all the leading proprietors... are determined to do their duty well, towards the people, during this season of unprecedented distress. I sympathise with you under your extraordinary wants and privations, I may say beyond human endurance.*

In referring to the local landlords he had the following comments:

> *I have never witnessed greater zeal or anxiety to do all in their power to administer to the wants of the poor during the summer. Those gentlemen not only contributed largely towards relief funds, but they also fed hundreds weekly at their own residences and actually superintended the cooking of food...in their own kitchens.*[9]

The riot of 28th September 1846
Over the following two weeks there were disturbances all over West Waterford (see chapter 11). On 28th September Howley attended

sessions in Kilmacthomas on his way back from Tramore with a troop of dragoons. However,

> *Knowing that the peasantry (in Dungarvan) would take advantage of my absence I begged of the magistrates to allow me to return with as little delay as possible.*

Before Howley arrived back in Dungarvan the crowds had been gathering. The *Cork Examiner* reported,

> *About 12 o'clock, the square and the streets began partially to fill up with people and at half past one, a body of labourers from Old Parish, Ardmore and Clashmore, to the number of something near seven hundred, entered the square and marched in procession down the quay and towards Mr. Flood's store, when they cautioned him against shipping corn.*

The group was led by a man known as '*Lame Pat Power*' from Killongford. The crowd proceeded up a lane to the Main Street. A baker named James Morgan offered the crowd whatever bread he had, but they refused his offer, replying that they only wanted employment and fair wages.[10]

When Howley arrived at about three o'clock, accompanied by a troop of about 40 of the First Royal Dragoons, he saw a large crowd of about three thousand attempting to break into the corn stores on the quay. He had a number of the ringleaders arrested and placed in the Bridewell. He then addressed the crowd and asked them to put their demands in writing which he would forward to the government. At half past three the crowd became very agitated on learning that two men had been arrested and put in the Bridewell. They raided bread shops owned by Roger Baker and James Morgan in Main Street, also Williams shop and Peter Moor Fisher in Blackpool.[11]

At about four o'clock a large group of labourers were observed coming into the town down William Street (the present Mary Street). It was said that they marched in procession dressed in flannel jackets and corduroys. Described as "*an ingenious and sensible friend to the public peace as well as the people*", James Byrne of William Street, suggested to them that they put their grievances in writing as suggested by the magistrate. They agreed to his suggestion.[12] What appears to be a copy of this list of demands is included amongst correspondence from Howley to the Under Secretary. It is titled:

> *The Memorial of the distressed labourers of the districts of Dungarvan and the surrounding districts:*

That our provision has failed as is too well known; that employment though often promised has not yet commenced. That the rate of wages offered is inadequate to the support of a single individual. That the rate of wages now offered is but ten pence a day; that the price of Indian meal is now selling at no less a rate than thirteen pounds per ton, retail price. That last summer, the price of Indian meal was but nine pounds per ton...[13]

Other sections of the crowd were not as pliable and insisted that the gaoled men be released immediately. *"Nothing would satisfy them short of giving up the prisoners, they commenced throwing stones at us, and I had to order the Police to clear the street."* The Police were beaten back by showers of stones and Howley ordered the Dragoons to the front:

I heard several voices cry out in Irish 'Kill them, kill them – they are only a handful'. I went myself in the midst of the rioters and besought of them... to cease stone throwing; all was in vain. One misguided man in the crowd was seen by a policeman to stoop for a stone. Sub-Inspector Rooney arrested him and in the handcuffing, a shower of stones were thrown at the policeman, when the dragoons charged the crowds through the square, making them fly in all directions.[14]

The military pursued the crowd up William Street: *When coming near Carroll's public house in the vicinity of the Christian schools, a fearful shower of stones was thrown at the Dragoons.* The crowd became more aggressive and Howley gave permission to Captain Sibthorp to fire: 'each round was returned by a volley of stones.' The Dragoons fired 26 shots into the crowd, hitting a number of them, two seriously. One of them had his thigh, just above the knee joint, shattered in pieces, the other received a bullet through the upper part of the thigh. These two were taken to the workhouse and attended there by Dr. Christian.[15] According to the magistrate the rioters than left to look for arms with the intention of returning to break into shops and stores.[16] Thus, the riot of 28th ended, but with much tension remaining.

Reportage of Riot and Sequel

The riot was reported in the editorial of the *Cork Examiner* on Wednesday, 30th September. It remarked that *'starvation is rendering the unarmed man a desperate enemy of the public peace. Towns and villages are invaded and plundered by armies of idle labourers, who famish for want of bread and who will not be put off.'* It concluded by

141

Illustrated London News **view of Dungarvan subsequent to the riot of
28th September 1846.**

stating that the riot was '*a fitting though calamitous sequel to the
excitement of the last month.*' The paper's Dungarvan correspondent
blamed the riot on the '*ill-advised and cruel curtailment of labourer's
wages.*'

Reports of the riot quickly reached London and were picked up by
the *Illustrated London News* which also sympathetically editorialised
thus:

> *The accounts of the state of Ireland grow darker and darker.
> Famine seems to be doing its worst and the extreme of want is
> producing revolt and riot: At Dungarvan it appears that the
> military have been obliged to fire on the people – with fatal effect.
> This is one of the horrors attending on scarcity; the rebellion it
> excites is of the worst kind; the aggressors find a certain amount of
> sympathy and excuse which, although against our judgement it is
> impossible to withhold...the mass makes a wild and desperate
> attempt to snatch a remedy at all risks with this sad and heart
> rendering result.*[17]

There had not in fact been a fatality although one of the wounded did
die later. Otherwise the accompanying report is accurate and put in the
context of the bands of starving people scouring west Waterford and
threatening an attack on Youghal. The journal sent an artist to sketch
the scenes of the riots. The first of these appeared in the *Illustrated
London News* on 7th November.

The comment, presumably from the anonymous artist, was –

> *The distress, both in Youghal and Dungarvan, is truly appalling in
> the streets; for, without entering the houses, the miserable spectre of
> the haggard looks, crouching attitudes, sunken eyes, and colourless
> lips and cheeks, unmistakeably bespeaks the sufferings of the people.*[18]

An interesting story concerning the police was recalled the following month. During the riot a number of people had attempted to break into a store on the quay only to be met by three policemen: James Downes, John Jennings and James Flanagan. However, instead of a violent confrontation the police took pity on them: *seeing their famished appearance each of them put his hand in his pocket and offered a crown to them, which was declined. Three cheers were given for the policemen.*[19]

One of the men shot, Michael Fleming, died in the workhouse four weeks later. An inquest was held on that day at the workhouse. One of those called as a witness was Beresford Boate J.P.. He recalled seeing a mob of about 6,000 coming into Dungarvan: *between four and five o'clock it was deemed expedient to clear the square... the mob rallied in William Street and commenced pelting both the military and police with stones...Some of them the size of the crown of my hat.* He stated that Howley went into the middle of the crowd, but after talking with some of them he decided it would be of no use so he read the Riot Act: *while so doing his horse was struck in the side with a large stone, which reeled him round, and caused him nearly to fall.* The troops fired on the crowd and *after it commenced the stone throwing rather increased than diminished until the Dragoons went in front of the Killongford road and fired a volley which made the mob give way.* Richard Walsh, the master of the workhouse, stated that Michael Fleming was a servant boy of William Walsh's of Kilmacthomas. Fleming had been sent to Dungarvan with the baggage of the Dragoons. Asked why he threw stones he replied that he did so because everyone else did.[20] The following was the verdict of the inquest:

> We find that Michael Fleming was one of a riotous mob who were throwing stones at the First Royal Dragoons, on the 28th September last...when he received a gunshot wound in the thigh. We also find that Michael Fleming died of disease of the heart brought on by said wound. We further find that no blame is to be attached to the magistrate in command...who used every forebearance towards the rioters.

The trial of all who disturbed the peace in Dungarvan and the surrounding area took place on Thursday, 27th October: *The courthouse was thronged, every available seat having been occupied and the greatest anxiety prevailed to know the issue of the trial of the fifty one persons charged.* They were charged with unlawful and riotous behaviour at Clasmore, Whitechurch and Dungarvan and interfering with trade by violence and intimidation. All of them pleaded guilty, regretting their actions. Eleven were ordered to be discharged on finding '*two securities of 40 shillings and themselves of £5 each to keep the peace*'. The counsel asked that the prisoners shouldn't be sentenced except the ringleader, Lame Pat Power. The judge found it '*his most painful duty to sentence him to 12 months imprisonment with hard labour*'. The *Waterford Freeman* reported that the '*unfortunate Power declared to the court that he was four days and four nights living on cabbages and salt previous to his misconduct.*[21]

The magistrate, P.C. Howley, had written several letters to the Under Secretary before the riot asking that measures should be implemented to prevent any disturbances. He complained that his letters had remained unanswered and that he was left with no choice but to go to Dublin to meet the Under Secretary in person. However, he was not allowed to meet him. The Under Secretary replied stating that all important letters from Howley had been answered and that they had received no letters with suggestions on how to prevent a disturbance in Dungarvan, nor had they any record of his seeking an appointment to meet with him in Dublin. It appears from this reply that the government were trying to protect themselves to avoid blame for the riot, by not acting on Howley's advice. However, on 1st October the Under Secretary wrote to Howley exonerating him from what had happened and stating how regrettable it was that troops should have had to fire on the crowd.[22]

Continuing Tensions

On 30th September Howley informed the Under Secretary that in the event of trouble he had arranged for seventy of the First Royal Dragoons, the 8th Hussars, 88 men of the 67th Regiment and 18 of the Constabulary to be on standby. He felt this number would be only barely sufficient: '*The shipping here requires to be protected as a mob have assembled on the quay to prevent any export trade.*' He warned that it was essential to have sufficient men on standby as '*the peasantry are enraged at being fired on.*' Five thousand people had assembled at Whitechurch, a few miles from Dungarvan, but Howley was afraid to send any troops there as the town would be left without adequate protection'. He appealed to the government to listen to the people's demands and to employ a sufficient military presence in Dungarvan. Four companies of the 47th Regiment had been ordered to proceed to Dungarvan by steamer to arrive on 2nd October.[23]

In spite of the shooting on the 29th, crowds were still gathering at the quay intimidating the merchants. On 1st October, it was reported that there were 110 Hussars and First Royal Dragoons stationed in Dungarvan besides 150 foot soldiers and policemen. However, the local people felt that all these troops were unnecessary and that the government should concentrate on giving the people adequate wages on the public works. On the same day a ship owned by McDonald of Liverpool was loading grain on the quay in Dungarvan. It appears that the fishermen had blocked any ships leaving with grain, but on this day they were out fishing. However, the fishermen's wives marched to the quay and *'threw the planks over, preventing them from continuing and have since kept watch, even at night, bodies of them relieving each other at intervals.'* The Dragoons, infantry and police were called to the scene. Some men were offered extra money to load the grain, but as soon as they began *'they were received with such a shout, from their fellow countrywomen, they could not stand the gaze and desisted.'* A small group of women remained and insisted they would not allow the ship to leave until a supply of Indian meal arrived in Dungarvan.[24]

A petition was sent to the Lord Lieutenant, the Earl of Bessborough, dated 1 October and signed by two of the leading corn merchants, Andrew Carbery and Joseph Donnell:–

> *That from the present state of mob excitement in this town, petitioners are not allowed to ship their corn, though fully protected by the military and police that the intimidation is so high that the men employed permanently and usually for this purpose of loading corn have refused to work thereby leaving the petitioners without the means of shipping their corn.*

Donnell and Carbery asked that the merchants should have proper protection when loading their ships to impress on the mobs that the *'country is fully protected in all its operations of trade and business'.* The Under Secretary replied that he would ensure that the merchants and their employees would be protected but insisted that the constabulary couldn't be used to guard business premises.[25]

Once the trial of the rioters was over, by the end of October, as it seemed that there was no threat of further violence, the 8th Hussars were transferred from Dungarvan to Cahir after five weeks of *'arduous and harrowing'* duty. It was said that their Commander, Lord Killeen, *'was loved and esteemed by all classes, particularly by the poor peasantry for whose condition he and his men manifest such compassion.'*[26] Resident Magistrate Howley was unhappy with this transfer and, fearing another outburst of violence, wrote to Dublin Castle stating that the peasantry could have guns next time. He sought reinforcements for the garrison, particularly cavalry, but was turned down.[27]

Perhaps Howley was being alarmist as nothing on the scale of the riot of 28th September did take place afterwards. Such tensions as occurred related to the workhouse which by early 1847 was overcrowded with hundreds of people waiting for admission. One commentator remarked: '*No longer can a pen describe the sufferings and destitution of our poor here. Their condition is daily getting more appalling and heartrending.*'[28] The fever hospital in Abbeyside was full and the public works had ceased in mid March. The Scots Greys had to be called to the workhouse because of the enormous crowd which surrounded it, some of whom tried to scale the walls.[29] The Board of Guardians appealed to the government to put the Temporary Relief Act into operation immediately as there would certainly be '*a fearful increase in crime and aggression by the starving population.*'[30]

In February the Dungarvan union was in financial difficulty and the guardians had to use their own personal security to obtain a loan. The local Poor Law Inspector observed that: '*it was heartrending to witness the mass of human suffering which the medical officer stated neither food nor medicine could save from death.*'[31] The following month the guardians informed the Lord Lieutenant of the '*indescribable destitution*' in the union. The workhouse was full and 2,000 people were claiming relief as a result of the closure of the public works.[32] By April, Andrew Carbery, Secretary of the Dungarvan Relief Committee remarked that most of his committee had abandoned them, leaving him, Father Halley, the Rev. Crofton and a few guardians to carry on the work. The condition of the people was desperate with reports of starving people falling collapsing in the streets and along the surrounding country roads. In certain cases in the country the bodies lay there unburied for weeks.[33]

Towards the end of October 1847 the police had to guard the entrance to the workhouse to allow the guardians to pass through the crowds of people seeking relief. It was remarked that:

> *The people have no sort of employment and are thrown on the rate payers for support. Before Winter is over one half of them will have starved. These poor creatures whose cabins the landlords tumbled down are in a most deplorable state of misery and are forced to live at the sides of the roads.*[34]

Because of the overcrowding in the workhouse the guardians had to rent Kiely's store in Quay Lane which accommodated 350 people.[35]

By January 1848 there was a breakdown in discipline in the workhouse. After one disturbance a number of paupers were jailed and the clerk suggested that the guardians acquire some guns for protection. The guardians felt they were unable to cope and asked that paid guardians be sent down to run the union and sort out the

Dungarvan workhouse in 1995, now St. Joseph's Hospital.
Top shows front of the original block and below shows the second block.

finances. By April 1, 184 paupers were being relieved in the work-house with a further 4,353 receiving outdoor relief.[36] Around this time the guardians rented another store to cope with the growing numbers. Some months later a Dungarvan resident stated that: '*utter misery still continues in our town and the grave daily opens up to receive the victims of famine and pestilence.*'[37]

In the latter months of 1848 there were numerous arms searches and arrests of suspected rebels. Gunpowder was found hidden in a ship at the quay, the captain, Mr. Whelan, and the crew were arrested. On the night of 13th September it was reported that: '*all the hills surrounding the town were lit with fires, the movement of the authorities here seemed to be full of alarm and consternation – Mounted policemen were sent to all the country stations... the barricades at the courthouse were again raised by the police.*'[38] (This may have been linked with Young Ireland activity – see Dermot Power's article).

By December 1848 the Poor Law Commissioner claimed that Dungarvan workhouse was one of the best kept under his supervision. However, the numbers of paupers continued to increase forcing the guardians to rent a further store in January 1849. This was certainly one of the worst years of the famine in the union. Along with the huge increase in numbers an epidemic of cholera appeared in April to exacerbate the problem and increase the mortality levels. The medical officer reported the first cases of cholera in April. The guardians leased Shandon House to the north of the town, as a cholera hospital. By May over 300 cases had been admitted. The epidemic was almost gone by August but by the time the hospital closed in September there had been a mortality rate of 50.2%.[39]

That there were still tensions in Dungarvan in 1849 is intimated by the fact that watchmen had to be hired to clear the streets of paupers. The reason why there were so many, the workhouse guardians suggest, was because of evictions in the surrounding countryside forcing those rendered homeless to gravitate towards Dungarvan. The watchmen were to be paid a miserly five shillings per week to round up these aggrieved people and lodge them in the workhouse, presumably against their wills.[40]

Further trouble in the workhouse was inevitable. A number of those lodged there refused to do any work. This was deemed "rioting" and a number of them were arrested and imprisoned in April 1850. Over the next ten weeks there was continuous tension with over three thousand people jammed into the workhouse. Cooking for them was a major problem with breakfast sometimes not being served until midday and dinners at midnight. Violence erupted on Sunday, 30th June:

The male adults rose at breakfast and smashed the trays containing their breakfasts and threatened the life of the lately appointed Assistant Master. The ringleaders to the number of 15 then broke out of their yard and paraded about the workhouse grounds uttering defiance to the officers. They then scaled the walls and went down to Keatings auxiliary store for the purpose of getting out some of the girls there. In this they were disappointed. About half past two p.m., they returned to the main house arriving with sticks, shouting and uttering threats and rushed into the yard where the taking of the roll was in progress. The Guardians on duty disarmed the ringleaders and they were incarcerated in a store room. Then a proper row broke out with the police being sent for. The ringleaders numbering 15 were arrested and marched off to the Bridewell.

Information for assault and riots was sworn against them, they were tried at the quarter sessions and condemned to twelve months imprisonment with hard labour.[41]

The removal of the ringleaders did not solve the problems but there were no further riots reported from inside the workhouse. However, a paradoxical situation arose in the Summer of 1850 where a number of inmates were trying to get out, while outside on 27th July a '*mighty assembly of vagrants*' was trying to get in. They had to be disbanded by the police. The problem continued over the next few weeks and regular patrols had to be inaugurated to dispel them.[42] It is not clear why they were not admitted as workhouse numbers were dropping at the time. Nevertheless the tensions continued and it was decided to punish all inmates on Christmas Day 1850 by not giving them meat soup due to their '*unruly behaviour*'. Shortly afterwards, a ton of broken glass was ordered for the top of the workhouse wall '*to keep paupers in and keep out vagrants*'.[43]

The males were not the only source of trouble – there were difficulties with the females as well. Part of the reason might have been the decision to ship two hundred of them out to Canada in 1850 – whether they wanted to go or not. Mary Snow and Mary O'Shea refused to go and were evicted from the workhouse.[44] The rest then consented to go and were sent in July to Liverpool where they transferred to the Essex bound for Quebec. However, the ship sprung a leak and had to put into Cork Harbour for repairs. The women had to disembark and seventeen of them availed of the opportunity to escape. Most of them however had no option but to make their way back to Dungarvan.[45]

Another manifestation of female discontent was a '*strike*' by twenty two of them who refused to do any more of the workhouse washing until they had been fed. They were immediately discharged.[46] Nine months later ten females described as '*nurses*' were found guilty of an unspecified '*insubordinate conduct*'. Four of them were to be brought before the magistrate and the rest left to the mercy of the master.[47] Margaret Power represented a different expression of hostility. When it

Reilig na tSléibhe, the graveyard that was opened on the hill above Dungarvan to accommodate the workhouse dead when all the other graveyards were full.

was discovered that she was pregnant, she immediately named the master of the workhouse as the father. This was deemed '*not entitled to credit.*'[48]

Conclusion

Violence is manifested in many ways. This article has drawn together available evidence on the violence of those driven desperate by hunger in September 1846 and of different forms of violence within and outside the workhouse over the following four years. Much of this must have been a response to the unreported violence of those who evicted cottiers from their homes and lands to take their chances on the streets of Dungarvan. There was also the violence of the workhouse guardians, for instance, in deporting those girls against their wills and arbitrarily discharging others into a society which had nothing for them.

In amelioration, it may be said that the situation around Dungarvan was desperate. The sheer effort of keeping so many alive may have dulled the finer sensibilities of those in authority. What they were remembered for, however, was not the number they saved, but the lack of humanity by which they did it. This is reflected in the song "*Amhrán na Prátaí Dubha*". The song refers to the workhouse in Dungarvan and the famine graveyard at Reilig an tSléibhe (The Mountain Graveyard) a few miles outside the town.

"Oh pity the proud ones, all earth possessing
That for these distresses must surely pay,
Oh, sad their fate, who the poor oppressing
Do richer grow by their moans each day,
The potatoes that failed, brought the nation to agony,
The poorhouse bare, and the dreadful coffin-ship,
And in the mountain graves do they in hundreds lie,
By hunger taken to their beds of clay."

REFERENCES
1. Dungarvan Union: Minute Book, 1 Nov. 1845 to 20 Aug. 1846.
2. Relief Commission Papers 1845-7, 2/442/7 and *Cork Examiner*, 23 September, 22 December 1845. This canal extended from Killongford for four and a half miles to Knockmaun and cost £10,000. It was intended to continue the canal to connect with the river Blackwater at a total cost of £40,000.
3. Dungarvan Union: Minute Book, 1 Nov. 1845 to 20 Aug. 1846.
4. Chief Secretary's Office, Outrage Reports 29/10565; Howley lived at Duckspool House, now owned by the Augustinian Community. The merchant was Robert Howell. His corn store, kiln and yard were leased from Edward Galwey. In this century it was used by A. Moloney as a corn store.
5. ibid, 29/10767.
6. ibid, 29/23895.
7. ibid, 29/204069.
8. ibid, 29/24081.
9. *Cork Examiner*, 23 September, 25 September 1846.
10. ibid, 2 October 1846; O'Rourke, John, T*he History of the Great Irish Famine of 1847, with notices of earlier famines* (Dublin 1902) pp 229-232. Patrick Flood was agent for Joseph Donnell & Co., corn and butter merchants. This store was leased from Edward Galwey. The site is now occupied by the C.A.B. garage.
11. Chief Secretary's Office, Outrage Reports 29/26315.
12. *Cork Examiner*, 30 September 1846.
13. Chief Secretary's Office, Outrage Reports 29/26323
14. ibid, 29/263115.
15. *Cork Examiner*, 2 October 1846.
16. ibid, 19 October 1846.
17. *Illustrated London News*, 3 October 1846, p.215.
18. ibid, 7 November 1846, p.293.
19. Chief Secretary's, Outrage Reports 29/26315.
20. *Cork Examiner*, 2 November 1846.
21. ibid, 30 October 1846.
22. Chief Secretary's, Outrage Reports 29/26323.
23. ibid, 29/26317.
24. *Cork Examiner*, 2 October 1846.
25. Chief Secretary's Office, Outrage Reports 29/26755; Andrew Carbery was one of the most important merchants in Dungarvan – a ship owner, corn merchant etc. He is particularly remembered for helping the fishermen before and during the Famine.
26. *Cork Examiner*, 4 November 1846.

27. Chief Secretary's Office, Outrage Reports 29/37017, 29/1.
28. *Cork Examiner*, 22 January 1847.
29. Woodham Smith, Cecil, *The Great Hunger: Ireland 1845-9* (London, 1962) p.285.
30. Dungarvan Union: Minute Book, 22 August 1846 to 22 July 1847.
31. Kinealy, Christine, *This great calamity: The Irish Famine, 1845-52* p.585.
32. Dungarvan Union: Minute Book, 22 August 1846 to 22 July 1847.
33. Relief Commission Papers, 1845-7 20.030.
34. *Cork Examiner*, 27 October 1847.
35. Dungarvan Union: Minute Book, 7 August 1847 to 10 February 1848.
36. Kinealy, Christine, op. cit. p.587.
37. *Cork Examiner*, 14 June 1848.
38. ibid, 20 September 1848.
39. Dungarvan Union: Minute Book, 23 December 1848 to 1 December 1853.
40. ibid, 18 September 1849 Re. Watchmen; 23 November 1849 Re. Evictions. These and the references which follow are courtesy of John Young, Dungarvan.
41. ibid, 13 April 1850; 30 June 1850.
42. ibid, passim and 27 July 1850; 3 & 10 August 1850.
43. ibid, 21 December 1850 and 22 February 1851.
44. ibid, 27 April 1850 and 11 May 1850.
45. ibid, 6 & 27 July 1850; 17, 24 & 31 August 1850.
46. ibid, 3 August 1850.
47. ibid, 3 May 1851.
48. ibid, 8 & 29 March 1851.

Chapter 9

The famine in Waterford as reported in the local newspapers

EUGENE BRODERICK

Introduction

The Famine, although one of the central events in modern Irish history, has been relatively ignored by historians, attracting very little serious research.[1] In particular, there has been a dearth of studies of the impact of this calamity on Ireland's counties.[2] Moreover, historians have tended to concentrate on official sources, ignoring others especially local newspapers. This essay seeks to trace the course and impact of the famine on Waterford, as they were reported in the local press.

Four newspapers were examined. Two of them, *The Chronicle and Munster Advertiser* and the *Waterford Mail*, were printed throughout all the famine years. The *Waterford Freeman* ceased publication in the summer of 1847, and the *Waterford News* began to be published in September 1848. Of these, three appeared twice weekly, on Wednesdays and Fridays; only the News was issued weekly, on Fridays. In addition, *The Cork Examiner* provided much valuable material appertaining to the west of the county.

All of the newspapers, except the *Waterford Mail*, were broadly nationalist in politics and outlook. They supported Daniel O'Connell and his campaign for Repeal. The *Waterford Mail* was hostile to O'Connell and Repeal, and was conservative in its political beliefs. The politics of a journal often had a significant influence on the style and content of its reportage and editorials.

1. Extent of the Famine in Waterford

1845-1846

Throughout the summer months of 1845, Waterford Newspapers carried reports of a strange disease attacking potatoes in various European countries. By August, its appearance in parts of England, notably Kent and the Isle of Wight, was being reported. Articles on the malady by Professor Lindley, who was regarded as an expert on blight, were reprinted from *The Gardener's Chronicle*.

There was no sense of alarm evident in the journals at the prospect of the disease spreading to Ireland. On the contrary, there was a prevailing sense of optimism due to the fact that the potato crop was unusually abundant. In early August, *The Cork Examiner* observed upon '*the luxuriant character*' of the crop.[3] In the middle of the month it was declaring that '*there never perhaps was a finer crop than the present*'.[4] This theme was repeated in early September.[5]

However, on 10th September *The Cork Examiner* carried a report on Waterford stating that

> *the blight of the potato crop so much complained of in Belgium and several of the English counties has affected the crop and that to a considerable extent in our immediate locality and the surrounding districts. We are assured by a gentleman of vast experience that the injury sustained by potatoes from blight on his domain is very serious – that they are entirely unfit for use and he suggests that the potatoes so injured should be immediately dug out for use of pigs as if they are allowed to remain in the ground they will become for the increase of blight not even suitable as food for swine.*

Later in the month the *Waterford Freeman* expressed the fear that a considerable portion of the crop in the county would be lost.[6] By the middle of October, *The Cork Examiner* was commenting that reports of the universal prevalence of the disease nationally '*multiply upon us*' and that the blight appeared to have spread '*North, South, East, West*'.[7]

The newspapers fully appreciated the seriousness of potato failure in a country where so many were dependent on the crop. In October, the *Waterford Mail* wrote:

> *We are no alarmists but all that we hear, read and see respecting the potato crop – the staff of life in Ireland – admonish us that precaution and economy are necessary; that distress is nigh at hand – that famine and pestilence stalk gauntly forward through the dark but not distant future......To about six million it (the potato) is the chief, if not only, article of diet......Famine stares us in the face; and unless money be forthcoming for the purchase of food from abroad, pestilence and death are the certain consequence.*[8]

The *Waterford Freeman* enunciated the view that there was a calamity overhanging the Irish people, with the prospect of '*fearful and direful*' results.[9] In a prophetic phrase the paper declared: "*Great famine threatens the land.*"[10]

In response to the perceived impending crisis, advice was published on how to store potatoes so as to ensure they would not be infected by disease. Articles were reproduced from scientific and gardening journals. While the blight was a mystery, it was the opinion of most botanists that excess moisture caused the tubers to rot.[11] Accordingly, the advice given in the local journals was, in the words of the *Waterford Mail*, founded on "*the principle that the disease in the potatoes arises from a superfluity of moisture; and that the remedy consists in the evaporation of this moisture.*"[12] In effect, farmers were advised on methods of storage to counteract what had been diagnosed as a kind of wet rot.

The incidence of blight varied considerably between different parts of Ireland, though historians are of the view that Waterford, together with Antrim, Monaghan, and Clare, were the most severely affected counties.[13] In late October, the *Waterford Mail* carried an account of a meeting of the Board of Guardians of the Waterford Union at which it was reported that the disease was more extensive than was generally imagined.[14] The same journal tried to quantify the disaster:

> *The crop in the ground was the most abundant ever known. It exceeded the average by a fifth, if not a fourth part of the whole. Some loss could therefore be sustained. But the sudden pestilence which has come upon the crop has destroyed the excess: it has reduced the average quantity by one third and as the destruction is still progressing, we cannot calculate on more than one half being housed in a sound state.*[15]

While general notes of alarm abound in the coverage of the crop failure throughout September and October, specific information is absent. What details may be gleaned from the newspapers on its progress in the county is unsatisfactory, even contradictory. In late October the *Waterford Mail* printed a letter from a visitor to the estate of Lord Stuart de Decies at Dromana, in which the correspondent expressed the opinion that the blight was very serious and extensive. The situation was deemed to be most pressing as the disease was spreading rapidly.[16] The Waterford Board of Guardians were informed in late November that the Portlaw area was not badly affected.[17] A report to the same guardians on conditions in the Parish of Crook stated that the crop was not damaged to the extent as had been thought a few weeks previously:

> *The amount of the produce of this harvest is estimated at least one fourth greater than late years, and although the prevailing disease has more or less injured the general crop, still, as far as we can*

collect, there does not appear to be above one-fourth on the average affected; consequently there is no immediate deficiency of potatoes to be apprehended as an article of food in this district.[18]

This report was presented in early December. It reflected a growing sense of confidence, which had begun appearing in the press in November, that circumstances were not as urgent as had been feared. A letter in *The Chronicle and Munster Advertiser* expressed the opinion that the disease was not spreading, it having been checked in the more mature potatoes.[19] The *Waterford Mail* editorialised:

> *This fertile subject of alarm appears to have been thoroughly threshed out; and separating the truth from the exaggeration, the result appears to be – in the first place: the subsidence of panic; and in the next, the fact that enough remains sound and good to cover the loss, and with due care to furnish abundant food for the people...........distress will neither be severe nor lasting.*[20]

The Board of Guardians were reported to have stated that the situation was not as bad as had been thought.[21]

The various expressions of confidence indicated that the impact of the blight had been mitigated by the fact that it did not spread widely until October and November, by which time the early potatoes had been lifted. Moreover, the crop had been particularly prolific.[22] In 1845, however, newspaper coverage of the crop failure had been effectively confined to the eastern part of the county. The western part had not featured to any great degree. This was to change in 1846, and a very different picture was to emerge.

The Chronicle and Munster Advertiser had dissented from the optimistic view that the threat presented by the blight appeared to have abated. On 10th December it commented:

> *The cry of the failure of the potato crop is not exaggerated. The failure will inevitably make itself understood before next summer....We are apprehensive that from March next, the unfortunate labouring population in the rural districts will be very badly off.*

However, it was as early as January 1846 that newspapers were carrying reports of distress in rural areas, particularly around Dungarvan. The *Waterford Freeman* reported that 400 families in the town, comprising 2,500 individuals, principally fisherfolk, were in want of the necessaries of life. The failure of the potato and the high price of provisions meant that they had to endure much misery. According to the same edition, the local Board of Guardians had sent a memorial to the Lord Lieutenant in which it was claimed that half the potato crop was unfit for human food.[23]

In early February *The Cork Examiner* printed a letter in which the correspondent wrote that he/she had not entertained any serious fears for the safety of the crop until recently. Now the writer was convinced of the spread of blight and was of the opinion that the inhabitants of the coastal districts would be left hardly a quarter of the crop. The potatoes stored in pits in Dungarvan had been destroyed.[24] The *Waterford Freeman* reported that upwards of 5,000 persons were in a starving condition, with no prospect of relief.[25] In an editorial comment it spoke of people in many places being *"consigned to the jaws of hunger".*[26]

It is ironic that the journal which had forecast hardship in rural areas for 1846 should deny the existence of widespread distress in Dungarvan. On 11th February *The Chronicle and Munster Advertiser* carried an article which rejected the truth of reports that 5,000 people were in a state of starvation. It was contended that such reports had libelled the town and injured the feelings of its inhabitants.

> *It is no crime to be poor but it is a contemptible thing for a town that at all times heretofore maintained a high and independent position to be represented with 5/6 of the inhabitants starving.*

The *Waterford Freeman*, in a reply, attacked *The Chronicle and Munster Advertiser* and re-iterated its claims.[27] By 21st February, *The Chronicle and Munster Advertiser* had modified its position. It admitted the existence of extreme poverty and sought to clarify its earlier disavowals. The journal complained that it was concerned about Dungarvan's commercial reputation and the damage which adverse publicity could do it. *The Chronicle and Munster Advertiser's* initial report, it would appear, had been influenced by a bourgeois mercantile perspective, and it's subsequent modification was a response to hostile criticism in other sections of the press and in the town itself.[28] This modified attitude meant that the newspaper's editorial perspective was now more consonant with that of the *Waterford Freeman* and *The Cork Examiner.*

If *The Chronicle and Munster Advertiser* had questioned, albeit temporarily, the prevalence of distress in Dungarvan, the *Waterford Mail*, (consistent with its view of the previous year that panic had subsided), was not satisfied that there existed any substantial evidence of potato shortages and famine conditions in the country.[29] It used the occasion of a parliamentary return on the price of potatoes to attack the Prime Minister, Sir Robert Peel, who seemed

> *determined to make parliament and country believe in the existence of famine and pestilence, though the latter is only 'apprehended' as yet; and the former has not given the usual symptoms of its application by the rise of the price of general staple of food.*

Readers were reminded that *'we have been already living for nine months out of the twelve on the produce of the late short crop.'*[30] The corollary of the rejection of the notion of famine was the absence of any reportage of misery in the county, including Dungarvan.

However, the *Waterford Freeman* was certain that there existed real suffering in that town. It reported Dr. Hally, the Parish Priest, stating from the altar that he knew of poor families living for several days on a meal of bran.[31] According to the newspaper, the condition of people in the rural districts was even more deplorable.

> *The accounts from the surrounding districts relative to the condition of the peasantry are heartrending and alarming in the extreme. In Killongford, Kilrossanty, Comeragh, etc. the stock of potatoes is consumed and the inhabitants of these places are now using their seed potatoes, which will last them but a very short time; this is the case with many of the farmers, but the condition of the cottiers and labourers is far more deplorable.*[32]

The *Waterford Freeman* wrote emotionally:

> *Famine and pestilence are preying on the vitals of the people. Hundreds of human beings – honest industrious men go forth in search of employment and again return to their wretched provisionless cabins to witness children crying out "Mother, give something to eat; I am hungry", but alas! the mother has nothing! Her husband is idle and could get no work and so the big scalded tear that marks her pallid and emaciated cheek silently answers the heart piercing appeal of the hungry child. They go to bed supperless and the morning sun rises and casts its bright beams on the gloomy cabin only to awaken them to a more poignant feeling of their condition and to make their misery look them more vividly in the face for they have no breakfast. This is the condition of thousands.*[33]

The evidence of the local newspapers regarding the potato failure of

1845/1846 in Waterford suggests that the abundance of the crop and the late arrival of the blight ensured that in many places the peasantry escaped undue hardship. However, this was not the case in Dungarvan and surrounding districts. It was the consensus view of the *Waterford Freeman*, *The Cork Examiner* and, however reluctantly, *The Chronicle and Munster Advertiser*, that there existed here misery on a considerable scale. If the journals were correct in the summer of 1846, another failure of the potato crop would have meant disaster for the peasants and poorer classes in many of the county's western areas. Such a failure occurred in 1846, more complete and widespread than in the previous year.

1846-1847:

The potato blight returned with virulence in the summer of 1846. In the middle of August the *Waterford Mail* reported that '*in some districts fields of potatoes which at night appeared perfectly healthy have next morning presented the aspect of withering blight.*'[34] Later in the month it declared the general crop to have failed everywhere.[35] *The Chronicle and Munster Advertiser* announced that '*by report, by inspection and by universal admission*' it was lost beyond recovery.[36] The *Waterford Freeman* painted a similar dismal picture.[37] This time there were no editorials as to the seriousness of the situation – it was obvious to all.

In late August various relief committees met in order to formulate a response to the unfolding crisis. The one responsible for the Barony of Upperthird was concerned about the fact that the labourer and cottiers classes had no grain crops on which to fall back.[38] The Committee for Clashmore stated that the potato crop was totally destroyed in its district and there was an urgent necessity for immediate action to prevent famine and destitution.[39] The central relief committee of the Barony of Decies-within-Drum met on 26th August to consider the prospect for the cottier classes.[40]

As with the previous season, Dungarvan and district dominated press coverage. On 3rd September the *Waterford Freeman* announced that the potato crop was destroyed in the locality. The same edition carried a report that not a morsel of bread was to be had in any baker's shop in the town. A few days later the same newspaper observed that deaths were more numerous in the locality at present than they were for many years as a consequence of bad food and hunger.[41] In early October *The Chronicle and Munster Advertiser* wrote of people starving and hundreds surviving on a meal of cabbage and salt in twenty four hours.[42]

By winter the situation had deteriorated dramatically. A correspondent of the *Waterford Freeman* wrote:

The cabins in this district are, indeed, miserable hovels. Their appearance denote the extreme wretchedness and destitution of their inhabitants, and afford them but a poor shelter against the inclemency of this weather. Fuel they have none – their food now consists chiefly of sprats that are brought to Dungarvan from the more western towns along the coast, and occasionally a scanty portion of Indian meal...... Fever has visited the people and carried off its victims. Starvation, it is said, has likewise, by its slow and terrible stages, caused two deaths.[43]

During the first six months of 1847, reports of deaths increase significantly. From the evidence of the newspapers, starvation and fever were widespread. In early January it was reported that 24 persons had died in Dungarvan and Abbeyside after three or four days illness.[44] Mortality was prevailing to an alarming degree, according to the *Waterford Freeman*. Scarcely a day went by that six or seven corpses were not buried in the old churchyard at Abbeyside. In the workhouse inmates were infected with dysentery.[45] Even the more circumspect *Waterford Mail* was moved to comment:

The fever cart is hourly through the town of Dungarvan; the poor room keepers are starving, as well as the industrious dealers in fruit, fish, turf, and knitting.[46]

In February conditions were no better. Deaths at the rate of half a dozen a day were being recorded. It was the opinion of the *Waterford Freeman* that Dungarvan ".*was bidding fair to out rival Skibereen in its dismal catalogue of destitution"*[47] By the last week of the month the Catholic Clergy were administering the last rites to no less than fifteen to eighteen persons daily. The *Waterford Freeman* put the weekly death rate at around thirty. The cause of death was not actual starvation, but a want of sufficiency of food.[48] This would suggest mortality was due primarily to fever.

The same newspaper carried a description of conditions at Abbeyside

The destitution at Abbeyside is even greater than in Dungarvan. We visited from fifty to sixty houses in some of the lanes of the village, and we solemnly declare we never witnessed such misery and destitution in any place before; every article of furniture, every stitch of bedclothes they had were sold and pledged; their bed, a sop of straw strewed on the damp, cold floor, without blanket or quilt, and the rain coming down through the roofs of wretched cabins. Many of the poor creatures were ailing with a bowel complaint, some of them in fever; but there was scarcely a house we entered that we were not assured that someone of the family died of the effects of want and cold. In the number of houses we entered there could not have been less than 300 human beings, and over 250 of whom we found to have been living eking out a miserable existence on three scanty meals of yellow meal stirabout, with hot water and sugar, in the week; and very often only two meals of the same meal and water in a week.

The correspondent entered the house of a man named Sheehy.

We found him on his knees offering up his privations and sufferings to his Creator; his poor wife was striving to console her famishing children by promising them that 'God would send them relief to-morrow.' They did not eat a morsel of food that day, and the mother said that herself and John, her husband, did not care about themselves, but the poor children; When they are asking for something to eat and when we have nothing to give them, their cries go through our hearts; they must (added the unfortunate woman in a subdued tone) go to bed supperless tonight, and 'tis long since they got anything like a supper or dinner before.'......When she got up to open the door, she faltered, and fell prostrate on the floor from exhaustion. This is but a faint idea of the condition of the poor of Abbeyside.[49]

In March *The Chronicle and Munster Advertiser* expressed the view that Dungarvan *'presented one of the most fearful exhibitions of extreme destitution, misery and starvation that was ever beheld in any country or age'.*[50] Surrounding areas were also affected. A correspondent recorded his/her impressions, having *'travelled much'* in the rural districts of the county, particularly Ring, Ballynacourty, Old Parish, and as far as Ardmore.

To particularize one or a dozen houses out of each locality would be impossible. Every house you enter (with the exception of the occasional strong farmer's) presents nothing but one black mass of the most deplorable wretchedness. Not a spark of fire on the hearths of nine out of every ten of the wretched houses. And where you do see a 'spark' of fire little larger than a tea-cup, you will behold the squalid and misery-stricken creatures crouching round it, like spectres, with not a human lineament traceable upon their countenances. As to food, good or bad, they have none.

The correspondent continued:

> *In the districts I have above enumerated......there cannot be less than TWENTY or THIRTY DEATHS from STARVATION each DAY. Coffin-making is the staple trade of the country; every turn you take you see them in dozens being brought to the rural districts; sometimes in cars, sometimes under men's arms, and not infrequently on women's heads. I lately met several times on the Slievegrine Mountain half naked women going home and the only commodity they were able to bring to Dungarvan was COFFINS ON THEIR HEADS.*[51]

In April *The Chronicle and Munster Advertiser* reported that the aggregate deaths daily from starvation from every part of the county, but more particularly Dungarvan, Abbeyside, and the surrounding rural district, were over 50.[52] On the 22nd April the *Waterford Mail* stated that mortality from fever and famine was on the increase in the town.

By May fever was raging. The *Waterford Mail* spoke of infected people lying in the streets and lanes.[53] According to *The Cork Examiner*, fever and dysentery were prevalent. It recorded the discovery of a dead body on the side of the road near Ballyduff. At Abbeyside two sisters died in the same house. The next day a father, son, and daughter died in the one house in Dungarvan, while four persons suffered a similar fate at Ballycurreen.[54] Later in the month the *Waterford Mail* reported on the body of a man who had died of typhus being left in a shed in Dungarvan for days.[55]

While fever was present everywhere, hunger was also casting its shadow. The *Waterford Mail* commented that starvation, combined with malignant sickness, presented itself to the observer wherever he/she looked.[56] In a sentence redolent of the horrors of famine the journal wrote:

> *There is no nettle, or a bit of water cress to be found near Dungarvan, as the starving strangers consumed them all.*[57]

In early June it was reported that a sixty year old man had died outside the town's workhouse, and that grass was discovered in his stomach and bowels.[58]

Lismore also featured in press reportage. On the occasion of the Presentment Sessions for the Barony of Coshmore and Coshbride, held at Lismore Courthouse, a crowd of peasants converged on the town. *The Chronicle and Munster Advertiser* stated that the '*deep marks*' of starvation and famine were to be seen on their countenances. People were described as '*hunger maddened*'.[59]

A letter, dated 18th January, 1847, and printed in the *Waterford Freeman*, remarked on the *'awful destitution'* prevailing in Lismore and the surrounding rural districts. Three thousand people were in a state of serious distress. It was claimed that a meal of turnips every 48 hours was the regimen on which two-thirds of the poor had to subsist; the remaining third had a meal of cabbage and turnips every 24 hours.[60]

It was reported in the *Waterford Mail* that on Good Friday twenty one inquests were held in the town. One of them concerned a Patrick Coleman, from near Tallow. He had been found dead on a public road near Lismore. A verdict of death by cold and starvation was returned. A woman, Margaret Flynn, making her way from Ballyduff to the poor-house, was overcome by exhaustion within 50 yards of the building. She fell senseless, and on being discovered was admitted. She died the next day. A verdict similar to that on Coleman was returned.[61] Fever and famine were reported in the town in May.[62] In early June the *Waterford Mail* reported that several people in the vicinity of Lismore had died or were dying in quarry holes and caves, of fever and destitution.[63]

The horrors of the famine visited Kilbeg and Kilcalf, near Tallow. *The Cork Examiner* published a dramatic letter in March. The correspondent wrote of a *'mass of squalid misery.'*

> *I am anxious to avail myself of the opportunity to inform the public of what, perhaps, it is not generally aware of; and it is that this ill-fated locality may for wretchedness be placed almost in the same rank with Skibereen and Mayo. While I am writing these few lines, in a miserable cabin there lie the gaunt and ghastly bodies of a mother and her son, found dead in each other's arms by the remaining little boy, who had gone out a day or two before to beg something for their relief. And this morning, before men had left their beds, the same sad postulant was at doors, begging wherewith to purchase coffins to consign them to their mother earth. In fact, as an intelligent farmer from the place remarked to me yesterday, it is impossible to walk in that part of the country without being frightened by the rabid, hunger-stricken faces which meet you on your way - faces which you can no longer recognise, so altered were they from what they were. Nor is the foregoing the only – no, not the tenth – instance of death from starvation which has occurred in this locality.*[64]

Newspaper evidence suggests real hardship and distress in the Bonmahon area. Coroner's inquests were held in February on the bodies of two persons, a man and a child, the jury returning verdicts of *'death from want of food.'* According to the *Waterford Freeman*

*There are twenty persons in such a miserable state at Bonmahon
that the Coroner told us he expected to be called out to hold
inquests on them before the end of the week.*[65]

More inquests were held in early March. Two persons were adjudged
to have died from starvation. This brought to five the number of victims
of starvation within a space of three days.[66] Two days later inquests
were being reported on the bodies of three persons, all of whom were
deemed to have starved to death.[67]

The evidence of the newspapers for 1846-1847 conveys the clear
impression that famine conditions prevailed in the western part of
County Waterford, particularly in Dungarvan and its locality. What is
significant is the broad consensus in the journals that a crisis existed.

While the *Waterford Freeman* was the most prolific and graphic in
its accounts of sufferings and destitution, and the *Waterford Mail* the
most restrained both in terms of the amount of coverage and the style
thereof, there was a substantial similarity in the reportage of the local
press.

Regarding famine deaths, reports in newspapers will not furnish
evidence which will satisfy the exacting criteria demanded by statistical
analysis. However, the general observation may be made that the local
press recorded a significant increase in the rate of mortality in 1847.[68]
The death rate peaked in the spring, and this is consistent with the
pattern nationally.[69]

The causes of death were starvation and fever. During the Great
Famine, only a minority of deaths can be attributed directly to
starvation. These remain the exception rather than the norm and were
concentrated in the most deprived localities.[70] In Waterford, on the
evidence of newspapers, people did starve to death. Such reports were
not always accurate, the cause of death having been attributed
popularly, rather than determined medically. Furthermore, the exact
number or anything approximating it, cannot be learned from the
journals. Notwithstanding these reservations and qualifications, the fact
is that people did die of starvation, and this is clear evidence of the
existence of severe destitution.

Fever accounted for most deaths. Three diseases became widely
epidemic between 1845-1850: dysentery, relapsing fever, and typhus,
the latter two often given the general designation 'famine fever'.[71]
Relapsing fever and typhus were carried by lice; and lack of cleanliness, unchanged clothing, and crowding together for warmth due to
lack of fuel provided the ideal conditions for lice to multiply.[72] Typhus
was the more fatal disease and during the famine years its mortality
rate in general was three or four times higher than relapsing fever.[73]

In their reports, the local newspapers rarely distinguished between the diseases. They just spoke of 'fever' as the cause of death. On the basis of the evidence of national trends and other local studies, it is reasonable to assume that typhus and relapsing fever were the most common diseases in the affected areas.[74] On the evidence of the press, fever had reached the county not later than December 1846, and had reached epidemic proportions by the summer of 1847.

Dysentery was widespread, particularly in Dungarvan. In January and May this disease was mentioned in the newspapers, and in the *Waterford Freeman's* account of Abbeyside in February, the reference to people ailing with a bowel disorder may be consistent with this malady. While the relationship between food deprivation and fever is rather imperfect, some relationship exists in the case of dysentery. Unsuitable food and inadequate diet can make people more liable to infection.[75] The dispensary doctor in Skibereen, Dr. Donovan, pointed out that *'starvation induces dysentery.'*[76] A recent medical historian of the famine has written that *'in most parts hard hit by famine, dysentery was rampant before fever had begun to spread.'*[77] In January, a *'vast number'* of the inmates of Dungarvan workhouse had this disease. This would suggest that people were starving or at least had a very inadequate diet.

Those who died in 1846-7 were predominantly labourers and cottiers. They were the most vulnerable to want of food and disease. The nexus between poverty and mortality during the famine has been well established by scholars. However, if the wealthy were immune to starvation, they were not to fevers. A Waterford physician, Dr. Carroll, observed that fever fatality increased in the ratio of rank and respectability of the individuals attacked.[78] Typhus, especially, took a severe toll.

Reports in the local press offer evidence to corroborate these general observations. In May a correspondent wrote in *The Cork Examiner*:

> *The rich for their own, if not for humanity's sake, should in time look to the frightful and dangerous condition of these poor creatures, from which (sic) malignant pestilence might find its way to their own door. By night some of them, though not actually recovered from fever, but driven the gnawings of hunger, leave the fetid straw on which they were stretched and go around the town clamouring for something to eat at the houses of the wealthy classes. And here let me observe that every rich person that got fever in this town died.*[79]

In the same month the *Waterford Mail* recorded:

> *Fever and pestilence have been doing the worst here among the upper classes, while famine and destitution are quickly thinning the numbers of the poor.*[80]

One further point might be made here. It may be remembered that parts of the county, especially Dungarvan and its locality were, according to the newspapers, severely affected by the blight of 1845-46. The events of the following season would suggest the accuracy of this reportage. The failure of '46-'47 was catastrophic because labourers and cottiers had no food reserves, these having been exhausted by the efforts to survive the blight of the previous year. Thus the circumstances of 1845-46, as reported in the local press, help explain the level of destitution of the following year; while those of '46-'47 suggest that the reports of the impact of the previous year's blight were substantially accurate, and offer another reason why they should be treated seriously.

1847-1848

The partial and total failures of the potato crop of the previous two seasons was followed by a virtually blight free one in 1847-48. In June, the *Waterford Mail* reported that the appearances of potatoes throughout the county was most promising.[81] The towns and adjoining districts of Tallow, Lismore, Cappoquin, and Dungarvan were visited by a correspondent of *The Cork Examiner*, who commented that the condition of the crop was most satisfactory.[82] A similar story was recorded in Whitechurch, Ardmore, Kilgobinet, and Ballinacourty.[83]

The blight free crop of 1847 was reported with enthusiasm. However, there was no analysis in the reportage. The facts are that the potato acerage planted in that season was small, though the yield was high. The total crop nationally would seem to have been less than in the disease ridden year of 1846.[84] Labourers and cottiers in 1847 had to suffer the cumulative effects of a small crop return, a total crop failure, and a partial crop failure in the space of three years. The circumstances of the peasants, therefore, could not have improved dramatically in the autumn of '47. This fact was only hinted at in the local press. While there were some reports of continuing suffering and deprivation, they were so intermittent and desultory as to be of no real value in assessing the extent of destitution in the county.

In September *The Chronicle and Munster Advertiser* reported that people were dying 'fast' in Dungarvan. Seventeen people had been prayed for on one Sunday. Dysentery was prevalent and all classes were attacked by it.[85] In January 1848 the skeletal body of a man who had died of starvation was found on the side of the road near Dungarvan.[86] In the same month a coroner's inquest was held on the death of a poor woman. She had been found in a state of exhaustion on the streets of Lismore. A bed was procured for her, but she died during the night. The Jury returned a verdict that she had died '*due to weakness and general debility, brought on by want.*'[87]

In February *The Chronicle and Munster Advertiser* commented:

> *The Coroner is likely to have much duty in Lismore Union during this season; the deaths from starvation are likely to be shortly so numerous that the coroner cannot find it convenient to attend them all.* [88]

Coverage of the famine in the local newspapers effectively ceased from June 1847. This, on reflection, should not cause surprise. The improvement in the crop in the summer was regarded as a signal of the return to normalcy, something which would have been widely welcomed. The readers of newspapers had been fed a diet of news concerning the diet of rotten potatoes, and very often the diet of nothing, which had been the plight of many in the county. Editors and readers were probably *'famine fatigued'*, i.e. emotionally drained from recording and reading about starvation, privation, and death. Any apparent respite from the dire tidings of famine would have been seized upon with alacrity and gratitude.

Furthermore, the absence of detailed reportage after June '47 is explained by the nature of newspapers themselves. They concentrate their attention on news items for a time, and then turn their attention to others. What are deemed more newsworthy reports will displace less *'interesting'* ones. For example, *The Chronicle and Munster Advertiser* had been reporting at reasonably regular intervals through the spring of 1847 on the condition of tenants at Ballysaggartmore, near Lismore. In May, after the absence of reports for a number of editions, it returned to the subject. The absence was explained thus: *"We since had not room, owing to the press of parliamentary and other reports, to return to the subject as we promised* [89] In the late summer of that year, and in subsequent months, politics elections, the death of Daniel O'Connell, and the divisions in Young Ireland were the concerns of editors – not the jaded facts of a famine, which had been so often retailed, and the probable end of which had been heralded by the advent of a healthy crop.

2. Relief Measures
1845-46

The British Prime Minister, Sir Robert Peel, acted promptly to address the possible problems associated with the failure of the potato crop in 1845, viz., price inflation and starvation. As early as November he had authorised the purchase of £100,000 worth of Indian meal. By January 1846, these supplies were stored in depots around the country. They did not open until the late spring, the first on 28th March. The food so supplied, usually a mixture of Indian meal and oatmeal, was seen as a guarantee against profiteering by local traders and as a last line of defence against starvation.[90]

The Waterford *News*papers contain little information on the operation of the relief measures locally. At a public meeting in the city in April, a Mr. Clark, a member of the corporation, commented that the importation of Indian corn by the government was having beneficial results.[91] This was not the opinion of the *Waterford Freeman*, however.

> *When will the famishing poor of this city and neighbourhood be able to obtain a single meal of good food......We know the government have stored Indian corn for their use, but they might as well have it in Van Diemen's Land. It is stated that it will be given at one penny per pound, but no time has been fixed to open the granaries; the poor are now paying 8 1/2d. per stone for potatoes.[92]*

It was reported that a ton and a half of maize was landed from a government cutter at Tramore in early June.[93] In the same month the *Waterford Mail* alleged that food was being sold by the relief committee in Dungarvan at 1s 4d. per stone, while local traders were charging only one penny more.[94] These criticisms were rejected by the *Waterford Freeman*. It claimed that the *Waterford Mail* was seeking to convey the impression that the committee afforded scarcely any relief to the town's poor. According to the *Waterford Freeman*, the shopkeepers charged more than 1s 5d., while the committee had made arrangements to sell the meal at one shilling per stone to upwards of 600 families.[95] This conflict of opinion was indicative of fundamentally conflicting perceptions. The attitude of the *Waterford Mail* was probably influenced by its belief that there was no serious privation, and consequently, it sought to disparage the efforts of the relief committee.

The main method of famine relief adopted by Peel's government was public works – a tried and tested remedy in dealing with Irish distress. The cabinet decided that the works should be jointly financed, with half the cost coming from local taxation, the balance in the form of a Treasury Grant. The administration of the scheme was entrusted to the Board of Works. Legislation facilitating these measures was enacted in March.[96]

Applications for government funding were made to the Board of Works by local grand juries. The Board, having examined the proposed schemes, accepted or rejected them. Employment on relief works was given to people who possessed relief tickets, which were issued by local relief committees – bodies composed of the gentry of a locality.[97] The Board of Works was deluged by applications. This caused delays, which adversely affected the efficacy of local relief efforts. The Tramore Relief Committee found it necessary to forward a memorial to the Lord Lieutenant requesting him to use the influence of the government in expediting the commencement of works already approved by magistrates and rate payers.[98]

The most serious problem in Waterford, however, was the apparent inadequacy of the provision of relief works. In late June, the *Waterford Freeman* carried the following report from Dungarvan:

> *At Abbeyside and Ringnasilloge there are only about 180 persons at works, including masons and carriers. These latter two are the only works which have begun in the immediate vicinity of this town.*[99]

The comments regarding the inadequate amount of public works locally would appear to have been correct. In March Mr. Dobree, the official in charge of relief in Waterford had written Trevelyan: *"From all that I can collect no measures whatever have been adopted in any part of this district (beyond private charities) to afford relief when the crisis may come."*100 More recently, Professor Mary Daly has examined the breakdown of expenditure on public works in the period up to August 1846, and has concluded that two counties badly affected by blight, Waterford and Monaghan, received very small sums.[101]

Peel's response to the potato failure has generally been praised in Ireland. As early as October 1845 *The Cork Examiner* expressed great confidence in the Prime Minister's abilities.[102] In July, 1846 after he had left office, the same journal commented:

> *But for the wise precautionary measures of Sir Robert Peel, it is now universally admitted that this country would have been plunged into all the horrors of the famine.*[103]

However, the *Waterford Freeman* was no admirer of the British politician. In November 1845 it wrote:

> *Great famine threatens the land, yet the great ones pause, rulers cogitate and their deliberations end in naught. We fear he (Peel) will delay in the vain hope that the evil hour will be removed.*[104]

In February it re-iterated its belief in government delay: *"Hunger with all its concomitant disease ravages the land and has taken prisoner a noble people whilst the government sits idly by until the evil may become irremediable.'*[105] This negative attitude owed more to politics than any considered assessment of Peel's actions.

1846-1847

The total failure of the potato crop in the summer of 1846 made the situation significantly more serious than in the previous season. There was a change of government in July, with Lord John Russell, a Whig, becoming Prime Minister. The Whig Administration was committed to the principles of free trade and private enterprise. He discontinued the importation of Indian meal, concentrating on the provision of employment, whereby people could secure the means to buy food.

In late August 1846, legislation was enacted whereby half the cost of public works in a local area was to be levied on Grand Juries. The balance was to be provided by central funds in the form of a loan, not a grant, as under Peel's administration. The effect of this policy was that all the cost of relief works were to be borne by local taxpayers. The Board of Works was to have more control over the operation of schemes to ensure greater efficiency.[106] The practical application of this policy in Waterford, on the evidence of the newspapers, was a disaster.

Delays

A real sense of urgency is evident in the local press in September. The second failure of the potato crop in as many years meant severe hardships for a large number of the county's population. The previous schemes of relief works had ceased by order of a treasury minute in July. The purpose of this cessation was to release people from public works to help save the harvest.[107] The fact that there was none was made worse by the absence of relief measures in September. The *Waterford Freeman* commented that most relief committees no longer furnished assistance and impoverished labourers were now left to their own resources.

Presentment sessions – bodies composed of local taxpayers with the ultimate responsibility of repaying relief costs – met in September to propose schemes to the Board of Works. Sessions were held at Dungarvan in mid-September; at Clashmore and Lismore later in the month. This represented a reasonably prompt local response given the date of the enactment of the enabling statute.

From mid October, complaints of delays in providing public works were quite common in the newspapers, particularly in the *Waterford Freeman*, which observed:

> *Nearly two months have elapsed since the extreme destitution that is upon us was foretold; the famine that has come was foreseen.*

Preparation for the approaching calamity was called....the task was commenced....the Board of Works had its orders; presentments were made.... and yet, nearly two months have gone by, and what is done for the dying man, or the wailing child.[108]

In December the same points were repeated. Despite the voting of large sums of money at presentment sessions, many destitute people still lacked employment.[109] A letter dated 18 January 1847, expressing concern about conditions in Lismore, urged

that the Board of Works should order their officials acting in this county to approve at once the roads already passed by a full bench of magistrates in last September, and for which a sum of 1,400 pounds has been granted.[110]

The delay in starting relief schemes was due to the centralisation of administration. Every proposed measure had to be examined by Board of Work's officials. As a result, distress was frequently far advanced before works commenced. It is the general consensus of historians that this was a major defect in the government's response, the consequences of which were publicised and criticised in the contemporary Waterford press.

Wages

The Treasury decided that those employed on relief schemes were to be paid by task work. Wages were fixed to enable the moderate worker earn from 10d. to 1s. per day. Most labourers were weakened by hunger and could only, with difficulty, earn 10d. which proved to be the average wage.[111] In Waterford as elsewhere, escalating food prices were a feature of the autumn and winter of 1846-47. However, between August 1846 and January 1847, the price of Indian meal doubled. Wages which were adequate to feed a family in August, could no longer do so by November. For those dependent on the wages paid by public works, the economics of survival were virtually impossible by January 1847.[112]

The Chronicle and Munster Advertiser and *Waterford Freeman* were very vocal in their criticism of the rate of payment on relief works. As early as September 1846, the former paper believed it would present real difficulties:

There is, however, one great stumbling block in the act, which renders its provisions in the main point totally inoperative, at all events, perfectly inadequate to the present emergency – that is the restricted form of the Treasury Minute which regulates the rate of wages. Never was there so unwise or so mistatesmanlike a restriction placed upon anything.[113]

In October it denounced the stubborn adherence to this method of payment.[114] Later in the same month a correspondent in Dungarvan wrote:

It (the rate of payment) is next to starvation according to the present price of food. It will scarcely support the labourer himself. What then will his wife and children do? In the name of God, I solemnly ask, must they, will they starve? The price of Indian meal is now two shillings a stone. The labourer had a shilling a day last summer under the Board of Works, when his meal was only ten pence per stone. So then instead of raising the wages in proportion to the rise in the price of food, they lower it as the food rises. What is the meaning of this?[115]

The *Waterford Freeman* also commented on the inadequacy of the wage rates, which made it impossible for a labourer to support himself and his family:

Indian meal is being sold a two shillings per stone and it is dearer than that in some places. We will suppose that a labouring man has four children, himself and his wife to feed on ten pence per day; and allowing him six full days to work in each week, he will be able to earn only five shillings. This would buy two stones and a half of Indian meal, which, divided by seven, the number of days in the week, would leave five pounds for the support of the family each day; and these five pounds divided again by six, the number of the family, would leave five-sixths of a pound to each member for a whole day; and, to carry out the calculation still further, if five-sixths of a pound be divided by three, the usual and ordinary number of the poor man's meals in the day, there will be only five-eighteenths of a pound for each repast. This slender supply would not be sufficient to feed a chicken.[116]

Thus the newspapers identified a major flaw in the government's response and engaged in a sustained criticism of it (the response). There was a call for a change of policy involving the payment of a living wage. Professor Cormac Ó Gráda has written that if labourers had been granted such a wage during the winter of 1846 '47 then no doubt an adequate supply of food would have been forthcoming from across the Irish sea or further afield.[117]

Reproductive Works

The most common form of relief works was the construction of roads. This was entirely consistent with the laissez-faire principles of the Whigs, by which care had to be taken not to convey undue benefit on any one person as a consequence of a public works scheme.[118] While the Treasury insisted on projects combining a high social and low private value, there were demands in Ireland for reproductive works, meaning land reclamation, drainage, and estate improvement.[119]

The *Waterford Freeman* wanted the construction of railways to be included in relief schemes.[120] In November 1846 there was a meeting in Dungarvan of the principal landed proprietors of the county, at which it was demanded that public works be of a *'reproductive'* nature and that tax not be expended on useless projects.[121] The *Waterford Freeman* denounced many of the schemes approved of by the Board of Works.

> *Heaven knows we have had enough of artificial employment, of hill cutting, and hollow filling, and useless road making. In the barony of Decies-without-Drum from £40,000 to £50,000 have been squandered on these artificial sorts of works......Look at the hospital road at Abbeyside. Why the place is now in a worse state than it was before any road was there.[122]*

It re-iterated these sentiments when it claimed that projects, in too many instances, were of positive injury to the county.[123]

The Treasury did modify somewhat the regulations governing a public works so as to permit some *'reproductive'* ones. However, the modifications were so circumscribed by conditions as to make little difference.[124] Drainage schemes could be included in certain circumstances, but these never represented more than 5 per cent of the total cost of relief schemes.[125] One landlord who benefited was Kiely Usher of Ballysaggartmore. Railways were also covered by the new regulations, and the Waterford-Limerick Railway took advantage. These concessions were no more than mere tinkerings with a flawed system. Press criticisms of the useless nature of many projects were justified. One historian of famine relief efforts has written:

> *Having decided to make the cost of public works a local burden, the government should have seen to it that the capital was not wasted. The opportunity to improve the country was lost, however, and the effect was to increase the demands on already heavily mortgaged property by leaving a heavy debt to be repaid out of rates.[126]*

Misery

Public works employed large numbers of people. There were 3,110 persons on relief schemes in Waterford by the week ending 8th November 1846.[127] This figure had risen dramatically to 8,535 in the county and 255 in the city by the week ending 26th December.[128] For many, if not the majority it was a miserable experience.

Hunger was widespread. The *Waterford Freeman* commented:

> *To expect that a man would hold out working on one meal a day is preposterous and heartless; yet any man working on the public works, having three or four in the family, cannot afford to have one morsel more than one meal of Indian meal, without milk or anything else, in every twenty-four hours. To our knowledge, numbers of labourers employed on the roads in this neighbourhood are lingering out a miserable existence in this deplorable condition; and we have heard them to say that, though they go at the appointed hours to breakfast and dinner they have to return again to the works without tasting a morsel of food, except merely a little Indian meal stirabout in the morning, in order to share the miserable pittance with the rest of the family in the evening.[129]*

The bureaucracy associated with the administration of the works often contributed to the hardship experienced by labourers. In January, 200-300 were discharged from the works at Comeragh because they did not have tickets from the official in charge. In addition, some labourers were taken off schemes near their homes and sent a distance of five or six miles to others. It proved to be difficult to be punctual in these circumstances, and tardiness was penalised by a deduction in wages.[130] Nor were wages always paid on time. It was observed by the *Waterford Freeman* in November 1846 that '*some of the pay clerks of the public works are very attentive in the discharge of their duty, whilst others of them are very negligent, and do not pay the labourers at the appointed time.*'[131] A few months later a correspondent in the same journal was complaining that payment was up to three weeks late at times.[132]

The fact that children sought employment was indicative of the extent of misery in parts of the county. It was reported in Dungarvan that

> *A large number of children, from ten years to thirteen years of age, is employed on the public works here breaking stones. It was really affecting to see those poor little creatures asking for tickets to get work, on Tuesday morning last. 'Give me a ticket, sir, I am in want' was the cry of these young labourers to the officers of the*

relief committee. What could have induced the parents of these children to have taken them from the schools of the Christian Brothers, that nursery of virtue and morality. Certainly nothing less than the direst necessity and want – their little hands are already blistered from hammers.[133]

While the conditions which prevailed on works schemes were often appalling in terms of human misery, the alternative – no employment – was worse. This was the fate of between 40 and 50 Abbeyside fishermen who were refused tickets for work. It was reported that as a consequence of an official's decision, they went hungry.[134]

End of Public Works

The scale of destitution overwhelmed the relief schemes, nationally and locally, as the administrative machinery could not cope. A policy of dependence on public works was simply inadequate and inoperable, the death rate affording visible proof of this fact. In January 1847 Russell's government decided to abandon them and have recourse to an emergency scheme of direct outdoor relief, the chosen model of which was the soup kitchen. The new policy could not become effective immediately. Public works continued in operation, but in March the authorities began dismissing those in such employment. While relief schemes had produced a catalogue of miseries in Waterford, the circumstances of the dismissed employees was even worse. Soup kitchens were not in place to offer basic sustenance. On 4th April the *Waterford Mail* commented that it knew of none yet in operation. Ten days later it reported that soup and bread had been given out for the first time in Dungarvan, on Monday, 19th April.

Dismissals in the absence of alternative relief measures meant widespread suffering. On the evidence of the newspapers one area adversely affected was Tramore. Heretofore, this town and district had not attracted any significant journalistic attention, there having been only one report of distress. This had been in January 1847, when the Parish Priest, Dr. Cantwell, announced that no less than four persons had perished of starvation in the locality.[135] In March the *Waterford Freeman* reported *'great distress'* as a consequence of the dismissal of 400 labourers.[136] A fortnight later it commented:

We are sorry to find that distress is now rapidly accumulating at Tramore......A large number of men have been thrown off the public works in so precipitate and reckless a manner that sufficient means of relief could not be procured from any private source in time to meet the emergency.[137]

The Lord Lieutenant was prevailed upon to issue a proclamation for the holding of an extraordinary presentment session at Tramore for the purpose of completing the unfinished works in the neighbourhood.[138] The session passed a sum of £1,500 to afford relief to the destitute of the district.[139]

The dismissals resulted in terrible scenes in Dungarvan. On March 18th over two thousand dismissed labourers came into the town, accompanied by their starving families, with a view to seeking admission to the workhouse, or getting outdoor relief. No such relief was available.

> *This melancholy news threw the people into black despair, and the scene which then followed was one of the most heart-rending and awfully deplorable sights that you could at all witness or even imagine. Children bawling with hunger and asking their parents for something to eat, and the parents crying out, 'what will we do at all – we will not be able to go home alive'. Not one in Dungarvan ever saw so much misery, wretchedness, and want collected together on any one day before. In fact, they were one vast multitude of living skeletons covered with rags; in vain you looked amongst them for a plump, ruddy cheeked Irish peasant.*[140]

People were reported to be starving to death. A correspondent of the *Waterford Freeman* wrote a few days later:

> *I saw a number of them on the strand, down from the high road, scraping a species of sea weed called doolamaun off the stones and eating it raw. These weeds are enough to kill them, but what will not the dint of hunger make men do. The strands here are now as bare from anything like human food as the very burning sands of Africa, having been picked and scraped by the famishing people in their vicinity a thousand times over.*[141]

Professor Mary Daly has criticised what she termed *'the hiatus'* in famine relief in the early months of 1847, during one of the most difficult periods of the famine, describing the government's actions as *'probably one of the most serious inadequacies in the whole relief programme".*[142] The local press in Waterford was trenchant in it's exposure of the inadequacy of the government policy in this regard Other aspects of Russell's response were subjected to vigorous criticism. The *Waterford Freeman* had denounced the decision to discontinue the purchase of Indian meal:

> *The government do not propose to buy up provisions this year as was done by them last year, lest it would interfere with men in*

trade. The lives of the people are to be looked upon as things less sacred than the interests of the 'men in trade'. We are afraid that the last ministry in their arrangements for the prevention of distress have had a decided advantage over the present.[143]

The more conservative *Waterford Mail* fulminated against Russell's adherence to the principles of laissez-faire and his pursuit of a policy dictated by considerations of political economy.

They would not, forsooth, meddle with the ordinary course of trade! Government would not turn merchant! They would enhance instead of diminishing evil! Admirable theory! Splendid philosophy! Inconceivable folly, say we. How in the nature of things could they have rendered matters worse than we now find them?[144]

The Chairman of the Relief Commission, Sir Randolph Routh, was subjected to a vitriolic attack in the same paper:

His political economy is but a poor substitute for the staff of life and we hope he may soon be consigned to the retirement of private life, where he may feast his soul and enrich his knowledge from the pages of Adam Smith, while more competent hands shall find for the evils of the day remedies, at once substantial and satisfactory.[145]

The whole concept of political economy was discredited in the opinion of the local press, as it was believed that people were being sacrificed for dogmatic considerations. It was argued that the legitimate concerns of the unfortunate destitute were not even entertained by those in authority as, in the words of the *Waterford Freeman*, '*the political economy of their humane and wise rulers must be carried out in all its ramifications.*'[146]

The reportage of famine relief measures in the Waterford newspapers during 1845-46 was a chronicle of human misery and a catalogue of criticism of government actions. The horrors of widespread starvation and destitution prompted the local journals to reject the response of Russell's administration as utterly inadequate.

3. Food Exports

Writing in his Jail Journal, John Mitchel claimed:

In every one of these years, '46, '47, and '48, Ireland was exporting to England, food to the value of fifteen million pounds sterling, and had on her own soil at each harvest, good and ample provision for double her own population, notwithstanding the potato blight.[147]

His sentiments were those of the enduring nationalist and populist lament that the fundamental problem during the years of the famine in Ireland was not the availability of food, but rather that agricultural produce, and grain in particular, was being shipped out of Ireland, often to pay rents to absentee landlords. Waterford newspapers, especially *The Chronicle and Munster Advertiser* and *Waterford Freeman*, articulated this perception, were vocal in their condemnation of food exports while people starved, and called for the closure of the ports in order to ensure the retention of food in the country. The distinguished historian of the famine, Austin Bourke, has commented that in the course of the critical years of the calamity little evidence is to be found in newspapers – with the exception of the Clare Journal – of any public demand for the closing of the ports.[148] Mary Daly has written that the call to prevent food exports was much stronger in retrospect than it was at the time.[149]

The general nature of these observations is contradicted by a study of the local press in Waterford. Indeed, the *Waterford Freeman* claimed to have been among the first papers in the country to express its views on the subject of exportation.[150] As early as November 1845, it had commented on the fact that the ports were open *and from north to south, from east to west, of this famine-threatened land our people's food is being wholesale exported.*

The '*murderous recklessness*' of the English government, whose policies '*set men's brains on fire and turn their hearts to fiercest rage,*' was denounced.[151]

Six months later *The Chronicle and Munster Advertiser* observed that in every issue it was recording the sailing from Waterford Port of vessels laden with food.[152] While Indian meal was being imported to feed the starving population.

> *Ireland must in return behold her best flour, her wheat, her bacon, her butter, her live cattle, all going to England day after day. She dare not ask the cause of this fatal discrepancy – the existence of famine in a country, whose staple commodity is food – food – food of the best – and the most exquisite quality.*[153]

The *Waterford Freeman* reproduced a table showing the level of exports of grain, flour, and oatmeal from September 5th to October 9th, 1846.

From:	Wheat Brls.	Oats Brls.	Flour cwts.	Oatmeal cwts.
Limerick	10,823	120,054	1,750	1,400
Cork	1,009	39,111	5,070	—
Belfast	1,685	9,059	815	—
Tralee	658	7,725	–	—
Galway	1,249	3,750	1,400	1,809
Wexford	—	7,143	–	860
WATERFORD	7,011	13,805	24,392	—
DUNGARVAN & YOUGHAL	5,009	10,000	—	7,180

Particular editorial comment was made on the exports from Dungarvan and Youghal, towns in which, it was claimed, people were starving. The figures prove that *'the pounds, shillings, and pence of the corn factors of Britain weigh heavier on the legislative balance of England than the interests and lives of Ireland's millions.'*[154]

The crisis in Ireland prompted calls for the government to prohibit food exports in order to alleviate food shortages. In February 1846, the *Waterford Freeman* supported demands made by a committee of Dublin citizens to close the country's ports.[155] In October it re-iterated these sentiments in the aftermath of riots in Dungarvan to prevent the shipment of food.

> *When famine is spreading its pall over the land, and death is visiting the poor man's cabin, it is not meet that the food of millions should be shipped from our shores. It is indispensably necessary that the grain should remain in the country while scarcity is apprehended. Will not a starving population become justly indignant when whole fleets, laden with the produce of our soil, are unfurling their sails and steering from our harbour, while the cry of hunger is singing in their ears? It is beyond human endurance to suffer it; and a wise government should at once issue an order prohibiting the exportation of provisions from this country, until the wants of the people have been sufficiently provided for.*[156]

In the same month the Board of Guardians of Waterford Union petitioned the Lord Lieutenant to issue a proclamation closing the ports:

> *We cannot avoid taking leave to express our serious and but too well-founded apprehensions that the total loss of the potato crop requires immediate and extraordinary legislative measures to*

avert, as far as possible, a more than probable scarcity of human food throughout the land. We should not, under ordinary circumstances, desire to interfere with the great principles of free trade, but as there is no rule without exception, so we believe that the present alarming emergency at once forcibly presents a powerful one in regard to Ireland, that should operate against the continued drain of corn from this country.[157]

The *Waterford Freeman* supported the petition and printed a letter from Sir Richard Musgrave, a prominent local landlord, in favour of port closure.[158]

The deteriorating conditions of 1847 witnessed renewed demands in the *Waterford Freeman* for government action in relation to the prohibition of food exports. It claimed in January that if the authorities had acted accordingly when it first became apparent, that the potato crop had failed, then famine would not have manifested itself.[159] In the spring the newspaper editorialised:

If the government took not an active part in providing a supply of food for their Irish subjects, they had a right to prohibit the extraction of any article of food from this country, but this they have not done and therefore, they are responsible for the lives of those who have perished from want.[160]

The government's continued failure to act elicited an even more pronounced note of bitterness in later editorials:

It will appear to our readers passing strange that wheat and flour is (sic) being shipped from a land where thousands are daily perishing of famine. The mammon worshipping speculators, whom Lord John Russell has taken under his special protection, deaf to the incessant appeals of the famishing millions, are sending the food to whatever portion of the globe it will bring the highest price......A million men may starve, but the rules which have regulated commercial enterprise must remain as immutable and fixed as the poles.[161]

The whole issue of what impact port closure would have had on the course of the famine, or the actual feasibility of such a policy, is a complicated matter to assess, but it is the considered opinion of some historians who have studied this matter that such a response by the government would have been of little value in the context of the serious crisis facing the country. Bourke has written:

It is beyond question that the food deficiency arising from the loss of the potato crop in 1846 could not have been met by the simple expedient of prohibiting the export of grain from Ireland, even if the difficult practical problems of acquisition, storage, milling and distribution could have been surmounted at short notice.[162]

Another historian, Margaret Crawford, offers four arguments in support of her opinion that the belief that prohibiting grain exports would have averted famine is a myth. Total exports fell during the famine years, and Ireland actually became a net importer of grain. Secondly, the government was ideologically committed to free trade; to believe that it could have interfered with private markets is anachronistic. Thirdly, the peasant had no money to purchase grain even if it had been diverted into the home market. Finally, the loss of potatoes was so great that the prohibition would not have made up the shortfall of food in its entirety.[163]

Whatever about a general prohibition, the *Waterford Freeman* called for at least a temporary embargo on exports in the critical autumn of 1846.

There was cleared out of the custom house in this city, for England, within the past week, 1,035 barells of wheat, 4,279 barells of oats, though thousands are starving in the west of the county. The government should put a stop to this drain, at least till some substitute is provided to replace this large export.[164]

This call should not be dismissed off as quickly as that for a more general one. Some historians have argued that a temporary surprise embargo in late 1846, in anticipation of imports already on their way, might have been of benefit.[165] Bourke acknowledged a small kernel of truth in this argument:

The grain crop of 1846, if entirely retained in Ireland, could have made an appreciable contribution to bridging the starvation gap between the destruction of the potato crop in August and the arrival of the first maize cargoes in the following winter.[166]

Bourke correctly emphasised that this retention in the country of all home-produced food could have served only as a temporary device, of short term duration.[167] While it would not have eliminated the huge problems associated with the potato failure, it would have alleviated them. Food shortages would have been reduced, with the consequent benefit to food prices, particularly during the early months of

'Black '47'. Thus the purchasing power of those dependent on public works would have been increased. A short term policy, moreover, would have obviated the difficulties presented by a more general prohibition. Such a response would not have required the government to abandon its principles, only to compromise them, something it was not adverse to doing later, as may be seen, for example, in its abandonment of relief works in favour of outdoor relief. Finally, there was a precedent for closing ports during a period of food shortages. During the crisis of 1782-4, an embargo was placed on the exports of foodstuffs by the Lord Lieutenant. As a consequence, food prices were reduced.[168]

The calls for the closure of ports which featured in the local press were not made by revolutionary nationalists. Newspaper editors, Poor Law Guardians, and a landowner, were not persons in the mould of John Mitchel. Some of them would have been considered pillars of the establishment, normally conservative in their outlook. By refusing to consider such a policy, even as a temporary device, *'the British government ensured that 'Black '47' was indelibly associated with suffering, famine, mortality, emigration and to some, misrule.'*[169]

4. Landlords, Tenants, and Evictions
1845-1846
If the nationalist and folk memories regard the famine years as ones of starvation amidst plenty, these same years are also seen as one of dispossession amidst starvation. There was a huge increase in the rate of evictions between 1846-54, though it is not possible to give an exact figure for the numbers of people evicted. The police began to keep official accounts only in 1849, and a total of 250,000 persons evicted from their holdings is recorded up to 1854. James Donnelly reckons that a figure of half a million for the entire period (1846-54) is not an unrealistic one.[170]

Economists and government inquiries had advocated the need for a more streamlined farming structure in the immediate pre-famine decades. The famine confirmed the validity of these proposals for many landowners. Furthermore, it (the famine) intensified the pressures on them as the burden of local taxation to finance relief schemes increased dramatically. The famine gave landlords the opportunity to effect clearances of unwanted tenants, not least because tenants, exhausted by the struggle to just survive, were unable to resist the owners actions. Such resistance in the past had intimidated landlords and prevented clearances.[171]

The key role of the landlords in society was acknowledged by the local press, as it exhorted them to assume a responsibility in the alleviation of the distress of their tenants. *The Cork Examiner*, as early as September 1845, declared that the owners of the land should be the legitimate protectors of the people, and called on absentees to forego rents for one year.[172] In January 1846 it stated that it was the solemn duty of the rich '*to succour the poor in the hour of their distress.*'[173] Such advice was given not so much in friendship as in hostility, which was the general attitude of the local newspapers to landlords, with the exception of the *Waterford Mail*. For example, in February 1846 the *Waterford Freeman* attacked wealthy absentee landlords who had done nothing to assist their impoverished tenants around Dungarvan.[174]

On the evidence of the newspapers local landlords did not wait long to begin clearances. On 10th April 1846 *The Cork Examiner* reported that within the last three weeks forty six houses had been taken down at Graigue Shoneen, near Kilmacthomas, on the property of the Marquis of Waterford. Each family was offered £2 to quit, which was accepted by all. This practice of giving inducements to tenants to quit their holdings became common throughout the country.[175] Five days later a more detailed account of the evictions was carried in the same journal, in which it was stated that 277 persons in all had been thrown out of their homes. Details were also given of evictions at Glenafoca, also near Kilmacthomas, which involved 80 persons in all. Many of those evicted did not owe any arrears of rent and were satisfied to continue paying rent to the landlord.[176]

By the autumn of 1846 actual starvation was facing many tenants and landlords were once again reminded of their obligations:

> *Every good landlord should be found at his post inspecting the condition of his tenantry. He should go from house to house – from farm to farm – and calculate the loss that his tenantry may have sustained. It is the duty of the landlord to protect those over whom Providence has placed him, from the dread effects of famine. It is his imperative duty to rush to the rescue with his presence, purse, and counsel.*[177]

The *Waterford Freeman* rejected landlords' claims that they were not as wealthy as was popularly believed. The journal declared that it had no sympathy for them and that they must assume their obligations in the relief efforts: '*They must, able or not able – willing or unwilling – contribute to the support of the destitute population of the country.*'[178] The *Waterford Mail*, as might have been expected, was more supportive of landlords, more sympathetic to their plight, and praised them as a class for what it regarded as their generous response to the crisis:

*The landlords of Ireland, in a manner above all praise, took on
themselves the setting on foot of relief undertakings, to their own
heavy loss, for the employment of the destitute.*[179]

1847

Newspaper evidence suggests a significant increase in the rate of
evictions in 1847. *The Chronicle and Munster Advertiser* reported in
January that Mr. Smyth of Ballintray was about to add to the *'horrible'*
number of evictions. Tenants unable to pay rents and arrears were to
be ejected.[180] In the same month the *Waterford Freeman* carried a
report of 50 ejectment processes being served in Ballyreilly, near
Ring.[181] The same journal condemned the conduct of some landlords in
Dungarvan as *'cruel and nearly incredible'* for serving eviction notices
by the hundreds.[182]

In March a correspondent of *The Cork Examiner* wrote of 19 families
under the threat of ejectment on the lands of Richard Gumbleton, near
Tallow. It was observed that there was already much destitution in
place, *'and yet with misery the most appalling and staring men in the
face, this is the place which Irish landlordism seems bent upon reducing
to a still more frightful condition for the future.'*[183]

In January it had been reported that notices to quit by 25 March had
been served on 57 tenants and their families – 477 persons in all – on
the estate of Kiely Ussher at Ballysaggartmore, in the parish of
Lismore.[184] On 3rd May *The Cork Examiner* carried reports that evictions
had begun. Over a period of three weeks 16 families – 87 persons –
had been ejected. The journal's correspondent wrote that the
demolition of cabins was a daily occurrence, and continued:

> *I counted from twelve to fourteen houses in some instances levelled
> to the ground, with the exception of portions of the walls; in other
> cases, the roofs torn off, the windows broken in, and the doors
> removed. Groups of famished women and squalid children still
> hovered round the place of their birth, and endeavoured to shelter
> themselves from the piercing cold of the mountain blast by
> cowering behind walls, or seeking refuge beneath chimneys.*

Typical of the tenants' plight was that of a man named Walsh, a
married man with 4 children. He farmed 32 acres of mountain. Three
weeks before, the steward of Mr. Ussher demanded the rent. The
dearness of provisions made it impossible for Walsh to meet the
demand. To ensure a peaceable eviction, he was promised £5 if he
unroofed his own cabin and levelled the walls. The tenant concurred in
this arrangement.

This report in *The Cork Examiner* was the first of many in this and in other journals on events at Ballysaggartmore. In 23rd May, 40 people were evicted. The whole occasion was one of absolute misery:

> *The lamentations – the loud cries of the men, women and children (some of the latter of the tenderest age and many of them suckling at their mothers' breasts) were heart-rending. Many of the poor people were sick and infirm; some of them, through extreme old age, were unable to walk when the walls of their houses were thrown down around them. They were carried out in the hands of men and were deposited on the field near the scene of the terrible act. The manifestations of misery were the most fearful that were ever witnessed in a Christian land.*

Kiely Ussher witnessed the proceedings from his carriage. The evicted tenants and their families were obliged to sleep by the sides of ditches that night, such furniture as they had being their only protection against the elements.[185]

Tenant Right

Reflecting upon these evictions, *The Cork Examiner* commented on the necessity of introducing a bill to regulate the relations between landlord and tenant in order to prevent such events happening again.[186] Even the *Waterford Mail* acknowledged that the existing law could not remain unchanged.[187] The conduct of some landlords was proving embarrassing and unacceptable to erstwhile supporters.

The horrors of famine brought the evils of the Irish land system to public attention. With widespread starvation and eviction, agrarian grievances could no longer be ignored. Greater security was required by tenants against landlords, and to that end a meeting was organised in County Waterford for Sunday, 24th October. The main movers were Roman Catholic clergy. The requisition for the meeting was signed by 91 priests and 600 gentlemen, including many liberal landlords.[188] The venue selected was Kilmacthomas, described, in the words of *The Chronicle and Munster Advertiser*, '*as the once busy, prosperous and wealthy village, now turned to pauper haunts, to charnel houses.*'[189] The purpose of the meeting, according to *The Cork Examiner*, was to establish '*a Tenant League to serve the rights of the landlord, and to petition the legislature on the same subject.*'[190] The meeting was awaited with a great sense of anticipation in the local press.[191]

According to *The Cork Examiner* the attendance at Kilmacthomas on Sunday October 24th was between 20-30,000 people.[192] The meeting was held in a field of several acres about a mile and a half from the village. A large platform had been erected, capable of accommodating 3-400 people. There was a very significant clerical presence.[193]

A number of resolutions were proposed and adopted. The first one declared that

> *The present state of relations between landlord and tenant is marked by contention, insecurity, injustice, misery, outrage, and alas! sometimes the spilling of blood.*

The fifth resolution lauded the custom of tenant right that existed in Ulster, as securing the landlord in his rent and the tenant in the improvement of his holding. Another resolution recognised that while a landlord's rights should be respected, it was imperative to respect the rights of tenants.[194]

The meeting received a very favourable reaction in the local press. The *Waterford Mail* commented that *'no same individual but must concur with the sentiments expressed at the meeting'*. The editorial agreed that while landlords' rights of property should be respected, it was *'as imperatively necessary that those of the tenant should be as strictly guarded.'*[195] *The Cork Examiner* praised the county of Waterford for taking the lead in this important issue. It called on every county in the southern provinces to assemble, to make known to parliament the opinion of the people on landlord-tenant relations.[196]

This meeting was a significant historical event. It would appear to have been one of the first occasions in the country on which tenants gathered to demand a recognition of their rights. There is no evidence in newspapers' accounts of the event of a league or society being formed, nor is there any subsequent evidence. It would seem that the primary purpose of the meeting was to petition the legislature. The gathering was characterised by moderation. It was not one at which landlordism was denounced. On the contrary there was a recognition of landlord's rights, what was demanded was a reciprocal recognition of the rights of tenants. The reasonable and moderate nature of the resolutions, together with a landlord presence, made it possible for even a conservative journal like the *Waterford Mail* to express its approval.

Related to tenant right activity was a fascinating letter which appeared in *The Chronicle and Munster Advertiser* of 22nd September. It was addressed to the *'virtuous women of the county of Waterford'*, informing them that a preliminary meeting had been held at Kilmacthomas on Sunday, 19th September to make arrangements for a Female Tenant League. The women were reminded that they have already witnessed their husbands and children reduced to the condition of *'walking skeletons, by oppression and wrong; they are now little better* than moving spectres and a living mass of bare bones, slowly sinking into the welcome grave.' It was asserted that this state of affairs could not be allowed continue. As the men 'wont do the work, it remains for us to accomplish it'. The calamities which had befallen Ireland were blamed on bad laws and on the cruelty of bad landlords and their agents. As a consequence, women had witnessed 'privations and sufferings during these years of famine, such as were not equalled in this or any other country since the time of Adam.'

The aim of the proposed Female Tenant League was to get all the women of Ireland to join in a united movement:

> We'll shame the men into action. We'll insist on love of country and kind in the tender hearts of our children. We'll control our husbands and command our daughters. We'll make a solemn vow not to rest our heads on the same pillow with our husbands until they become ardent members of the Tenant League.

It was intended that the Female League would compile facts and grievance relating to agrarian conditions in the county, which would be embodied in a memorial to Queen Victoria. This appears to be the only reference to the Female Tenant League in the local press. No further evidence is to be found therein as to whether the organisation ever came into existence.[197] Notwithstanding these facts, the letter is a significant document, not least because it purported to speak for women to women. The role perceived for women represented a rejection of the one which traditional nineteenth century male dominated society imposed on them. The language used was confident and purposeful, there being no sense that women were in any respect less able than men. Rather, the writer envisaged women giving men a lead. The preliminary meeting mentioned in the letter to organise the league took place one month before the much publicised Kilmacthomas meeting, and the proposed Female League was regarded by the writer as a response to male inactivity in the face of landlord oppression. Moreover, the language sought to create a strong sense of female solidarity, the readers being addressed as 'sisters'. Letters such as this are rare in the first half of the last century. That one should emerge from a rural village during a period of catastrophe is noteworthy, if not extraordinary.

The tenant meeting at Kilmacthomas in October did not make any apparent difference in relation to evictions, which continued apace. One landlord, however, Lord Stradbroke, expressed the view that the gathering had an unfortunate effect on some of his tenants. In a later dated 14th December 1847, addressed to his tenants in the townlands of Kilbarrymeaden, Ballymurrin, and Kilbeg, he regretted that

> Some of the tenants have put me to the great expense of serving
> ejectments, when I knew they had the means but not the
> inclination to pay their rents. These men have no persons to blame
> but themselves; and I believe that the effect of the great public
> meeting at Kilmacthomas was to make some men pursue a
> dishonest course, which they would not otherwise have done.[198]

1848

On 1st February 1848 *The Chronicle and Munster Advertiser* carried a
report on evictions in the area of Dungarvan. The writer spoke of pau-
perised human beings left to perish in ditches. In Ballynalahessery over
200 had been evicted. At Abbeyside the number was more than 100,
while 50 to 60 had been thrown out near Kilgobinet. A similar number
had experienced the same fate at Cushcam. The peasantry were being
swept off Slievegrine *'like rotten sheep and their cabins tumbled down.'*

At Ballyduff, on the property of Mr. Woods, 58 persons were ejected,
some of them receiving a sum of £2 if they acquiesced in the decision
and left without demur.[199] In the same parish, 113 persons on the estate
of Captain Barry were thrown off their holdings. In the same edition of
The Chronicle and Munster Advertiser, a figure of 280 was given as the
number evicted at Ballysaggartmore in 1847.[200] Kiely Ussher was also
reported to be responsible for evicting 132 persons at Kinsalebeg.[201]

Landlords were assisted in their campaign of clearances by the
Gregory Clause, which stated that no tenant holding more than a
quarter acre of land was eligible for public assistance, either inside or
outside the workhouse. Of this legislative provision it has been written:
*'A more complete engine for the slaughter and expatriation of a people
was never designed'.*[202] *The Chronicle and Munster Advertiser*
commented, *'To Gregory's quarter acre clause be traced much of the
pauperism by which the country is at present overrun.'*[203]

The Local Press and Evictions

The press played a very significant role in relation to evictions by
creating a public awareness of what was happening on some of the
county's estates. Reportage was not always dispassionate and objective.
Most newspapers were openly sympathetic to the plight of tenants,
describing landlords; actions as *'extermination'*. By their evocative and
often dramatic accounts of the circumstances of those who had been
evicted, they strove to elicit a strong sense of compassion in their
readers:

> It is an undeniable fact that on the roadside at Ballysaggartmore
> in the severest part of the winter, whole families were seen lying on

188

stone benches in small sheds, with a stream of water running
through the centre of the horrible abodes. There are but few of
those poor people alive to-day to corroborate whay we say.
Dysentery and fever carried them off.[204]

The corollary of sympathy for the tenant was hostility towards, even hatred of, landlords. The press contributed in a major way to the creation of the stereotype of the landlord as a heartless tyrant and to his demonisation as one of the bogeymen of Irish history. This overt hostility and the regularity of editorial attacks on them created and reinforced a public perception of them as unfeeling purveyors of doom. Commenting on landlords' use of the Gregory Clause, *The Chronicle and Munster Advertiser* observed:

As well might the government unkennel a pack of bloodhounds on
the defenceless peasant, as arm agents and landlords with the
unlimited powers they now possess.[205]

Such invective both accorded with public prejudice and sowed even more seeds of bitterness.

The Catholic clergy were in the forefront of the campaign of opposition to evictions. While they denounced clearances from the altars, they also used the press to expose what they regarded as landlord tyranny. They were the probable authors of detailed lists of evicted persons which appeared with some frequency in local newspapers in 1847 and 1848.[206]

Whoever was responsible for their authorship, the compilation of such lists was a conscious attempt to appeal to public sympathy and to secure widespread rejection of landowners' actions by employing the power of the press in a very deliberate way. These lists had the effecting of humanising abstract figures. Those evicted were no longer lost among a morass of numbers – they were women and men with names and families. The following was printed in *The Chronicle and Munster Advertiser* relating to Ballysaggartmore.[207]

Name of Tenant	No. in Family
Denis Duggan	6
John Liddy	6
Garret Roach	7
Owen Guiry	4
Matt Daly	7
John Browne	5
William Walsh	3
Edmond O'Donnell	8
James Fitzgerald	3

Only part of the list is reproduced. Another more detailed type of list was sometimes compiled. The following is part of one relating to the property of Mr. Woods at Ballyduff, Lismore:[208]

1. *John Ryan had 7 in family – he had 13 acres of land. The annual rent of his small holding was £8 p.a.; he not only owed no rent, but actually offered to pay the ensuing gale, and still was he refused; mercy could not be extended to him, or his.*
2. *Richard Barry, 6 in family – held only one cabin, which was levelled, and himself and his dependants turned on the world to starve, or to seek some shelter in some poorhouse.*
3. *John Bute, 6 in family – owed nothing – got £2 and was turned adrift with his starvlings.*
4. *Michael Mahony, held 4 acres; had 9 in family; paid £1 per acre for his holding; owed £6 and got £5 when leaving.*

Estate clearances added greatly to the level of suffering experienced by many in County Waterford. To hunger, starvation, and pestilence, must be added evictions, the latter contributing to the mortality rate by depriving people of even the meagre shelter against inclement weather afforded by their wretched hovels and cabins.

5. Crime and Disorder

1846-1848

Dr. Kevin Nowlan's observation that '*the famine years were to prove conspicuous for their tranquillity rather than their turbulence*[209] has been described by Professor Mary Daly as '*perhaps something of an overstatement.*'[210] Agrarian crime rose during 1846.[211] This fact is reflected in Waterford's local press. The prevalence of so much misery and destitution resulted in incidents of disorder, particularly in the autumn of that year. Many of these were acts of collective violence, some of them organised and orchestrated. Such crime as characterised the later years of the famine in the county was of a more sporadic and isolated nature.

1846

Many of the presentment sessions convened under the terms of the relief act enacted in August 1846 became occasions of disorder by virtue of demonstrations by large numbers of desperate people seeking to impress on the magistrates and ratepayers, the urgency of the need for immediate relief schemes. The Dungarvan session in early September attracted a large assembly of impoverished labourers. Their riotous conduct created considerable alarm and the majority of shops remained closed during the day. The local authorities ordered out the military and police, but the soldiers and constables were pelted with stones. A number of people were arrested and tensions remained high. The *Waterford Freeman* described the day '*as one of uncertainty and intimidation, and one that threatened lives and property with certain destruction*'. It denounced the actions of the protesters as likely to cause delays in the provision of public works.[212]

Later in the same month the sessions for the Barony of Decies-Within-Drum, held at Clashmore, saw more disorder. From an early hour

> *hundreds of the peasantry from the neighbouring hills and surrounding country began to pour into the village. The Courthouse was crowded outside, and the excitement was alarming and menacing; whilst cries of 'we are starving and we must get work or food – we cannot hold patient and famishing any longer' were exclaimed, in Irish, both within and outside the Courthouse.*

After the completion of business at five o'clock, the assembled crowd of 3,000 persons, acting ' *in a most furious and determined manner*' attempted to assault the Lieutenant of the county, Lord Stuart de Decies. A party of dragoons, which had been sent from Cork, in anticipation of disturbances, charged and injured many of the rioters. The soldiers were met by a volley of stones and several were hurt. (see William Fraher's article for further details)

The presentment sessions for the Barony of Coshmore and Coshbride, held at Lismore in late September, exhibited all the potential for a repeat of the Clashmore riot. According to *The Chronicle and Munster Advertiser*, '*the town was crowded to suffocation; on every road leading to it, bodies of the peasantry were collected from all the surrounding districts for miles around.*' There was confusion in the courthouse soon after the commencement of proceedings.

> *A formidable body of peasants forced its way into the court, and furiously exclaimed that they must at once get employment and food, that their condition was awful and that they could not or would not endure it much longer, as they are actually starving. Their cries, their screams, their fury were really fearful and frantic, and beyond measure.*

Only the intervention of the Parish Priest, Dr. Fogarty, who calmed the intruders, helped restore order.

There were reports in the newspapers of concerted efforts to prevent corn being sent to market and to secure refunds on rents. The *Waterford Mail* declared that '*Mob law seems to be in the ascendant and order at an end.*' It reported that 2,000 persons had assembled at the chapel of Grange and issued the following '*regulations*':

> *That farmers were not to thresh or send out any corn to market. That no milk should be given by the farmers to their pigs, but kept and given to the labourers without any charge for same. That no bailiffs were to be allowed to distrain for rent. That the farmers should at once refund all money paid for conacre land; and also the value of the seed and labour; and all able-bodied labourers should get two shillings a day, and the old men and boys ten pence, provided meal was one shilling a stone, and, if higher, the wages to increase accordingly; and every person to be employed, or paid if allowed to remain idle. That no process should be served for any debt, on pain of the plaintiff's ears being cut off.*

The principal farmers in the locality were warned that if they failed to comply with the regulations, they should prepare their coffins. Two '*respectable*' farmers were so terrified that they at once paid back the money for the conacre on their land; other farmers promised to do so in less than a week.

The *Waterford Mail* reported on '*mobs*' going through the parish of Ardmore, most of them with firearms, stopping all corn going to market, cutting the bags, spilling the corn on the road, and not allowing the owners to take it up.[213]

The Chronicle and Munster Advertiser observed that bands of peasants were nightly visiting the homes of farmers and intimidating them into refunding the rents paid for conacre, alleging that no value had been received due to the failure of the potato crop.[214] The *Waterford Freeman* carried a report of a meeting of over 600 peasants at Whitechurch, for the purpose of compelling farmers to refund the money paid by cottiers for dairy ground which produced no crop.[215]

At the Dungarvan Quarter Sessions, held in October, 55 persons were charged with various offences, including intimidation, rioting, and lawless assembly. The defendants were tried in batches of 11 and 12. All pleaded guilty, but most explained that they had been driven to commit the offences by starvation. The court acted sympathetically; all the defendants, except one, being fined and bound to the peace. The exception was Patrick Power, described as the ring leader, who was sentenced to one year's imprisonment.[216]

In late October *The Chronicle and Munster Advertiser* commented that Dungarvan and the adjacent western districts had been for the last six weeks *'the very headquarters of Irish excitement.'*[217] The incidents of disorder were the response of the peasantry to the threat of starvation, and deplorable destitution. The disturbances at the presentment sessions were products of the sheer desperation of starving crowds, transformed into riotous mobs by hunger pangs. The attempts to prevent food going to market and to seek refunds on rents were prompted by the urgency to secure the means of subsistence and the wherewithal to purchase them.

However, in the same edition of *The Chronicle and Munster Advertiser* it was observed that *'the country districts have again regained their usual tranquillity.'* As famine conditions worsened, militancy gave way to the struggle for survival. In September and October people faced the threat of hunger, but were still in a position to engage in protest; by late October the access to food became difficult and mere survival became the primary concern. The energy formerly devoted to agitation was now devoted to securing food. This is not unusual in famine conditions.

During the Russian famine of 1918-22 it has been estimated that the search for food occupied up to 95 per cent of a person's time.[218] Hunger also brings with it listlessness and apathy, and people so afflicted have no inclination to agitate. The physical debilitation wrought by starvation can make the most militant agitator quiescent.

1847-1848

Throughout 1847-48, the crimes reported in the local press were sporadic in character, robbery being the most common. At the Quarter Sessions at Dungarvan in January 1847, the absence of disorder in the county was noted by the presiding judge; the only offences which prompted a comment were those relating to sheep stealing. In the judicial remarks it was observed that the animals were stolen from parties whose condition was little better that that of the perpetrators.[219] At Killossragh, near Dungarvan, a cow belonging to a farmer named Flynn was killed and the carcass taken away, the head and hide being left behind.[220] In the autumn there were reports of sheep stealing at Grange.[221] In February 1848, the *Waterford Mail* reported the robbery of turnips from a field near Lismore and the attack on the watchman guarding the crops.[222] In the same month a farmer at Ballylaneen thwarted attempts to rob his sheep.[223] Occasional reports of the robbery of money appeared in the journals. In November 1847 eight armed men forced entry into the house of a poor man near Lismore. The occupant was ordered to kneel and a pistol held to his head. Money was demanded and the gang made off with one pound and six shillings.[224] A man was attacked near Dungarvan around the same time and 39 shillings were stolen.[225]

A noteworthy feature of press reportage was the apparent absence of any significant level of agrarian crime in spite of evictions. Two incidents were reported in the *Waterford Mail* in December 1847. A land agent was fired upon near Cappoquin[226] and a group of eight to ten men attacked and beat two keepers of a property near Carrick-on-Suir, which have been seized for non-payment of rent.[227] The infrequency of such outrages was not unique to Waterford. Other counties were the same.[228] The neighbouring county of Cork, for example, was also relatively tranquil.[229]

The crimes reported in 1847-48 were generally acts of desperation, proving that for some people, in the words of the *Waterford Freeman*, '*the maddening and desperate influence of protracted want will drive its despairing victims to the perpetration of lawless deeds and outrages.*'[230] Some evidence that the offenders came from the most deprived sections of society is to be found in a report of the 736 persons returned for trial at the Quarter Sessions and Assizes throughout the county in 1847. Of these, 100 males and 4 females could read and write; 23 males and 11 females could read only, 423 could neither read nor write; and the education of the remaining 175 was not ascertained.[231] However, their state of education may be taken to be on the same average. Social historians have established a link between illiteracy and income per capita, the inability to read and write often being the concomitant of a low income. The *Waterford Mail* contended that ignorance (meaning illiteracy) and crime went hand in hand.[232] Ignorance in the circumstances of Waterford in 1847 may be taken as a definite indicator of poverty and deprivation.

When Waterford journals denounced crime[233] and discussed the merits and demerits of coercion legislation,[234] they were concerned more about the national rather than the local situation. After 1846, denunciations were usually unnecessary and coercion hardly warranted in what was essentially a relatively peaceful county.

6. Emigration

1845-1850

Between 1845-50 over one million people emigrated from Ireland. The Emigration Commissioners estimated the figures for the famine and immediate post famine years were as follows:[235]

1847 ——	219,885
1848 ——	131,316
1849 ——	218,842
1850 ——	213,649

The scale of the flight had no precedent in the history of international migration. David Fitzpatrick has written that 'even in the period of heaviest famine-induced mortality, emigration was equally important as a source of the decline in Ireland's population.'[236] However, the local press coverage of this momentous event was disappointing, being sporadic, vague, and at times, inaccurate.

Emigration did not truly commence until 1846. Even though blight did not strike until the usual passage season was over, 100,000 left the country for North America.[237] On 18th April the *Waterford Freeman* commented on the increased port activity in Waterford:

> *Perhaps so large a number of persons never emigrated at any time from this country for America as at present. Our quays have been crowded during the week with emigrants embarking in the several ships.*

A list of the vessels which had sailed in the past week was published.:

Name	Destination	No. of Passengers
Velocity	St. John's New Brunswick	24
Bolivar	Quebec	30
Admiral	,,	480
Medina	,,	257
Despatch		240
Thistle		121
Nancy	Miramichi	29
Sophia	Halifax	84
Rose Macroom	Quebec	30
		1,295

All the berths in the remaining ships had been already engaged.

The *Waterford Mail* observed in an editorial in May 1846 that never before had so many people sought to improve their condition by emigration.

> *For on no occasion within the past few weeks has our Liverpool Steamer (William Penn) taken her departure from our quays, that her decks have not been crowded with all ages and grades of persons, on their way to join some vessel, either for Canada, or the United States.*[238]

The numbers leaving Ireland in 1847 represented a 100 per cent increase on those for 1846. In the words of Canon John O'Rourke: '*Emigration played a leading part in the terrible drama of the Irish*

Famine of 1847'.[239] The local journals made references to the considerable activity evident in Waterford Port and to the volume of emigrants. On 20th March, the *Waterford Freeman* commented on the *'great number'* which sailed the day before for Liverpool. Several vessels bound for American were taking on passengers. *'From the number of applications for berths it is quite certain that they will bring out a full complement.'* An editorial at the end of the month spoke of every passing day witnessing thousands leaving for America.[240] *The Chronicle and Munster Advertiser* reflected on the situation thus:

> *Day after day our quays are crowded with people seeking for American ships, and no sooner is a ship's departure for that prosperous land announced than she is filled. Never did the 'oldest inhabitant' – whoever he may be – witness so many emigrants, at any one period, as swarmed the quays on Wednesday and Thursday.*[241]

Occasionally, the newspapers gave the precise number of emigrants on a vessel. In March, the Sophia sailed with 80 persons for New York.[242] On the 9th April, the William Penn departed for Liverpool with 600 emigrants.[243] On 21st April the *Waterford Freeman* reported the departure of several vessels with a full complement of passengers, the total number exceeding 2,000. On 4th August the *Waterford Mail* carried a list of all emigrant ships which arrived at Quebec from Waterford and New Ross, between 14th May and 10th July. It was compiled by the Canadian Port's Chief Agent for Immigrants.

The reportage of emigration in the local press for 1848 was most inadequate. *The Chronicle and Munster Advertiser* reported on 1st April that the first spring ship, the Countess of Durham, had departed for New York with an immense number of passengers. The extent of the flight from Ireland during the next few months was virtually ignored by the newspapers. However, there were reports on emigration in the autumn and winter – one of the effects of the Famine being the extension of the passage season. The Liverpool steamer, which sailed on 23rd September, was crowded with passengers.[244] On 7th October *The Chronicle and Munster Advertiser* commented that the quays were swarming with emigrants. A week later it carried a report that an extraordinary number of passengers – 1,200 – left on 12th October on board the William Penn. In November, the Victory sailed for Bristol with 300 emigrants.[245]

The exodus continued through 1849-50. In January 1849 two vessels, the Helen and the Frances, sailed for New Orleans with 147 persons on board.[246] In April of that year, 90 passengers sailed for New York on the

Name of ships	Date of arrival 1847	Number of days on voyage	Male	Female	Children under 14	Total	Infants
					Number of emigrants		
Dunbrody	20 May	44	128	85	84	297	15
Erin	07 June	60	57	28	28	113	7
Thistle	10 June	54	78	49	36	163	6
Stanlard	18 June	55	129	115	111	355	10
Dispatch	19 June	59	88	70	76	234	12
Pacific	19 June	46	73	60	50	183	14
Juverna	25 June	42	97	50	24	171	9
Laurence Forristall	11 June	38	48	40	46	134	
Trade	27 June	42	57	41	23	121	11
John Bell	30 June	49	116	73	52	241	13
Solway	30 June	35	135	101	162	338	23
Agent	02 July	47	146	116	111	373	13
Margaret	03 July	50	208	163	128	499	45
Aberfoyle	04 July	44	151	89	68	308	12
WS Hamilton	07 July	52	87	45	60	192	17
Margaret	07 July	54	150	99	130	379	23
Progress	10 July	66	173	174	190	537	18

Velocity; 70 on the Harmony for Boston, and 200 on the Orinoco for New York.247 In May 1850 the *Waterford News* stated that 600 persons a week were leaving Waterford by steamers alone.[248]

Destinations

An analysis of the destinations of Irish emigrants during the famine has shown that the United States was the prime one, with approximately 80 per cent choosing to go there. The next most significant destinations were Britain and British North America (Canada).[249] Most pre-famine emigration had been to Britain. The re-direction of emigrants from there to America during the famine years was an accident of timing. A serious economic rescession between 1847 and 1851 made the neighbouring island unattractive. Notwithstanding Britain's economic difficulties, however, hundreds of thousands of poor Irish still flocked to that country's cities.[250]

An examination of local journals would appear to confirm that emigration from Waterford Port conformed to this general trend. Apart from the evidence of reports on the departures of vessels, the newspapers carried numerous advertisements for transatlantic passages. Moreover, many of those who travelled to Britain did so as the first step in emigrating to America. Cheaper fares were to be found in British ports. The *Waterford Mail* of 27th May, 1846 commented that persons bound for Liverpool were going thither with a view to joining some ships either for Canada or the States. The *Waterford Freeman* made a similar observation a year later,[251] while *The Chronicle and Munster Advertiser* reported on 18th November, 1848 that 20 families were heading for America via Liverpool.

Canada was cheaper to travel to than the United States because Canadian vessels were subject to fewer regulations. Once arrived, emigrants who were healthy enough could walk across the border into America. Accordingly, Canada became a favoured destination whereby a person of limited means could enter the United States.[252]

The Voyage

One of the most vivid folk memories of the famine is that of the *'coffin ships'*. Steerage passengers, in particular, endured disgusting conditions, and already diseased emigrants succumbed to the primitive hardships of the voyages. Accordingly, mortality rates were high. However, the fact is that the horrors of the *'coffin ships'* were mainly restricted to vessels bound for Quebec in 1847.[253] Cheap fares, which were a product of lax shipping regulations, attracted some of the poorest passengers and made this emigration route a lethal one. Of over 100,000 persons who made this journey, one sixth died.[254] Five per cent died at sea; 3.46 per cent on the emigrant station at Grosse Isle, and 8 per cent in Canadian hospitals.[255]

Regarding the fate of emigrants who sailed from Waterford Port, it is impossible to make anything but the most tenuous assessment based on the scanty evidence of the local newspapers. *'Coffin ships'* were not an issue in the pages of the journals. This may be significant as most of them would not have been adverse to reporting *'horror'* stories of ship board conditions, as they (newspapers) were strongly condemnatory of what they regarded as *'forced emigration'* (see below). More important, the return of the Chief Agent for Immigrants at Quebec, listing all ships arrived at that port from Waterford and New Ross between 14th May and 10th July 1847, and reprinted above, carried the following observation by the Canadian official: *'The numbers from your port (Waterford) have arrived generally in good health.'*[256] This observation covered a crucial period and related to a crucial route as regards the phenomenon of the *'coffin ships.'* Therefore, on the basis of the absence of journalistic criticisms, and the remarks of the Chief Agent at Quebec, it can be tentatively suggested that Waterford, at least, was not one of the worst ports.

Voyages to the United States were much less dangerous to the health of passengers, largely because of stricter regulations applying to

***Illustrated London News* sketch of scene at Liverpool docks. Many emigrants from Waterford went first to Liverpool and from there to Canada or the States.**

shipping.[257] Shipboard mortality on most routes seldom exceeded one in fifty.[258] There was even a dramatic improvement on vessels bound for Canada. In 1848 the death rate fell to barely more than 1 per cent, largely because of stricter regulations.[259]

Social Composition of Emigrants
Reading the local journals, there was a consensus that the 'better class' of farmers and the most industrious members of the population were preponderant among the emigrants. This perception represented one of the most enduring newspaper themes of the famine years.

As early as April 1846, the *Waterford Freeman*, commenting on emigrants bound for America, observed that '*they are seemingly respectable looking farmers and persons of the more comfortable grade of society......who have plenty of money.*'[260] A year later the same journal remarked that those embarking for the United States '*belong to the hard-working, comfortable farming classes.*'[261]

The Chronicle and Munster Advertiser, reporting on the departure of the Sophia for New York in March 1847, expressed the view that it was taking with her 80 of the '*most industrious of the population.*'[262] In the same month the following report was published:

> *We are informed, on the authority of a highly respectable gentleman from the county of Waterford, that upwards of 200*

tenants of the Duke of Devonshire have tendered their leases, being resolved to emigrate this spring to America. They are solvent and substantial farmers, and therefore, of the class which Ireland can least afford to lose, and furnish, we fear, an index to those from among whose ranks emigration is likely to prevail.[263]

Recent historical research on emigration has revealed that the belief that *'respectable farmers'* were leaving Ireland in droves was exaggerated.[264] An examination of the manifests of vessels sailing to New York in 1846 has revealed that three quarters of the Irish passengers were either labourers or servants; artisans made up 12 per cent and farmers only 9.5 per cent of the remainder.[265] According to Professor James Donnelly: *'The conclusion is inescapable that in both the late 1840s and the early 1850s the overwhelming majority of emigrants were drawn from the lowest classes of Irish society'.*[266]

These findings indicate that newspapers are not a reliable source for determining the social composition of emigrants. On reflection, this is not surprising. Reports on emigration were few. Reports which referred to the social class of emigrants were even fewer and related to only a tiny proportion of the persons leaving the county. There is, therefore, insufficient evidence in the press to allow the formulation of a definite and precise opinion regarding the social origins of emigrants.

Moreover, the local press regretted and lamented the fact of emigration and denounced its prevalence. The departure of the *'respectable classes'* was emphasised to validate the opinion that their flight from Ireland was a disaster of major proportions. Journalistic requirements demanded a certain misrepresentation of facts to corroborate the preferred editorial position.

In any case, the departure of the poorer classes was not viewed by middle class contemporaries with any real concern, and this attitude was reflected in the newspapers. The press effectively ignored the fact of the emigration of poor people, while at the same time it stated that they lacked the means to emigrate. Commenting on a report which had appeared in a Dublin journal, *The Chronicle and Munster Advertiser* wrote:

> *We fully agree that the poor who are considered a burden cannot emigrate and that those persons who will are only impoverishing the country that they leave behind.*[267]

This inaccurate comment was replete with bourgeois attitudes and prejudices; newspapers like *The Chronicle and Munster Advertiser* articulated them because they – the newspapers – were essentially bourgeois in character and spoke with the middle class accent of their predominantly middle class readership.

Geographical origins of Emigrants
References to the geographical origins of emigrants who departed from Waterford Port were very rare in newspaper reports. However, it can be stated with some certainty that the majority were not natives of the county, which reportedly had one of the lowest emigration rates in the country.[268] Many of those who sailed from the port in search of a new life were likely to have been from the neighbouring counties of Kilkenny and Tipperary, both of which demonstrated one of the largest increases in emigration over their pre-famine levels.[269]

There are cursory references to inhabitants of both counties in press reportage. *The Chronicle and Munster Advertiser* commented on a group of *'fine athletic young men'* leaving for America, many of whom were from Kilkenny and Tipperary.[270] In April 1849 many of the 300 passengers on the Liverpool steamer were from these counties,[271] as was the case with the 200 passengers who departed for New York on another vessel in the same month.[272]

Newspaper reaction to Emigration
The local newspapers were strident in their denunciations of emigration, which they stigmatised as forced exile. Attacks on what was regarded as a great evil were quite common from 1847 onwards, as the numbers leaving Ireland reached hitherto unprecedented levels. Blame was attached to the British Government for allowing this state of affairs arise and continue.

On 31st March 1847, the *Waterford Freeman* editorialised thus:

Every day that passes witnesses thousands of emigrants leaving our shores for America. They are going to labour in a distant clime for that support which, through the instrumentality of foreign rule, they are unable to procure at home. They are leaving behind the entire wretchedness and poverty of the country, and solacing themselves with the reflection that in no part of the globe will they be compelled to witness the heart-rending scenes of destitution which abound in unhappy Ireland. In flying from Saxon bondage they leave no flesh pots behind, nor carry with them the golden treasures of their enslavers. Before them is unremitting toil, danger and uncertainty; behind them an amount of human misery which it would be impossible for the pen of a Defoe or a Carleton to depict, much less exaggerate.

A few days later the same journal stated that the comfortable farmers departing for America were not leaving of their own accord, but were being forced '*to fly from a land where nothing is to be found, save the chaotic elements of misrule, pestilence, and death.*'[273] *The Chronicle and Munster Advertiser* wrote of farmers being '*obliged to run out of Ireland*,'[274] and the country's '*best men and loveliest women floating to the wilds of America.*'[275] The News mused on how the British Government viewed '*the interminable drain upon the hearts blood of the country*', and concluded that '*they will, as usual, be half an hour too late in a remedy for what must inevitably turn out a calamity.*'[276]

Assisted Emigration
During the famine years there was much discussion of, and numerous plans for, assisted emigration, whereby distress would be alleviated by removing the '*surplus*' population of various districts to some relatively unpopulated areas of Canada or America. Nothing came of all this talking and planning as only a small minority of famine emigrants received any assistance. In all, less than 40,000 people were in receipt of subsidies either from the state or landlords between 1846 and 1850, to facilitate their departure from Ireland.[277]

It is hardly surprising that there was an absence of reportage of instances of assisted emigration from Waterford, given the paucity of schemes. There is reference to one in the *Waterford Freeman* of 17th February 1847:

> *The barque Pons, which left our river yesterday, took out 90 passengers for New York, several of whom were hitherto employed as curers in the bacon trade and were enabled to find a comfortable livelihood; but, in consequence of the total failure of that branch of trade, they have been thrown idle, and their employers have kindly offered them means to emigrate.*

The reaction of the local press to the whole concept of assisted emigration was unremittingly hostile. If '*forced*' emigration was regarded as reprehensible, assisted emigration was anathema. Rumours that some such scheme would form part of government relief measures prompted the *Waterford Freeman* to declare its opposition to any proposals of this nature in January 1847. It was opposed to the idea while the resources of the country remained undeveloped. The money so employed would, in the words of an editorial, 'go *a great length in reclamation of our waste lands.*'[278] A month later *The Chronicle and Munster Advertiser* attacked those '*inhuman theorists*' who were seeking to promote emigration '*under the pretence that Ireland is not*

The teeming decks depicted in this *Illustrated London News* sketch does not seem typical of the experience of the Waterford emigrants.

able to support so large a number of rural people in the country at present, without the potato.'[279]

Emigration – A Fact of Life

One of the effects of the famine was to extend massive emigration to every county and parish of Ireland. While editorials might fulminate against evil, there was also a recognition of a reality – that this massive exodus of people was becoming a part of Irish life. Accordingly, information and advice for emigrants began to feature in some newspapers.

The Chronicle and Munster Advertiser published a letter in September 1846 from a Waterford emigrant to Canada in which much information was given about the country.[280] The *Waterford Mail* carried an article in May 1847 with particulars of the same place.[281] A year later it cautioned emigrants about the difficulties they may encounter in New York,[282] and it gave helpful hints to those bound for Canada.[283] The News had advice for those contemplating emigration to America.[284]

As emigration continued, there was a change in attitude towards it. There was a transition from the initial panic-driven expulsion to a more calculated pursuit of economic betterment.[285] The dramatic dislocation of economy and society caused by the famine made Ireland a less attractive place than foreign lands. The News conveyed a sense of this change while commenting on the departure of the Orinoco for New York on 3rd April 1849, with 200 passengers on board:

There was not that incessant crying on the departure of the emigrants that we have been wont to witness. Formerly, the leaving of one's country was deemed an awful epoch – but now men rejoice for having the means wherewith to leave it.[286]

The report was probably exaggerating when it stated that '*men rejoice*', but it was reflecting a truth: later emigrants had taken a more deliberate choice than earlier ones; having considered their economic future in Ireland, they had decided to depart for a country which seemed to offer the opportunity of a brighter future.

David Fitzpatrick has commented that there was an oddly jaunty tone about many of the letters sent home by emigrants.[287] Newspapers occasionally published ones they received. In the News of 13th April 1849, a letter appeared, written by a man who had left Waterford three months earlier. He recounted how the voyage had taken six weeks, during which three persons died. He had been unemployed in New York for some time, but had eventually found work about 20 miles from Boston. The writer concluded by saying that '*those who have industry, perseverance, and a little money can do right well in America.*'

Another letter was published in the same journal on 21st June, 1850. The correspondent stated that most of his fellow passengers had been from Waterford. The passage had been '*excellent*', with only one fatality. All other emigrants had arrived in good health. The writer stated that there was work for all tradesmen.

The Chairman of the Emigration Commissioners observed in 1849 that '*Emigration begets emigration.*'[288] Letters such as these served as a stimulus to encourage people to leave their native land, by presenting an optimistic view of the emigrant's lot. The journey was no longer hazardous; '*if it was scarcely a pleasure cruise, neither was it a death sentence.*'[289] Work was available in foreign lands, the wages were adequate, and there was a prospect of a prosperous future.

The reason for the sporadic nature of press coverage of emigration is the same as for the absence of detailed treatment of the famine after 1847 – the nature of newspapers themselves, which is not to give prolonged attention to a subject. The fact that readers were probably already aware of the prevalence of emigration meant that occasional reports served the purpose. In effect, there was no need to overstate the obvious. Furthermore, regular reports would have made dull reading, these being essentially a litany of the departure dates of vessels and their passenger complements. Editors were influenced by their assessment of news-worthiness and readers' interest, and both these considerations suggested that the extent of reportage was adequate.

The Local Newspapers and the Famine:

This essay has shown that the newspapers were often trenchantly critical of government policy in respect of its response to the crisis caused by the failure of the potato crop. The wages policy adopted on public works, the official attitude to reproductive projects, the undue delays in beginning relief schemes, and the rigid adherence to political economy were severely criticised. The ideological assumptions and their practical applications were deemed gravely deficient.

In addition to a body of coherent criticisms of the government's response, there were proposals in the newspapers for alternative policies. Editorials and articles advocated the payment of a living wage, the sanctioning of works which would be of benefit to their respective areas, less bureaucratic administrative structures, and an abandonment of strict political economy. These proposals were generalised in character, but they were real alternatives nonetheless.

It is important to realise that there existed this quite extensive contemporary criticism of government policy. It may have implications for historical research. Many historians have tended to be inhibited in their critique of the official response. Perhaps they believe that critical judgement may be based on hindsight. However, the fact that contemporaries exposed the deficiencies and limitations of Russell's actions, and challenged the prevailing Whitehall orthodoxies, may persuade historical researchers to be more critical without the fear of judging events anachronistically.

Extreme nationalism has interpreted the famine as an act of genocide against the Irish people by their British rulers. The Young Ireland movement was primarily responsible for politicising the events of 1845-49, especially its appalling mortality, which was invested with genocidal intent. The seeds of such a belief were sown, however, before many of Young Ireland's pronouncements. The famine generated great bitterness towards England, a bitterness reflected in, and fuelled by the newspapers. In the local press in Waterford charges of incompetence and indifference were levelled on a frequent basis against the government. Belief in an incompetent and inadequate response was easily transmuted, in an atmosphere choked by death, starvation, and disease, into a belief in a deliberate policy of genocide. On the evidence of the Waterford newspapers, the press played a significant role in creating a climate of opinion which gave the genocide charge credibility and acceptability.

Likewise, the interpretation of famine emigration as banishment and forced exile found some of its most vociferous exponents among extreme nationalists. However, Waterford newspapers articulated such sentiments also. Moreover, evictions had been termed *'extermination'* in the local press. Such views arose spontaneously out of bitter common experiences shared by significant numbers of the population, but the press gave them a wider currency and respectability. In effect, newspapers, by reflecting and influencing public opinion, helped create a climate conducive to the spread of the ideas of a more extreme nationalism.

In an editorial of 10th December 1845, *The Chronicle and Munster Advertiser* sought to define the role it and other newspapers should play in relation to the unfolding distress caused by the potato failure:

> *We and the press of Ireland must do our duty. We must give the alarm and, as it were, keep firing the signal guns of distress, and ringing the alarm bells continuously, until the dreadful danger is made known to those who may render assistance.*

The self-defined role assumed by *The Chronicle and Munster Advertiser* was also effectively adopted by all other journals in Waterford, to a greater or lesser degree. They sought to publicise the full horrors of the famine, and in so doing bring them to the attention of the appropriate authorities. When a correspondent in a letter to *The Chronicle and Munster Advertiser* described the press '*as the only safety valve of the poor*',[290] a reality was being recognised and acknowledged – the only forum for the publicity of their destitution and the articulation of their needs was the newspapers. Though this '*safety valve*' could be distorted, and at times seriously so, by editorial considerations and middle class prejudices, the newspapers, by giving public testimony to the sufferings surrounding them, highlighted the plight of the famine's victims and became, after a fashion, a voice for the destitute.

The local press was frequently emotive in its coverage of the famine. In some of the more recent scholarly accounts, what has been termed '*a retreat from emotiveness*' has become apparent.[291] Descriptions of sufferings and starvation, often to be found in newspapers, have been omitted. A more sanitised approach to the events of 1845-49 is favoured. Perhaps there is the fear that the use of emotive descriptions may result in the works being termed '*nationalist*' and '*anti-British*'. A more clinical attitude is therefore deemed more desirable, even necessary. However, there is a danger of the sufferings of those who were most directly affected being minimised and unappreciated. Just as wallowing in their misfortunes may lead to the distortion of historical fact and perspective, so too may deliberate minimisation.[292]

Conclusion
On the evidence of the local newspapers there was a famine in Waterford. It caused much hardship, especially in the western part of

the county. Hunger and disease were widespread. Evictions and emigration compounded the misery. The government response was deemed inadequate by the press, and there was much criticism and condemnation of the official relief policy. The reportage in the same press conveyed something of the horrors of a terrible period. The newspapers of these years became, after a fashion the chroniclers of the poor and destitute, providing later generations with one of the few authentic records of the sufferings and privations which were visited on the people of Waterford during the years of the Great Hunger.

REFERENCES

Newspapers: *The Cork Examiner* (hereafter *CE*)
Waterford Freeman (hereafter *WF*)
Waterford Mail (hereafter *WM*)
The Chronicle and Munster Advertiser (hereafter *WC*)

1. Ó Gráda, Cormac, *The Great Irish Famine* (Dublin, 1989) p.10 for his observations on this fact.
2. A recent publication commemorating the event, Cathal Póirtéir (Ed.), *The Great Irish Famine* (Cork, 1995) has only one essay relating to a local area – Skibereen, Co. Cork.
3. *CE*, 8 Aug. 1845.
4. ibid, 18 Aug. 1845.
5. ibid, 3 Sept. 1845.
6. *WF*, 17 Sept. 1845.
7. *CE*, 15 Oct. 1845.
8. *WM*, 25 Oct. 1845.
9. *WF*, 1 Nov, 1845.
10. ibid, 12 Nov. 1845.
11. Ó Gráda, Cormac, op. cit. pp. 39-40.
12. *WM*, 1 Nov. 1845. For advice see, ibid, 25 Oct. 1845; 8 Nov. 1845.
13. Daly, Mary E., *The Famine in Ireland* (Dundalk, 1986) p.53.
14. *WM*, 22 Oct. 1845.
15. ibid, 1 Nov. 1845.
16. ibid, 22 Oct. 1845.
17. ibid, 26 Nov. 1845.
18. ibid, 10 Dec. 1845.
19. *WC*, 5 Nov. 1845.
20. *WM*, 15 Nov. 1845.
21. ibid, 26 Nov. 1845.
22. Daly, Mary E., op. cit. pp.53-54.
23. *WF*, 17 Jan. 1846.
24. *CE*, 2 Feb. 1846.
25. *WF*, 4 Feb. 1846.
26. ibid, 11 Feb. 1846.
27. ibid, 14 Feb. 1846.
28. *The Chronicle and Munster Advertiser was* attacked by members of the relief committee and local repealers. See *WF*, 25 Feb. 1846; *WC*, 25 Feb. 1846.

29. See above.
30. *WM*, 21 Mar. 1846.
31. *WF*, 2 May 1846.
32. *CE*, 29 Apr. 1846.
33. *WF*, 2 May 1846.
34. *WM*, 12 Aug. 1846.
35. ibid, 26 Aug. 1846.
36. *WC*, 29 Aug. 1846.
37. *WF*, 3 Sept. 1846.
38. ibid, 19 Aug. 1846.
39. ibid, 29 Aug. 1846.
40. ibid, 3 Sept. 1846.
41. ibid, 9 Sept. 1846.
42. *WC*, 7 Oct. 1846.
43. *WF*, 2 Dec. 1846.
44. ibid, 6 Jan. 1847.
45. ibid, 9 Jan. 1847.
46. *WM*, 13 Jan. 1847.
47. *WF*, 17 Feb. 1847.
48. ibid, 24 Feb. *1847.*
49. ibid.
50. *WC*, 20 Mar. 1847.
51. ibid.
52. ibid, 7 Apr. 1847.
53. *WM*, 5 May 1847.
54. *CE*, 10 May 1847.
55. *WM*, 22 May *1847.*
56. ibid.
57. ibid, 12 May 1847.
58. ibid, 2 June 1847.
59. *WC*, 30 Sept. 1846.
60. *WF*, 23 Jan. 1847.
61. *WM*, 7 Apr. 1847.
62. ibid, 12 May 1847.
63. ibid, 2 June 1847.
64. *CE*, 10 Mar. 1847. The letter was dated 3 March.
65. *WF*, 20 Feb. 1847.
66. ibid, 6 Mar. 1847.
67. ibid, 8 Mar. 1847.
68. According to Christine Kinealy, in *This Great Calamity*, median rate for mortality in each county in 1847 was 2.6 per cent. Waterford exceeded this average with a rate of 3.3 per cent.
69. Daly, Mary E., op. cit. p.101.
70. ibid, p.102.
71. MacArthur, W., "Medical history of the Famine", in R. Dudley Edwards and T. Desmond Williams (Eds.), *The Great Famine Studies in Irish History, 1845-1852* (Dublin, 1994).p.275.
72. Daly, Mary E., op. cit. p.104.
73. MacArthur, W., op. cit. p.266.
74. In Skibereen, for example, post mortems for 1846-47 recorded that 44 per cent of deaths were caused by fever *and* 22 per cent by dysentery. (See P. Hickey,

"Famine, Mortality and Emigration: A profile of six parishes in the Poor Law Union of Skibereen, 1846-7" in P. O'Flanagan and C. Buttimer (Eds.) *Cork History and Society* (Dublin, 1993), p.901.
75. Daly, Mary E., op. cit. p.103.
76. Quoted in P. Hickey, op. cit. p.901.
77. MacArthur, W., op. cit. p.286.
78. Cited in L. Geary, 'Famine, Fever and Bloody Flux' in C. Póirtéir (ed.), *The Great Irish Famine*, (Cork, 1995) p.83.
79. *CE*, 10 May 1847.
80. *WM*, 12 May 1847.
81. ibid, 16 June 1847.
82. *CE*, 11 June 1847.
83. ibid, 16 June 1847.
84. Daly, Mary E., op. cit. p.55.
85. *WC*, 29 Sept. 1847.
86. ibid, 22 Jan. 1848.
87. *WM*, 26 Jan. 1848.
88. *WC*, 16 Feb. 1848.
89. ibid, 15 May 1847.
90. Daly, Mary E., op. cit. pp.70-71; G. Ó Tuathaigh, *Ireland before the Famine 1798-1848* (Dublin, 1972) pp.209-210.
91. *WM*, 15 Apr. 1846.
92. *WF*, 11 Apr. 1846.
93. *WM*, 3 June 1846.
94. ibid, 6 June 1846.
95. *WF*, 6 June 1846.
96. Daly, Mary E., op. cit. pp.73-74.
97. ibid, p.74.
98. *WM*, 4 July 1846.
99. *WF*, 27 June 1846.
100. Quoted in Daly, Mary E., op. cit. p.75.
101. ibid.
102. *CE*, 8 Oct. 1845.
103. ibid, 26 July 1846.
104. *WF*, 12 Nov. 1845.
105. ibid, 11 Feb. 1846.
106. Daly, Mary E., op. cit. p.76.
107. *WF*, 3 Sept. 1846.
108. ibid, 21 Oct. 1846.
109. ibid, 2 Dec. 1846.
110. ibid, 23 Jan. 1847.
111. O'Neill, Timothy P., "The Organisation and Administration of Relief, 1845-1852", in Edwards and Williams (eds.), *The Great Famine*, p.228.
112. Daly, Mary E., op. cit. p.80.
113. *WC*, 26 Sept. 1846.
114. ibid, 7 Oct. 1846.
115. ibid, 17 Oct. 1846.
116. *WF*, 11 Nov. 1846.
117. Ó Gráda, Cormac, op. cit. p.62.
118. Daly, Mary E., op. cit. p.77.
119. Ó Gráda, Cormac, op. cit. p.44.

120. *WF,* 21 Oct. 1846.
121. *CE,* 18 Nov. 1846.
122. *WF,* 23 Jan. 1847.
123. ibid, 8 Mar. 1847.
124. O'Neill, Timothy P., op. cit. pp.230-31.
125. Daly, Mary E., op. cit. p.77.
126. O'Neill, Timothy P., op. cit. p.234.
127. *WF,* 21 Nov. 1846.
128. ibid, 9 Jan. 1847.
129. *ibid,* 17 Oct. 1846.
130. ibid, 9 Jan. 1847.
131. ibid, 11 Nov. 1846.
132. ibid, 23 Jan. 1847.
133. ibid, 17 Oct. 1846.
134. ibid, 11 Nov. 1846.
135. *WC,* 20 Jan. 1847.
136. *WF,* 17 Mar. 1847.
137. ibid, 31 Mar. 1847.
138. ibid.
139. ibid, 7 Apr. 1847.
140. ibid, 20 Mar. 1847.
141. ibid, 24 Mar. 1847. A recent researcher has written that "starving people ate several varieties of seaweed. Beaches were stripped bare of the tidal crop". See E. M. Crawford, "Food and Famine", in Cathal Póirtéir (ed.), *The Great Irish Famine,* p.65.
142. Daly, Mary E., op. cit. p.88.
143. *WF,* 26 Aug. *1846.*
144. *WM,* 16 Dec. 1846.
145. ibid.
146. *WF,* 17 Oct. 1846.
147. Mitchel, John, *Jail Journal, or five years in British prisons* (Dublin, 1982), p. xlix.
148. Bourke, P.M. Austin, *The Visitation of God? The potato and the Great Irish Famine* (Dublin, 1993) p.165.
149. Daly, Mary E., op. cit. p.115.
150. *WF,* 24 Oct. 1846.
151. ibid, 29 Nov. *1845.*
152. *WC,* 22 Apr. 1846.
153. ibid, 16 May 1846.
154. *WF,* 24 Oct. 1846.
155. ibid, 11 Feb. 1846.
156. ibid, 3 Oct. 1846.
157. *WM,* 24 Oct. 1846.
158. ibid.
159. *WF,* 9 Jan. 1847.
160. ibid, 10 Mar. 1847.
161. ibid, 10 Apr. 1847.
162. Bourke, P.M. Austin, op. cit. p.165.
163. Crawford, E.M., op. cit. pp.65-66.
164. *WF,* 3 Oct. 1846.
165. Ó Gráda, Cormac, op. cit. p.61. Professor Ó Gráda summarises the opinions of other historians.

166. Bourke, P.M. Austin, op. cit. p.165.
167. ibid.
168. Kinealy, Christine op. cit. p.354.
169. ibid.
170. Donnelly, James S. Jnr., "Mass Evictions and the Great Famine", in Poirteir, Cathal (ed.), *The Great Irish Famine* (Cork, 1995) pp.155-156.
171. Daly, Mary E., op. cit. pp.109-113.
172. *CE*, 12 Sept. 1845.
173. ibid, 21 Jan. 1846.
174. WF, 4 Feb. 1846.
175. Donnelly, James S. Jnr., op. cit. p.157.
176. *CE*, 15 Apr. 1846.
177. *WF*, 3 Sept. 1846.
178. ibid, 12 Sept. 1846.
179. *WM*, 30 Sept. 1846.
180. *WC*, 2 Jan. 1847.
181. *WF*, 6 Jan. 1847.
182. ibid, 13 Jan. 1847.
183. *CE*, 10 Mar. 1847.
184. *WC*, 2 Jan. 1847.
185. *CE*, 24 May 1847.
186. ibid.
187. *WM*, 3 July 1847.
188. *WC*, 22 Jan. 1848.
189. ibid, 6 Oct. 1847.
190. *CE*, 8 Oct. 1847.
191. *WC*, 13 Oct. 1847; *CE*, 22 Oct. 1847.
192. *CE*, 24 Oct. 1847.
193. *WM*, 27 Oct. 1847.
194. ibid.
195. ibid.
196. *CE*, 5 Nov. 1847.
197. The letter outlined an organisational structure for the proposed league. There was to be a central committee composed of one lady representative of each townland; this representative was to be elected by the female inhabitants. The duties of the elected committee members were to receive funds, collect facts, and bring local grievances before the central committee.
198. *WC*, 22 Jan. 1848.
199. ibid, 12 Feb. 1848.
200. ibid, 16 Feb. 1848.
201. ibid, 27 May 1848.
202. O'Rourke, John, *The history of the Great Irish Famine of 1847, with notices of earlier famines.* (Dublin, 1989) p.171.
203. *WC*, 12 Feb. 1848.
204. *WC*, 1 Jan. 1848.
205. ibid.
206. Donnelly, James S. Jnr., op. cit. p.166.
207. *WC*, 16 Feb. 1848.
208. *WC*, 12 Feb. 1848.
209. Nowlan, Kevin B., "The Political Background", in Edwards and Williams (eds.), *The Great Famine: Studies in Irish History* (Ireland, 1956) p.138.

210. Daly, Mary E., op. cit. p.86.
211. ibid.
212. *WF*, 16 Sept. 1846.
213. *WM*, 30 Sept. 1846.
214. *WC*, 7 Oct. 1846.
215. *WF*, 3 Oct. 1846.
216. *WC*, 31 Oct. 1846.
217. ibid.
218. Daly, Mary E., op. cit. p.87.
219. *WF*, 16 Jan. 1847.
220. ibid, 9 Jan. 1847.
221. *WM*, 16 Oct. 1847.
222. ibid, 9 Feb. 1848.
223. ibid, 16 Feb. 1848.
224. ibid, 17 Nov. *1847.*
225. ibid, 24 Nov. 1847.
226. ibid, 11 Dec. 1847.
227. ibid, 18 Dec. 1847.
228. Donnelly, James S. Jnr., "Landlords and Tenants", in Vaughan, W.E. (ed.), *A New History of Ireland V.: Ireland under the Union, 1801-70*, (Oxford, 1989), p.337.
229. Donnelly, James S. Jnr., *The Land and People of Nineteenth Century Cork: The rural economy and the land question* (London, 1975) p.117.
230. *WF*, 10 Mar. 1847.
231. *WM*, 5 Jan. 1848.
232. ibid.
233. *WM*, 27 Nov. 1847; *WC*, 24 Nov. 1847.
234. *WM*, 15 Dec. 1847; *WC*, 15 Dec. 1847.
235. Kinealy, Christine, op. cit. p.298.
236. Fitzpatrick, David, "Flight from Famine", in Poirteir, Cathal (ed.), *The Great Irish Famine*, (Cork, 1995) p.175.
237. Ó Gráda, Cormac, op. cit. p.55.
238. *WM*, 27 May 1846.
239. O Rourke, John, op. cit. p.246.
240. *WF*, 31 Mar. 1847.
241. *WC*, 27 Mar. 1847.
242. ibid, 10 Mar. 1847.
243. *WF*, 10 Apr. 1847.
244. *WC*, 23 Sept. 1848.
245. ibid, 18 Nov. 1848.
246. *WN*, 26 Jan. *1849.*
247. ibid, 13 Apr. 1849.
248. ibid, 17 May, 1850.
249. Kinealy, Christine, op. cit. p.297.
250. Fitzpatrick, David, op. cit. pp.176-177.
251. *WF*, 20 Mar. 1847.
252. Daly, Mary E., op. cit. p.107.
253. Fitzpatrick, David, op. cit. p.179.
254. Litton, Helen, The Irish Famine: An Illustrated History, (Dublin, 1994), p.105.
255. Daly, Mary E., op. cit. p.107.
256. *WM*, 4 Aug. 1847.
257. Donnelly, James S. Jnr., "Excess Mortality and Emigration", in Vaughan, W.E.

(ed.), *A new history of Ireland (Vol. V): Ireland under the Union 1801-1870* (Oxford, 1989) p.356.

258. Fitzpatrick, David, op. cit. p.179.
259. Donnelly, James S. Jnr., "Excess Mortality and Emigration", in Vaughan, W.E. (ed.), *A new history of Ireland (Vol. V.): Ireland under the Union 1801-1870* (Oxford, 1989) p.356.
260. *WF*, 18 Apr. 1846.
261. ibid, 10 Apr. 1847.
262. *WC*, 10 Mar. 1847.
263. ibid, 20 Mar. 1847.
264. Daly, Mary E., op. cit.106.
265. Donnelly, James S. Jnr., "Excess Mortality and Emigration", in Vaughan, W.E. (ed.), *A new history of Ireland (Vol. V.): Ireland under the Union 1801-1870* (Oxford, 1989) p.353.
266. ibid, pp.353-54.
267. *WC*, 10 Mar. 1847.
268. Donnelly, James S. Jnr., "Excess Mortality and Emigration", in Vaughan, W.E. (ed.), *A new history of Ireland (Vol. V.): Ireland under the Union 1801-1870* (Oxford, 1989) p.355.
269. Kinealy, Christine, op. cit. p.299.
270. *WC*, 27 Mar. 1847.
271. *WN*, 13 Apr. 1849.
272. ibid, 6 Apr. 1849.
273. *WF*, 10 Apr. 1847.
274. *WC*, 27 Mar. 1847.
275. ibid, 8 July 1847.
276. *WN*, 26 Jan. 1849.
277. Fitzpatrick, David, op. cit. p.178.
278. *WF*, 9 Jan. 1847.
279. *WC*, 10 Feb. 1847.
280. ibid, 5 Sept. 1846.
281. *WM*, 1 May 1847.
282. ibid, 13 May 1848.
283. ibid, 13 Sept. 1848.
284. *WN*, 22 Dec. 1848. This advice included: "*An Emigrant going to America should always provide for a 60 day passage, although he may not be half that time crossing. It is always better and safer for Irish people to emigrate at Irish ports. When you arrive on the new soil, get into the heart of the country. Do not refuse any situation that may turn up.*"
285. Fitzpatrick, David, op. cit. pp.180-181.
286. *WN*, 6 Apr. 1849.
287. Fitzpatrick, David, op. cit. p.178.
288. ibid, p.180.
289. Ó Gráda, Cormac, op. cit. p.57.
290. *WC*, 22 Sept. 1847.
291. Ó Gráda, Cormac, op. cit. p.41.
292. Kinealy, Christine, op. cit. p.342.

Chapter 10

The Quaker relief effort in Waterford

JOAN JOHNSON

Introduction

The Ring graveyard was full of life and celebration that fine August day in 1994. The people of Ring wished to mark the life and famine relief work of the Rev. James Alcock and I was amongst those invited as a Quaker presence to share with them. He was *"a friend to all"* we were told and had worked ardently to save the Ring fishing community at the time of the famine. With local relief practically gone, he had appealed to the Quakers in Waterford. They responded positively and a strong link was forged between James Alcock and Joshua Strangman, Secretary of the Waterford Quaker Relief Committee, known as the Waterford Auxiliary Committee. The Waterford Auxiliary Committee comprised –

Richard Allen	George White
Joshua William Strangman	James Walpole
Thomas W. Jacob	Samuel White
Joseph S. Richardson	Thomas H. Strangman
Thomas Robinson White.	

They provided grants and loans through the Rev. Alcock to retrieve the pawned boats and gear; they encouraged new and more effective methods of fishing; they worked towards having restrictive and discriminatory fishing laws changed. This was sustained through the famine years and its immediate aftermath, enabling the Ring community to survive and thrive down to this present day.

I stood during the Ecumenical Service, humbled by the gratitude of the present Ring community, for events that took place five generations ago and aware of my limited knowledge of that time. During the day a story unfolded, which set me on a route of enquiry to discover the broader picture of the Quaker famine relief effort in Waterford.

First Steps toward Relief, October-November 1846

By September/October 1846 it was obvious that the total failure of the potato crop was going to have disastrous effects on the labouring population. At their Quarterly Meeting, on 19th October, Munster Friends decided that something should be done to help. Three days later a Waterford committee was established to alleviate the "*destitution which the poor are now suffering and likely to suffer in the approaching winter*. Joshua Strangman and George White were to gather subscriptions.[1] Within five weeks they had raised £815, mainly from among their own numbers. Some further money was raised over the following months, including a collection from the pupils of Newtown School. (Appendix 1)[2] They put initial contributions to immediate use; by 26th November they had visited the most deprived parts of the city, had selected 180 people in desperate need of immediate food and established a soup kitchen for them. They anticipated that within two weeks they would have to feed five to six hundred people.[3]

A start had therefore been made in Waterford when the Society of Friends in Dublin decided that direction should be given to such local efforts and on 13th November, a Central Relief Committee was formed comprising such well-known names as Bewley, Pim, Allen and Jacob. They were to be advised by twenty one *"Corresponding Members"* from around the country. Corresponding from Waterford City were Joshua Strangman and Thomas White Jacob; from Portlaw was Joseph Malcomson; from Clonmel Benjamin Grubb; from Youghal Thomas Harvey; and Joseph Haughton from Ferns.[4]

The Waterford Quaker Relief Committee therefore became part of a co-ordinated national plan. In Munster three other auxiliary committees were established, in Clonmel, Cork, and Limerick. To the Cork committee was assigned responsibility for County Waterford west of Dungarvan while the Clonmel committee were to look after the adjoining area of Waterford (Barony of Glenahiry and Upperthird).The Waterford Auxiliary Committee were assigned the rest of County Waterford as well as all of Counties Wexford and Kilkenny.

Before the end of November 1846 Joshua Strangman had drawn up an extensive report on the consequences of potato failure locally. Its effects on Waterford City he tellingly expresses thus:

> .... *we may class the distressed and destitute under several heads. The first comprises the aged, infirm and widows. This class have been accustomed to subsist partially on the produce of a little knitting, but principally 'on the charity of the neighbours'; and this latter source being now, from the pressure of the times, dried up, they may be looked upon as really the most destitute, and consequently to them the attentions of Friends here has been, in the first instance, directed.*
>
> *Another class comprises the poorest of the peasantry compelled by dire necessity to seek refuge in the towns. They mostly consist of women with children, the husband being perhaps employed at a distance on some of the public works and whose weekly stipend is*

insufficient to support them. For these classes gratuitous relief seems the only remedy for they possess no means of payment and good soup, with portion of bread, will be found perhaps, the most economical.

The third class consists of the families of the men employed in public works whose earnings (one shilling per day) are inadequate to provide sufficient food at its present high price for their large families.[5]

Our issue of food commenced on 21st instant. It is given out four times per week and consists of 1 quart of good soup and half a pound of bread and costs about two pence farthing per ration.[6]

Strangman goes on to describe how such people buy up *"Flummery"* which he says is waste from starch yards sold at one penny per gallon, *"poor watery substance"* but yet in such demand that police are often called in to maintain order. These people have also pawned all clothing, furniture and bedding, stating that it was necessary to do so to feed their children –

and indeed the wan features and sharpened countenances of the children bore ample testimony that theirs was no exaggerated tale.

Joshua Strangman did not claim such direct knowledge of country districts and could only judge by the quality of products such as *"half-fed pigs"* coming to the market in Waterford. He feared, however, that bad as the distress was in the city, *"it will be much exceeded in the country parts, especially in the mountain districts"*. His colleague, Thomas White Jacob, informing the Society of Friends in London about the situation in the Waterford area, wrote in November:

I fear the accounts you have received in England of the calamitous state of the potato crop are not exaggerated. What remains of the potatoes is (with scarcely any exception) unfit for human food....[7]

Extension of Relief Effort, 1847

By the beginning of January Quaker women in Waterford city had visited nine hundred people in possible need of relief and had selected five hundred and eighty of them. These were provided with a ration of a quart (just over a litre) of soup and half a pound of bread four times a week (later five times), at a cost of 2d. per ration. By February 1847 four hundred and fifty gallons of soup per day was being distributed to six hundred and fifty of the very poorest citizens as well as 2400 lbs of bread.[8] Whatever difficulties there might have been at the beginning –

The recipients soon acquire the system of quietude and order we have adopted. The issue is effected without difficulty at the rate of eight or nine per minute. Not a loud word is spoken and scarcely a voice heard except that of grateful acknowledgement for the relief dispersed.[9]

Three hundred and fifty beds of straw were also issued in early January and in March bedding for one thousand persons.[9]

There were other feeding operations in the city. One was the Fish House on the Quay which fed 319 people daily. Another, as the childhood memory of Thomas N. Harvey recollects was,

going up to the Fanning Institution in Waterford City with my father to assist in giving out soup and bread to long rows of starving creatures.[10]

The Waterford Auxiliary Committee acknowledged the role of two other voluntary relief committees in the city as

embracing the classes immediately outside the circle to which our attention has been particularly directed.

One sold bread at one penny per pound and the other sold bread and coal at reduced prices.[11]

The Society of Friends in Waterford could well have felt that they had fulfilled their obligation by looking after the needy in the city area where they had a presence, but in compliance with the objectives of the Central Relief Committee they sought to extend their efforts into the seething unknown of the countryside. Of particular concern was Bonmahon which Strangman visited in early March 1847 in order to set up a soup kitchen. Eight people had died there a few days before his visit, all having been put off the public works. An increase of fever in the area meant that further fatalities were to be expected.[12]

One report of early January 1847 fatalistically expressed what their religious philosophy committed them to:

the flood of desolation pouring its accumulated torrent, but so utterly disproportionate are all our efforts that many would shrink in dismay were they not animated by a measure of that love which transcends all other motives of human action.[13]

Joshua Strangman himself expressed the foreboding and trepidation with which they undertook this enormous task, thus:

with regard to the future, although of a hopeful temperament and disposed to look on the bright side, yet on the present occasion seeing how much distress exists so early in the season (late November 1846) I may candidly admit I cannot contemplate the advance of winter and spring without feeling much solicitude.[14]

Most immediately in need of help was the parish of Grange in the Slieve Grine highlands. This fell under the care of the Cork Auxiliary Committee and was visited in January 1847 by Friends from Youghal. Around Newtown *"many widows and children quite destitute...the men on the public works earning 10d. per day, quite insufficient for their support"*. One hovel they visited had a family of six *"without furniture, utensils for cooking, straw to lie on...and without food"*. The man of the house *"was hardly able to raise his head from exhaustion"*. In another house the body of a child was found. The father had gone the eight miles into Youghal for a coffin which meant sacrificing two or three days vital pay. Assistance was given to all these people. Discussions were held with the local priests and arrangements made to provide boilers for soup kitchens both at Grange and at Old Parish helped by two grants of £10.

Soup too continued to be distributed on an increasing scale in the city. The soup made by the Youghal and Waterford committees was probably quite similar to that recommended by the Dublin Committee with its emphasis on nutritional quality, as follows –

Receipt for 200 gallons
Beef, 150 lb.
Peas, 70 lb.
Oatmeal, 42 lb.
Scotch Barley, 42 lb.
Ground pepper and allspice, 1½ lb.
Salt, 1¼ stone.

To make the soup, fill the vessel about half full of water, when boiling put in the meat, having been previously cut into small pieces about the size of a walnut, and the bones broken small; an hour after put in the peas, first dividing them into bags, containing about 14 lb. each, and tied at the top, but leaving sufficient room for the peas to swell; in about four hours afterwards take out the bags and turn the peas into a tub; have them bruised into a paste, and put them back into the boiler along with the barley; keep it boiling gently for four or five hours, then put in the oatmeal, which should be first blended with cold water, and fill the boiler with water to the quantity required; put in the salt and spices an hour after the oatmeal; keep all well stirred for about half an hour, when it will be ready for delivery.[15]

The soup was made in boilers provided by the various auxiliary committees which came originally from the English Quaker Foundry in Coalbrookdale. By early 1847 the Waterford Committee had supplied boilers, similar to the surviving one illustrated here, as well as cash, to

Quaker soup boiler in the possession of Mrs and Mr Sheridan of John Hill, Waterford. The fire door is closed.
(Photograph courtesy Iris Graham).

fifteen locations. Six of these were in Waterford, one in Dunkitt and four in County Wexford. Cash assistance was also provided to named individuals who were running bona fide soup kitchens under other auspices. The biggest sum was £50 to Thomas Harvey of Youghal for his relief efforts in the stricken highlands between Dungarvan and Youghal. Eight other grants were made in Waterford totalling £115. Another £80 went to aiding four other soup kitchens in Wexford and £60 to three others in Kilkenny.[16] The Waterford Auxiliary Committee distributed a total of fifty five boilers, ten in County Wexford, twelve in Kilkenny and the thirty-three in Waterford.[17] An English Quaker, William Bennett visited Waterford in March 1847 and remarked on *"the admirable soup kitchens established under the care of Friends in that city"*.[18] Meanwhile, the Clonmel Auxiliary Committee had been distributing money and boilers to selected personnel not only in Tipperary but in the following parts of Waterford:

Clonmel Committee (February-March 1847)[19]

Place	Sponsor	Money	Boiler
Carrick-on-Suir	John Grubb	£10	
Kilsheelin	Thomas Ryan	£20	
Ballymacarbery	Robert Sparrow		2
Kilmanhan	Robert Sparrow		2
Kilsheelin	Thomas Ryan		2
Carrickbeg	Patrick Hayden		1
Carrickbeg	James N. Wall	£10	
Clogheen	W.G. Fennell	£10	1
Ballyporeen	Joseph Armstrong	£10	1
Ballymacarbery	Robert Sparrow	£10	1
Ardfinnan	Ch. Hart	£20	
Clogheen	Wm. G. Fennell	£10	
Carrick-on-Suir	Eliz. Jellico	£5	
Burncourt	Wm. G. Fennell	£15	1
Carrick-on-Suir	John Grubb	£15	1

One interesting aspect of the Quaker relief effort, with respect to current attitudes, was the role that women were free to play at a time when all official relief committees and all Boards of Guardians were exclusively male. In Clonmel on 5th March, *"Sarah Malcomson and Charlotte Moore attended from nine to eleven (o'clock); about 380 gallons of porridge disposed of, the quality good and the demand great"*. Ten days later they dispensed 690 gallons. Sometime later a further report from Clonmel is signed by Eliza Sargint and L.H. Strene:

> *We have attended here since ten o'clock this morning; tasted the soup and found it excellent and the demand for it was very brisk. We suggest for Fridays the manufacture of porridge made of Indian meal, oatmeal, water, pepper and onions with the addition of some salt herrings boiled in it and also that three or four wooden seats would be provided for the attendants.*[20]

Elizabeth Ridgeway in Ballygunner and Mary Owen at Cheekpoint were each granted £10 to organise relief in these places with a boiler also being given to Mary Owen for her to initiate a soup kitchen. Similar barrels of American Quaker aid were sent from Waterford for distribution by Jane Carr of Castle Annagh, New Ross (five bags of meal, one of beans) to Dorcas Nixon of Freshford (two of meal) and to Margaret Johnson of Fethard-on-Sea (four of meal). The Auxiliary Committee in Clonmel likewise supported the relief efforts of local women by providing money and food. In Carrick-on-Suir Elizabeth Jellico was given £5 *"for private distribution of food to poor housekeepers"* a like sum being given to the Fennell sisters of Cahir for *"private distribution of food to the poor"*. Eliza Fennell and her sisters in Ballybrado were given £5, one and a half cwts of rice and two cwts of meal to distribute in their area. The Waterford committee gave £10 to Margaret Mathews of Rockview and two barrels of meal to Ann Lynberry for distribution at Reisk.[21]

In early March 1847 Joshua Strangman revisited some of the rural areas *"within a circuit of 20 miles of the city"* where relief was being provided, hoping also to promote further soup kitchens. Since his last visit (the previous October?) he was shocked by *"the rapid descent in the scale of suffering"* but touched that

> *amidst this increased misery and woe I never witnessed or heard of such patient submission and endurance to outrages committed.... no murmuring, no reproaches on rulers or landlords – 'It is the Will of God' being the simple touching response to our enquiries.*

Joshua Strangman also reported on the relief effort in the city in March

1847. Up to then the three classes that he had reported as in need of relief the previous October (i.e. what he now called *"the sick, aged, infirm and widows with helpless families"*, those to whom the benefits of the Labour Act did not extend) were being given 713 rations per week comprising two pints of soup and half a pound of bread five days a week which cost £35. Also one thousand straw beds were given out during that bitter winter and some fuel. However –

> *In consequence of the still increasing distress several instances have recently come to our knowledge in which assistance is now required, where a few months since, the parties were in comparative comfort......among tradesmen such as tailors, shoemakers etc., who, having parted with all their little comforts, now severely feel the extreme pressure of the times.*

Joshua Strangman reports that in Waterford dysentery and fever were on the increase, with the numbers in the Fever Hospital quadrupling (53 to 212) in the first three months of 1847. Sixty more of the newly destitute were to be aided which would put further strain on the resources of the small Quaker community in Waterford. How widely their contribution was appreciated is indicated by the fact that the Church of Ireland Bishop of Cashel and the Catholic ex-mayor of Waterford, Thomas Meagher both asked the local auxiliary committee to apply to the Government Relief Commission in Dublin for a grant under the matching-funds system. Strangman said that they were unwilling to do so, *"least it might be supposed that our object was to publish abroad what little we have been able to accomplish."* Finally, he was persuaded to apply but was then turned down, as they were not an officially constituted relief committee.[22]

However, aid from a different source came to hand three months later. The Central Committee in Dublin had written to the Quakers in America sending copies of their reports, including Strangman's on Waterford. The reports were printed as an appeal in the Philadelphia-based Quaker journal The Friend in December 1846, and Famine Relief Committees were immediately set up over there to collect food and money to send to Ireland. The Westminster Government offered to transport the food across the Atlantic at their expense. Most of it landed in Liverpool and two transhipments from there arrived in the William Penn in Waterford at unspecified dates during the summer of 1847. Thirty seven ships came directly to Irish ports, mainly landing in Cork and the West of Ireland, but two shipments arrived in June 1847 in Waterford harbour for the use of the local Auxiliary Committee.

First to arrive was the Minerva from New York (13th May) followed a few weeks later by the William and Sarah, from Baltimore. The following are the details:[23]

Cargo	Minerva Shipment date 13th May, 1847	William and Sarah 29th May, 1847
Cwts* of meal	62	1685
Cwts* of corn	1032	3856**
Cwts* of pork	40	
Packages Clothes	28	2
Sundry packages	7	

*Figure given in barrels which are taken as equal to 280 lbs for grain and 200 lbs for pork.
**Original figure given in bushels which is taken to be 2 cwts.

Once this aid arrived it was distributed to responsible local personages between 19th June and 31st July 1847 for their distribution amongst the poor. The area serviced by this aid ran from Cashel through Freshford and Gowran to Bunclody and Enniscorthy to Ferns, embracing most of South East Ireland. About half of it went to County Waterford as follows:[24]

Waterford Committee

Date June	Place	Sponsor	Meal (barrels)	Beans (barrels)	Other
19	Kilronan	C. Fry	1		£5+1 rice
19	Clonmel	C. Phipps			2 rice
19	Dungarvan	T. Christian	10		
21	Ring	J. Alcock	10		
22	Stradbally	J.R. Smith	10		
22	Dunkitt	P. Rennie	3		
22	Cappoquin	L.F. Keane	2		
23	Ballinaparka	T. Fitzgerald	10		
24	Ballinacourty	M. Crofton	6		
30	Kilrossanty	W.J. Ardagh	20		
30	Kilmacow	J.T. Bourke	3		
30	Belmont	S. Roberts	1		
30	Annestown	W.E. Shaw	2		
30	Slaterbridge	R. Chearnley	6	1 pork	

July

1	Woodstock, Cappoquin	T. Walsh	2	
2	Waterford City	C. of I. Bishop	80	
3	Dungarvan	J.W. Strangman	175	20
5	Richmond	J.H. Alcock	3	1
9	Knockmahon	J. Petherick	6	1
9	Seskinane	R. Chearnley	10	2
10	Waterford City	R.C. Bishop	40	
		(Dr. Foran)		
16	Annestown	J.B. Palliser	5	1
24	Cheekpoint	Mary Owens	1	
28	Cappagh	R. Ussher	6	2
31	Dunkitt	O.P. Rennie	3	1

One lesser known aspect of the Quaker relief effort was the distribution of seed of both root and green crops as alternatives to planting solely potatoes. Early in 1847 the Waterford Committee pioneered this idea of seed distribution to small land-holders in the adjoining counties. This Waterford initiative which proved so successful was then followed by the Central Relief Committee in March '47 and the following year seed was distributed free of charge by Bianconi. The number of persons helped overall is most impressive.[25]

		lbs. of seed	Acres sown	Persons supplied
Barony of Forth				
Co. Wexford		120	24	60
Tipperary		720	158	430
Kilkenny		432	96½	141
Wexford		492	106	279
National	(1847)	36,196	9,652	40,903
	(1848)	133,796	32,446	148,094

The Ring Fishermen: (i) 1846-'48

Amongst others contacted about local conditions by Joshua Strangman was the Rev. James Alcock, Vicar of Ring. He described the appalling conditions that existed in Ring in Autumn 1846.

> *When your Honorary Secretary first applied to me for information respecting the fishermen of this district, I went in person to inspect their boats and fishing appointments and found that in almost every instance these latter had been pawned or sold for the purposes of food during the winter months and that the oars and lining of the boats had been used as fuel, so that of a fleet consisting of about one hundred fishing boats, not more than six*

or eight could be procured on this whole line of coast that might be considered seaworthy.

I observed the fishermen wandering along the cliffs in idleness with apathy or despair fixed on every countenance. They had neither nets nor lines nor hooks, all having been long since disposed of for food. Famine was raging at its height, while fever and dysentery, whose virulence was much increased by the impurities so prevalent in fishing hamlets, was hurrying many to a premature grave.

Our local subscriptions had long since been expended on the purchase of food. We had no relief to expect from resources that were already drained to the dregs.[26]

The Waterford Auxiliary Committee then devised a scheme whereby £1 to £3 would be loaned to each boat to be repaid weekly out of fishing earnings with one quarter of the loan remitted for reasonable punctuality in repayment – gratuitous relief was discouraged. Also *"each boat's crew received two stone of Indian meal per week to render them independent of outdoor relief"* which would have cost them time away from fishing. So successful was this scheme that by the Summer of 1847, having received aid and applied it locally, Alcock was able to tell Strangman, *"...your very liberal donation has been attended by success beyond my most sanguine expectations."* Forty nine boats were thus reportedly helped, totalling 150 crew.[27] The immediate sequel is conveyed by James Alcock thus:

Our ship's carpenters were immediately set to work. The fishermen might be observed making every preparation for the approaching season while their wives and daughters were busily engaged in spinning and making nets...

One boat's crew who had been compelled by extreme destitution, to sell during the winter, for less than half its value, a large sweep net, which was their only means of support, obtained a loan of £3, which enabled them to purchase another, and with this at the very first drought they obtained about 4000 mackerel, worth nearly £10. Another party to whom a similar advance had been made, took in one evening £50 worth of mackerel and scads.

A very poor man who obtained a loan of 15 shillings from the fund caught a turbot, for which he received the full amount of the sum advanced. A fourth party came to inform me that his whole substance, consisting of a little stack of corn and some household furniture, had been distrained by his landlord for rent, and that consequently, if not speedily assisted, he was inevitably ruined. He

225

got as much money as enabled him to procure at a pawn office some herring nets, and in two days he came to inform me that he had taken £15 worth of herrings, a sum almost sufficient to purchase the fee simple of the small holdings on which he had been living. It is scarcely necessary to add that the bailiffs were immediately withdrawn and the rent paid. I could mention many similar cases, but sufficient I trust has been said to prove, if proof were wanting, what inestimable benefits your munificent liberality has conferred on the poor fishermen of this district.[26]

Six months later Rev. Alcock was able to assure his mentors of the Waterford Friends' community that the fate of so many other short-term ventures had not befallen the Ring fisheries:

We have had, thank God, no destitution up to the present time; all are beginning once more to look cheerful, robust, and comfortable. They are provided with a sufficient supply of fishing gear for their immediate wants, and therefore constantly employed whenever the weather permits. I might almost add that no weather prevents them from putting to sea in search of fish so great is their anxiety and ambition to be distinguished for industry, hardihood and perseverance. It has been remarked that there were many more persons engaged in taking haddock, cod, and ling on this coast during the late inclement season than in any former year.

A very visible improvement is, I say, now observable among the fishermen. Their houses have been all newly thatched, and the whitened walls, and neatly sanded floors, give an appearance of cleanliness and comfort to those humble dwellings, to which the inmates were hitherto strangers.[28]

Other efforts were made in the Summer of 1847 to improve the lot of the Ring fishing community, as a selection from Alcock's description that July indicates:

Preparations are being made at Helvic under the management of a Scotch company for the purchase and curing of fish so that our prospects are brightening every day.....Money has been expended primarily on making nets and on the purchase of ropes......the barrel of clothes has done much to promote cleanliness amongst those who are in fever or recovering from it...

Alcock also comments on the reluctance of the fishing community to avail of the fever sheds there, comments on how punctual the fishermen are in making their repayments, but also makes it clear that he was running the relief and development operation there on very tight lines.[29]

Ring Fisheries (ii) Development 1848-'52

In 1848 the Quakers terminated their relief effort across the country. However, the egregious success of the collaboration between the Auxiliary Committee in Waterford and Rev. J. Alcock in Ring caused this particular relief effort to be continued. Furthermore, it pioneered new developmental patterns.

In Strangman's words –

> *That numerous efforts made within the last two years by benevolent individuals to benefit Irish fishermen have been unsuccessful is unhappily true, but whether its failure has been occasioned by the intractable character of the persons whose condition it was sought to ameliorate or by the unskilful application of the means to effect that object, the following case appears to me to afford an apt illustration. During the famine year of 1847, the neighbourhood in which I reside was placed under the supervision of the Waterford Auxiliary Relief Committee of the Society of Friends and they being anxious to encourage industrial employment at an early period directed their attention to the promotion of the coast fishery. With that object a sum of money was placed in the hands of a gentleman residing at Ballinacourty at the Eastern side of the entrance of the bay of Dungarvan to assist the fishermen of that locality – He was a very benevolent person and, considering the poorest and most destitute man stood the most need of aid, he made his selection from this class – thus practically holding out an inducement to every applicant to appear as wretched and as miserable as possible. The result was similar to what it has been in many other places – after a few months trial he pronounced them to be indolent, lazy and ungrateful and that further efforts would be unavailing and he therefore returned the balance remaining in his hands. On the opposite side of the same bay at a distance of about two miles is the Ring district and the wretched condition of its inhabitants, a hardy race of fishermen was at the same period brought under the notice of the Committee by the Vicar of the parish, James Alcock. He stated that their boats were out of repair, their oars had been burned as fuel, their clothing, furniture and fishing gear had been pledged for food and in one village alone one hundred families were daily receiving public relief. Besides a supply of twenty barrels of meal – the sum*

of £20 (subsequently increased to £57) was forwarded to him, to try what could be effected by means of small loans to enable the fishermen to repair their boats and resume their usual occupation thus making them producers of food instead of mere consumers of it. The judicious vicar who possesses the talent (a qualification much needed in Ireland) of being able to assist persons without making them dependent and also teaching them to rely upon their own exertions, made his selection solely from among the well conducted, sober and industrious – those who were anxious and willing to help themselves and truly important have been the results of his valuable exertions.[30]

Thus the vision had been formulated that relief was not just about feeding the starving but of enabling them to support themselves by promoting a permanent fishing industry at Ring. To achieve this an infrastructure was required and a wide ranging development plan emerged from the collaboration between Alcock in Ring and Strangman in Waterford. It may be divided into a number of elements, most of which ran concurrently.

Most urgent perhaps was the need for a pier. Surveys of the suggested site at Ballinagoul took place in late 1847 into early 1848. Alcock estimated that its completion *"will relieve of hundreds of those now congregated within its gloomy walls and raise the labouring classes from that degraded and servile position to which the late distressing trials had reduced them."*[31] He reported the urgency of the pier as witnessed by a visiting engineer in the winter of 1847-'48:

The pier at Ballinagoul built in 1848-'49 as part of the infrastructural development for the Ring fishermen at the behest of the Waterford Quakers and Rev. James Alcock.

It was blowing a gale of wind accompanied by severe showers of snow and sleet on the day when he visited Ballinagoul, and great was his surprise to see those brave fellows advancing towards the shore in their little yawls; nor was his astonishment less when he observed them casting anchor...and wading through the water with the fish on their back.[31]

When Joshua Strangman visited there in December 1848, work was under way using rock quarried locally, *"and the superintendent in charge gave us a gratifying account of the honesty and industry of the men employed, about sixty in number."*[32] By January 1849 it seems that the work was sufficiently finished for the pier to be in use.[33] Rev. Alcock and Joshua Strangman tried to promote the development of other aspects of the fisheries. Two fishing boats of unusual design for the locality (costing £60 each) were commissioned for construction at Ring and Alcock intended sending to Scotland for a skipper for each. Little detail survives about this endeavour. A fishing shop for gear, selling hooks, kemp, etc., was established, as well as a curing house at Helvick, following a £200 grant.[34]

Attempts were also made to provide more effective nets for deep-water fishing in addition to the shallow trammel nets already being used. However those were under threat from what seems to be the extraordinary conservatism of the Dungarvan fishing interests who, with the backing of an anachronistic law, objected to the success of the Ring fishermen and would have had them use old-fashioned hand lines as they themselves were using. Much energy was expended by the two patrons of Ring in fighting these interests. In October 1847 Rev Alcock informed the Waterford Auxiliary Committee that a recent bye-law had forbidden the Ring fishermen from using their nets in the hours of daylight. They were faced with confiscations of their nets and a £5 fine for failing to comply.[34] Alcock called on the Fishery Board to be induced to relax the laws. and in September 1848 asked whether the Quakers could help to have the law changed.

Joshua Strangman made many efforts to do so through correspondence with Dublin and London. Finally on December 1848, an enquiry was held by the Fisheries Board in Dungarvan.

The extraordinary nature of these proceedings are not relevant here, but in the course of the background evidence, Strangman made clear the importance of the trammel net.

A careful inventory of each man's stock was made for us...we found ...that the value of it amounted to £1,500. The fishermen assured us that if the 'absurd daylight restrictions' had been

Central Relief Committee of the Society of Friends
43 Fleet Street Dublin 10th of 3rd month 1848

Fishermen's Clothes & Nets forwarded to Joshua
William Strangman Waterford for distribution,
by Prizes, or otherwise, as may be deemed advisable,
for encouragement of the coast Fisheries

Item	Rate	£	s	d
5 Best Monkey Jackets — Blue & Linsey Woolsey lining @ 15/		3	15	
5 Good Monkey Jackets Grey & Linsey Woolsey lining @ 12/6		3	2	6
5 Good Monkey Jackets Blue & Drugget lining @ 12/6		3	2	6
5 Good Monkey Jackets — Black & Grey lining @ 10/		2	10	—
10 pairs strong Blue Flushing Trousers @ 7/6		3	15	—
20 pairs Linsey Woolsey do @ 4/		4	0	0
30 South Wester Hats @ 1/2		1	15	—
30 Coats oiled @ 3/4		5	0	0
30 Trousers do @ 2/6		3	15	—
		£ 30	15	—

2 Herring Nets Each 20 Fathoms
long 4 Fathoms deep, 1 Inch
mesh — Well Twine Barked Roped &
Corked Complete — Made by the
Manufacturer Jo Bridport Dorsetshire
for this Committee — @ 114/6 £ 11 . 9 . —
£ 42 . 4 . —

Errors Excepted
10th / 3rd month 1848

William Todhunter

Example of ledger sheet from the Central Relief Committee, Society of Friends, 10 March 1848.

relaxed that nearly double the quantity of fish would have been captured and 'that thrice the number of boats would have eagerly embarked in the same lucrative employment.[35]

While the Dungarvan hearing was not immediately successful, change did come about. In 1852, Rev. Alcock was able to state in his final report

the bye-law recently passed by the Commissioners of Fisheries has worked with a most beneficial effect......Our fishermen are now in as prosperous and thriving condition as they were before the famine. The fishermen are to be distinguished from the same class of persons around by their robust and healthy appearance;....and that their boats and gear are in good working condition.[36]

The Quaker Central Relief Committee more modestly described the Ring operators as having had *"a measure of success"*.

Alcock tried to deal with what he saw as health hazards posed by *"the slovenly habits and absence of neatness so manifest in these fishing hamlets"* by distributing brushes and lime free to each household. When this did not work he withheld all aid from those who refused to whitewash their houses *"This at length had the desired effect"* by early 1848.[37] When Joshua Strangman visited there in December 1848 he was understandably gratified to find –

the people comfortably off......several of the houses have been newly thatched and the whole place wears a thriving aspect.[38]

Conclusion

Research on the Quaker famine relief effort has shown that important aspects of their mid-19th century methods and beliefs were exposed for the first time to a wider public; these included making business decisions by consensus, keeping accurate records, the degree of their religious tolerance, their attitudes towards women and the value of the individual. Their work during the famine was not restricted by religion or gender, or by political or economic considerations; rather it was driven by a strong concern towards *"enabling the strong more effectively to help the weak"*. They had decided that they should *"extend their relief to those that were ready to perish"* and that *"their willing labours may be so directed as to effect the largest amount of good with the means at their disposal".*[39] Furthermore, wherever possible (as in Ring) they tried to look beyond the distress and address its cause. Perhaps it was here that they first realised that to give a man a fish, you feed him for a day; but to teach a man to fish, you feed him for his life.

The Friends community in Waterford City was about two hundred and fifty people. Between them they initially raised £854 and financed the initial relief effort in late 1846. They then distributed money and supplies from the Quaker Central Relief Committee in Dublin to local relief groups in Waterford City and County in 1847 (total amount £3,114-5s.-5d.) as well as the foodstuffs from America in June and July. Altogether 154 tons of food were distributed in Waterford, generally made into soup, porridge or bread. Its total value, including the price of thirty-three boilers, was £2,640. Also the Waterford Auxiliary Committee distributed in Wexford and Kilkenny a further eighty-five tons of food and twenty-two boilers at a total cost of nearly two thousand pounds.[40]

The Alcock memorial in the Church of Ireland graveyard near Ring.

However, by early 1848 Waterford Auxiliary Committee reported to the Central Relief Committee in Dublin that their funds were *"very much reduced"* and that none of the soup kitchens for which they had provided boilers were still in operation, nor had been *"for several months past"*. Meanwhile, the workhouses had expanded their operations to include soup kitchens. The Quakers own resources being as they put it *"much reduced"* they decided that the destitute *"should be induced to avail themselves"* of workhouse relief measures while they provide *"good warm clothes, particularly flannel, and shoes at half price"* to those *"struggling to support themselves and to maintain their independence"*.[41]

How successful were their efforts? How did they rate their own success? During the whole of this time, some 37,000 letters, recommendations or reports were dispatched.[42] The later ones reflect a certain amount of disillusionment and regret that their efforts were not creating a more permanent improvement on the condition of those they had been able to reach – despite having distributed £200,000 worth of direct aid, established soup kitchens, distributed food and intervened in a number of other practical ways.[43]

Perhaps the Quakers may not have given themselves credit for saving an unknown number of lives after the total failure of the potato crop in August 1846, through the bitter winter that followed and over the next twelve months when changes in government policy left gaps in the relief programme during which families starved to death. By the end of that time government relief agencies had belatedly been providing similar relief to that piloted by the Quakers for the survivors. Nevertheless, exhaustion of energy, morale and resources caused the Central Relief Committee to reduce their overall effort in 1848. Yet Strangman and Waterford Quakers continued their connection with the fisheries at Ring up to 1851. Alcock's anticipation of the future of the fisheries in April 1848 was –

What a vast field for employment will this open for our dense population! How it will relieve the workhouse of hundreds of those now confined within its gloomy walls and raise the labouring classes of the district from that degraded and servile position to which their late distressing trials had reduced them. The fisheries, if properly worked, contain inexhaustible treasures...[44]

By 1851 he was able to report to the Quaker Relief operation:

there has been no diminution of the population from eviction, no emigration, no abandonment of premises through distress, no dilapidation of houses, a reduced poor rate, a large stock of cured fish on hands.....it may fairly be inferred that much good has been affected in Ring through your means...and the fishermen have continued to support their families in comparative comfort for a considerable period even after your favours were discontinued.[45]

The fruits of Rev. Alcock's labours were acknowledged at the ecumenical service in the old Church of Ireland graveyard overlooking the still thriving and flourishing community of Ring, which might have disappeared along with so many others were it not for his dedicated work and his concern for all in the parish of Ring. He would have been gratified to see that the *"much good"* which *"had been effected in Ring"* through Quaker support and his own dedication, had continued for the intervening 150 years (*"a considerable period"*) through the Ring

Fishermen's *"perseverance and hardihood of which they are distinguished".*[46]

I can now begin to appreciate the sense of gratitude to the Waterford Quakers for help given. In early 1847 with deprivation and destitution increasing, lives swung precariously on the edge in Ring. The relief from Waterford Quakers seemed to tilt the balance. Small loans and grants for fishing gear was the initial response. With new and effective fishing methods encouraged, the restrictive fishing laws resolving, a pier at Ballinagoul completed and two modern boats provided, Ring community was revitalised in the subsequent years.

Those gathered that day in Ring paid tribute to Rev. James Alcock, M.A.

Who for 60 years was the faithful and zealous Vicar of this Parish. For the above period during the scourge of famine and cholera he proved himself the generous friend, the wise guide and councillor of the sick, distressed and afflicted of all classes and creeds.

(Died March 23rd 1893 aged 88 years)
(On the tombstone in the old graveyard – Ring)

Subsequent to my visit to Ring in August 1994 my route of inquiry led me to discover the broader aspects of Quaker Famine relief in Waterford; their approach at that time was more than simply to give relief; they tried to look behind the immediate distress and address the cause as a modern historian has expressed it (1) *"Quakers....were advanced in their conception of poverty, disaster, limitation of philanthropy and the responsibility of the State and also in their ability to look beyond the individual to the cause."*[47] Was this approach to relief, the seed about which Joshua Strangman wrote? *"The seed may be actively germinating in the soil, though hidden from our view...we must be content to sow in hope and patiently to wait."*[48] Has this seed germinated? (2) *"It is their (Quakers) kind of intervention which is now accepted world wide as the appropriate method of assisting in relief development".*[49]

REFERENCES

1. Waterford Monthly Meeting of Friends, 22nd Oct. and 26th Nov. 1846. Copies of minutes are in the Friends Meeting House in Waterford but contain no further references to famine relief, indicating that this was minuted separately. These are not extant.
2. Society of Friends Relief of Distress Papers; 2/506/42-45; Also *Cork Examiner* 13/11/1846, reporting on contract with Mr. Thompson to supply beef.
3. Friends Historical Library, Swanbrook House, Morehampton Road, Dublin 4 (henceforth FLH) houses much of the surviving famine archive of Quaker relief.

"Distress in Ireland" (London), Pamphlet Box 20, No. 133. I would like to thank the staff of the library there for their kind and diligent assistance.

4. Society of Friends, *Transactions of the central relief committee of the Society of Friends during the Famine in Ireland in 1846 and 1847* (Dublin, 1852), pp.33, 129, 130.

5. The Friend (Philadelphia Jan. 1847), p.110. Letter dated 25 November published as part of Report from CRC.

6. F.H.L., Distress in Ireland (Dublin, 1846), Pamphlet Box 20, No. 130, 13 Nov. 1846.

7. ibid, Address from the committee of the Society of Friends in London on the subject of the Distress in Ireland. Pamphlet Box 20, No. 133.

8. Society of Friends, *Transactions of the central relief committee of the Society of Friends during the Famine in Ireland 1846 and 1847* (Dublin, 1852) p.183.

9. F.H.L., Pamphlet Box 7, No. 27, Extracts from correspondence published by the Central Relief Committee of the Society of Friends on the subject of Distress in Ireland, No. 1, p.24. Also Society of Friends Relief of Distress Papers 2/506/6-32 D5183.

10. Harvey, Thomas N., *Autobiography of T.N. Harvey* (Waterford 1904) *The Waterford Chronicle* 2 Jan. 1847.

11. Extracts from correspondence published by the Central Relief Committee of the Society of Friends on the subject of Distress in Ireland No. 1 (FHL) Pamphlet Box 7, No.27 p.24.

12. *Waterford Chronicle*, 13 March 1847: Report of Public Meeting.

13. Extracts from correspondence published by the Central Relief Committee of the Society of Friends on the subject of Distress in Ireland (FHL) No. 2 pp.23, 25.

14. F.H.L., Distress in Ireland (Dublin), Pamphlet Box 20, No. 130, 13th Nov. 1846.

15. F.H.L. Pamphlet Box 7, No. 43, Extracts from correspondence published by the Central Relief Committee of the Society of Friends on the subject of Distress in Ireland, No. 2, p.41.

16. ibid, pp.56, 62, 63.

17. Society of Friends, *Transactions of the central relief committee of the Society of Friends during the Famine in Ireland 1846 and 1847* (Dublin, 1852) pp.472-3.

18. Bennett, William, *Narrative of a recent journey of six weeks in Ireland in connection with the subject of supplying small seed to some of the remoter districts: with observations of the people and the means presented for the permanent improvement of their social conditions* (Dublin, 1847), p.135.

19. Society of Friends, Relief of Distress Papers 2/506/45.

20. F.H.L., Box 52, Grubb Collection, Clonmel Famine Relief Book 1846-'47.

21. Society of Friends, Relief of Distress Papers 2/506/43 & 45.

22. ibid, 2/506/6-32, D5103, D5183, Also the Waterford Chronicle, 13 March 1847.

23. Society of Friends, '*transactions of the central relief committee of the Society of Friends during the Famine in Ireland in 1846 and 1847* (Dublin, 1852) pp.293, 342, 349.

24. Society of Friends, Relief of Distress Papers 2/506/43.

25. Society of Friends, *Transactions of the central relief committee of the Society of Friends during the famine in Ireland in 1846 and 1847* (Dublin, 1852) pp.75-77 and pp.386-388.

26. Tuke, James H., A Visit to Connaught in the Autumn of 1847 (A letter addressed to the Central Relief Committee of the Society of Friends, Dublin), (London 1847). Appendix which is reproduction of letter from James Alcock of Seaview, Dungarvan to the Waterford Auxiliary Committee dated 7th Oct. 1847.

27. F.H.L., Mss. Box 59, Hodgkin Correspondence, Box 1, Folder 1, No. 20. The names of twenty three of these boats, their skippers, number of each crew and sum bestowed is given by Micheal Ó Cionnfhaolaidh in Beatha Mhíchíl Turraoin, (Dublin 1956), pp.136-7.

28. Facts from the fisheries, part second. Being the third quarterly report from the Ring District, County Waterford (Waterford 1848) pp.3-4.

29. F.H.L., Mss. Box 59, Hodgkin Correspondence, Box 1, Folder 1, No. 20, Alcock to Strangman 20 July 1847.

30. ibid, Folder 5, No. 276. Copy of letter written by Strangman to the Times, dated Waterford, 15 Dec. 1848.

31. Facts from the fisheries, part second. Being the third quarterly report from the Ring District, County Waterford (Waterford, 1848) pp.4, 7.

32. Society of Friends, Relief of Distress Papers 2/506/41, letter from Strangman dated 18th Dec. 1848.

33. Facts from the Fisheries, part fourth being the fifth quarterly report from the Ring District, County Waterford (Waterford 1849) this being the published report of Alcock to the Waterford Auxiliary Committee, dated 21 April 1848, pp.9-10.

34. F.H.L., Hodgkin Correspondence, Box 59, Folder 5, No. 276.

35. Society of Friends, Relief of Distress Papers NA 2/506/41 18 Dec. 1848 re visit the previous week.

36. Society of Friends, *Transactions of the central relief committee of the Society of Friends during the Famine in Ireland in 1846 and 1847* (Dublin, 1852) pp.395-6

37. Facts from the Fisheries, part second. Being the third quarterly report from the Ring District, County Waterford (Waterford, 1848) p.5.

38. Society of Friends, Relief of Distress Papers 2/506/41.

39. F.H.L., Distress in Ireland Pamphlet Box 20, No. 130, 13 Nov. 1846.

40. Society of Friends, *Transactions of the central relief committee of the Society of Friends during the Famine in Ireland in 1846 and 1847* (Dublin, 1852) pp.472-3

41. ibid, p.374.

42. F.H.L., Distress in Ireland Pamphlet Box 20, No. 131, Dublin, 19 June 1848.

43. Society of Friends, *Transactions of the central relief committee of the Society of Friends during the Famine in Ireland in 1846 and 1847* (Dublin, 1852) Alcock, Final report p.396

44. Society of Friends, Relief of Distress Papers 1848, p.7.

45. Society of Friends, *Transactions of the central relief committee of the Society of Friends during the Famine in Ireland in 1846 and 1847* (Dublin, 1852) p.47.

46. F.H.L., Mss. Box 59, Hodgkin Correspondence, Box 1, Folder 4, No. 228.

47. Hatton, Helen E., *The largest amount of good* (Canada, 1993), p.261.

48. F.H.L., Mss. Box 59, Hodgkin Correspondence, Box 1, Folder 5, No. 269, Strangman to J. Hodgkin, 25th Nov. 1848.

49. Hatton, Helen E., *The largest amount of good* (Canada, 1993) p.268.

Appendix 1

List of subscriptions from the Society of Friends in Waterford for alleviating the wants of the Poor and Destitute in that City

	£	s	d
Joseph Malcomson	60	0	0
John Malcomson	60	0	0
William Peer	60	0	0
Joseph S. Richardson	60	0	0
E.& E. V. Strangman	30	0	0
J. W. Strangman	30	0	0
Albert White	40	0	0
George White	40	0	0
Samuel White	30	0	0
Thomas N. Jacob	24	0	0
Mary M. White	24	0	0
Thomas Barnes	20	0	0
Sarah N. Ridgway	20	0	0
Henry White	18	0	0
I. & E. Clifford	15	0	0
Maria Jacob	15	0	0
Sarah Strangman	15	0	0
Samuel Strangman	15	0	0
Richard Allen	12	0	0
George Courtenay	12	0	0
Thomas Hill	12	0	0
Joshua Jacob	12	0	0
William B. Jacob	12	0	0
Elias. Ridgway	12	0	0
J. J. Strangman	12	0	0
Thomas H. Strangman	12	0	0
Samuel J. White	12	0	0
William Walpole	12	0	0
A. Friend	10	0	0
William S. Hill	9	0	0
George Saunders	9	0	0
Thomas R. White	9	0	0
Joshua Barton	6	0	0
S. & J. Courtenay	6	0	0
Henry Davis	6	0	0
Thomas S. Harvey	6	0	0
M. & A. Hill	6	0	0
Sarah Newsom	6	0	0
James Walpole	6	0	0
Maria Waring	6	0	0
Joseph Waring	6	0	0
M. & D. Walpole	6	0	0
H. White	6	0	0
Elisabeth Courtenay	5	0	0
Rebecca Davis	5	0	0

Henry Dennis	5	0	0
Sarah Knight	5	0	0
Benjamin Morse	5	0	0
George R. Penrose	5	0	0
Hannah Davis	3	0	0
Lucy A. Goff	3	0	0
Thomas Gooch	3	0	0
William Gooch	3	0	0
Samuel Harris	3	0	0
D. H. & E. Moore	3	0	0
Hugh N. Nevins	3	0	0
J. P. Penrose	3	0	0
Ann Waring	3	0	0
Richard White	3	0	0
Deborah S. Allen	2	0	0
A. Friend	2	0	0
T. Hancock	2	0	0
Children at Newtown School	1	9	10
J. & S. Abele	1		
Rachel Barnes	1		
Margaret Blain (Illeg)	1		
A. Friend	1		
Jane Hutchinson	1		
Hannah May (Illeg)	1		
Susanna Moore	1		
Henry Gatchele		10	
Robert J. Green		6	
	854	5	10

Waterford 23rd of 3rd Month (March) 1847
Joshua Strangman
Treasurer

Chapter 11

Some local responses to the famine, 1846-48

DES COWMAN

Introduction

For the purpose of this study, local society may be divided into two groups – those that were capable of surviving the famine on their own resources and those that were not. The first group comprised landlords, strong farmers and merchants along with their families; agents and associates. Whatever compassion individuals among this group might have had for the teeming masses of the starving poor, their collective priority was to ensure that there was no threat to the social order which gave them status. The response of the lower orders, the victims of famine, goes largely unrecorded though we catch occasional glimpses of them through the eyes of the more privileged.

The limited range of responses treated of here, therefore, are mainly those from the better-off in their roles as magistrates, secretaries of relief committees or other official positions that would cause them to report to Dublin Castle. The partial famine of 1845 in Waterford caused them no particular problems to judge by their lack of written response to whatever exigencies it created. There is one exception to this however – the case of Carrickbeg.

The Case of Carrickbeg

What distinguishes Carrickbeg is the benevolent indignation of one man, Patrick Hayden, secretary of the local Relief Committee. Had the inhabitants of areas like the Slievegrine Highlands between Dungarvan and Youghal got a similar activist in their midst, we would know more about their plight in that first Spring, after the partial potato failure of 1845. It is unlikely that Carrickbeg was much worse than there.

It's relief committee was re-formed on 15th April 1846 with Hayden as secretary. Within two days it had collected £110, much of this from Lady Waterford who had been helping to relieve distress over the previous three months. The new secretary sought further government aid, *with as little delay as possible......as the distress in this district is frightfully urgent it is confidently hoped you will give this matter your immediate attention* (his emphasis).[1]

The following day he had a circular out to local landlords looking for subscriptions (fig. 1). Two days later he had a census of destitution in Carrickbeg in the post to Dublin (fig. 2) and the next day a letter apologising for not having similar details for the three parishes of Dysert, Kilmolleran and Fenough that comprised its hinterland. He states that there are –

2,403 men, women and children destitute, many of whom are willing to work, but no employment. Within the last fortnight, three have died of want in Carrickbeg – John Ryan a stonecutter leaving a wife and eight children, and an aged couple Thomas Carbery and his wife. A man of the name of Kelly living at Ballyquin......has also died of want leaving a widow and nine children. No doubt more have died from the same cause...

He says that the funds are being quickly exhausted selling food at half price. He wants immediate relief works and a supply of Indian corn. Four days later again (23rd April) he writes that the parish of Dysert has opted out of their relief district as it refused to support the destitute of Carrickbeg.[2]

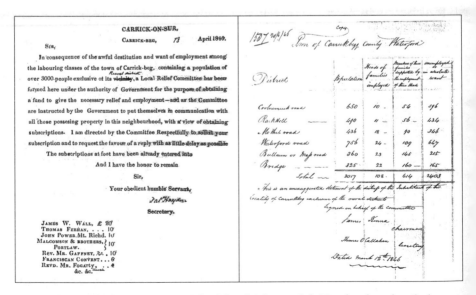

Examples of the type of material with which Patrick Hayden bombarded Dublin Castle on behalf of the destitute of Carrickbeg.

The Relief Commission in Dublin granted £65 aid to Hayden's committee. He wrote immediately asking them to reconsider this "*totally inadequate*" sum, threatening *On the reply to your letter will depend whether or not the committee will be under the painful necessity of discharging about 150 wretched individuals*" from the public works. He adds a telling detail which he underlines "*though there are several landlords of great wealth who have properties in this vicinity no contribution has been received from them*".[3] Further correspondence follows, successfully looking for further funds. Some phrases from his letter of 23rd June 1846 sum up the response of three of the four groups involved:

The landlords (with exceptions): "*have contributed nothing – they have been grossly deficient.*" Those who have helped: "*Exhausted – a second collection quite out of the question*".

Government Relief: "*Were it not for the bounty of government the people would have been suffered to perish.*[4]

There is no response from "*the people*" on record nor is it recorded what happened when the full horrors of famine struck in the Autumn of 1846. Hungered mobs ranged over the other badly affected areas but there is no record of this happening in the Carrickbeg area (see next section). Strangely, however, it is when the worst of the famine had passed in 1848 that the area around Carrickbeg to Clonmel enters official records again, first because of the Young Ireland agitation (see Dermot Power's article) and in 1849 because of casual crime. Clearly there are social forces at work which are still undetermined.

How successful were the efforts of Hayden and his colleagues? In 1841 there were 2878 people in Carrickbeg town and adjoining townlands. Hayden gives the figure as 3017 for a similar area in March 1846. The census of 1851 gives the figure as 2207. Thus 810 people disappeared from the area over those five years. Put another way, however, local and government response to the famine, inadequate though it may have been, did keep up to 2000 people alive there.

Response to total crop failure Sept/Oct. 1846

As reports of drastic crop failure reached Dublin from all around the country, the police were circularised on 19th August to quantify the extent of the blight. The seven responses extant for Waterford indicate what faced those totally dependant on the potato. The questions asked of the police were as follows:[5]

> 1. *Is the acreage of potatoes planted in 1846 the same as in 1845?*
> 2. *What proportion of 1846 crop is affected by blight?*
> 3. *Is the early or late crop affected?*
> 4. *Is the surviving crop fit for food?*

	1	2	3	4
Ballinamult	No	3/4	both	some of early
Dungarvan	1/4 less	all	both	little
Kilmacthomas	1/3 less	all	both	no
Cappoquin	No	3/4 gone	late gone/ early 1/2 gone	part early
Tramore	No	3/4 blighted	mainly late	1/2 early o.k.
Waterford City	No	all	some early	little
Waterford (?)	No	whole crop	part early/ all late gone	little

(It is not clear whether this last report is a summary of the county. It does mention the smell from the fields.)

The provision made in 1845 for local committees of landlords, agents, strong farmers and clergy in each locality to set up relief committees were in place over most of the county by October 1846. The largest tract of land not covered by any such relief committee was the impoverished stretch of highland between the stricken Dungarvan (see William Fraher's article) and Ardmore (which itself was "*in a lamentable state*"). Thus while the better-off did respond well to the emergency and raised from amongst themselves the money which would be matched by the government, they did not have the authority to take positive initiatives to relieve the destitute. The Relief Commission in Dublin was swamped with applications from all over the county for matching funds as was the Board of Works, whose officers had to give approval for any work undertaken. Meanwhile, people were starving. When work did get started (usually on road making or maintenance) it was to a set maximum payment per day which did not reflect the soaring price of food. Right across most of the county lying west of Kilmacthomas, groups of desperate peasantry did what they could to protest against these difficulties; the response in east Waterford was comparatively muted.

From early September 1846 trouble was reported from Dungarvan (see William Fraher's article). In mid September seventeen grain carts on their way to Waterford were stopped near Kilmacthomas by a crowd. Instead of taking the wheat, however, they scattered it over the road. Other attempts were made, about the same time, to prevent corn being moved along the same road and a cart load of oats had also been stopped near Stradbally.[6] One local landowner commenting on this latter incident wrote that if the government did not control prices, "*I tremble for the consequences*". He described the people around Stradbally as "*actually starving*" (his emphasis), adding, *The unfortunate people fear that if they allow the corn to go out of the country, that bye and bye there may not be any to purchase........The people are beginning to get sulky and determined.*[7]

Further west, according to landlord Henry Villiers Stuart, there was a more organised conspiracy to stop the transport of corn. Youghal bridge had been blocked by a crowd who stopped two tons of Indian corn from going to Ardmore. An alarmed Villiers Stuart states that a

> *system of signal fires was again....had recourse to by the peasantry during the night past* (i.e. 21/22 September) *when a great extent of country stretching from Youghal to Lismore and towards Fermoy was lighted up.....*

He does not explain this but adds his own concern about the stoppage of the movement of corn:

> *The answer of the farmers is, when called upon to pay any portion of their rents, that they are deterred from doing so by the difficulties which have been interposed in the way of them sending corn to market.*[8]

On 24th September *"a mob of thousands"* marched to Fisher's Mill at Piltown opposite Youghal, demanding that meal be sold for one shilling per stone. They then went to Ferry Point and seemed to threaten to attack Youghal. The magistrates there had sent a message to Cobh looking for naval protection which arrived that afternoon. They filled the ship's boats with armed marines and a nine pounder, upon which the *"mob"* dispersed. The next day the naval launches went up the Blackwater and recaptured a lighter of corn which had been seized by the local people above Ballinatray. This was brought to Youghal where the townspeople feared a retaliatory attack from Waterford. They responded to this by raising several thousand pounds to buy Indian meal immediately for the people.[9]

On that same day (25th September), Henry Villiers Stuart as Lieutenant of the county was presiding over Presentment Sessions in Clashmore, to decide on the raising of money for that area which was largely his own estate. The Cork Constitution graphically sets the scene which is very revealing about the response of the cottiers and small farmers –

> *The scene at the Extraordinary Presentment Sessions, for the Barony of Decies within Drum, held yesterday in Clashmore...was frightful. Thousands were congregated there, most of them Lord*

Stuart's tenants on Slievegrine mountains. These wretched people have held small patches of the mountain at a mere nominal rent, are quite paupers and have lost their entire supply of food. At best they are not of the most orderly or quietly disposed.

The people were so dense it was almost impossible to get close to the court. Many were clamorous and violent for their food, which was supplied to not a few from shops and houses in the village, but in such a small place to so great an assemblage it was no more than a drop in the ocean...In the sessions nearly every work asked for was granted, to the amount of thousands of pounds. As the proceedings were drawing to a close, it was apparent a bad spirit was abroad amongst the people. Several expressions of a violent nature were made respecting Lord Stuart's small subscription of £5 only to the Relief Fund, and also as to his having stated from the chair that 10d per day was ample wages and that the work could not be commenced in less than 10 days. With the Hussars standing by, the Magistrates tried a speedy departure, but when Lord Stuart appeared, the crowd's excitement grew to an intense pitch. Menaces, threats and opprobious epithets were showered on him, which was succeeded by attempts at violence.

The account goes on to describe how he barely escaped with his life and how the Hussars were forced to retreat and barricade themselves in a local farmyard.[10]

Over the next two days there were systematic stoppages of corn shipments along the Blackwater.[11] One such stoppage at Old Strancally was

.....by a large number of persons from both sides of the river who threatened and threw stones at the boatmen, prevented the lighters proceeding to Youghal and obliged them to return to Lanville Quay near Tallow.[12]

Villiers Stuart persuaded the admiralty to send another steam gunboat from Cobh to patrol the river.[13] It arrived on 25th September amidst great excitement, with himself and Richard Musgrave of Cappoquin on board.[14] According to the latter, the gunboat itself would have been attacked also except that a public works programme had just started, as outlined below.

When crowds like those along the Blackwater assemble to right one grievance, they are likely to turn their attention to other matters, as the landed classes well knew. On the same day as the gunboat was on the Blackwater, further east

> *About five hundred men assembled in the parish of Grange and marched to Ballymacart.......They visited all the farmers in that locality and warned them not to sell corn but to keep it for themselves. And that if landlords distrained for rent, that they would deal with them. They also required of them (i.e. the farmers) to refund what had been paid of con-acre rent.*

This latter may well have been their main objective. They threatened or inflicted violence on five farmers of Ballymacart. The opinion of farmers, police and magistrates was that "*it would not be desirable to take any step in the matter until there is sufficient force in the county*".[15] In other words, only the symptoms were to be dealt with, not the causes. Other roving gangs, one of two hundred, another of three hundred, were reported as intimidating landlords and farmers along the east bank of the Blackwater only two days after the visit of the gunboat.[16] At about the same time, a large "*mob*" stormed through an unidentified parish near Dungarvan and a group of about two hundred men split from them. "*Armed with sticks and bludgeons*" they terrorised a strong farmer named Lewis FitzMaurice of Glenard (?) House.[17] At the end of September, Cappoquin farmers and gentry were terrorised by a band of "*five or six hundred... (who) marched in procession*" while another band of about four hundred intimidated the better off in the Aglish area. Over the following week at least two farmers received visits at night and anonymous notes were given to them: "*Take notice that any person or persons paying rent in this neighbourhood will suffer severely for it*".[18]

What principle was involved in this is not clear but the main demand seems to have been to get back the money paid in advance to farmers for each conacre which had been manured and prepared for the useless potato crop. According to one magistrate, "*There are a great number of these cases not reported...as the farmers are afraid to do so and when I oblige them to come forward, they are quite reluctant to prosecute*". He suggests that the labourers are formally organised into "*gangs*", each under a "*captain*". "*In my opinion the entire British army cannot preserve tranquility*", the magistrate adds.[19] That there was some degree of formal organisation is confirmed by both a landlord and police. Outsiders were brought in to intimidate farmers while their own labourers were threatening farmers elsewhere. Thus the 1500 men who rampaged through Ballinamult on 2nd October were known to have come from Aglish and Clashmore.[20]

That same day the magistrates were meeting in Dungarvan. They expressed their own perspective thus:

245

Anonymous threatening letter, Mogeely, Sept. 1846.

> *The labouring classes of this county have been reduced to a state of absolute idleness and that this circumstance, combined with the decay which renders that potato unfit for human food, has had the effect of diffusing such a spirt of insubordination amongst the peasantry throughout a large portion of the county as appears to us fraught with extreme peril to both life and property.*[21]

The lives in peril of course, are those of their own class, their being no mention of the perils to the peasantry arising from the aforesaid potato failure. Charles Walsh, J.P., writing from Mogeely Castle on 26th September provides an example: "*the state of excitement here amongst the populace is very great and indeed alarming*", he writes, repeating this again and enclosing an anonymous letter that was in circulation.

> *It is requested that the labourers of Mogeely will attend the meeting of 25th inst. on their (?) and I do forewarn Edmond Hayes that if he does not mind his manners he will be rewarded in time for all his doings and before long he may procure himself a coffin for indeed the boys do intend to pay him the 1 visit.*[22]

To what extent this represents old vendettas is impossible to say. Certainly the Caravat faction was involved in a fracas that occurred after the fair of Ballykeeroge on 2nd October.[23]

On that same day Villiers Stuart, after a meeting of Resident Magistrates in Dungarvan, refers to *"large bodies of men marching unchecked throughout the county"*. The magistrates themselves state that it is impossible *"to preserve even the semblance of public order"* and also refer to how law and order in west Waterford *"must be considered altogether in abeyance"*. Intimidating as this would have been for the landed interests, the magistrates were able to identify some probable causes. Firstly, they had to distinguish the *"industrious and well-disposed from the temptation of identifying their cause with that of the disaffected"*. Secondly, the public works were only sporadically starting. By way of resolution towards a resumption of public works they state –

> *Whilst the people have remained thus unemployed it is notorious that they have devoted their leisure to the practice of assembling in large bodies for the purpose of devising measures of their own for the redress of alleged grievances and that the result of their deliberations may readily be traced in the organisation of a widespread conspiracy (which has hitherto proved entirely successful in the Baronies of Coshmore and Coshbride, of Decies without and Decies within Drum) for preventing the transit of corn, in the serving of threatening notices upon the tenantry with*

Dromana House, home of the lieutenant of the county, Henry Villiers Stuart, Lord Stuart de Decies. On his instructions gunboats patrolled the Blackwater on 24th and 25th September, 1846.

a view of compelling them to withhold the payment of rent from their landlords, in the extorting from farmers the money received of them in advance on account of con acre, in the assembling of such mobs at gentlemens' houses on the plea of demanding employment, in the intimidation experienced towards labourers employed upon the public works and in a scheme which we believe is in the contemplation of the disaffected for securing the registered arms throughout the county in furtherance of their insurrectionary prospects.[24]

This last suggestion would seem to have been purely speculative on the part of the magistrates. Later, one of them seeking reinforcements for the barracks in Dungarvan makes the point that the current force of twelve dragoons *"could be of little service acting against a large body of the peasantry who it is probable when they go plunder will do so with fire arms which they now have rich possibilities to obtain".[25]* However, no other evidence of this emerges in 1846, though as we shall see, events two years later would serve to lend them retrospective verification.

There is some justification for the other points made by the magistrates. A letter referring to events of October/November in west Waterford mentions *"combination against the rights of property"* as well as *"intimidation as to payment of rent".[26]* This reactionary response ignored factors which were identified by P.C. Howley, a perceptive, though generally unsympathetic, magistrate. He says that those employed in public works around Dungarvan –

find that their wages are so much disproportioned to the price of food, Indian corn being 1/8d per stone while the wages of an able bodied man is from 8d to 10d per day.......At present a few individuals have command of the markets and charge what prices they please.

He realised that he was going against official policy at the time in advocating the setting up of government depots which would sell food at a fair price thus forcing the merchants' prices down, or else paying a realistic rate to those on public works.[27]

The point about employment and wages is forcibly taken up by Richard Musgrave of Cappoquin. He writes that those on public works there complained to him *"much and justly of the low rate of wages".* Referring to the episode of the gun boat on the Blackwater he goes on –

I do not think the labourers look for more than the bare necessities of life. The same men that were prevented from attacking the man

248

of war boats with stones were, when employed at one shilling per day, as quiet as possible shouting for the queen and for the officers whom they would certainly have assailed a few days before. It is lamentable to risk insurrection and destruction of property for the sake of two pence per day.

He goes on to describe the stretch from Ardmore to Dungarvan as being *"in an awful state of destitution"* and castigates the government for giving *"wise maxims of political economy"* instead of food. He sensibly suggests that the authorities should buy up the grain which was being exported and simply sell it at the purchase price. Not alone would this help to solve the food problem, but it *"would calm the minds of the people".*[28]

Thus, it would seem that there was a greater benevolence locally than was manifest in the immediate response of government to the total failure of crop. However, more testing times were to come.

Responses to the bitter Winter, 1846-'47

To add to the calamity of failure of the potato crop in 1846 the weather during the following winter was the bitterest in living memory. It coincides with a paucity of reportage to Dublin. There seems to have been no more *"mobs"* rampaging around west Waterford from November on. The relief works may have contributed to this but the most likely reason is that the people were weakened by cold and hunger so that they did not have the energy to pursue strategies that had done them little good in any case.

A few isolated responses to immediate grievances are reported but in insufficient detail to produce any pattern. On the relief works near Tallow about fifty workers acted *"in a tumultuous and riotous manner"* and stopped working at 9.00 a.m. on 7th December. However, Thomas Ross, a Board of Works inspector, visited them, and listened to their complaints, the main one being that their wages were insufficient to buy them enough food. He sacked ten ringleaders and *"lectured the others on the impropriety of their conduct. They seemed very penitent and promised not to transgress again".*[29] Not all protest by the peasantry ended as easily. An inquest was held in Clashmore on 28th December into the deaths of two local men and the verdict was that *"they met their deaths from gun-shot wound inflicted by a party of police in discharge of their duties* (sic) *on 26th inst.".* What happened next is not reported but a strong presence of military and police during the hearing ensured that the anticipated trouble did not break out.[30]

These may have been isolated incidents. Certainly from February 1847 when the local relief committees were empowered to feed the people directly much of the difficulty associated with relief work passed to them. Insufficient evidence has survived to build up a clear picture of how well these committees coped with destitution on their own doorsteps but probably it varied with place and circumstance. The Kinsalebeg committee were able to announce that due to the measures they had taken *"the district has been from the present time preserved from the calamity of death arising from starvation"*. However, they had *"only been a short time in existence".*[31]

Other committees were unable to cope from early on. In February from Ardmore it was reported as impossible to get food for nine hundred families in the parish which extended into the densely populated Slievegrine highlands. Fifteen tons of food per week would be needed but only six could be obtained so that:

> *in consequence of the anxiety of the poor to get a share of what remained for distribution yesterday our depot was broken into and the police assaulted. (Otherwise) the people are in general bearing their privations and suffering with wonderful patience but such cannot be expected to continue unless some steps are taken to provide a more regular supply of food.*[32]

In Tallow it was reckoned that there were 393 families (2183 people in all) depending on the *"precarious employment"* of 576 labourers. Normally they would eat over 2500 stone of potatoes per day. By the end of January many of these were

> *hurried into untimely graves from want of food......while others are fast hastening towards the same melancholy fate.*[33]

Not all the peasantry were prepared to acquiesce in this fashion to the inevitable, to judge from a traveller in early 1847. He says that the only business being done around Clonmel was the sale of guns. According to him all farmers and provision dealers in the area were buying guns to protect grain, either in barns or in transit. Ordinary travellers were also arming themselves because of the increase in highway robbery. He himself joined a military escort to a convoy of grain carts going from Clonmel to Dungarvan, *"arming himself"*, as he put it, with only bread and cheese. He describes crossing the thickly populated Comeraghs:

> *Groups of squalid beings were seen at road corners, or running from the multitudinous houses, hovels, huts, or cabins dotted on the slopes......to see the meal go past them under the protection of*

bullets, bayonets and cavalry swords on its way to feed people beyond the mountains, hunger stricken like themselves but to whom they would not let it go if bullets, bayonets and cavalry swords were not present.[34]

This suggests the opportunistic nature of many of the robberies, the bulk of which did not find their way to the files of Dublin Castle. A series of robberies on provision carts on the road between Waterford and Kilmacthomas or Bunmahon between February and June 1847 went unreported until one Marcus Jackson and his assistant fought them off, but most importantly, were then prepared to give testimony against their assailants:

> *of all the outrages that took place at that time against the provision carts, no party could be persuaded to come forward in prosecuting parties well known to be concerned in these outrages, until Marcus Jackson and his boy voluntarily did so on this occasion.*

Such, it seems was the power of intimidation. Once convictions were secured, those robberies then ceased. However, the reason these were recorded was that compensation was being sought by Jackson in the context of the death of his assistant from fever.[35]

A further example of this comes from the Cappoquin area where again compensation was sought. Charles O'Connell, a baker from Cappoquin bought, as usual, his flour from the mill at Clogheen. Four sacks (value £19-6s-0d)were coming by cart to him on 30th January 1847 when *"the country people....plundered the cart"* just a mile from Clogheen. This, the baker said, was part of *"a system of plunder, unhappily too prevelant in these times of famine..."* His own circumstance he defined as *"a man of humble circumstance with a large family"* and most unusually he expressed some sympathy that this robbery was *"arising from prevailing distress"*. This was generous because he himself, having identified the robbers to the police was now *"obliged to have an escort to protect him from the vengeance of a people, proverbally lawless"*.[36]

There is, however, alternative evidence that order had been restored. Three officials connected with the public works happen to comment on various parts of the county on 12th and 13th December 1846. Towards the north of the county, *"Should the men receive their weekly payments regularly there will be no cause of complaint and things must go on well"*. Around Dungarvan: *"found the people perfectly quiet...."*. In the county at large, *"The people are peaceful and well-disposed"* and a week later he confirmed *".....the demour of the people quiet"*.[37]

Landlords' responses (with two case studies)

Landlords served on relief committees and on the boards of guardians of the three workhouses in the county. Sixty or more Waterford landowners had to sell their estates between 1850 and 1855. Some of them may have impoverished themselves through famine relief but there is no means to quantify this.[38] Most of the evidence is of landlords who showed little sympathy for tenants or cottiers although once again the percentage that actually did so cannot be ascertained. Some casual references however suggest that the unsympathetic response was fairly widespread.

Catholic landlord Power O'Shee of Gardenmorris, Kill, owned part of the land on which Bonmahon mines stood and, while he took royalties from the mine, he would not allow the company to build houses for the miners on his land. According to the mine manager's report in 1847, *"he would not allow a single pauper on his estate".*[39] That landlords used the famine to clear such paupers from their land is suggested from a reference in December 1847:

> *It might not be generally known that when many people came into the (work)house their cabins were thrown down and as soon as they left the (work)house they were obliged to return or become wandering paupers having no place to shelter themselves.*[40]

According to a contemporary opinion the response of absentee landlords in Waterford (with the major exception of the Duke of Devonshire) conformed with every stereotype about them. Resident landlord, Sir Henry Winston Barron, stated that –

> *Unless the absentee landlords did something towards improving the condition of their tenantry and alleviating the present condition of the poor in these times of appalling distress, they would lose their estates, and very justly. The conduct of some of them was most disgraceful. They did not expend a shilling beyond what is compelled them to pay. The land let under them is daily crying out for improvement whilst the unfortunate tenantry are famishing from want.*[41]

However, the two case studies that follow concern resident landlords. There is no means of knowing how typical of attitudes towards tenants in times of stress was the behaviour of the apoplectically righteous Francis Wyse or the more calculatingly cynical Arthur Ussher. Something of the response of tenant farmers towards ruthless landlords also emerges but not in their own words.

On 17th August 1847 Francis Wyse wrote to John Clarke, the Police Inspector in Dungarvan:

> *I am now about to cut the crop of the evicted tenant, Patrick Whelan, who owed nearly two years rent and have reason to believe when saved it will either be destroyed or carried away and an example to other tenants similarly circumstanced of which they will scarcely be loth to take advantage.——*

The somewhat confused syntax and punctuation in all his correspondence are possibly diagnostic of his social attitudes. The next day the inspector replied that the police from Bunmahon would keep an eye on things but that essentially it was not their problem as *"The police cannot interfere in cases which involve the rights of property"*. He suggested that Wyse contact the magistrates. Wyse's reply of 21st August was most sarcastic stating that since *"the rights of property"* were beyond their brief they might at least police the district as they had *"good reason to apprehend a forcible seizure and carrying away of my property"*, or its destruction by fire. He got no immediate reply to this but eight days later (29th August) wrote in haste to the inspector in Dungarvan –

> *information has this moment reached me of a great part of the crop of Castlecraddock which had been cut and saved was on last night between the hours of 10 and 12 forcibly carried away by a large concourse of people assembled for that purpose and permitted through the supineness and neglect of the police force or the entire inefficiency...*

The Inspector replied by return (30th Aug.) that Wyse should have then and should now approach the magistrates. Wyse had written to one of them, in fact, that –

> *A large body of men with cars (&) horses.... feloniously took and carried away twelve large stacks of wheat and one of oats, my property. There is still a large amount of produce cut and saved upon these lands that I have reason to believe if not protected by police intervention will also be taken away.*

He called for *"prompt and decisive action"*. On the same day he made a sworn statement before a J.P. in Tramore adding in it that he had reason to suspect that his thirteen stacks of corn

> *were conveyed to the lands and premises occupied by John Power*

as also to the lands occupied by John Whelan brother to Patrick Whelan aforesaid, both of Kilsteague ....

A week passed and nothing happened to the growing fury of Wyse. On the 4th Sept. 1847 he decided to write to the Chief Secretary in Dublin Castle. He filled five and a half sheets of very large writing paper (almost A3 size) with a prolonged rant against the ineptitude of everybody with whom he had been dealing. He filled a further six and a half pages with copies of his letters and the replies.[42] A sampling conveys the incoherent tone and something of the disproportionate indignation of this man in the midst of a disaster in which 37 of the sixty people, who had been living in that townland, simply disappeared about that time. He quotes the Inspector's remarks about the police not intervening in matters concerning the rights of property, and rants

> *The rights of property questioned – the rights of, property feloniously taken or about to be taken away, and in the hands of a public robber – taken in defiance of every defined law and in the enforcement of a system of outrage and general combination of which the history of no other civilised country and of laws afford any near example ....*

and he goes on immediately to accuse the Police Inspector of being an

Kiely-Ussher's elaborate gate lodge.

"actual abetter". Eight days later (12th September, (which he mis dated as 6th)) he wrote again complaining that he hadn't yet had the courtesy of a reply from Dublin Castle. He also mentioned that a shot had been fired into the home of one of his employees. He got a reply on 14th and wrote again on 17th, expressing his dissatisfaction and proceeded to lecture the Chief Secretary for Ireland on the duties of the police.[43] However the end result was that an instruction came from Dublin to the Police Inspector in Dungarvan to appease Wyse, particularly as the shot fired at the house was a worrying development. In a reply of 20th September to the Inspector's enquiry as to what to do, Wyse wanted three policemen on permanent duty for a least three weeks while he was preparing the rest of the crop for market. He would provide accommodation for them. This was done, but another incident took place regardless. The outraged Wyse dashed off another letter to the Chief Secretary for the attention of the Lord Lieutenant, no less, and states that *"Upon Her Majesty's government must rest the responsibility".* He fulminates against

> .....*dangerous acts of insubordination....the state of anarchy and wild disorder to which this district of the country has been reduced....public justice made a scoff and byword through the country.*[44]

Meanwhile, people were starving. What actually happened was that on the night of 23rd September the three policemen were on duty in Wyse's store house in Castlecraddock. Wyse's agent, John Roe was there as well, since he had to arrange for the wheat in barrels to be transported to Waterford the next day. The house was suddenly attacked by what Roe estimated to be about a hundred men, one of whom said *"the corn or your life".* When they would not open the door some men came in through the thatch and shots were fired. Roe and the police retreated into another room which they secured. The men then took twenty six barrels of wheat from the building as well as two stacks of wheat from the haggard. A group kept Roe and the police trapped inside the house all night, threatening to burn them out and firing at them occasionally. By the time they were released after daybreak, the corn had disappeared, reportedly into Tipperary.[45] Presumably it was never recovered and Francis Wyse had no option but to express his apoplectic wrath to every authority figure he met.

By way of sequel it seems that the police decided that such a lawless district needed a police barracks since Bunmahon was too far away to patrol it properly. Seven men were allocated to the area. However, *"owing to a system of intimidation and conspiracy among the peasantry they could not obtain a house"*. No more information is given about this but the local magistrates decided to recommend that a barracks be built at Kill. Wyse offered to build a barracks at Savagetown Cross and this was the preferred option by Dublin Castle. Meanwhile, it was deemed urgent to get police into the area and an offer of immediate premises at Kill by the landowner there, was taken up.[46] The police presence has remained at Kill right up to the present day.

The other case study of landlord response to distress achieved greater notoriety at the time, mainly through the agency of the *Cork Examiner.*[47] This was on the estate of Arthur Kiely Ussher at Ballysaggartmore. The entrance to his demesne is now a well known tourist attraction, signposted *"towers"* but leading to the spectacular gate-house and gothic bridge (illustrated here) meant to impress Ussher's visitors. His name too was meant to impress – he had originally been a plebeian Kiely but had changed it by 1820 to the more socially presumptuous one of Ussher. And most impressive of all was meant to be his demesne. This he kept expanding from about 1820 onwards through the process of evicting tenant farmers. Instead he offered them land on the wild hill slopes to the north, promising them leases once they had cleared it. When they had reclaimed the mountain, however, all he offered them was a yearly lease.

When, from 1846 his tenants could not pay the rent on the land they had wrested from wilderness, he evicted them or tolerated them to go survive as best they could on the upper slopes of the Knockmealdowns. Thus he availed of the famine to take into his own possession all the good land on the estate. The resulting depopulation is starkly borne out by the census statistics. Fourteen of the sixteen families in Coolisheal were cleared; nine families out of the ten in Glenmore went; the entire population of twenty two persons in South Park vanished as did 124 of the 129 inhabitants of Coolenagh. Some may have crawled to the upper slopes of the mountain, though how they subsisted to 1851 must remain a mystery. The most dramatic change was on the desolate highland of Deerpark North which increased from a population of 71 to 259.[48] The human stories behind all this go largely unrecorded,[49] especially the plight of the labourers who lived on the farms. There is mention of just one household who *"lived in a cabin on a tenant's farm whom they paid by labour. Mr. Smith (Ussher's agent) ordered the tenant to pull down the cabin. The family erected two sheds alongside* a ditch but these were also levelled by Mr. Smith." However, the tenants at will were just as vulnerable when Ussher decided to avail of their distress to clear them. He evicted one John Walsh but offered him £5 if he unroofed his own house and levelled the walls:

All that remained of the Kiely-Ussher house in the 1950s.

> *Neither submission or entreaty could avert the decree of the landlord and the poor farmer at last consented to destroy the only shelter the family possessed and the only shelter in the neighbourhood they could hope to obtain, for the landlord....(had) the heaviest displeasure on any of his dependent tenants who would afford shelter even for one night to any family evicted from their own homes.*

The Walsh family therefore spent the night of their eviction under the chimney of their ruined house. The next morning they asked Ussher for the promised £5, but he *"indignantly repudiated the obligation until they should clear themselves from his property"*. How or whether they could then recover the £5 goes unrecorded. Another tenant, Maurice Murphy, whose mother and grandmother had been born on the estate under the previous landlord was evicted about 1835 and the farm added to Ussher's demesne. He was given the option of reclaiming mountain land and was orally promised a twenty one year lease once this was done. However, following the total failure of the 1846 crop he was unable to pay the rent on his mountain land and so Ussher seized his cattle. Murphy then borrowed the rent money and redeemed them. However, food still had to be bought in substitution for the potato and by March 1847 once again he had not got the rent money and had to sell cattle and sheep. This still was not enough, so, as he told the Examiner reporter –

257

The missus had to bring a blanket to town to pledge if for 4/6d. That was the first time she had gone to such a place and I was as much ashamed as if I stole it. I was born and bred on Ballysaggart and if Mr. Ussher can say that I ever defrauded him of a ha'penny, I am willing to give it all up to him.

All the evidence would seem to indicate that these were decent hard-working people who now found themselves helpless in the face of a callous egotistical landlord. One old man appealed to Ussher's better nature and put it to him: *"After spending my whole life upon your property will you let me die of hunger?"* The reply was *"Give it up and go into the workhouse".*

Thus for Kiely-Ussher the famine merely presented an opportunity to achieve goals which had been set out beforehand and no doubt Francis Wyse was equally irascible with those who crossed him pre-1845. What they probably had in common with most other local landlords was that they continued to apply the thinking processes which had characterised them before the famine, into the changing circumstances of 1845-49. Whatever short-term response they had to the violence of their tenants and their labourers in Autumn 1846, or sympathy for their suffering thereafter, evidence does not survive that there was a real response to the famine in the sense of active accommodation to the circumstances which brought it about.

1848: No further response to famine?

The Outrage Papers and Famine Relief Commission material on which most of the previous chapters are drawn fall silent about the famine from 1848. However, a unique insight into the problem that was being ignored comes from Kilmacthomas. The Kilmacthomas Relief Committee had been justifiably proud of the practical way in which they had used the money they had raised over the bad winter of 1846. Instead of buying imported meal from traders they had bought good quality wheat directly from local farmers for distribution.[50] This response would seem to have paid off to judge from the statistics. The census of 1841 gives a population of 1197 in Kilmacthomas. By 1851 it had dropped by only 160 to 1037 persons.[51] The existence of a separate census taken by a local doctor in November 1848 casts a very different light on this, however.[52]

Dr. Coughlan gives a population of 1321 people in Kilmacthomas at a time when the worst of the famine had passed – an *increase* of 124 on the pre famine total. While the areas covered may not be exactly the same, that the population actually grew over those years is affirmed by his division into "*Locals*" and "*Strangers*". The latter number 224 and comprise people who moved into Kilmacthomas within the previous two years. Why they should have done so goes un-stated – the workhouse there had not yet been built.

This raises the question, therefore, as to whether there was a migratory movement through the county in response to potato failure, particularly along main roads such as that on which Kilmacthomas stood. Certainly there was nothing particular to attract the *"strangers"* there – 138 of the 220 *"local"* households were defined as *"destitute"*. That there was movement out of there is clear from Dr. Coughlan's notes: either one member or all of 27 of these local families had moved on, some to workhouses, some to Portlaw or Bunmahon and some had emigrated. About the same ratio of *"stranger"* households also moved between 1846 and 1848 – six out of fifty-seven. Presumably one only stays in a place if it offers either security or some comfort, otherwise one moves on in search of these, no matter how vain the search. That there was no security for the destitute is self-evident. The lack of comfort, particularly for the *"strangers"* is apparent from the doctor's comments. The fate of some is given below.

Name	Number in household	Comments
Dowley/Hart	16	house 10 feet square
Dee/Bryan	16	house only 10 feet square
Coughlan/English	15	house 8 feet square
Finn/Fenissy	9	this house is 4ft by 9ft
	(Mg. Finn's family of 4 "the robbers")	
Kirwan/Connors	11	all these people live in a small cellar of Higgins house.
Rich Maguire	6	the house is roofless with people still resident
Mary Linehan	2	house down; one found dead in ditch, other in poor house.
Matt Lannigan	4	house lately thrown up, also down – natives ditto. A happy riddance.

Of the second house mentioned above, he notes that all sixteen had gone to the workhouse, but the abode was taken over by a tinker named Donovan with a family of six.

These *"houses"* probably had low sod walls and a roof comprising sods across sticks. By our standards it is difficult to see how so many people could crowd into such small spaces, assuming Dr. Coughlan is correct. At least the motives are explicable in terms of traditional sharing in the face of a common privation which reduced them all to the lowest level of existence.

However, these are the people who left no written or structural record of their plight. While Dr. Coughlan chose to record them, what is probably most significant about local response is that his is a lone record in 1848.

Conclusion

John O'Donovan the antiquarian was born just outside Waterford City, his family having lived in south Kilkenny for at least three generations. He wrote of the fierce sense of pride in family lineage which people like his great-grandfather, William O'Donovan of Drumdowney, nurtured. This book was published in 1851. On his own copy of the book, John O'Donovan wrote the following marginal note:

> These feelings of ancient pride and family distinction existed ... but the late famine has almost obliterated them.[53]

However, there are too few chance survivals such as this to be certain how widespread the demoralisation was among the solid, rooted farming classes who survived the famine. The psychological reaction of the more vulnerable class of small farmers can only be guessed at but it was they, mainly, who turned their backs on Ireland and sought better futures elsewhere. The cottiers left no notes, marginal or otherwise, to record their response to famine before disappearing into oblivion.

The normal response to trauma is denial, then anger followed by acceptance. Only the second of these is likely to leave a firm stamp on the historical record. However, the denial must have been short-lived after the total failure of the crop in August 1846 as the hunger quickly followed. The anger showed itself most strongly in the disturbances of September and October 1846 and sporadically thereafter.

Acceptance manifested itself more subtly and more clearly emerges from other articles in this book. The Quakers gave up their relief work in 1848 (Joan Johnson); the newspapers cease to write about the famine during 1848 (Eugene Broderick); there is no mention of the famine in the records of Young Ireland activity in the county that year (Dermot Power). For many famine had become the norm. They no longer saw the crowds which flocked in increasing numbers to the three workhouses in 1848, '49 and '50 (Rita Byrne, Tom Nolan and William Fraher). The misery which Dr. Coughlan solely records for Kilmacthomas had become the natural order of things, perhaps for the unfortunate people themselves, and probably for those who like Patrick Hayden of Carrickbeg had written such angry letters in 1845-'46.

However, this framework is offered very tentatively in the awareness that it is based on a limited range of evidence which contains many anomalies. There is still much research to be done on local responses to the famine.

REFERENCES

1. Relief Commission Papers 1845-7.
2. ibid, 1587 and 1708.
3. ibid, 1887, 27 April 1846.
4. ibid, 2904, 3081 and 3553 quoted.
5. ibid, II/1, 5705-5782, September 1846.
6. Chief Secretary's Office, Outrage Reports Waterford, 184629/25035, P.C.; Howley, R.M. 18 Sept. 1846 & 29/25425, Magistrate's report, Dungarvan 19 Sept. 1846 .
7. ibid, 29/25267, signature illegible, 19th Sept. 1846.
8. ibid, 29/25731, Villiers Stuart, 22 Sept. 1846.
9. *Illustrated London News*, 3 Oct. 1846 p.215.
10. The Cork Constitution, 26 Sept. 1846. I would like to thank William Fraher for this reference.
11. Chief Secretary's Office, Outrage Reports 29/26961, undated (early Oct.) from Villiers Stuart.
12. ibid, 29/27299, police report 4 Oct. 1846.
13. ibid, 29/25931, instructions for *Stromboli* to sail from Cobh 24 Sept. and accompanying. documentation. This seems separate from the boats from the *Myrmidon* which were on the river the same day.
14. ibid, 29/25987, four items of 25 Sept. re gunboat.
15. ibid, 29/26193, police report, Dungarvan 26 Sept. 1846.
16. ibid, 29/26341, police report, Cappoquin 27 Sept. 1846.
17. ibid, 29/263359, Villiers Stuart from Dromana 26 Sept. 1846. He said the ringleader of this group had already attacked he, himself, at Clashmore.
18. ibid , 29/26761, various items dated 2-4 Oct. 1846.
19. ibid, 29/26911, /26921 & 26959, J.C. Howley, R.M., Dungarvan, three letters dated 3rd Oct. 1846.
20. ibid, 29/27091, letter Villiers Stuart and police report 3 Oct. 1846.
21. ibid, 29/27155, resolutions of the magistrates, Dungarvan 2 Oct. 1846.
22. ibid, 29/25975, Walsh's letter 26 Sept. and enclosure.
23. ibid, 29/26917, Howley, Dungarvan 4 Oct. 1846.
24. ibid, 29/27155, resolutions of the magistrates, Dungarvan 2 Oct. 1846.
25. ibid, 29/37017, P.C. Howley.
26. ibid, 28/58, Padworth 11-2 1847, signature illegible.
27. ibid, 29/2659, enclosure from Howley dated 16 Sept. 1846.
28. ibid, J/I 1846, 2/442/13 from nos. D5881 to 7501 passim.
29. ibid, 29/35119, Ross' report and 29/34997 Howley' comment.
30. ibid, 29/4 of 1848, from Howley dated 29 Dec. 1847.
31. Relief Commission Papers, 1845-7 II, 28/9062, 12 June 1847.
32. ibid, 11589, from the Glebe Ardmore 20 Feb. 1847.
33. ibid, 1742 of 23 April 1846 re numbers and /9836, 30 Jan. 1847.
34. Summerville, Alexander, *Letters from Ireland during the Famine of 1847* (Dublin 1994) pp.40-41 and 51.
35. Chief Secretary's Office, Outrage Reports 29/301 Statement by Jackson and letter signed R.F. Fanning, Tramore.
36. ibid, 29/335 (Clogheen).
37. British Parliamentary Papers, *Correspondence relating to measures adopted by Her Majesty's government for the relief of distress arising from the failure of the potato crop in Ireland with similar correspondence: Commissariat series (first Part) and an index 1846-47* (Shannon, 1970) p.426 Reports respectively Lt. Primrose, Lt. Downman and Capt. Hay. Also Downman 19th Dec., pp.454-5.

38. N.A., Index to O'Brien Rentals for Waterford.
39. *Waterford Mail*, 13 March 1847, p.2; also passim 1845-'48 Mining Company of Ireland half annual reports to its shareholders, in NLI.
40. ibid, 22 Dec. 1847, p.4, Board of Guardians, opinion of Capt. Newport.
41. ibid, 16 Jan. 1847, p.2, Board of Guardians. However, Barron may not be entirely trustworthy (see References to him in R. Byrne's article).
42. Chief Secretary's Office, Outrage Reports, 1848-9 29/301 which contains Wyse's transcripts of all his correspondence.
43. ibid, 29/304. Census of population 1851, Castlecraddock, Parish of Dunhill, Barony of Middlethird.
44. ibid, 29/221 or /231.
45. ibid, 29/331.
46. ibid, 29/341, 349 & 379.
47. The reports in the *Cork Examiner* were collated and published as a pamphlet by the *Dungarvan Observer* in 1946.
48. Ireland Census of Population 1851, Parish of Lismore & Mocollop, Barony of Coshmore & Coshbride.
49. Feeney, Patrick, "Ballysaggart Estate: Eviction, Famine and Conspiracy", *Decies* XXVII (Autumn 1984), pp.5-12 for wider context and sources of what follows.
50. Relief Commission Papers, 1845-7 II, 2B/1165, 20th Feb. 1847.
51. Ireland Census of Population 1851, Barony of Decies Without Drum, parishes Ballylaneen and Rossmire (i.e. Kilmacthomas West and East off the River Mahon).
52. Reproduced by Sheila and Seán Murphy in *The Comeraghs – Fact and Famine* (Waterford 1975), pp.39-44. This had been in the possession of a descendant of Dr. Coughlan in Kilmacthomas but has since been mislaid.
53. O'Donovan, John, *Tribes and Territories of Ancient Ossory* (Dublin 1851). The copy in NLI is annotated by John O'Donovan himself.

Chapter 12

The demographic impact of the famine in county Waterford

JACK BURTCHAELL

(Centrefold map inserts are central to this chapter)

Introduction

The Great Famine has been seared into the Irish consciousness both at home and abroad for a century and a half. Historians have seen it as one of the great watersheds in Irish history. On this fulcrum, Irish nineteenth century experience neatly divides into two equal but contrasting periods. The 1840s were years of shortage, deprivation and hunger all over Europe, but nowhere else was the experience as catastrophic, pervasive and enduring as in Ireland and among the Irish overseas. Widespread starvation, mass destitution and wholesale emigration were unique to Ireland in their intensity and scale.

For a century and a half, social, religious, cultural, economic and political development have been seen as irrevocably influenced by the Famine. Scholars and others have sought to apportion blame, a phenomenon which began almost as soon as the famine itself. Depending on one's perspective, the blight, the potato, farming practices, the social structure, the ignorant Irish, the landlords, the British Government and its administrators, or God have all been held responsible. Culpability has frequently been utilised to sharpen political axes, and some recent historians have downplayed the significance of the famine. Popular perceptions have inevitably been coloured by the politics and historiography of the famine. A frequent misconception is to see the famine as culminating late in 1847. This may be due to British Government policy at the time, the Famine was called off in the autumn of 1847, and was declared officially over a little later. In reality the famine continued only slightly abated during 1848, reaching a new peak in 1849, and continued at a horrific level in parts of Ireland in 1852.[1].Another aspect of popular perception of the event in parts of eastern Ireland, is that the famine is largely forgotten as having occurred in the immediate locality. Such horrors have been externalised to areas further west. Such historical amnesia is paradoxical given the importance the famine assumes in the national psyche.

Population and Land

This essay seeks to place Waterford in the context of the famine nation-wide, and to examine the variations of its impact on a local scale across the county. The population of Ireland was 8.2 million in the early 1840s, of which 196,187 people lived in Waterford City and County in 1841.[2] In 1991 this same area had a population of 91,624.[3] The city population in 1841 stood at 23,216 which left 172,971 in the county. Twenty six towns were recognised by the census enumerators, but it makes more sense to amalgamate Knockmahon with Bunmahon and Scrothea with Clonmel, leaving twenty four towns and villages ranked by population in Table 1.

Table 1

Rank order of Warerford Towns and Villages – 1841 Census

1.	Waterford City	23,216
2.	Dungarvan	8,625
3.	Portlaw	3,647
4.	Lismore	3,007
5.	Tallow	2,969
6.	Carrickbeg	2,680
7.	Cappoquin	2,341
8.	Bunmahon-Knockmahon	2,026
9.	Kilmacthomas	1,197
10.	Tramore	1,120
11.	Stradbally	814
12.	Environs of Clonmel	739
13.	Ardmore	706
14.	Passage East	624
15.	Aglish	458
16.	Kill	338
17.	Villierstown	328
18.	Ballyduff Upper	302
19.	Dunmore East	302
20.	Cheekpoint	74
21.	Ringville	264
22.	Tallowbridge	258
23.	Annestown	149
24.	Rathgormack	130

Outside the towns and villages, 139,673 people lived in rural County Waterford, the overwhelming majority of whom derived all or part of their livelihood from agriculture, or servicing the agricultural industry. This figure is an underestimate, as many people who lived in towns, and especially in the smaller villages, were farmers or farm labourers.

The average rural population density albeit involving wide variations was 207 people per square mile in 1841, compared with 44 people per square mile in 1991. The county wide average of 207 per square mile was a fairly typical figure for rural population density in pre-famine Ireland. Large areas of the drumlins in South Ulster, and much of the west coast had significantly higher concentrations, while most of eastern Ireland had similar or lower scores. Population density alone however does not give an accurate picture of how resources were divided among individuals or classes. Farms varied considerably in size, productivity, value and labour requirements. Indeed population densities were frequently low on some of the very finest agricultural land, as it was often occupied by large pastoral farms. Small farm areas obviously had more farmers per square mile, but their labour needs from outside the family were usually low. Large tillage farms employed vast numbers of labourers which often concentrated in neighbouring townlands at very high population densities.

Waterford in 1841 contained 10,729 land holdings of above one Irish acre in extent.[4] These figures were compiled in Irish acres, for statute acre equivalents multiply by 1.62. Of these, 3,190 or 30% were of less than five Irish acres (8.1 statute acres). These farms were almost purely subsistence holdings heavily devoted to potato cultivation, and their occupiers frequently depended on seasonal labour on larger farms or non agricultural work to sustain themselves. These people known as cottiers swelled the multitude of labourers and landless spailpins in the agricultural jobs market each year. Some 3,024 farms or 28% of holdings were between five Irish acres (8.1 statute acres) and fifteen Irish acres (24.3 statute acres). These small farms straddled the chasm between commercial and subsistence holdings. Economically vibrant during the tillage boom of the era before 1815, falling tillage prices in the three decades after Waterloo had pushed this sector to the margins of viability by the 1840s. Without either the acreage or the capital to move into more profitable pastoral farming, this small farming class largely sustained the huge expansion in grain exports during the decades before the famine in a valiant bid to increase production in the face of falling prices. In County Waterford, these small farmers also produced large surpluses of potatoes for pig rearing, and human consumption in urban markets.

The holdings of small farmers and cottiers made up a majority of all farms in pre famine Waterford. Together with the large numbers of labourers and spailpíns, they were the dominant element numerically in the population, but were increasingly peripheral to the economy as it evolved in nineteenth-century Ireland.[5] Much of the violence and lawlessness in pre-famine Ireland was an increasingly desperate response by such marginalised people to worsening conditions. In other countries these were the people filtering into the expanding industrial towns, but Ireland was in fact going through a process of de-industrialisation following the introduction of free trade in the mid 1820s. So very few opportunities existed for non agricultural employment short of emigration. Emigration overseas, while significant and growing, was as yet prohibitively expensive for the poorer social classes. Emigration had taken large numbers to Newfoundland in the eighteenth century, and increasingly to Atlantic Canada, the United States and Britain in the years before the Famine, particularly from the east of the county, but its impact in mid and west Waterford was considerably less.

The remaining 4,515 farms of over fifteen Irish acres (24.3 statute acres) were commercial holdings developing apace and of growing importance to the economy. These strong farmers were well integrated into the market economy and well attuned to fluctuations in the demands of the market. They also increasingly assumed leadership roles in the political, religious and social spheres. These farms constituted 42% of all farms in County Waterford on the eve of the famine and they were better equipped to weather the coming storm. As Table 2 illustrates, Waterford had the most commercially viable farming structure of any Irish county at this date. Within this vibrant commercial sector, 2,179 or 20% of all farms were between fifteen Irish acres (24.3 statute acres) and thirty Irish acres (48.6 statute acres). Farms with over thirty Irish acres (48.6 statute acres) numbered 2,336 or some 22% of all holdings in the county. Some of these were lavish holdings of several hundred acres, but most were not much above the thirty Irish acre threshold. These farms were the employers of large quantities of farm labourers and had the acreage and capital to respond quickly to changing market conditions. These larger holdings of the strong farming class were heavily concentrated on the best agricultural land.[6] Since 1815, many of these farmers had begun to move away from commercial tillage towards less labour intensive and more profitable pastoralism. Some who wished to do so, could not face the fury of the labourers that would be displaced, and held their hand.

This strong farming element of the agricultural population was better represented in Waterford than in any other Irish county. Only the grazier county of Kildare had a higher percentage of its holdings above thirty Irish acres. Just two counties, mountainous Wicklow and Waterford had over 40% of farms in this larger more comfortable commercial farming sector. Eight other counties, all (with the exception of Limerick), in the east of the country, had over 30% of their farms in this sector. At the other end of the Irish agricultural spectrum Galway,

Roscommon, Sligo, Leitrim, Monaghan and Mayo all had less than one in ten of their farms which exceeded thirty Irish acres (48.6 statute acres). In Mayo an overwhelming 73% of farms were in the cottier class of less than five Irish acres (8.1 statute acres). Most of these were in the partnership or rundale system so despised by commentators and improvers at the time.

Table 2
Irish Farm Structure 1841

County	Farms	(1.62-8.1st ac.) No. 1-5 A	(8.1-24.3 st ac) 5-15 A	(24.3-48.6 st ac) 15-30 A	(>48.6 st ac) >30 A	Comm. Farms >15 A
Waterford	10,729	30%	28%	20%	22%	42%
Wicklow	9,433	28%	31%	20%	21%	41%
Dublin	5,002	37%	26%	15%	22%	37%
Wexford	18,140	29%	35%	23%	13%	36%
Kildare	8,063	39%	26%	12%	23%	35%
Cork	45,526	30%	35%	23%	12%	35%
Kilkenny	16,490	31%	35%	22%	12%	34%
Carlow	6,296	31%	37%	17%	15%	32%
Meath	13,501	40%	29%	12%	19%	31%
Limerick	19,727	35%	35%	18%	12%	30%
Westmeath	11,375	38%	36%	14%	12%	26%
Antrim	23,993	29%	45%	18%	8%	26%
Tipperary	33,717	39%	38%	15%	9%	24%
Kerry	25,759	34%	42%	16%	8%	24%
Laois	13,601	41%	36%	13%	10%	23%
Offaly	12,746	44%	35%	11%	10%	21%
Derry	20,439	38%	43%	13%	6%	19%
Down	31,117	44%	39%	12%	5%	17%
Louth	7,841	51%	33%	8%	8%	16%
Donegal	33,724	46%	38%	11%	5%	16%
Longford	10,732	41%	45%	10%	4%	14%
Tyrone	34,141	43%	43%	11%	3%	14%
Clare	26,928	43%	45%	8%	4%	12%
Fermanagh	18,136	41%	47%	9%	3%	12%
Armagh	23,798	49%	39%	9%	3%	12%
Cavan	25,641	42%	48%	8%	2%	10%
Galway	44,330	63%	29%	4%	4%	8%
Roscommon	27,346	64%	30%	3%	3%	6%
Sligo	18,584	61%	33%	4%	2%	6%
Leitrim	18,423	51%	43%	5%	1%	6%
Monaghan	25,510	52%	42%	5%	1%	6%
Mayo	46,521	73%	22%	3%	2%	5%

Paradoxically, despite its relatively affluent farming structure, County Waterford produced more potatoes (0.46 acres per capita) than any other county.[7] A large part of the crop was used to fatten pigs and to supply early crop potatoes to Irish towns and cities. With more potatoes per capita, and with a better farming structure, the county seemed to be better positioned than most others to survive the potato blight of the late 1840s. In years of dearth, such surplus potatoes could be withheld from market and used as a subsistence crop.

Deaths due to Famine?
The census of 1851, by which time starvation if not destitution, had passed in the county, shows a decline in population of 17% from the 1841 figures for the county and city. The city population increased by 2,081 during the decade, but almost all this increase was accounted for by the destitute in public institutions which amounted to 1,958. Outside the city the population fell by 20% during the decade. Only a proportion of these people had died during the famine, as many had emigrated.

The estimation of famine mortality is fraught with danger, and many results are contradictory. Questions remain unanswered. How accurate was the 1841 census? Was population still increasing by 1845-6?, How accurate is the 1851 census?, Does the first edition Ordnance Survey of the 1840's show every habitation?, What was the ratio in a given area of mortality to emigration?. Joel Mokyr's statistical analysis of mortality during the famine places Waterford in thirteenth place nationally with excess mortality figures of between 20.8 and 30.8 famine deaths per thousand.[8] The census of 1851 implies a natural increase of population annually of 1.03% for the 1840s. If this is correct the population of Waterford would have reached 220,000 people by 1845, an increase of almost 24,000 since 1841. If we apply Mokyr's figures of excess mortality to this population we get estimated famine mortality in the county of between 4,576 and 6,776 deaths above the normal average mortality for the city and county of Waterford. This Waterford rate of between 20.8 and 30.8 per thousand compares with excess death rates of between 58.4 and 72.0 per thousand for Mayo, and 1.7 and 6.6 per thousand for Wexford. The census commissioners themselves estimated death rates in the city and county for the decade 1841-51, their method was by personal recollection, but they stated *"a correct statement....can never be procured by such an inquiry."*[9]

These figures are an estimate of all deaths and are usually considered a marked underestimate. No figures were collected from families which had all died or emigrated by 1851. Yet these figures show dramatically how terrible the years 1845-51 were in comparison to the previous years. If we average out the death rate for the three years prior to 1845, we get an annual death rate in Waterford City and County of 1,980 deaths per year. This figure of 1,980 would be natural mortality and if we subtract it from reported mortality for the years 1845-50, we get excess mortality. However this is not accurate, the figure of 1,980 for normal mortality implies an annual death rate of 10 per thousand, when the true rate was close to 25 per thousand. Such a figure would give an annual death rate of 4,950 for the years before the Famine. If the latter figure is applied to reported mortality 1845-1850 it completely discredits the data collected in 1851.

Table 3
1851 Cenus: Estimate of deaths in Waterford 1841-51

Year	County	City
1841	324 (208 days) 569 full year	127 (208 days) 223 full year
1842	1,551	417
1843	1,504	419
1844	1,595	453
1845	2,124	507
1846	2,792	703
1847	5,764	1,162
1848	4,532	1,032
1849	6,197	1,565
1850	3,289	880
1851	1,094 (89 days) 4,487 full year	233 (89 days) 956 full year

Using the 1851 census data, the excess deaths in the last column gives a total of 18,667 deaths due to famine in the city and county, compared to Mokyr's figures of between 4,576 and 6,776, the latter estimates are much closer to the mark. There are so many inaccuracies with the memory based methods of the 1851 census, that arriving at any real excess mortality rates from this source is impossible. The disparity of over 12,000 in the figures is compounded by the fact that the above figures are based on data which has traditionally been viewed as underestimates. However, the greatest bias is probably the dramatic under recording of deaths prior to 1845. The figures presented in Table 3 cannot be taken as estimates of famine mortality, at best they may be used as rough indices of the severity of the famine when comparing one year with another.

Table 4

Estimate of severity of the famine
(annual percentage of estimated excess deaths)

1845	3%
1846	8%
1847	27%
1848	19%
1849	31%
1850	12%

It is incontestable that Famine victims, be they deaths through hunger and disease, or the paupers in workhouses or aboard emigrant vessels were not random victims. They were primarily the cottiers and labourers and their dependants. Using any criteria the impact of the Famine was relatively more severe in Waterford as a whole than it should have been given its farming structure and market oriented economy. The consequences of the disaster within the county showed marked social and spatial variation.

Rural population density is illustrated on map 1. While the average rural population density for the county as a whole was 207 persons per square mile, huge variations were found even within very small areas. This information is mapped at the townland level and shows how inappropriate and misleading average county figures can be in any given locality. Two large uninhabited areas emerge, the Comeragh-Monavullagh mountain massif in mid county, and the less extensive Knockmealdowns in the west. Other uninhabited areas were the Burrow at Tramore, Ballydermody and Castlecraddock bogs, the bog beside Gardenmorris in Kill and Knockanagh near Kilmeadan. In the west of the county, rocky outcrops such as Monang, Carnglass, Glengoagh and Corrannaskeha in Knockanore area were uninhabited. Along the Blackwater valley, quite good land such as at Knocknagappul and Ross were uninhabited as they were demesne land. Along the southern flank of the Knockmealdowns, a ragged frontier of cottiers had colonised parts of the lands just below the mountain proper. This upland plateau of between six and eight hundred feet is an extensive area of marginal land perched between the Blackwater valley and the barren mountain. This was still a moving frontier in the 1840s, and quite heavily populated townlands such as Glenknockaun and Knockaniska East were interdigitated with uninhabited areas like Monalour Upper and Knockaungariff.

The carefully run estates along this section of the Blackwater were not congested and therefore were not too badly affected by the famine. Towns like Cappoquin here did not develop shanty suburbs.

Very high population densities in particular townlands were found throughout the county, 218 townlands had population densities of over 400 people per square mile (Appendix 1). Of these grossly overpopulated townlands twenty four were in the Tallow-Knockanore area, with another thirty four such townlands in the Lismore-Ballyduff-Cappoquin district. The barony of Decies within Drum contained fifty or (one quarter) of the county total of grossly overpopulated townlands. The Sliabh gCua uplands of Seskinane and Modeligo only contained nine such townlands in marked distinction to the Drum Hills across the valley. The miniature townlands of the Dungarvan-Ballinacourty area were significantly overpopulated. The entire barony of Gaultier had fourteen townlands with population densities of over 400 per square mile many of them in the densely populated area around Killea parish centre. The remote Nire valley and its adjacent lowland in the barony of Glenahiry had only five such townlands. Middlethird had fifteen such congested townlands, and Upperthird fourteen mostly on the fringes of Carrick and Clonmel.

Many of these teeming townlands were along the coast in cottier/fisher communities such as Coxtown East and Portally in Gaultier, through Newtown and Garrarus near Tramore, to Knockane, Dunabrattin and Tankardstown, to Ballyvoyle and the Ring peninsula. Such huge maritime concentrations were also common on the Ardmore coastline, at Hacketstown, Ballymacart Lower, Crobally Lower, Crushea, Ardoginna, Ballysallagh, Monatray and Shanacoole. The copper mining activities at Knockmahon concentrated population in Knockmahon itself and in the neighbouring townlands of Rathquage, Kilduane, Templevrick and Ballynarrid.

Away from the coastal belt, townlands with over 400 people per square mile girdled the towns of Dungarvan, Carrick and Clonmel as well as Waterford City. The more carefully administered estate towns of Lismore and Cappoquin did not develop this shanty ring of poverty though nearby Ballyduff Upper and Tallow did have highly congested townlands at the urban fringe.

A significant zone of overpopulation occurred in the Modeligo district, in the middleman – dominated townlands of Graigavurra, Derry Upper and Lower, Staigbraud, Scart (Hely), Graigmore, Ballyard and Boherawillin. This was an area of fragmented ownership, and middleman domination of leasing arrangements. John Greene, Thomas Hely, Christopher D. Griffith, Richard Chearnley, Beresford Power and Richard O'Brien wove a complex web of interests, which in several instances supported two layers of middle interest between the proprietor and the occupier of the soil. Nearby Canty in Whitechurch contained 35 houses in 1841 and a population of 210, made up of six strong farmers, two small farmers, and twenty seven cottiers and labourers.

With the exception of the Bonmahon area, gross overpopulation was an isolated phenomena in east County Waterford. Knockaderry Upper in Middlethird, Ballyduff West and Adamstown near Kilmeadan are examples but these townlands sit in swathes of country where population densities of between 100 and 200 people per square mile are the norm. Ballynabola and nearby Knockboy are similar examples from Gaultier barony. The entire Upperthird barony is almost entirely free of the agricultural congestion of the west Waterford area, with the exception of the urban fringes of Clonmel, Carickbeg and the nearby industrial village of Portlaw.

By far the most overpopulated part of the county relative to its resources in 1841 was the barony of Decies within Drum. The Drum Hills themselves were massively populated given their limited agricultural potential. The Mountstuart district had a population density of 104 people per square mile in 1841 and in 1991 it stands at less than eight people per square mile. Indeed most of West Waterford has a rural population density today of about twelve people per square mile. Before the famine the marginal acidic lands on the sandstone flanks of the Drum Hills supported over 300 people per square mile in townlands such as Barnastook, Gowlaun, Scrahans, Boherboy, Grallagh and Monalummery. Along the northern face of the Drum Hills similar figures occur at Ballyguiry West, Ballycullanebeg and Ballycullanemore. Even the heathery wastes of Monaculee, Clashbrack and Carronadavderg held population densities of close to fifty people per square mile on terrain only fit for turf cutting. Here on the mountain reaches of the estate of Lord Stuart de Decies, pre-famine conditions were almost identical to the west of Ireland. The fact that population densities on very marginal land such as Lagnagoushee in the Drum Hills, or Scartadriny Mountain near Kilbrien or Glendeish in the Knockmealdowns, could equal or exceed that found on some of the most favourable agricultural areas such as Dromana, Headborough, Woodhouse or almost the entire Clodagh valley, starkly illustrates the inequalities and injustices in pre-famine Ireland.

The massive overpopulation in certain parts of County Waterford illustrates the interplay of a poorly diversified economy in these areas and weak, non existent or misguided estate management. Even on highly organised estates, the position of middlemen rentiers with long leases frequently precluded effective control of galloping subdivision and increasing dependence on subsistence potato cultivation. Some estates were far more effective in checking this trend than others, but few were totally successful in eliminating it. The Marquis of Waterford was the most effective landlord in the county at limiting overpopulation on his estate. Despite intense management the Duke of Devonshire's estates at Lismore were not quite as successful in practice as at Curraghmore. Some fourteen townlands on the main estate directly managed by his agent Currey had excessive population pressure. However, the constellation of smaller estates along the Blackwater and Bride Valleys were frequently grossly overpopulated in parts. John Kiely of Strancally Castle owned three such townlands, William More of Sapperton another three, Captain Henry Parker owned five in the Tallow-Knockanore area. The Gumbletons, Georgiana and Richard also owned five townlands with population densities of over 400 per square mile. In the barony of Decies within Drum, Lord Stuart de Decies and his entourage of middlemen such as Thomas Anthony, Francis Kennedy, Anthony Fitzgerald presided with Edward O'Dell, Astle Walsh and Sir Richard Musgrave over a torrent of overpopulation. In the Dungarvan area the estate of Sir J. Nugent Humble carried vast numbers of people.

Across the county gross overpopulation tended, with few exceptions, to be a feature associated with small estates and the prevalence of middlemen. Estates held by military officers also tended to be overpopulated i.e. Captain James Barry, Major General Thomas Kenah, Captain Henry Parker, Captain William Chearnley, Colonel Palliser and Major John H. Alcock. These men were probably absentees in many instances, carving out careers in a military milieu which was highly expensive and time consuming, leaving little energy or interest in the effective management of their Irish estates.

Now (1995) uninhabited, portions of the Slievegrine highlands between Dungarvan and Youghal had population densities of up to fifty per square mile. This was the worst affected part of Waterford.

Distribution of Famine Loss

The 1851 census coincides with the end of the worst years of the famine in Waterford and throughout most of Ireland. It records 6,552,385 people in Ireland, a decrease of 1,622,739 from the figures of 1841. The census estimated that, had there been no famine, the Irish population would have exceeded nine million by 1851, though this is questionable. If half such an increase had occurred by 1846, then Ireland's estimated population on the eve of the famine was circa 8.6 million. Some two million people had vanished. If Waterford's population could have reached 220,000 by the outset of the famine, the 1851 census shows a drop in population of 55,949. The 1851 census shows a population of 164,051 in city and county. If we assume that the population of 1841 did not increase at all prior to the onset of the famine, the 1851 figures reveal 32,136 victims of the trauma. The thorny problem of exact figures rears its head again. Was the total number of famine victims in Waterford almost 56,000 or as low as 32,136, and how many died? Mokyr's computations of between 4,576 and 6,776 are probably as close as we can get.

Nationally, it has been estimated that half the population loss was due to mortality and half to emigration. In Waterford, however, emigration accounted for far more than the average nation-wide. A long tradition of emigration to Atlantic Canada, easy access to the ports of Waterford, Dungarvan and Youghal and cheap fares across

St. George's Channel to the colliery ports of South Wales, and the Cumbrian coal ports would augment the emigration opportunities of Waterford people.

One of the maps at the rear shows the dramatic impact of the famine years on the population of County Waterford. Especially striking is the variability of experience from townland to townland. Some townlands experienced population increase, but if we raise the mesh of analysis to the civil parish scale, many of the anomalies are ironed out. At the civil parish scale, only two parishes experienced population increase in the county area. Kilrush parish, which is within Dungarvan town, increased its population due to the location of the workhouse within its confines. Clonagam parish on the Suir Valley also saw a population increase of some 5.8%, but this is entirely due to the expansion of the bustling cotton town of Portlaw, the rest of the parish saw a decline of some 39.5%. Waterford City parishes saw slight population decline overall, with the exception of St Johns Without, again largely due to the location of the workhouse there.

In general terms the east of the county suffered least in this traumatic decade with the exception of the Drumcannon area and adjacent Kilmacleague. The population of Gaultier barony fell by only 4%. Further west the barony of Middlethird varied enormously, the northern parts of the barony close to the river Suir and the city suffered least, while the rocky heart of the barony experienced heavy losses. Population loss was almost as heavy along the coastal belt from Tramore to Annestown. Overall the barony of Middlethird lost 14% of its population total of 1841. Upperthird barony lost 10% between 1841 and 1851, its eastern parishes near the city losing least, with Clonagam actually increasing. Further west the Rathgormuck-Dysert areas had lost over 35% of its population.

The barony of Glenahiry incorporating Nire Valley and its adjacent lowland had the highest losses in percentage terms of any Waterford barony. The parish of Kilronan lost 37% of its population, most of it from the better endowed riverine townlands. Change on the whole was less dramatic on the hill margins and in the Nire Valley. The Glenahiry part of Reanadampaun Commons was actually settled for the first time during the decade 1841-51, while nearby Carrigroe showed dramatic population increase. Yet, equally close Curraghteskin, Castlereagh and Graignagower saw their populations plummet by 51%, 33% and 62% respectively.

Glenahiry along with the baronies of Decies Without, Decies Within and Coshmore and Coshbride are markedly different in their demographic history at this time, than the eastern baronies which fared better. In the barony of Decies without Drum, the territory between Kill and Cappoquin, the famine decade took 21% of the population. The

Fews-Ballylaneen area lost over 30%, Stradbally 26% over the entire parish. Kilgobinet lost 22% and nearby Colligan saw one third of its 1841 population gone, neighbouring Modeligo fared little better. Whitechurch lost 21.5% and Affane 27.4%. The more mountainous Seskinane and Kilrossanty had declines of just under 20%.

The barony of Decies within Drum lost 30% of its population in the famine decade, making it the second worst barony after Glenahiry. But it is a far bigger area over three times as large and having over four times the pre-famine population. Large parts of the Drum Hills saw 50%, 60% or 70% of their population gone by 1851. Ballynagleragh in Ardmore lost 93% of its 1841 population, Carronadavderg 83%, Duffcarrick 88%, Knocknamona 80%, and Knockaunagown 87%. While the mountainous areas of Ardmore civil parish suffered worst and the parish as a whole lost over 35% of its population, the Blackwater Valley portion of the barony did somewhat better. Kinsalebeg civil parish lost 22%, Clashmore civil parish 22% and Aglish 26.8%. The civil parish of Ringagonagh had a population decline of 25.8% over the decade 1841-51, with losses more severe further inland, and less drastic in the more maritime townlands of Helvick, Ballyreilly and Killinoorin.

The western barony of Coshmore-Coshbride saw a cumulative loss of 25% of its 1841 population by 1851. Lismore parish lost 21.3% of its population, much of it from the area south of the Blackwater river, and in the Ballyduff-Mocollop area. The area to the north of Cappoquin town saw significant population increases in townlands such as Tooranaraheen, Glenfallia, Feddaun, Scrahans, and Lyre East. The hilly watershed between the Araglin and Blackwater valleys also saw population expansion in townlands such as Knockadoonalea, Ducarrig, Knocknabrone and Knockcorragh.

To the south of the Bride river in the hills of Knockanore, the experience matched that of the Drum Hills further east across the Blackwater. Tallow lost just over 20% of its population, Kilcockan lost 19.6%, and Kilwatermoy lost 37%. The civil parish of Templemichael had the highest population collapse of any parish in the county with a deficit of 45.1%. In Templemichael, every single townland lost population during the decade, from Rincrew which lost 8% to Ballyknock which lost 89%. The following townlands in Templemichael lost over 50% of their populations, Ballynatray Demesne, Ballycondon Commons, Ballydassoon, Ballyknock, Bridgequarter, Castlemiles, Coolbeggan East, Garryduff, Harrowhill, Lackaroe and Propoge. Appendix 2 lists all the townlands in County Waterford which lost 50% or more of their populations between 1841 and 1851.

Appendix 1 lists townlands which had population densities of over 400 people per square mile in 1841. It contains 218 townlands, together with their landlords and the percentage population change during the decade. Appendix 2 lists the 336 townlands in the county which lost over 50% of their population between 1841 and 1851, together with their landlords. If gross overpopulation prior to the famine was the dominant factor in population decline during the catastrophe, one would expect a very strong correlation between both lists. If this were the case most, if not all 218 townlands of gross overpopulation would appear on the list of high population loss, but this is not the case. Only 76 of the 218 grossly overpopulated townlands appear in Appendix 2. Less than 35% of the teeming townlands suffered high population loss in County Waterford. There is very little variation in this correlation across the county. In fact huge population loss was as likely in Waterford townlands with population densities of less than 200 people per square mile as it was on the most densely settled areas.

Some townlands with high densities of over 400 people per square mile such as Scart in Kilcockan, Knocknamuck South in Lismore, Knockanroe and Lissarow in Ardmore, Coolboa in Clashmore, and Springfield Lower in Kinsalebeg saw increases in population during the Famine. Further east Burgery and Kilminnin North in Dungarvan saw their already bloated population densities double. In Inishlounaght, Grennan townland saw its 1841 population density of 407 per square mile increase by 12% by 1851. However most population increases were on townlands of less than 200 people per square mile in 1841.

Conclusion
Population decline in County Waterford during the famine decade cannot be directly correlated with extreme crowding prior to the blight. In fact of those townlands which lost over half their populations during the decade, only 25% had over 400 people per square mile in 1841, while 36% of such townlands had population densities of less than 200 people per square mile. Depopulation can only be explained by the provision or retention of aid and the willingness of government, landlords, large farmers and others to render assistance. Not all the exploiters were distant or alien, shopkeepers, merchants and strong farmers did well out of the famine. The Ireland of the late nineteenth and early twentieth century was of their making and in their image. The draconian operation of the Poor Law together with the 1843 provisions on rates and the Gregory Clause were opportunities presented by central government. Many, but not all landlords along with others, took those opportunities to all but banish a social class from the landscape. The interplay of government policy, estate practice and individual greed determined whether communities persevered or perished during this dreadful decade.

REFERENCES
1. Kinealy, Christine, *This great calamity: The Irish Famine 1845-52* (Dublin, 1994).
2. Ireland: Census of Population 1841.
3. Ireland: Census of Population 1991.
4. British Parliamentary Papers, *Correspondence relating to the measures adopted by Her Majesty's government for the relief of distress arising from the failure of the potato crop in Ireland with similar correspondence: Commissariat series (First Part) and an Index 1846-47* (Shannon, 1970) p.449.
5. Burtchaell, Jack, "Nineteenth Century Society in Co. Waterford part 3" *Decies* Vol. XXXII, (1986) pp.48-58.
6. Burtchaell, Jack, "A typology of Settlement in Co. Waterford c.1850" in Nolan, W. & Power, T. (eds.), *Waterford: History and Society* (Dublin, 1992).
7. Mokyr, Joel, *Why Ireland starved: A quantitative and analytic history of the Irish Economy 1800-1850* (U.K., 1983).
8. ibid.
9. Report of the Census Commissioners 1851 Census.

Appendix 1

Townlands > 400 persons per sq. mile 1841

Civil Parish	Townland	Pop density	Landlord GV 1851	% change
Kilcockan	Ballyphilip East	451	John Keily Esq.	-45%
	Newport West	514	John Keily Esq.	-62%
	Scart	443	John Keily Esq.	+19%
Kilwatermoy	Ballyclement	467	William Moore Esq	-4%
	Ballymuddy	412	John T. Greaves Esq	
			{Edward Lane Esq.}	-14%
	Dunmoon	461	{Willaim Moore}	
			{W.H.R. Jackson Esq).	-8%
	Fountain	412	William Moore Esq.	-55%
	Kilwatermoy	773	Robt. D. Perry Esq.	-63%
	Knockaun North	479	James Parker Esq.	-87%
	Moorehill	404	William Moore Esq.	-9%
	Tircullen Upper	856	Arthur Ussher Esq.	-54%
Leitrim	Inchinleama West	445	Thos. St. Jn. Grant Esq.	-61%
Lismore	Ballinaleucra	721	Georgiana Gumbleton	-46%
	Ballinlevane West	633	Georgiana Gumbleton	-66%
	Ballinwillin	808	Sir Rich. Musgrave	-37%
	Ballyduff Lwr.	483	Sir Rich. Musgrave	-70%
	Ballyduff Upr.	459	Sir Rich. Musgrave	-62%
	Ballyea East	507	Duke of Devonshire	-64%
	Ballygalane Upr.	527	Duke of Devonshire	-36%
	Ballyin Upr.	1236	Duke of Devonshire	-64%
	Ballynaraha	486	Richard Oliver Esq.	-22%
	Burgessanchor	1436	Pat Heffernan Esq.	-82%
	Camphire Hill	948	Christ. Ussher Esq.	-45%
	Carrigane	470	Capt. James Barry	-51%
	Carrignagower Nth.	474	Duke of Devonshire	-33%
	Coolishal	484	Arthur Ussher Esq.	-84%

	Coolnaneagh	573	Arthur Ussher Esq.	-81%
	Flowerhill	420	Nelson T. Foley Esq.	-81%
	Garrisson	424	Maj. Gen. Thos. Kenah	-40%
	Glenasaggart	475	Christ. Ussher Esq.	-34%
	Glengarra	410	Duke of Devonshire	-16%
	Glenshaskbeg	443	Duke of Devonshire	-44%
	Glentaun E & W	575	Duke of Devonshire	-70%
	Knockaun	936	Benjamin S. Wood Esq.	-86%
	Knocknamuck Sth.	419	Duke of Devonshire	+4%
	Lismore (rural)	516	Duke of Devonshire	-100%
	Lisnagree	629	Capt. James Barry	-48%
	Lyre West	529	Georgiana Gumbleton	-73%
	Monalour Lwr.	444	Duke of Devonshire	-73%
	Monaman Lwr.	444	Duke of Devonshire	-26%
	Parknoe	439	Rich. Chearnley Esq.	-60%
	Sruh West	515	Duke of Devonshire	-11%
	Tooradoo	532	Benjamin S. Wood Esq.	-59%
	Toornagoppoge	543	Duke of Devonshire	-10%
	Tourin	1122	Townsend R. Keily Esq.	-92%
Tallow	Ballinaha	407	Capt. Henry Parker	-15%
	Glenaglogh	407	Rich. Gumbleton Esq.	-17%
	Hunthill	503	Capt. Henry Parker	-35%
	Kilbeg Lwr.	425	Rich. Gumbleton Esq.	-17%
	Kilwinny	489	Capt. Henry Parker	-14%
	Moanfune	1006	Duke of Devonshire	-71%
	Parkdotia	528	Capt. Henry Parker	-32%
Templemichael	Boola	423	Richard Smith Esq.	-31%
	Bridgequarter	1144	Spottswood Bowles Esq.	-85%
	Lackaroe	4173	Capt. Henry Parker	-86%
	Newtown	490	Nicholas P. Stout Esq.	-24%
	Stael	779	John Hudson Esq.	-48%
	Templemichael	473	John Pollack Esq.	-22%
Aglish	Ballingown East	452	Lord Stuart de Decies	-55%
Ardmore	Ardoginna	400	Dirs. of Nat. Bank	-39%
	Ballintlea South	696	Earl of Donoughmore	-75%
	Ballynagleragh	885	Robert Graves M.D.	-93%
	Ballynamona	576	Robert Graves M.D.	-75%
	Crobally Lower	558	Earl of Donoughmore	-51%
	Crushea	445	Sir Robt. J. Paul	-43%
	Duffcarrick	1560	Edward O'Dell Esq.	-88%
	Farranlounty	530	Astle Walsh Esq.	-16%
	Garranspick	518	Declan Tracey	-15%
	Hacketstown	537	Astle Walsh Esq.	-52%
	Knockanroe	576	Astle Walsh Esq.	+5%
	Lissarow	564	Anthony Fitzgerald Esq. & others	+38%
	Moanfoun	506	Astle Walsh Esq.	-35%
	Rodeen	880	Sir Richard Musgrave	-11%
Ballymacart	Ballymacart Lwr.	808	Pierce N. Barron Esq.	-91%
Clashmore	Blackbog	722	Pierce Smyth Esq.	-60%
	Coolboa	444	Earl of Huntingdon	+100%
	Kilmore	712	Earl of Huntingdon	-47%

	Knockaniska	929	G.L.P. Mansfield Esq.	-61%
	Lackamore	729	G.L.P. Mansfield Esq.	-86%
	Pillpark	400	Trus. of Mrs. Osborne	-40%
	Raheen	3692	Earl of Huntingdon	-100%
	Shanacoole	467	Lord Stuart & others	-24%
Kilmolash	Keereen Lwr.	425	Lord Stuart & others	-7%
Kinsalebeg	Ballysallagh	565	Arthur Ussher Esq.	-32%
	Glebe (7 acres)	3200	Rev. Hamilton Beamish	-49%
	Monatray East	624	Pierce S. Smyth (minor)	-24%
	Monatray West	777	Pierce S. Smyth (minor)	-62%
	Mortgage	506	Pierce S. Smyth (minor)	-84%
	Pilltown	627	Reps. of Sir J. Kennedy	-16%
	Springfield Lwr.	487	Pierce S. Smyth (minor)	+51%
	Springfield Upr.	1067	Pierce S. Smyth (minor)	-52%
	Tobergoole	512	Declan Tracy	-100%
Lisgennan/				
Grange	Ballybrusa West	406	Sir Richard Musgrave	-37%
	Bawnard	691	Sir Richard Musgrave	-47%
	Cappagh	821	Lord Stuart de Decies	-45%
	Mill & Churchquarter	498	S. Bagge & J. Gee	-58%
	Tinnalyra	522	Thomas Longan Esq.	-42%
Ringagonagh	Ballynacourty West	501	Edmond B. Roche Esq.	-6%
	Ballynagaulmore	1450	Lord Stuart de Decies	-84%
	Ballyreilly	504	Edward O. Dell Esq.	-9%
	Helvick	928	Lord Stuart de Decies	-9%
	Knockanpower Lwr.	1816	Lord Stuart de Decies	-35%
	Knockanpower Upr.	554	Lord Stuart de Decies	-31%
	Moat	933	Edward O. Dell Esq.	-95%
	Rathnameenagh	607	Lord Stuart de Decies	-35%
	Shanacloon	1086	Michael Anthony	-18%
	Shanakill	516	Lord Stuart de Decies	-40%
Affane	Affane	439	Samuel B. Power Esq.	-23%
	Kilderriheen	400	Court of Chancery	-27%
	Knockacronaun	577	Pierce Power Esq.	-35%
	Mountrivers	547	Sir Rich. Musgrave	-71%
Ballylaneen	Ballydowane East	446	College of Physicians	-48%
	Ballynarrid	611	College of Physicians	-35%
	Carrigcastle	409	Mining Co. of Ireland	-63%
	Cooltubbrid East	427	David O Neill Power Esq.	-50%
	Templevrick	956	College of Physicians	-24%
Clonea	Ballyrandle	1877	Rev. Walter Maguire	-14%
	Kilgrovan	442	Rev. Walter Maguire	-28%
	Acres (7 acres)	1097	Robert Seaward Esq.	0%
Dungarvan	Ballinure	452	Trus. of Mrs. Osborne	-5%
	Ballymacmague East	528	Lord Cremorne	-24%
	Ballynacourty	1014	Thomas Wyse Esq.	-27%
	Ballynaskehamore	1703	Sir J. Nugent Humble	-96%
	Burgery	683	Sir J. Nugent Humble	+112%
	Clonanagh (10 acres)	2752	Reps. Perigrue Butler	+11%
	Clonmore (17 acres)	753	Edward Galwey Esq.	-75%
	Crussera	816	Thos. J. Fitzgerald Esq.	-97%

	Currane (12 acres)	800	Sir J. Nugent Humble	+54%
	Cushcam (46 acres)	1336	Sir J. Nugent Humble	-70%
	Garrynageragh West	467	Sir J. Nugent Humble	-21%
	Gorteen (30 acres)	448	Mrs. Eliza Hobbs	-62%
	Kilminnin North	977	Sir J. Nugent Humble	+86%
	Knocknagranagh	537	Sir J. Nugent Humble	-69%
	Loughanunna	627	George Boate Esq.	-34%
	Monroe Glebe (9 acres)	711	Duke of Devonshire	+20%
	Parkatluggera (17 acres)	715	Marquis of Waterford	-43%
	Parklane (8 acres)	960	Sir J. Nugent Humble	-67%
	Shanakill	670	John P. O'Shea Esq.	-36%
	Skehanard (Barron 29 acres)	794	P.M. Barron Esq.	-100%
Kilbarrymaiden	Dunabrattin	458	Pierce Power Esq.	-8%
	Knockmahon	1658	Mining Co. of Ireland	+20%
	Rathquage	485	John P. O'Shea Esq.	-18%
	Tankardstown	482	Trus. of Mrs. Osborne	-10%
Kilrossanty	Briska Upr.	540	Col. Palliser	-20%
	Ballynevoga	468	Robt. P. Ronayne Esq.	-26%
	Kilcomeragh	630	Col. Palliser	-37%
Kilmolash	Bewley	414	Capt. Wm. Chearnley	-39%
Kilrush	Curraheen Commons	530	Duke of Devonshire	+12%
	Gallows Hill	1434	Sir John Power	+28%
	Kilrush (Marquis)	1134	Marquis of Waterford	-25%
	Loughmore	1002	Duke of Devonshire	+469%
	Luskanargid	492	Marquis of Waterford	-100%
	Spring (Duke)	1567	Duke of Devonshire	-5%
	Spring (Marquis)	520	Marquis of Waterford	-70%
	Springmount	823	Marquis of Waterford	+22%
Modeligo	Boherawillin	436	Robt. O'Brien & partners	-27%
	Brooklodge	591	Robt. O'Brien & partners	-25%
	Derry Lower	837	John Greene Esq.	-22%
	Derry Upper	534	John Greene Esq.	-40%
	Graigavurra	419	John Greene Esq.	-4%
	Graigmore	463	Christ. D. Griffith Esq.	-8%
	Scart (Hely)	505	Christ. D. Griffith Esq.	-67%
	Staigbraud	845	Thomas Hely Esq.	-59%
Monksland	Kilduane	1527	John P. O'Shea Esq.	-12%
Seskinane	Ballynamult	673	Earl of Huntingdon	-63%
Stradbally	Ballyvoyle	447	Sir Edward Kennedy	-16%
	Kilminnin Lower	463	Robert Uniacke Esq.	-70%
Whitechurch	Ballintaylor Upr.	1311	Richard Musgrave Esq.	-89%
	Ballyard	411	Beresford Power Esq.	-76%
	Ballylemon Wood	463	Thomas Foley Esq.	-91%
	Canty	421	Cooper Penrose Esq.	-7%
	Farranabullen (13 acres)	541	Lord Cremorne	-28%
	Killeeshal	729	John O Keeffe Esq.	-15%

	Whitechurch	823	Florence McCarthy Esq.	-18%
Ballygunner	Knockboy	528	Jos. Mackessy M.D.	+10%
Crooke	Crooke	507	Marquis of Waterford	-1%
Kilbarry	Coolgower	443	Thomas Carew Esq.	-34%
Killea	Auskurra Big (39 acres)	1034	Earl Fortescue	-40%
	Auskurra Little (9 acres)	1564	Earl Fortescue	-55%
	Coxtown East	560	Earl Fortescue	-5%
	Glebe (15 acres)	1237	Congreve Rogers Esq.	+155%
	Killea (2 acres)	8320	Lord Stuart de Decies	-50%
	Portally	954	Earl Fortescue	-15%
	Nymphall	1246	Earl Fortescue	-2%
Kill St. Nicholas	Ballynabola	689	Maj. John H. Alcock	-26%
	Ballycanvan Little (3 acres)	6187	Miss Eliz. Bolyon	-66%
Kilmacleague	Kilmacleague East	430	Edwin Newman Esq.	-23%
Rathmoylan	Graigue	889	Sir H. W. Barron	-19%
Inishlounaght	Glenabby	526	Richard Carey Esq.	-77%
	Greenan	407	J. Phillips & S. Moore	+12%
Kilronan	Castlequarter	798	Earl of Stradbrooke	-11%
	Clogheen	460	Earl of Stradbrooke	-59%
	Creggane	434	Earl of Stradbrooke	-13%
Drumcannon	Crobally Lower	1020	Geo. Lane Fox Esq.	-90%
	Garrarus	417	Edw. J. O Neill Power	-30%
	Newtown	543	Edw. J. O Neill Power	-15%
Dunhill	Dunhill	423	Rev. John B. Pallisser	-35%
	Knockane	411	Reps. of F. Sullivan	-30%
Kilburne	Munmahoge	451	E. Tottenham & T. Carew	-57%
Killotteran	Bawndaw	477	Waterford Corp.	-47%
Kilmeaden	Adamstown	412	Wm. Christmas Esq.	+3%
	Ballyduff West	599	Vis. Doneraile	-29%
	Kilmeaden	572	Vis. Doneraile	-29%
Lisnakill	Whitfield South	505	Wm. Christmas Esq.	-3%
Newcastle	Knockaderry Upr.	588	Maurice Roynane Esq.	-77%
Clonagam	Coolroe	434	Rev. J.T. Medlicott	-61%
Dysert	Common (1 acre)	9600	Free	+73%
	Corraginna	434	James Wall Esq.	+26%
Fenoagh	Crehanagh North	589	Francis Mulcahy Esq.	-21%
Killaloan	Lisheen	1185	Earl of Glengall	-32%
	Tickincor Upr.	465	Ralph B. Osborne Esq.	-69%
St. Mary's	Croan Upr. (45 acres)	825	Reps. of Robt. Dudley	-63%
	Glenagad	748	John Bagwell Esq.	-2%
	Kilgainy Lwr.	538	Ralph B. Osborne Esq.	-65%
	Knocklucas	1299	Samuel Gordon Esq.	-20%
	Knocknagriffin	1345	John Bagwell Esq.	-61%
	Scrothea East	726	Clonmel Corp.	+9%
	Scrothea West	1188	Clonmel Corp.	-11%
	Spa	970	John Bagwell Esq.	-60%

Appendix 2

Townlands ≥ 50% decrease 1841-1851

Civil Parish	Townland	1841 density	Landlord GV 1851	% change
Kilcockan	Killeenagh Mountain	272	John Keily Esq.	-52%
	Newport West	514	John Keily Esq.	-62%
	Strancally Demesne	375	John Keily Esq.	-69%
Kilwatermoy	Ballymoat Lower	97	Rich. L. Perry Esq.	-68%
	Ballymoat Upper	306	Robt. D. Perry Esq.	-65%
	Ballynafineshoge	229	Earl of Shannon	-76%
	Fountain	412	William Moore Esq.	-55%
	Kilwatermoy	773	Robt. D. Perry Esq.	-63%
	Knockaun North	479	James Parker Esq.	-87%
	Knockaun South	150	Earl of Shannon	-64%
	Paddock	185	Arthur Ussher Esq.	-100%
	Sapperton North	76	William Moore Esq.	-76%
	Shanapollagh	82	Robt. D. Perry Esq.	-100%
	Tircullen Upper	856	Arthur Ussher Esq.	-54%
Leitrim	Inchinleama West	445	Thos. St. Jn. Grant Esq.	-61%
	Raspberry Hill	375	Reps. Robt. Campion	-59%
Lismore	Ballinlevane West	633	Georgiana Gumbleton	-66%
	Ballinvella	252	Duke of Devonshire	-54%
	Ballyduff Lower	483	Sir Rich. Musgrave	-70%
	Ballyduff Upper	459	Sir Rich. Musgrave	-62%
	Ballyea East	507	Duke of Devonshire	-64%
	Ballygally	86	Duke of Devonshire	-60%
	Ballyin Upper	1236	Duke of Devonshire	-64%
	Ballyin Lower	67	Duke of Devonshire	-55%
	Ballynoe	320	Duke of Devonshire	-73%
	Ballyrafter	112	Duke of Devonshire	-70%
	Barrysmountain	203	Georgiana Gumbleton	-82%
	Bawnagappul	314	Christ. Ussher Esq.	-100%
	Bawnbrack	145	R.H. Gumbleton Esq.	-100%
	Boola	142	Sir Rich. Keane	-67%
	Boolakiley	270	Christ. Ussher Esq.	-74%
	Burgessanchor	1436	Pat Heffernan Esq.	-82%
	Carrigane	470	Capt. James Barry	-51%
	Cloonbeg	137	R.H. Gumbleton Esq.	-100%
	Coolishall	484	Arthur Ussher Esq.	-84%
	Coolnaneagh	573	Arthur Ussher Esq.	-81%
	Coolydoody South	295	Duke of Devonshire	-57%
	Curraghreigh South	257	Duke of Devonshire	-52%
Lismore	Deerpark	298	Arthur Ussher Esq.	-92%
	Deerpark Hill	324	Duke of Devonshire	-80%
	Fadduaga	140	Richard Chearnley Esq.	-59%
	Feagarid	78	Aruthur Ussher Esq.	-53%
	Flowerhill	420	Nelson T. Foley Esq.	-81%
	Glenaknockaun E & W	137	Duke of Devonshire	-61%

	Glencullen	293	Capt. James Barry	-62%
	Glendeish West	28	Duke of Devonshire	-56%
	Glenmore	139	Arthur Ussher Esq.	-93%
	Glenmorrishmeen	95	Duke of Devonshire	-63%
	Glentaun West	575	Duke of Devonshire	-70%
	Gortnapeaky	309	Georgiana Gumbleton	-54%
	Killahaly East	39	Townsend R. Keily Esq.	-100%
	Knockaniska East	176	Arthur Ussher Esq.	-90%
	Knockaniska West	153	Capt. James Barry	-74%
	Knockaun	936	Benjamin S. Wood Esq.	-86%
	Knockaun East	48	Sir Richard Keane	-100%
	Knocknaboul	29	Arthur Ussher Esq.	-100%
	Knocknafallia	18	Sir Richard Keane	-79%
	Knocknaglogh	66	Nelson T. Foley Esq.	-69%
	Knocknamuck North	197	Duke of Devonshire	-56%
	Liss	267	Capt. James Barry	-52%
	Logleagh	29	Arthur Ussher Esq.	-100%
	Lyre West	529	Georgiana Gumbleton	-73%
	Mocollop	169	Capt. James Barry	-84%
	Moanabreeka	386	Sir Richard Keane	-93%
	Monalour Lower	444	Duke of Devonshire	-73%
	Monataggart	209	Arthur Ussher Esq.	-72%
	Monatarriv East	292	Duke of Devonshire	-64%
	Okyle	263	Christ. Ussher Esq.	-70%
	Paddocks	44	Capt. James Barry	-90%
	Parknoe	439	Richard Chearnley Esq.	-60%
	Poulfadda	59	Duke of Devonshire	-53%
	Scart	655	Christ. Ussher Esq.	-100%
	Scartnacrooka	256	Capt. James Barry	-56%
	Seemochuda	266	Arthur Ussher Esq.	-68%
	Sheanbeg	232	R.H. Gumbleton Esq.	-50%
	Sion	256	R.H. Gumbleton Esq.	-50%
	Southpark	112	Arthur Ussher Esq.	-100%
	Tobber	182	Sir Richard Musgrave	-100%
	Toor	297	Capt. James Barry	-65%
	Tooradoo	532	Benjamin S. Wood Esq.	-59%
	Tourin	1122	Townsend R. Keily Esq.	-92%
Lismore	Tubrid	168	Townsend R. Keily Esq.	-86%
	Woodville	50	Arthur Ussher Esq.	-100%
Tallow	Carrigroe	210	Rev. William Percival	-60%
	Glennaglogh	407	Rich. Gumbleton Esq.	-67%
	Kilcalf West	158	Rich. Gumbleton Esq.	-60%
	Kilcalf Mountain	192	Rich. Gumbleton Esq.	-67%
	Moanfune	1006	Duke of Devonshire	-71%
	Parkgarriff	213	Rich. Gumblelton Esq.	-100%
	Racecourse	255	Rich. J. Maxwell Esq.	-88%
Templemichael	Ballynatray Demesne	204	Richard Smith Esq.	-50%
	Ballycondon Coms.	187	Richard Smith Esq.	-56%
	Ballydassoon	390	Capt. Henry Parker	-56%
	Ballyknock	330	Richard Smith Esq.	-89%
	Bridgequarter	1144	Spottwood Bowles	-85%

	Castlemiles	186	Richard Smith Esq.	-75%
	Coolbeggan East	150	Richard Smith Esq.	-51%
	Garryduff	295	Thomas Garde Esq.	-77%
	Harrowhill	233	Richard Smith Esq.	-50%
	Lackaroe	4173	Capt. Henry Parker	-86%
	Propoge	383	Richard Smith Esq.	-75%
Aglish	Ballingown East	452	Lord Stuart de Decies	-55%
	Ballingown West	391	Lord Stuart de Decies	-65%
	Ballycullane	251	Lord Stuart de Decies	-61%
	Bleach	206	Lord Stuart de Decies	-50%
	Killatoor	158	Thos. J. Fitzgerald	-73%
	Lisgriffin	159	Lord Stuart de Decies	-68%
Ardmore	Ardocheasty	82	Walter P. Carew Esq.	-55%
	Ballintlea South	696	Earl of Donoughmore	-75%
	Ballykilmurry	317	Earl of Donoughmore	-88%
	Ballynagleragh	885	Robert Graves M.D.	-93%
	Ballynamona	576	Robert Graves M.D.	-75%
	Ballytrisnane	385	Earl of Donoughmore	-70%
	Carronadavderg	52	Lord Stuart de Decies	-83%
	Carronbeg	106	Lord Stuart de Decies	-50%
	Cloghraun	73	Lord Stuart de Decies	-70%
	Crobally Lower	558	Earl of Donoughmore	-51%
	Crobally Upper	63	Earl of Donoughmore	-74%
	Drumslig	178	Lord Stuart de Decies	-60%
	Duffcarrick	1560	Edward O Dell Esq.	-88%
	Farrangarrett	332	Edward O Dell Esq.	-58%
	Hacketstown	537	Astle Walsh Esq.	-52%
	Knocknafreeny	208	Lord Stuart de Decies	-74%
Ardmore	Knocknaglogh Lower	137	Lord Stuart de Decies	-50%
	Knocknaglogh Upper	105	Lord Stuart de Decies	-65%
	Knocknahoola	51	Lord Stuart de Decies	-64%
	Knocknamona	130	Lord Stuart de Decies	-80%
	Lackenagreany	87	Lord Stuart de Decies	-66%
	Loskeran	198	Walter J. Carew Esq.	-51%
	Monageela	32	Lord Stuart de Decies	-50%
	Monalummery	319	Lord Stuart de Decies	-87%
	Monameean	202	Lord Stuart de Decies	-54%
	Monamraher	60	Lord Stuart de Decies	-50%
	Monaneea	60	Lord Stuart de Decies	-57%
	Monea	310	Eccles. Comms.	-62%
	Mountstuart	117	Lord Stuart de Decies	-56%
	Moyng	237	Lord Stuart de Decies	-50%
	Prap	186	Robert Graves M.D.	-58%
	Reamanagh West	79	Lord Stuart de Decies	-52%
	Reanaboola	263	Lord Stuart de Decies	-71%
	Toor South	165	Lord Stuart de Decies	-60%
Ballymacart	Ballycurreen South	354	The Misses McGrath	-60%
	Ballymacart Lower	808	Pierce N. Barron Esq.	-91%
	Liskeelty	164	Robert Dower Esq.	-64%

	Reamanagh	307	The Misses McGrath	-67%
Clashmore	Ballinure	316	G.L.P. Mansfield Esq.	-65%
	Blackbog	722	Pierce Smith Esq.	-60%
	Coolbagh	322	Lord Stuart de Decies	-66%
	Knockaniska	929	G.L.P. Mansfield Esq.	-61%
	Lackamore	729	G.L.P. Mansfield Esq.	-86%
	Raheen	3692	Lord Stuart de Decies	-100%
Kilmolash	Ballynicole	130	Thos. J. Fitzgerald	-58%
	Keereen Upper	250	Francis Kennedy Esq.	-50%
	Kilmagibboge	276	Lord Stuart de Decies	-58%
Kinsalebeg	Monatray West	777	Pierce S. Smith Esq.	-62%
	Mortgage	506	Pierce S. Smith Esq.	-84%
	Rath	336	Pierce S. Smith Esq.	-53%
	Springfield Upper	1067	Pierce S. Smith Esq.	-52%
	Toberagoole	512	Declan Tracy Esq.	-100%
Lisgennan/ Grange	Ballykilmurry	271	Earl of Donoughmore	-100%
	Bawnagarrane	304	Lord Stuart de Decies	-55%
	Crossford	183	Simon Bagge Esq.	-66%
	Glenwillian	258	Richard Fuge Esq.	-65%
	Knockaunagoun	343	Sir Richard Musgrave	-87%
	Mill & Church Quarter	498	James Gee Esq.	-58%
Ringagonagh	Ballyharrahan	271	Arthur Ussher Esq.	-58%
Ringagonagh	Ballynagoulmore	1450	Lord Stuart de Decies	-84%
	Leagh	285	Edward O Dell Esq.	-88%
	Moat	933	Edward O Dell Esq.	-95%
	Readoty	178	Arthur Ussher Esq.	-80%
Affane	Carrigeen	287	Sir Richard Keane	-53%
	Cluttahina	207	Sir Richard Keane	-63%
	Coolaneen	257	Capt. James Barry	-70%
	Coolnacreena	99	Sir Richard Keane	-50%
	Crinnaghtaun East	323	John & Edmond Power	-53%
	Knockyoolahan	265	Capt. James Barry	-53%
	Moneygorm East	111	Capt. James Barry	-82%
	Moneygorm West	163	Capt. James Barry	-50%
	Mountrivers	547	Sir Richard Musgrave	-71%
	Quarter	381	Abraham Coates Esq.	-98%
	Sunlawn	62	Geo. Beresford Power	-100%
Ballylaneen	Ballylaneen	306	Sir Edward Kennedy	-63%
	Ballyogarty	121	John Power O'Shee	-53%
	Carrowtassona	261	Cols. Palliser & Clements	-93%
	Carrigcastle	409	Mining Co. of Ireland	-63%
	Cooltubbrid East	427	David O Neill Power	-50%
	Graigshoneen	274	Marquis of Waterford	-100%
Clonea	Clonea Middle	347	Rev. Walter Maguire	-86%
	Clonea Upper	234	Rev. Walter Maguire	-77%
	Kilbeg	226	Rev. Walter Maguire	-57%
Colligan	Carrowgarriffmore	137	Trus. Mrs. Osborne	-70%
	Colligan Wood	146	Lord Cremorne	-77%
	Knockanpower Upr.	345	Trus. Mrs. Osborne	-64%

	Knocknamaulee	247	G.T. Baker Esq.	-63%
Dungarvan	Ballycullanemore	379	Lord Stuart de Decies	-51%
	Ballynaskehabeg	300	Sir J. Nugent Humble	-100%
	Ballynaskehamore	1703	Sir J. Nugent Humble	-96%
	Barranlira	289	Reps. Mr Walsh Esq.	-63%
	Boherard	215	Miss Cath. Giles	-63%
	Clonmore	753	Edward Galwey Esq.	-75%
	Crussera	816	Thos. J. Fitzgerald Esq.	-97%
	Currane	800	Sir J. Nugent Humble	-54%
	Cushcam	1336	Sir J. Nugent Humble	-70%
	Duckspool	378	George Boate Esq.	-69%
	Garrynageragh East	326	Sir J. Nugent Humble	-92%
	Glenbeg	156	Miss Cath. Giles	-85%
	Glenmore	264	Arthur Ussher Kiely	-56%
Dungarvan	Gorteen	448	Mrs. Eliza Hobbs	-62%
	Kilminnin South	819	Denis Flynn Esq.	-57%
	Knocknagranagh	537	Sir J. Nugent Humble	-69%
	Lisheenoona	188	Sir J. Nugent Humble	-100%
	Loughaniska	112	Sir J. Nugent Humble	-65%
	Parkeenaflugh	197	Sir John Power	-100%
	Parklane	960	Sir J. Nugent Humble	-67%
	Ringaphuca	284	Sir J. Nugent Humble	-100%
	Scartore	382	P.M. Barron Esq.	-93%
	Skehanard (Barron)	794	P.M. Barron Esq.	-100%
Fews	Rathmaiden	312	Lord Cremorne	-71%
Kilbarrymaiden	Ballingarry	371	John Power O'Shee	-82%
	Farranalahersery	119	James Barron Esq.	-73%
	Kilbeg	175	Earl of Stradbroke	-51%
	Kilmurrin	369	Pierce Power Esq.	-58%
Kilgobinet	Ballintoor	68	Sir J. Nugent Humble	-56%
	Ballyknock Lower	357	Lord Cremorne	-70%
	Bohadoon Mountain	86	Sir J. Nugent Humble	-50%
	Bohadoon North	302	Sir J. Nugent Humble	-58%
	Carrowcashlane	172	Thos. Kiley & partners	-64%
	Coolnasmear Mtn.	99	Richard Musgrave Esq.	-50%
	Gliddanebeg	76	Lord Cremorne	-82%
	Kilnafrehan Middle	101	Sir H.W. Barron & partners	-62%
	Knockaunagloon	123	Sir J. Nugent Humble	-58%
	Scartadrinny Mtn.	95	Richard Chearnley Esq.	-89%
Kilmolash	Knocknaskagh Upr.	126	Richard T. Keily Esq.	-54%
Kilrossanty	Comeragh House	27	Col. Palliser	-74%
	Curraun	105	Denis O'Keefe Esq.	-90%
	Englishtown	369	Sir Edward Kennedy	-81%
	Knockanacullin	244	Col. Palliser	-74%
	Paulsacres	224	John Power O Shee	-100%
Kilrush	Bawnatanavoher	190	Marquis of Waterford	-50%
	Clogherane	294	John Kiely Esq.	-50%
	Lackenfune	320	Duke of Devonshire	-56%
	Luskanargid	492	Marquis of Waterford	-100%
	Spring (Marquis)	520	Marquis of Waterford	-70%
Lickoran	Lickoran Mountain	27	Richard Chearnley	-100%

Modeligo	Eaglehill	298	Patrick Power Esq.	-56%
	Killeagh	159	Reps. Patrick Keefe	-51%
	Knockgarraun	152	John Keefe Esq.	-79%
	Lisroe	194	Denis O Keefe Esq.	-97%
	Newtown	368	Christ. D. Griffith	-75%
Modeligo	Scart (Hely)	505	Christ. D. Griffith	-67%
	Staigbraud	845	Thomas Hely Esq.	-59%
Monksland	Ballynasissala	322	Mining Co. of Ireland	-67%
Rossmire	Carrignanonshagh	161	Pierce N. Barron Esq.	-89%
	Parkeennaglogh	268	—Keefe (A minor)	-63%
	Whitestown	262	Marquis of Waterford	-86%
Seskinane	Ballynamult	673	Earl of Huntingdon	-63%
	Broe Mountain	57	Earl of Huntingdon	-59%
	Lackendarra	337	Richard Chearnley Esq.	-65%
	Reanadampaun Coms.	129	Earl of Huntingdon	-62%
	Tooreen East	82	Richard Chearnley Esq.	-50%
Stradbally	Ballyvalloona	355	Trus. Mrs Osborne	-60%
	Carrickarea	190	Col. Palliser	-51%
	Faha	259	Rich. T. Barron Esq.	-56%
	Kilminnin Lower	463	Robert Uniacke Esq	70%
	Sheskin	195	Robert Uniacke Esq.	-56%
	Williamstown	252	Richard Jebb Esq.	-54%
Whitechurch	Ballintaylor Upper	1311	Richard Musgrave Esq.	-89%
	Ballyard	411	Beresford Power Esq.	-76%
	Ballylemon Wood	463	Thomas Foley Esq.	-91%
	Ballylemon Lower	747	Sir Richard Keane	-63%
	Ballymullala East	395	Lord Stuart de Decies	-56%
	Ballymullala West	246	George Boate Esq.	-72%
	Ballynacourty	90	Sir Richard Keane	-56%
	Ballynamintra Lower	914	Richard Musgrave Esq.	-100%
	Kilcannon Hely	289	Pierce Hely Esq.	-58%
	Kilcannon Osborne	157	Trus. Mrs Osborne	-57%
	Kilcloher	245	Chas. M. St. George Esq.	-71%
	Kilnafarna Upper	353	Edward Foley Esq.	-80%
	Knocknacrooha Lower	179	Richard Ussher Esq.	-64%
	Parkeenagarra	112	John O Dell Esq.	-54%
Ballygunner	Ballygunner Castle	116	John P. Fitzgerald Esq.	-69%
Ballynakill	Grantstown	348	Rt. Rev. Robt. Daly	-50%
Crooke	Knockparson	331	Marquis of Waterford	-52%
	Raheen	320	Marquis of Waterford	-50%
Killea	Auskurra Little	1564	Earl Fortescue	-55%
	Fornaght	338	Marquis of Waterford	-51%
	Killea	8320	Lord Stuart de Decies	-50%
	Knockacurrin	185	Earl Fortescue	-100%
Kill St Laurence	Kill St Laurence	106	David O'Neill Power	-100%
Kill St Nicholas	Ballycanvan Little	6187	Miss Elizabeth Bolton	-66%
Inishlounaght	Glenabbey	526	Richard Carey Esq.	-77%
	Kilnamack East	224	John Bagwell Esq & Earl of Donoughmore	-62%

Looking south from Cappoquin on the Blackwater (Cambridge University Collection of Air Photographs).

Co.Waterford Rural Population Density per Sq.Mile (by townland) 1841

	>400 per sq.mile
	300 – 399 per sq.mile
	200 – 299 per sq.mile
	100 – 199 per sq.mile
	1 – 99 per sq.mile
	Uninhabited

PASSAGE EAST

DUNMORE EAST

WATERFORD

TRAMORE

PORTLAW

Bunmahon

Kilmacthomas

Stradbally

Helvick Head

COMERAGH MOUNTAINS

DUNGARVAN

MONAVULLAGH MOUNTAINS

Ardmore

KNOCKMEALDOWN MOUNTAINS

Mount Melleray

CAPPOQUIN

Lismore

Ballyduff

TALLOW

Source: Townland Index Map Waterford; Census of Ireland 1851